PUBLIC NATURE

PUBLIC NATURE

SCENERY, HISTORY, AND PARK DESIGN

Edited by Ethan Carr, Shaun Eyring, and Richard Guy Wilson

University of Virginia Press | Charlottesville and London

University of Virginia Press

© 2013 by the Rector and Visitors of the University of Virginia

All rights reserved

Printed in the United States of America on acid-free paper

First published 2013

9 8 7 6 5 4 3 2 1

Library of Congress Cataloging-in-Publication Data

Public nature : scenery, history, and park design / edited by
Ethan Carr, Shaun Eyring, and Richard Guy Wilson.

    pages   cm

  Includes bibliographical references and index.

  ISBN 978-0-8139-3343-6 (cloth : alk. paper)

    1. National parks and reserves—United States—Design—
History. 2. Parks—Design and construction—History.
3. Recreation areas—Planning. I. Carr, Ethan, 1958– editor
of compilation. II. Eyring, Shaun, editor of compilation.
III. Wilson, Richard Guy, 1940– editor of compilation.

  SB482.A4P83 2013

  712'.5—dc23

                    2012034378

CONTENTS

FOREWORD

It is perhaps arrogant of humans that we strive to improve on the design of nature. When we are tone deaf to nature's song or blind to her temper, she reminds us by sweeping our creations downstream in flood or into the air as smoke. When we attempt to compete with her grandeur we wind up looking crude. But when we use her as a teacher, we find a great guide, for nature has been designing our planet for a very long time. Teddy Roosevelt said of the Grand Canyon: "Leave it as it is. The ages have been at work on it and man can only mar it."

But in order to accommodate the recreation of all people as they stand along the rim of the Grand Canyon, there need to be roads, trails, and facilities of the sort constructed by the National Park Service. Park professional organizations at the city, county, and state levels must similarly build for the public's comforts and safety and enjoyment within nature. All these organizations do their job best when they draw their design from the lessons of nature. The natural parks of our country, in addition to offering their intrinsic beauty, remind us of the importance of these lessons. For example, President Abraham Lincoln set aside Yosemite during our Civil War, perhaps because he knew our country would need such places for healing.

Recently, scientists have been documenting that the historic range of variability of climate is no longer a viable standard upon which to design our park infrastructure. Nature is telling us that we need more flexibility and that in order to be sustainable into the future, we need to be ready to adapt and in some cases mitigate. Sustainability in our design and operations is now an imperative, not only to respond to the changes in climate but to demonstrate our leadership and sensitivity.

So too in our most important cultural sites must the design draw from sensitivity to the time, place, and people, and the events of the site that shaped our heritage. The cultural parks of our country are the places where civic engagements, often confrontational, occasionally bloody, have shaped who we are as a people: Selma to Montgomery, *Brown v. Board of Education,* Manzanar, the Statue of Liberty, and Flight 93. At such parks, national, state, and municipal, we learn not only of the people who left their marks on our future but also, through this intimate contact, how to take the next generation to a higher and better place.

The National Park Service encourages wide-ranging dialogues on the design and preservation issues in our national parks, and we learn from them. We do not necessarily endorse any specific opinions contained in the essays in this book, but we do support the spirit of inquiry they represent. Our parks are a collective expression of who we are as a people, where our values were forged in the hottest fires. They deliver messages to future generations about the foundational experiences that have made America a symbol for the rest of the world. They are an aggregate of what we Americans value most about ourselves, including the willingness to impose self-restraint in setting aside these places of instruction, inspiration, and commemoration. Our great parks are also places where we pursue happiness, as a respite from a fast-paced and congested world. Never in its two hundred years has this nation needed more the National Park System and the other parks throughout our nation. They stand as a collective memory of where we have been, what sacrifices we have made to get here, and who we mean to be. By investing in the preservation, interpretation, and restoration of these symbolic places, we offer hope and optimism to each generation of Americans.

Jonathan B. Jarvis

Director, National Park Service

September 2012

PREFACE

The twenty-first century ushers in a renewed and intensified need for healthy, vibrant public parks. The design of parks and open space respects and responds to societal expectations most effectively when it profits from an awareness of the past. Previous park design decisions, overlaid with centuries of use, create a unique perspective to inform our decisions about the future character of public space. The view through the lens of these essays illustrates our rich, textured, yet complicated historic relationship with public parks and their role in society. The goal of *Public Nature: Scenery, History, and Park Design* is to provide public park managers, scholars, professors, practitioners, civic leaders, and others an opportunity to better understand the story of park design over time as it relates to current and future park designs.

The idea for this publication sprang from the creative synergy of a group of practitioners, academics, public park managers, and community activists—all of whom believe strongly that well-designed public parks and healthy communities have a direct and measurable relationship. Through this shared vision, the *Designing the Parks* partnership was born, comprised of innovative thinkers from the National Park Service, The Cultural Landscape Foundation, the University of Virginia, the Golden Gate National Parks Conservancy, the Van Alen Institute, the National Parks Conservation Association, and the George Wright Society. Two conferences were held in 2008—one in Charlottesville, Virginia, and one in San Francisco—to explore the past, present, and future of park planning and design. Combined, these conferences attracted more than six hundred participants and inspired an international dialogue on public parks, their meaning throughout history, their influence on society, and their future design. Six design principles emerged from the conferences and have now become the cornerstone of Designing the Parks programs and activities. Moreover, participants were united in the belief that a foundational understanding of park design history is integral to any new park design process.

We would like to acknowledge the Designing the Parks partnership, whose focused vision, innovative thinking, and steadfast commitment gave this volume the staying power needed to move forward through its publication. In particular, Richard Guy Wilson's idea of researching the history of parks was the seed for the initiative; from this sprout, it grew into the much larger, robust Designing the Parks vision. Ethan Carr, Shaun Eyring, and Wilson selected and edited these essays and ensured that the publication contained a rounded, illustrative body of scholarship.

Jon Jarvis, Director, National Park Service; Sam Whittington, Director, Denver Service Center; and Sandy Walter, former NPS Northeast Regional Director (now deceased), brought leadership and credibility to the Designing the Parks initiative, as well as support for the bicoastal conferences and subsequent Designing the Parks pilot projects. Steve Whitesell, Dennis Reidenbach, and Randy Biallas provided continued support, national leadership, and perceptive insights as the initiative grew. All were strong voices in bringing diverse views into the discussion.

Charles Birnbaum, Executive Director of the Cultural Landscape Foundation, and Cathie Barner of the Golden Gate National Parks Conservancy brought their extraordinary design talents and ability to reach diverse audiences to enrich this dialogue. Jamie Hand, formerly of the Van Alen Institute, and Alex Brash of the National Parks Conservation Association both pushed the partnership to be inventive and think outside the box.

Maurice Cox contributed crucial perspectives both as a university professor and as the former Design Director of the National Endowment for the Arts. Randy Mason of the University of Pennsylvania offered ways of connecting to school design programs and including youth in the discussion. Eric Tamulonis, Principal, Wallace, Roberts, and Todd, provided constant support and offered the valuable insights of a private practitioner.

Rolf Diamant, Bob McIntosh, Woody Smeck, Elaine Jackson-Retondo, and Craig Kenkel of the National Park Service all provided support and ideas that enriched the Designing the Parks idea and gave life to the initiative at the park and region level. Emily Dekker-Fiala of the George Wright Society and Jan Harris, Pat Kenny, and Kerri Cahill of the National Park Service provided critical support for the design and facilitation of the two conferences.

Our indebted thanks to Kenny Marotta and the Cultural Landscape Foundation for providing outstanding copyediting and shepherding this publication through its final phases.

Finally, special thanks and recognition to Stephanie Toothman, National Park Service, Associate Director, Cultural Resources; and Rodger Evans, National Park Service, Chief, Design and Construction, Denver Service Center, Western Division. Stephanie's inspiring leadership engaged a national audience to think about park design broadly and inclusively. Rodger encouraged the Denver Service Center to rediscover its immense historical role and influence in park planning and design. Together, their unflagging support and creative ideas have ensured the agency's prominent role in the Designing the Parks initiative.

Please read this volume with a critical eye toward future park design.

Thank you.

PUBLIC NATURE

Introduction

The study of the history of park design has been hindered by uncertainty about what exactly defines a "park" and also about what would constitute "design" in such a setting. The word "park" is used to describe almost any landscape whether small or large, pastoral or paved. "Design" can mean almost any creative effort that involves a degree of utility as well as beauty and inspiration. The essays in this volume, which are remarkable for their diversity as well as their content, suggest that parks of very different types share related formal characteristics, cultural aspirations, and social implications. The places called parks are indeed various. But the histories of their implementation—their acquisition, planning, and development—reveal continuities with particular clarity. The histories presented here describe the physical and conceptual transformations of certain places into parks. Park design history, in this sense, allows us to appreciate how very different parks sometimes express common ideological purposes and economic motivations through related formal strategies of development. The practice of park making can be identified by shared theory and technologies applied within many realms, including urban parks, memorial landscapes, recreational meccas, and scenic reservations all over the world.

The thesis that binds these essays together is that park history is primarily a design history. This is not an assertion of human values over biological or other significance, but merely a recognition that parks often share a history of complex and continuing development and interpretation. This cultural attention, usually exercised for the benefit of a visiting "public,"

is the common attribute that allows for comparison, periodization, and other historical analyses of park landscapes. A remote wilderness area, as much as a municipal park or a commemorative battlefield, is a landscape set aside and managed ultimately for some level or type of public enjoyment and benefit. Enjoyment of one type of area obviously differs from that of another, and the phenomenon of tourism is as diverse as the individuals who undertake it. But parks share the attribute that they are defined by designations and designs that express cultural values. They are established through the thematic identification, bounding, and interpretation of a place, and by development (sometimes quite limited) intended to facilitate and shape the park experience. Governments and individuals design parks, in this sense, for ideological and economic purposes usually expressed in terms of a doctrine of public interest.

Park design, then, is not limited to the "designed" landscapes of urban parks, in which a site is typically altered to a significant degree. Central Park in New York would be the prototype of such a "man-made" landscape in the United States. As such it might be considered the antithesis of the "natural" landscape of, for example, the roughly contemporary state reservation created at Yosemite Valley in California. But these two great icons of park history—both of which were advocated in similar terms for their public benefits—neatly illustrate the continuity between two ends of a conceptual spectrum of park design. In the first case, the site required massive soil amendments, an extensive subsurface drainage system, excavations

1

to create lakes, and grading and planting that resulted in pastoral expanses that the designers, Frederick Law Olmsted and Calvert Vaux, prescribed in 1858 as a necessary complement to the frantic and more enclosed spaces of the modern metropolis. These extensive improvements were nevertheless predicated on the existing conditions of the site chosen to become a park. Local geology, in particular, interested the designers, who used outcrops of bedrock to structure their plan and to create visual effects. The site was dramatically transformed, but also preserved as an "improved" iteration of itself: an idealized version of the preindustrial landscape of Manhattan Island. While in some areas this required extensive engineering, in others, such as the woodlands in the north end of the site, it required very little.

This process is comparable to the strategy Olmsted devised while in California in 1864 for how Yosemite Valley also could be transformed into a public park. Park design, in this case, involved some of the same features and policies as at Central Park, such as carriage drives, pedestrian paths, and a proscription of any building that would detract from the appreciation of landscape scenery. The purpose of this landscape design was also essentially the same, despite the vastly different geographic contexts of the two sites. Government acted in both examples to allow for thousands of park visitors at a time to have relatively free access to the area, move through it, and enjoy the emotional effects and benefits of appreciating scenery without destroying the landscape in the process. At Yosemite, of course, the scenery required no enhancement and any attempts to "improve" it in this sense would have been disastrous. But Olmsted knew that one day visitation to the valley would be counted in the millions, and the minimal park development he suggested for Yosemite Valley—park drives, paths, overlooks, camping amenities—would have facilitated public appreciation of the existing landscape while minimizing the degradation of the scenic but fragile wet meadows and oak woodlands that were essential elements of it.[1]

Olmsted and Vaux described their profession as "landscape architecture," and from the beginning the theory and practice they developed was closely linked to the implementation of park plans of all types. The purpose of large parks specifically, as Olmsted defined it, implied the physical development of a site—to a greater or lesser degree—in order to facilitate meaningful experiences of landscape scenery and effects. As the practice of park making evolved, the careful selection of sites for parks in advance made it possible for less to be done to achieve the same purposes. At Franklin Park in Boston in the 1880s, for example, the cost per acre to create the park was almost one-fifth of what it had been at Central Park. The result, nevertheless, was arguably more successful, at least in terms of creating powerful, inspiring experiences of large, pastoral landscapes. This was because the site had been carefully selected for its existing scenic qualities (mainly upland pastureland interspersed with wooded ledges of exposed rock), which then became the basis for the park landscape Olmsted developed. Elaborate subsurface drainage was unnecessary and the need for grading and soil amendment was reduced.[2]

To a significant degree, the history of park design is the history of landscape "preservation," particularly in the United States, where both scenic and historic places were often preserved by turning them into parks. In some cases this might require as little improvement as possible, such as drives and paths to make an already scenic area more accessible. In others, major infrastructural or recreational programs required far more engineering and expense in the creation of public landscapes. The Back Bay Fens, for example, another of Olmsted's Boston parks of the 1880s, had major flood control and water quality improvement functions. Runoff from a large urban drainage area was rechanneled, retained, and released into the Charles River in a public landscape that operated as a tidal wetland (which the site had once been), as well as a naturalistic respite from surrounding urbanization. To realize this heavily engineered landscape, the cost was significantly higher per acre, roughly on a par with Central Park. But just a few years later, Olmsted's former apprentice (and later partner) Charles Eliot was also planning and advocating "scenic reservations" in the metropolitan region around Boston. These far larger, suburban parks were selected as representative examples of a typology of regional scenery, and Eliot's designs called for roads, paths, and other minimal park improvements that provided access for the public—and protected the landscape from them—but otherwise changed little.[3]

What Olmsted sometimes described as a "natural style" of landscape design was adaptable to the development of different large municipal parks, as well as larger scenic reservations outside cities. By the end of the century this practice of park making had been adapted to the "preservation" as well as the "improvement" of a wide range of selected scenic and historic places, which typically became parts of comprehensive "systems" of public parks that attempted to include representative examples of natural (and vernacular) landscape types, and also of historic scenes that embodied chosen narratives of group identity. In the setting of national parks in the United States, this approach underlay the National Park Service mandate in 1916 to preserve landscapes and wildlife "unimpaired" for the purpose of public "enjoyment," a core mandate for many park agencies still today.[4] For state parks, Frederick Law Olmsted Jr.'s 1929 plan for California epitomized a comparable approach to scenic and historic landscape preservation, which in this case became a model for New Deal comprehensive state park planning all over the country in the following decade.[5]

Seeing the connection between park design and landscape preservation requires an understanding of preservation as itself an active, essential transformation of a place, even if the intent of that transformation was to change as little as possible about an area's cultural character and natural condition. This is one of the most valuable insights that the study of park history can offer park managers and conservationists today. Landscape preservation implied some level of landscape design, whether that design was expressed in extensive, engineered improvements or in minimal development intended to allow public access while preventing that use from degrading places already considered significant for their historical or biological resources. Preservation—when it involved park making—entailed conceptual and, at least limited, physical change of a place to be effective, at least if any form of public "enjoyment" was involved. From a historical perspective, then, landscape preservation and landscape design have never really been separate projects.

The investigations of the history of park design offered in this volume, however, come at a time of historical shifts in the practice. Many conservation organizations today prefer to describe their activities as "protecting landscapes," not making parks.[6] The former phrase implies a more flexible, humanistic approach to conservation, working with indigenous peoples and local economies. The latter recalls the "Yellowstone model," now often disparaged because the approach required the absolute appropriation of a place (with attendant dispossessions) in order to achieve a nevertheless imperfect biologic or historic preservation.[7] But this distinction indicates an inadequate appreciation for some of the complexities of park design history. Whatever it is called, the imposition of a set of values on a place in order to "preserve," "protect," or merely "interpret" it inevitably involves the abrogation of at least some rights and access by one group in favor of another. The condemnations and evictions that partly defined park making in the nineteenth century were done with an overt ideological conviction that a larger and justifying interest was being served. At the very least, some aspects of the belief in a larger good that ethically supersedes at least some local preferences must remain even in the "new paradigm" of protecting cultural landscapes.

Park making has changed dramatically in recent decades, but only in some ways. The notion of a public interest, for example, also remains the most effective justification for true public funding. If a public interest is not served by conservation activities, why should public taxation support them? If only a select group benefit, then fees collected from visitors or donations given by interested parties, not general treasury funds, should support landscape protection. A related observation can be made regarding the economic importance of parks. New models of landscape protection emphasize sustainable forms of economic exploitation that create vibrant local economies on a long-term basis. This was exactly the kind of suggestion that Progressive Era preservationists made in the United States, promising that "scenery" was the one "natural resource" that could be fully exploited for local and national economic benefit without significant depletion of it.[8] Park improvements at many national parks in the United States included the construction of roads and hotels to facilitate regional tourism, which advocates pointed out would more than make up economically for the loss of logging and grazing opportunities. Proponents of the sustainable exploitation of tropical forest resources and the development of "eco-tourist" resorts evoke similar, if updated, potentials.

The history of park design should be of interest today not only because it contrasts with newer models for conservation and urban planning but because of the cogent lessons we can abstract from it to provide a thicker context for current practices. For example, historians have provided increasingly nuanced accounts of how powerful political and economic interests sponsored parks in the nineteenth and early twentieth centuries.[9] The historical links between urban park planning and real estate speculators and developers, if not often described explicitly in contemporary records, have been well established subsequently. The creation of national parks all over the world just as plainly served ideological and economic interests of governments and of influential individuals. Park making has always been a collaboration of good and greed as much as a struggle against "the Almighty Dollar," as Muir would have it.[10] Throughout this volume, convergence of diverse political, economic, and

more selfless interests characterizes the histories of how and why parks were established and designed. Since the 1980s the success of public-private partnerships of many types has demonstrated that identifying and exploiting mutual benefits and converging interests have continued to be essential to making public parks.

Parks were made, not born, which is why these essays can be considered design histories. Through park making, governments have elaborated and deployed the most powerful of cultural constructions: nature and history. Parks have been a means to preserve apparently unimpaired past conditions—whether cultural or ecological—but they have done so as agents of modernization, that is, as components of larger patterns of landscape and social change. The great eras of park making in different parts of the world have come at different times, but always during eras of social, geographic, and ecological disruption. Preservation and park making, the scholars contributing to this volume remind us, are among the most remarkable of all cultural activities, since the landscapes they produce simultaneously enable, critique, embody, and reject violent, large-scale adaptations of geography and society for the purposes of modern, capitalist, and urban civilization.

The Essays

In the first section, John Dixon Hunt and Elizabeth Barlow Rogers explore the early cultural context for park design and establish essential continuities to European garden theorists and cultural figures who created an intellectual foundation essential to how a park designer such as Frederick Law Olmsted perceived landscapes. The picturesque as a mode of experience as well as of design, Hunt asserts, was linked to the phenomenon of modern tourism. The picturesque was indeed "about movement," physical mobility as well as the "movement of the mind." Landscape itself may not travel, Hunt concludes, but ideas do. European thought and design precedent are fundamental to considering American park design in the nineteenth century. No cultural current, in this regard, was more powerful than the Romantic movement. As Rogers describes in her essay, Romanticism defined a revolutionary shift in responses to the natural, as well as the political, world. Romanticism reconstructed the idea of nature, its relationship to society, and above all the individual's place in it; it is the essential cultural context for the ideology and practice of park making. If the most profound expressions of Romanticism were in philosophy, poetry, and fine arts, landscape directly manifested the sensibility by embodying the otherwise abstract virtues of a wild nature. It perhaps follows that the largest expressions of the Romantic landscape would not be in Europe, but in its former colonies, including the United States, where the park movement that began in New York in the mid-nineteenth century would find its ultimate expression in an unprecedented national park system across the continent.

As Hunt observes, since the eighteenth century the perception of landscape has been inseparable from the fact of physical mobility: movement is the modern mode of landscape perception. The second group of essays presented here explores the changing means and technologies of movement in the landscape. Timothy Davis indicates that the growth of tourism and shift in landscape perception often associated with the rise of the automobile in the twentieth actually began much earlier, in the seventeenth and eighteenth centuries in Europe. Parks in the United States were designed with roads because movement through the landscape was a fundamental component of the park idea, not a compromise of it. The "emphasis on roads and vehicles" in national parks may offend today, Davis concludes, but it is "rooted in centuries of design theory and social practice." Again, it is the history of design that yields significant analyses and continuities in park history that otherwise would not be as apparent.

In the second essay of this section, Theodore Catton critically examines the history of design in the U.S. national park system, above all by reevaluating the essential—and increasingly problematic—reliance on automobiles as a primary means of accessing and experiencing parks. Catton notes that the national parks became a modern system of public parks in the twentieth century, especially after World War I as car ownership among the middle class made the parks more accessible. Not everyone saw this as progress, and at least some negative reaction to automotive tourism began immediately. But Catton closely examines reactions that followed World War II, and the more significant responses to this second, larger wave of postwar automotive tourism. He describes the 1960s as a "time of questioning" the assumptions and design principles that led to the accommodation of ever larger numbers of tourists and their cars in national parks. By the 1970s, imaginative new park designs challenged old certainties and promised "alternative" means of moving through the landscape that would leave cars behind. This is a history of particular relevance for park planners today, since many of these plans have been shelved or only partly realized, and they remain a priority for protecting parks and enhancing the experience of them. The conviction that automobile use in the parks was too pervasive was established and remains; but during the 1980s, new political realities in Congress mostly stalled or defeated plans to replace cars with other transportation technologies.

Perhaps the most significant difference between park design and other design disciplines involves the inherently open nature of public landscapes: in program and purpose, parks are inherently, inescapably political. Olmsted described landscape architecture as a "public art," but he might have added that it was an ideological one as well. In the third section of this volume, Esther da Costa Meyer takes as her subject the nineteenth-century modernization of Paris under Napoleon III and his prefect Georges-Eugène Haussmann. Da Costa Meyer analyzes the complex and unprecedented ways in which park design was used to deploy a heavily engineered, even mass-produced "nature" that was central to the redevelopment of the city. They were not "imitating nature," da Costa Meyer observes of these designers, but "constructing it according to the economic precepts of modernity." The parks were not an "exercise in mimicry" but were, rather, "parading their own truths" in the form of concrete lake beds, elaborate floral displays, and engineered rockeries.

Great park makers, such as Haussmann, were also great modernizers of societies, of cities, and of landscapes. Franklin Delano Roosevelt, who otherwise bore little comparison to Napoleon III, shared a profound sense of the ideological power and utility of park design. While the nineteenth-century French autocrat remade the modern city, the twentieth-century president oversaw the development of a national landscape. Neil M. Maher and Heidi Hohmann each contribute essays that explore how Roosevelt's Civilian Conservation Corps—literally an army of park makers working across the United States in the 1930s—created other natures, mainly in the form of state parks and an expansion of the national system. Maher's interest is in Roosevelt as a master politician as well as perhaps the greatest sponsor of park creation in U.S. history. These two aspects of his career were not unrelated. Bear Mountain State Park in New York was a prototypical New Deal landscape: a balanced composition that integrated the improvement of both natural resources and society as part of one ideal. The resulting park made "New Dealers out of poor New Yorkers," who came from the city by the thousands to use the park, while it also built rural political support by infusing federal money into the local economy.

To see another remarkable fusion of CCC labor and New Deal park design, Hohmann brings a landscape architect's analysis to Platt National Park (now part of the Chickasaw National Recreation Area). In this case the streams, springs, pools, and pavilions of a remote, nineteenth-century mineral springs resort of Sulphur, Oklahoma, were recast in the "rustic" masonry and naturalistic landscape design typical of the period. Hohmann suggests that in the process the landscape was raised from a substandard, unwanted "pariah" in the national park system to a "paragon" of park design:

one of the most remarkable examples of the "aesthetic achievements and transformative abilities of the naturalistic landscape design of the CCC and the New Deal–era National Park Service."

In the last essay of this section, Catharina Nolin describes the creation of "nature parks" in Sweden at the beginning of the twentieth century. In a parallel to William Robinson's "wild garden," the Swedish nature park rejected the carpet bedding and gardenesque design of Victorian-era park design in Europe. Instead these parks were based in the native characteristics of a site and its communities of plants, at a point in Swedish political history when a modern national identity was coalescing. As was the case elsewhere, a rapidly urbanizing society found increased significance in a nature that could be described and studied as specific to the nation. In urban parks in Gothenburg and other Swedish cites, that nature became the basis of distinctive public landscape design, one steeped in traditional cultural associations as well as possessing contemporary political significance.

The fourth section of this book presents other case studies in which public landscape design is strongly linked not only to politics but also to the formation of group identity. There are many ways of defining the perceived meanings or importance of park landscapes, but perhaps the most comprehensive is to consider them as the location and means of cultivating individual, group, and national identities. Landscapes are most meaningful to us when our being in them, or remembering that experience, directly affects or enhances our sense of who we are. Lucienne Thys-Şenocak describes the events and associations that permeate the landscape of the Gallipoli Peninsula Historical National Park, a commemorative battlefield in Turkey. Gallipoli was the scene of fierce fighting during World War I, and Atatürk's victory there laid the groundwork for the formation of the modern, secular state. Located on the Dardanelles, Gallipoli is also a vast archaeological site that has been fought over since the days of ancient Troy. The landscape continues to be contested ground. Designated a national park in 1973, the battlefield is revered for many reasons, and its management and interpretation are complicated by its role in the construction of multiple national and religious identities.

Katherine Solomonson and Brian Katen provide contrasting studies in landscapes associated with the formation of very different identities in the United States. Solomonson describes how Itasca State Park in Minnesota created a birthplace landscape not for a person, but for the Mississippi River. Although the headwaters of the river encompassed a wide area, Solomonson observes that a "single source" (Lake Itasca) usefully served the "single narrative" of the park's interpretive program in the 1930s. In his essay, Katen discusses a group of landscapes in Virginia that were part of a "statewide fabric of recreation sites" that served African Americans from the end of the Civil War through the end of the segregation era. These landscapes were important places of congregation and recreation at a time when African Americans were denied access to "public" landscapes, with the exception of limited and usually not equal segregated parks.

The next essay in this section involves the construction of national identity on a continental scale. Nicole Porter and Catherin Bull describe the transition of the Blue Mountains in Australia from "land" to "park." "The nature of national parks is inextricably linked," they explain, "with the evolution of cultural practices including naming, writing, image making, and spatial design," a statement that could introduce this book as well as their essay. Within sight of Sydney, the Blue Mountains were early subjects of attention by colonists, who were visiting the area as tourists by rail by the 1860s, although national park designation followed only in 1959. As landscape architects, Porter and Bull are particularly adept at illustrating how physical development has been inseparable from other cultural practices in the transformation they describe. Taken together, the construction of park narratives, through many media, practices, and activities, "as well as the physical form of the park itself," comprised park making in the Blue Mountains.

The last essay in this section also describes how the acquisition and development of national park landscapes played a role in the formation of national identity. In her essay on the Israeli national park system, Tal Alon-Mozes describes national park making as a fundamental tool of nation building. Her analysis of Gan Hashlosha al-Sakhne National Park offers an opportunity to observe "contrasting processes in the dynamic between park design and cultural identity," the latter a particularly complex subject as Israeli identity has become increasingly "fragmented and varied [and] less reflective of the hegemonic early settler society."

The essays in the final section of this volume are grouped around the sometimes uneasy relationships of monumental architecture and park landscapes. In a wilderness park, for example, even the presence of a building, regardless of its architectural merit or historical significance, can be considered inappropriate. Richard Longstreth describes the preservation of the historic Camp Santanoni complex in the Adirondack Forest Preserve, a park with perhaps the strongest wilderness protection provision in the United States. One of the largest and most significant of the Adirondack "camps" built in the late nineteenth century, Santanoni was a major monument of American architecture that, once it was acquired by the state in 1972, fell under the state's wilderness management policies. Longstreth describes the long struggle to recognize the cultural value of the camp within the context of the wilderness reservation. The experience yields a "particularly insightful case study of the ongoing debate between natural and cultural affinities" and ultimately shows "how both spheres can exist in harmonious relationship with each other."

The construction of new architecture in a park can be just as controversial as the preservation of historic buildings, as Elizabeth Flint Engle shows in her essay on Gilbert Stanley Underwood's Jackson Lake Lodge (1955) in Grand Teton National Park in Wyoming. Now a National Historic Landmark and considered one of the finest works of national park architecture in the United States, its modernist design originally caused an outcry among conservation groups and others who felt the prewar tradition of "rustic" design better harmonized with park settings.

In the last essay of this section, Christine Madrid French explains the history and controversy that surrounds another extraordinary work of modernist design in the U.S. national park system, Richard Neutra's Cyclorama Center building (1962) in Gettysburg National Military Park in Pennsylvania. In this case, the building's contemporary design and its location near the center of the battlefield site eventually became controversial. The perceived inappropriateness of the development has led the National Park Service to seek the building's demolition. A new visitor center complex, designed to resemble a group of farm buildings, has already been built in a less sensitive area of the battlefield.

* * *

The passionate and contrasting responses to postwar modernism in the U.S. national park system are a reminder that the setting of a park landscape creates significance—and sometimes controversy—for works of landscape and architectural design. Parks express the values, aspirations, and interests of their makers. Whether mostly made or mostly left unaltered, park landscapes are among the most telling and evocative of ideological expressions. Park landscapes embody cultural constructions of nature and history, and at the same time they model and comment on society's place in these grand narratives.

The history of park design, however, is prone to being misinterpreted as a history of styles, concerned merely with the outward appearance of buildings, structures, and other park landscape features. The essays presented here make it clear that the significance of the history of park design relates to defining what parks—clearly a diverse and multifaceted category of places—are intended to achieve. Park design,

in other words, is how parks work. Design is what has made it possible for people to have meaningful experiences of nature and history without destroying or impairing the landscapes they experienced. In other cases, park design made daily patterns of urban life more healthful, beautiful, and meaningful. Above all park design has been a means of landscape preservation: of stabilizing and interpreting places of perceived natural or cultural significance for a visiting public, whatever the interpretive program and whoever the visiting public might be.

The purpose of this volume, then, is to recover and expand these meanings of park design and to define what have been, historically, some of the essential purposes and processes of park making. This is a task of concern not only to designers and historians also but to park managers and, in fact, to anyone who cares about the fate of park landscapes of the past or of the future. Park design is too important to the task of stewardship to be dismissed as a matter of stylistic preferences. The expanded definition of design these scholars, together, elucidate is a necessary means of successful preservation, interpretation, and management.

Notes

1. Olmsted's plan was not implemented. For the text of his recommendations, see Frederick Law Olmsted, "Preliminary Report on the Yosemite and Big Tree Grove" (1865), in *The Papers of Frederick Law Olmsted,* vol. 5, *The California Frontier,* ed. Victoria Post Ranney (Baltimore: Johns Hopkins University Press, 1990), 488–516.

2. The comparative cost analysis of the Boston and New York parks was Olmsted's own. See Frederick Law Olmsted, "Notes on the Plan of Franklin Park and Related Matters" (1886), in *The Papers of Frederick Law Olmsted, Supplementary Series,* vol. 1, *Writings on Public Parks, Parkways, and Park Systems,* ed. Charles Beveridge and Carolyn Hoffman (Baltimore: Johns Hopkins University Press, 1997), 460–534.

3. Eliot's most significant description of his design intent for the metropolitan reservations around Boston was published shortly after his death. See Charles Eliot, *Vegetation and Scenery in the Metropolitan Reservations* (Boston: Lamson, Wolffe and Company, 1898).

4. The 1916 National Park Service legislation describes the purpose of the U.S. national parks, famously, as "to conserve the scenery and the natural and historic objects and the wild life therein and to provide for the enjoyment of the same in such manner and by such means as will leave them unimpaired for the enjoyment of future generations." See Lary M. Dilsaver, ed., *America's National Park System: The Critical Documents* (Lanham, Md.: Rowman and Littlefield, 1994), 46–47.

5. Frederick Law Olmsted Jr., *Report of State Park Survey of California* (Sacramento: California State Printing Office, 1929).

6. For perhaps the best description of this new paradigm for protecting landscapes, see Adrian Phillips, *Management Guidelines for IUCN Category V Protected Areas, Protected Landscapes/Seascapes,* World Commission on Protected Areas (WCPA) Best Practice Protected Area Guidelines Series No. 9 (Gland, Switz., and Cambridge, UK: IUCN, The World Conservation Union, 2002).

7. The 1872 legislation that established Yellowstone National Park specified that the vast wilderness of the Yellowstone plateau be "dedicated and set apart as a public park or pleasuring-ground for the benefit and enjoyment of the people." See Dilsaver, ed., *America's National Park System,* 28–29.

8. Stephen T. Mather, the first director of the U.S. National Park Service, for example, described in 1925 a "great flow of tourist gold" that would follow the routes of automotive tourism and add "new life to communities unprogressive for years." The flow, he added, was "a particularly dependable annual source of income for many Western States." See U.S. Department of the Interior, National Park Service, *1925 Annual Report,* 1.

9. For a comprehensive account of political and social dimensions of municipal park creation in New York, see, for example, Roy Rosensweig and Elizabeth Blackmar, *The Park and the People: A History of Central Park* (Ithaca: Cornell University Press, 1992).

10. John Muir, *The Yosemite* (New York: The Century Co., 1920), 262. However, even Muir knew when to enlist the most powerful capitalists of his day. See Richard J. Orsi, "'Wilderness Saint' and 'Robber Baron': The Anomalous Partnership of John Muir and the Southern Pacific Company for the Preservation of Yosemite National Park," *The Pacific Historian* 29, nos. 2 and 3 (Summer/Fall 1985): 137–56.

PART I

NATURE AND DESIGN IN EUROPE AND AMERICA

The Influence of Anxiety

Keeping Europe in the Picture in North American Landscaping

It is a commonplace that a change in land-scape taste and in landscape design occurred during the eighteenth century in Europe, with England initially providing the most conspicu-ous theoretical and practical manifestation of this modern mode.[1] And the picturesque was, by 1800, a central element in both the practice and the thinking of landscape design and land-scape experience. The poet Robert Southey wrote in 1807 that there was a "new science" of landscape (i.e., a new way of knowing land-scape), for the expression of which knowledge "a new language had been formed."[2] He meant, obviously, that there was a lot of talk and writ-ing about the picturesque; but equally he im-plied that the picturesque itself provided a lan-guage in which to articulate something new. It was more than just a language for the eye, but rather one (in Olmsted's words about Yosem-ite) to express that "with which on every side [sight] is *associated*."[3] Picturesque language, rather than being simply a fresh style of de-scribing or of doing something with the land, was relished as a means to knowledge; such knowledge was in itself new—an awareness, even self-consciousness about the mind's pro-cesses in themselves; yet it was also a means of articulating matters that had not hitherto found such an apt vehicle. What is at stake here, I believe, is that the picturesque for the first time in landscape discussions provided a means of talking not only about physical in-terventions by a landscape designer but about visitor responses to landscapes; it connected design to those who experienced it; it linked exterior effects and forms to imaginative and mental habits. And it did this by its reliance upon several mechanisms—yet we tend today to treat these mechanisms as if they were ends in themselves. The mechanisms of the pictur-esque upon which we tend to focus are, first, its promotion of static pictures, that is, of a land-scape fixed and captured in a series of pictorial moments, perhaps (but not necessarily) ones that remind us of paintings or seem suitable subjects for pictures; secondarily, its delight in merely formal properties, the textures of a land's basic materials, its stones, plants, sur-face gradations, and the endless modulations of the sky throughout the day and the sea-sonal round. Both of those prescriptions were certainly in play, but neither of them quite so starkly or so predominantly as we like to think.

The picturesque was above all about move-ment, movement through a landscape, and the movement of the mind: Southey said that "a course of summer travelling" was looked upon as "essential" for learning the new language. It insisted upon the spectator's constant mobil-ity in search of picturesque scenery, whether that was traveling in a coach through whose open window flashed images of countryside or wandering on foot through a parkland; this was as much what we might now call "moving pictures" as a sequence of isolated "stills." The young William Gilpin, later of course to publish his picturesque tours of different areas of Great Britain, published his first piece as a dialogue between two visitors moving through the gar-dens of Stowe in 1747. It is an instructive piece, for its insights into how the meaning of a land-scape is determined by the dialogic exchange

13

between its elements and visitors, and how the two visitors themselves debate and share responses during their lengthy stroll; but above all, the dialogue follows them *through* the gardens, a territorial exploration that is paralleled by the movement of their minds. One amusing moment draws attention to this: when a blank hedge momentarily hides further views, one of them explains it is like the pause of an orchestra in mid-piece or between movements.[4]

Certainly, the picturesque landscape involved the discovery of prime and special moments in a landscape that the connoisseur spotted and celebrated by stopping to contemplate them, but these moments were taken within a progress or process through some territory. The identification in American national parks of spots appropriately named "Artist Point" (on the eastern rim of the Grand Canyon of the Yellowstone) or "Inspiration Point" (in Yosemite) was a fossil of this picturesque strategy; in picturesque jargon they were "stations." But they were not, especially in the much larger territory of western national parks, anything but moments in a longer journey, as the effort to devise routes through those parks, combining carriages drives, bridle paths, and footpaths, made clear. In his recent work on the approach to Yosemite Falls, Lawrence Halprin has been focused precisely on the haptic experience of negotiating the territory as visitors move towards the falls.[5]

The love of rough and variegated materials derived undoubtedly and indeed etymologically from the origins of picturesque—the manner of applying paint roughly to a canvas was in 1685 termed "working A la pittoresk, that is boldly."[6] This emphasis upon the performance of the medium, which becomes of concern to many landscape painters in the eighteenth century, can be seen both in the detailed finish of a canvas (Thomas Gainsborough called it providing "business for the eye"[7]) and in the relish for the busy work of the engraving tool's incisions on the plate (fig. 1). In its turn this preference for texture and intricacy was transferred to and sought in the physical landscape. It was indeed hard to have a picturesque land-

scape that was not textured and *mouvementé*—it contained its own movements, just as the picturesque strollers or tourists had theirs. This is why the wonderfully and enormously satisfying materials of the Yosemite—its rocks, its streams, its tree forms—appealed immediately to picturesque taste like that of Ansel Adams, Carleton Watkins, or William Henry Jackson and continue to call for a responsive photography (fig. 2).

But that does not explain why people sought out both picture-like moments in the landscapes they visited and, further, looked for those moments to be variegated and textured; what had those purely formal experiences to do with the picturesque as Southey's "science" or mode of knowledge? The reason was that it was through the stimulus of the eye that the mind and imagination of the visitor could be touched. It was, as we shall see, an essential understanding of the new empirical philosophy, which had its most significant de-

FIG. 1. A detail of one image of a picturesque landscape design, by Benjamin Pouncy after Thomas Hearne, illustrating Richard Payne Knight's poem "The Landscape" (1794). The painter Thomas Gainsborough called the bold and busy work on painted canvases a "business for the eye," but this effect was also much employed by engravers, as here. (© Trustees of the British Museum)

FIG. 2. Two scenes in the Yosemite Valley, 2000. The temptation to photograph Yosemite by responding to its picturesque textures has always been strong. (Author photo)

velopments in Britain during the eighteenth century. Frederick Law Olmsted was squarely within this epistemological tradition when he said that "landscape is arranged to please the eye" so that it will also be "pleasing to the mind," or, again, when he insists upon the need for appropriate "associations" with a designed landscape like Prospect Park, or that Yosemite must arouse and occupy the mind in ways different from ordinary circumstance.[8] In short, the picturesque was not simply or only a visual language; it was a holistic experience that included responses for which words were sometimes better suited.

John Muir in a chapter titled "The Glacial Meadows" in *The Mountains of California* exemplifies this complex and rich experience with extraordinary subtlety. He evinces the standard picturesque delight in the texture of the landscapes, the "littered bits," the curving lines of

forest edge, which he appreciates as he moves through them in search of the glacier meadows themselves. How his associations were called into play becomes one of his themes: maybe the meadows are "gardens," "carefully tended lawns of pleasure grounds," yet words are neither "fine enough" to capture the effects nor does the handy vocabulary of garden art prove useful. He also celebrates the visual pleasures or the "picture" of the meadows—where "You are all eye" and where the lines are "such as Nature alone can draw"—only to gather them all into a state of "discriminating consciousness" where "the mind is fertilized and stimulated and developed like sun-fed plants."[9] And it is, finally, in the mind ("imagine yourself . . .") that the fullest meaning of these landscapes is grasped, in a prose that is agile, detailed in its descriptive moments, carefully scientific (even noting something "as yet almost unknown to science"), plying between the objective and a hinted transcendence ("divine alpen glow"; "winged representatives overhead" [i.e., insects!]). And if he stays his gaze in a quasi-pictorial gaze, he is equally quick to register the process-driven ecology of the Yosemite.

The chapter, in short, does not consist of statements *about* associationism, of the sort one can find in theoretical works by Uvedale Price and Richard Payne Knight (the leading English exponents of the psychological effects of the picturesque). Rather, writings like this chapter of Muir's actually *perform* associationism; they capture and articulate how it works; they are in short "picturesque interpretation" in process.[10] What we see significantly in American responses to landscape is the active reliance upon associative habits rather than a discussion of their mechanisms. The practice was beginning to emerge in European picturesque publications like the collections of imagery by William Watts (. . . *a Collection of the most interesting and Picturesque views* of 1779) or William Angus (1787), when words amplified the busily engraved image and volunteered appropriate associations for the viewer of the images or for the tourist who visited the sites themselves.

This, I think, represents the biggest misunderstanding of the original picturesque by modern commentators, especially those (and they are legion) who despise it. The picturesque was not primarily or only about physical forms and visual apprehension of them, whether static in "pictures" or taken in movement; it was about stimulating or moving the mind, promoting associations and ideas and emotions and sentiments. And this must inevitably continue to be an aim of landscape architecture in the twenty-first century. There were many ways in which that could happen, and they underwent significant changes during the eighteenth and early nineteenth centuries. Basically this change, as theorized by landscape writers like Thomas Whately,[11] went like this: once there had been landscapes into which a variety of items were inserted—statues, temples, inscriptions, etc.—that would stimulate but also direct the visitor's responses

along lines that were assumed to draw upon a shared cultural knowledge; but more recent fashion has turned towards landscapes where visitors were granted more freedom of response and indeed encouraged to bring their own associations to bear—this could be either in landscapes largely devoid of the prompts and triggers once fashionable, or in the same old emblematic landscapes but now without any obligation to respond (even if that were still possible) in ways that presumed a shared and collective culture. And this change in how landscapes were experienced may be paralleled also in the slightly earlier history of landscape painting, with a corresponding impact on the new picturesque science of landscape: Nicolas Poussin and Claude Lorrain, even Salvator Rosa, painted landscapes where figures, events, and even buildings had significance for those who could read them and so contributed to some meaning; increasingly, and influenced more by northern Dutch and Flemish painters, the preference was for landscapes not freighted with meaning, not focused upon historical or mythological narrative, but where viewers could identify with much more commonplace and quotidian events and characters.[12] In the American context, the absence (as Europeans presumed) of those markers of older cultures and civilizations, the absence of ruin, for example, or temples in the landscape, necessarily forced attention back (or forward) onto the land itself and upon whatever associations with it newly arrived Europeans could entertain.

What is happening then by the end of the eighteenth century in England and by extension in the United States, in both painted landscapes and, more important, in designed ones, is that the "control" or burden of responsibility for prompting ideas and associations had passed from the landscape designer to the visitor in ways that bereft the poor designer of a traditional responsibility to provide "content" and forced him back (they were usually men) to a concern with the play of forms and shapes and materials. The contents page of Thomas Whately's *Observations* says it all with his primary focus on "convex, and concave shapes of ground," varieties of wood, "effects and species of water," and the character of rocks. It was left to visitors to supply content or meaning, and handily available to them both theoretically and as a practical mechanism was a brand new strain of empirical philosophy.

Associationism was *the* philosophical or psychological development of the eighteenth century and was largely driven and achieved by a succession of empirical British thinkers, upon whose work the landscape theorists drew gratefully and substantially, thereby consolidating the British claim to have cornered the market in this new and modern science of the picturesque. Its basic assumptions need to be better grasped by landscape critics today (significantly, my computer's spell-check simply refuses to acknowledge the word "associationism"). Put briefly, British empirical philosophy from John Locke onwards, but especially in the later work of the Scots Archibald Alison, Alexander Gerard, and Hugh Blair (widely read in the United States), asserted that the individual human is not, as had been previously assumed, born with a set of preconceived ideas but acquires them through his or her own physical experiences that in their turn stimulate ideas and associations and thereafter combine in a series of complex maneuvers to constitute individual mind-sets. This theory was able to promote and sustain two essential elements of the new landscape experience: it gave primacy to all of our own, personal experiences, most notably those we received through the eyes; and it granted a hitherto unappreciated authority to the individual's responses and imagination. Consequently, it also promoted the idea that every person had a legitimate, plausible, or worthwhile way of responding to situations, including landscape situations. It was, if you will, inherently democratic.

The democratic value of this new landscape response was obviously well adapted to the American scene. However, at the same time, the idea that anyone's ideas and associations were equal to anybody else's was constrained by the need for people to be guided, coached, or otherwise directed by those who saw themselves as the guardians of taste, with the expertise and moreover the obligation to understand landscape. This had been true in Great Britain, where the whole landscape movement of the late eighteenth and early nineteenth centuries was understood by many as an education in national values and appreciation. It was true, also, of various manipulations of the picturesque cult throughout Europe, where German, Italian, and Russian territories sought to celebrate a particularly local terrain and its cultural significance. And it was at work, too, in North America, where, as the title page of A. J. Downing's *Treatise* (1841, 1844, 1849) made clear, available (European) landscape notions were to be "adapted" to the different circumstances of the United States.

We can track this double response—the reception of sense impressions; then their formation of mental ideas—in some early responses to Yosemite. These constituted an astonishing range of personal reactions, yet all were conditioned by a need somehow to get a more public, civic, or national handle on the meanings of this astonishing location. It was not simply a question of how on earth inherited modes of graphic representation could cope with its extraordinary scenery, but even more crucially how to grasp its significance. The range of associative imagery trotted out was quite extraordinary—at least for us today when we think we have found better means of articulating their meanings or perhaps do not see the need to do so: Yosemite had battlements, so it was America's answer to European mediaeval architecture, or perhaps a site naturally defensible; it was a temple, therefore a place to worship in; a textbook (biblically based), wherein to read quasi-sacred scripture; a (natural) sculpture museum, with exhibits to be viewed. Each of these responses was accompanied or sustained by an already available vocabulary and set of assumptions. As Yosemite was also hailed as a natural garden or park, this, too, allowed visitation in more or less established ways. Indeed, one practical consequence of thinking of Yosemite as a garden or park was that it came to be developed along the familiar lines of European-derived landscape architecture: paths, carriage drives, viewing stations were all downloadable devices from landscape architecture in Europe. This essentially touristic response—opening territory to visitation—underlay another early strategy, which involved promoting American scenery in the light of European assumptions: as when Olmsted, in his efforts to convince the California authorities to assume responsibility for Yosemite, invoked the commercially uplifting example of Switzerland's exploitation of its mountain landscapes. However, in all cases the associations and their practical consequences were driven by a need to understand and promote the Americanness of the landscapes; the Swiss had made their name, reputation, and economic stability by means of (exploiting) their landscape; the States could also do so in Yosemite, the Hudson Valley, or at Niagara.[13]

This understanding of the public meanings of landscape also had European origins that went beyond the mere appreciation of landscape for its own sake. In his book *The Political Theory of Painting from Reynolds to Hazlitt,* the English scholar John Barrell recalls that by the early eighteenth century, painting had a civic role, that its success was to be judged by its ability to constitute its viewers as members of a republic or community of taste and thereby confirm, indeed enable, their membership of a political public; in such matters the individual and personal are subordinated to the permanent and universal, and those who can grasp these abstract principles and ideas are the privileged citizens. Such considerations were readily carried from painting itself to the study of landscape viewed in the picturesque manner. But, as we have already seen, such collective standards and beliefs faltered and were essentially called into question by the early nineteenth century, not least by the growing popularity of landscape painting itself, which Barrell shows that Sir Joshua Reynolds allowed as a genre released or absolved from those civic responsibilities (Reynolds was arguing for the specific case of Gainsborough). However, I would argue that in the United States, the political and civic perspective continued to preside—one has only to think of the work of Thomas Cole, the Hudson River School, or paintings that confronted the railroad developments to see how they were committed to political and civic meanings of the American land.[14]

* * *

The picturesque mode of viewing, designing, or just thinking about landscape had been nurtured within the European culture of country seats. Though there were essential differences between say, nobility and gentry in England and their counterparts in Germany or France, for our purposes it is more important to recall that the new science of landscape flourished and spread outwards from the private estates of landed gentry, who, in England at least, constituted the power base of parliamentary democracy. This did not, I think, translate readily onto American soil, and one particular English artist and immigrant to Philadelphia in 1794, William Birch, demonstrates how this was so.

Back home Birch had participated in the cult of the picturesque by publishing a fine example of the landscape book: the *Délices de la Grande Bretagne* in 1791. Like other explorations of the English countryside—such as Gilpin's tours, innumerable guidebooks, and other collections of views by Watts or Angus mentioned earlier —Birch's images were accompanied by texts that explained the historical significance and associations of sites throughout England (fig. 3). The *Délices* offered its readers engravings of already existing paintings of significant places, most of which took a picturesque approach, and annexed to them a letterpress in which historical associations and significant features of the places were spelled out. It is a veritable repertoire of picturesque "science." Once he arrived in Philadelphia Birch followed the same practice, producing first a highly successful sequence of plates of the *City of Philadelphia* in 1800 and then, eight years later, his *The Country Seats of the United States of America,* which completely flopped.[15]

What is particularly interesting, then, about Birch's picturesque response is that at this

FIG. 3. A site engraved and annotated in William Birch's *Délices de la Grande Bretagne* (1791). The text is a transcription of the page succeeding this image in the original. (© Trustees of the British Museum)

"Roslin Castle. Situated five miles south-west of Edinburgh. The time this castle was built is not certain, but it existed about the year 1100: it stands on a rock decorated with the richest verdure, and almost round which flows the river Esk, after forming a beautiful cataract down its steep near the castle; from which it winds in luxurious streams to the distant lawns. The beauties of this place have inspired poets with pastoral delight; one of whom, in a favorite song (called Roslin Castle), speaking of it as the abode of rural felicity, writes thus:

'Twas in the season of the year,
When all things gay and sweet appear,
That Colin, with the morning ray,
Arose and sung his rural lay:
Of Nanny's charms the shepherd sung,
The hills and dales with Nanny rung;
While Roslin Castle heard the Swain,
And echoed back the cheerful strain.

Within the walls of this mouldering fabric has been reared a noble race of heroes, whose valiant deeds are still preserved; and often, as the villager recounts their glory, and the glory of his ancestors who fought under their banner, his breast glows with the patriotic ardour of his brave forefathers. This view was taken from the south, on the opposite bank of the river, in 1786."

early stage of the nineteenth century it was the public city and its emblematic buildings and institutions of the first federal capital that captured his new compatriots' attention, while private country estates along the neighboring rivers of Schuylkill and Delaware were of far less consequence to the fashioning of a national identity, unlike the country seats and landscapes of Great Britain. Birch's approach to the country seats around Philadelphia tried to exploit the full repertoire of picturesque science and technique that he had learned in England: busy engraved work on the page was easy enough, as were responding to dense and variegated territory (as his text points out) and ensuring a collaboration of word and image (fig. 4). More difficult was drumming up a selection of rich associations both historical and aesthetic for each site (again the text sometimes struggles to elaborate on these themes). But fundamentally the role of an American country estate was not at all the same as back home, where the English nobility and gentry ruled the country from their country seats and where those private retreats were the basis of communal power. The publication in 1808 of a picturesque anthology of *Country Seats* did not succeed in finding sufficient ways to high-

FIG. 4. An image from William Birch's *The Country Seats of North America* (1808). The text is a transcription of the page succeeding this image in the original. (Emmet Collection, Miriam and Ira D. Wallach Division of Art, Prints and Photographs, The New York Public Library, Astor, Lenox and Tilden Foundations)

"Woodlands. This noble demesne has long been the pride of Pennsylvania. The beauties of nature and the rarities of art, not more than the hospitality of the owner, attract to it many visitors. It is charmingly situated on the winding Schuylkill, and commands one of the most superb water scenes that can be imagined. The ground is laid out in good taste. There are here a hot house and green house containing a collection in the horticultural department, unequalled perhaps in the United States. Paintings &c. of the first master embellish the interior of the house, and do credit to Mr. Wm. Hamilton, as a man of refined taste. . . . It is about a mile from the city of Philadelphia."

light the significance and lessons of American scenery for the new nation. More time would be needed before the associative potential of the American landscape could be convincingly exploited; and this involved—as evinced in the much later imagination of Wallace Stevens—the bifocal skill to register the "poem of pure reality, untouched/By trope or deviation" as well as "the spirit's alchemicana/Included," the palpable quiddities of the American land as well as its meanings ("not merely the visible").[16] There would also be time needed to appreciate the lessons of bigger and more resonantly American sceneries, perhaps because they were public, like those at Niagara, White Mountains, Yellowstone, and Yosemite; all such landscapes responded to the approaches of European picturesque but now with a more carefully adumbrated sense of their national significance. So Birch's attempt to translate the culture of country seat picturesque to Pennsylvania is symptomatic of a cultural démarche that has two key elements: the landscaped private demesne was not the ground where public identity was primarily sought or created; and it was sites where indigenous natural features dominated rather than where designers remodeled sites for merely private consumption that inspired nationalistic attention, which is why in the early days of the nineteenth century, towns and cities were sometimes the more crucial emblems of the new nation and in their turn became the sites for major public parkland.

* * *

The European contribution to the reformulation or refashioning of American ideas of parks and park design, then, was neither direct nor directly transferable. In adapting landscape concepts and practices (as Downing registered) to the circumstances and conditions of this newfound land, three considerations were of consequence. First, the "natural" or naturalistic taste in landscape design lost its primacy. Second, new importance was given to a long-standing view (though little remarked in modern landscape criticism) that most territories consisted of a series of differently handled zones, each of which determined how the others might be understood; no longer was one particular mode of landscape preferred, and the immediate opportunities to experience one kind allowed others to be treated or encouraged. Third, given those developments, there arose the issue of how best to introduce the countryside into the town—the old *rus in urbe* of ancient Rome—as well as how the urban dweller might be encouraged and led to respond to the wealth of undesigned landscapes throughout the United States.

The English climax of eighteenth-century enthusiasm for the new landscaping glorified "natural" effects (though often created artificially) and vilified obvious art or meretricious design. This new naturalism was deemed an advance in civilization: a view promoted by Horace Walpole, and much repeated around Europe, was that landscape design had enjoyed an inevitable, teleological, and utterly admirable and unstoppable progress from rigid, formal, autocratic, and unnatural design to loose, informal, "free" democratic, and natural design, of which we are (so this story goes still for some folk) the lucky heirs today.

Such an attitude and indeed ideology were subjected during the nineteenth century to some tough challenges. The naturalistic style was associated, if only subconsciously, with the elite and wealthy landowner, and needed modifications if it was to be used in the public domain. Above all, there was the double charge that a totally natural landscape was simply boring and if it was indeed designed, then the design did not read as any different than the non-designed—in the third quarter of the eighteenth century, Williams Chambers, admittedly a political antagonist of Lancelot "Capability" Brown, voiced the objection that Brown's work was "no different from the common fields." Sir Joshua Reynolds made the same point, more philosophically, when he argued in 1786 that "Gardening, as far as Gardening is an Art, or entitled to that appellation, is a deviation from nature; for if the true taste consists, as many hold, in banishing every appearance of Art, or any traces of the footsteps of man, it would then be no longer a Garden."[17] Whether consciously or not, much landscaping sought to adjust design so as to escape that kind of stricture.

We know, in fact, that the Brownian mode of greensward to the very door was not as ubiquitous as is sometimes stated in landscape histories (we still exist too much in the thrall of Walpole's Whiggish and teleological narrative). But Brown's successor, Humphry Repton, worked frequently to pull the grass back from the house and to introduce gravel walks, terracing, and other elements of a more obviously "garden" character. Since Repton was also forced to work for clients no longer solely among the big landed gentry, but for industrialists and suburban bourgeois, his design adjustments made considerable sense. So the hold of a totalizing naturalism upon landscape design was conspicuously relaxed. This was increasingly evident in the landscaping of smaller, often suburban grounds, ill-suited to the generous expanses of Brownian grassland. And by the end of his career Repton was, of course, at work redesigning London squares. And it is the Reptonian legacy, mediated via John Claudius Loudon, who would eventually in 1840 republish Repton's writings, that underpinned A. J. Downing's introduction of adapted landscape gardening to the United States.

But these changes in design thinking, which provided more stimulating elements nearer the house, not to mention more useful areas to be enjoyed on foot, returned people to an old aspect of landscape understanding: where one responded to any kind of land by understanding it in relation to—or even seeing it juxtaposed with—another. Yet the basic concept was very old, on both a pragmatic and aesthetic level. Anyone who worked with the land knew that its different segments, for geological or topographical reasons, required various treatments, yielding different crops or allowing different activities. On the aesthetic level, the sudden flourishing of designed gardens in the Italian Renaissance had pushed their critics to invent a new vocabulary which distinguished

between the world of garden making and the world of larger cultural infrastructure—villages, ports, bridges, roads, and so on.[18] The garden was understood precisely in terms of its difference from the other zones—a point graphically rendered by many seventeenth-century and later engravings of country seats, where both the aesthetic distinctions and the practical ones obviously coalesce in one's reading of such imagery. Painting treatises, too, like that of Roger de Piles, established a taxonomy of different landscapes that had a marked effect upon later landscape design, as we can see in Thomas Whately's treatment of different situations to be treated by designers.[19]

These developments had several consequences for how parks were conceived and designed. If the "naturalistic" became a less favored way of representing "nature," partly because what one may term "real nature" was more and more accessible by road and later rail to more and more of the general public, and if one kind of landscape is appreciated the more because we know others to compare with it, then it became of the utmost interest to determine what kind of garden and park elements to establish both in remote landscapes and, as was increasingly the need, in a variety of modern urban contexts.

The landscape or picturesque garden had been touted throughout the late eighteenth and early nineteenth centuries as self-evidently *modern* and promoted endlessly as such. It was therefore a strong candidate to use in modern cities, and indeed it enjoyed that role widely across Europe from Munich to Birkenhead, from the French Republic's seizure and reformulation of royal parks and gardens to the various German states that saw its aptness for a whole new cluster of modern sites like cemeteries, academies, and town and city squares. Yet the picturesque or "English" style was by no means the only suitable mode for public parkland. Indeed, the European repertoire of parkscape and public garden that would have been familiar from their countries of origin to newly arrived immigrants in North America was considerable and various, and more often than not these useful and adaptable models were (not incidentally) rather more practical than picturesque.

Memories of village greens in England or urban squares and courtyards throughout European cities and towns, these latter often laid out in front of important public buildings like churches, cathedrals, or courthouses, sustained similar developments across the Atlantic. Furthermore, by the mid-eighteenth century at least, there were throughout Europe significant public pleasure grounds, such as Vauxhall Gardens in London, that were imitated in cities like Philadelphia and New York; there were promenades like the Cour de Reine in Paris or the Pincian Hill in Rome, not to mention the general availability for limited public use of royal or aristocratic lands (Hyde Park, for instance, or the Tuileries). By the early nineteenth century there were also very attractive new developments in public parks, sustained by a new theoretical literature which sought to translate the design and use of private, aristocratic land into proposals and plans for public use—the German C. C. L. Hirschfeld devoted a considerable part of his *Theory of Garden Art* (1779–85) to this subject, and the work was widely pillaged by writers in other European countries. The Englischer Garten in Munich was an early move to provide genuinely public parkland as opposed to simply opening royal and aristocratic parklands for public consumption. In the 1810s the city of Venice got its first public gardens from the conquering Emperor Napoleon; not insignificantly his architect, Giannantonio Selva, was determined to create a truly modern park, but in his case opted for the by then routine French strategy of combining a regular section with more deliberately picturesque sectors. Later landscapers still thought the "naturalistic" mode was better and offered to replace the more regular avenues of Selva's project with alternative "picturesque" designs.[20] Some of these examples—Munich notably (fig. 5)—were acknowledged by Americans, but it was probably Birkenhead Park, the first so-called people's park, near Liverpool (fig. 6), hailed by both Downing and Olmsted,

that inspired the proliferation of urban parklands throughout the United States. Its specifically egalitarian promotion and character, along with its shrewd exploitation of real estate around the edges of its parkland, made it an especially apt model for Americans to imitate.

But what seems particularly interesting and generally not much discussed is how the sheer variety of landscapes in North America impacted the design and implementation of public parks throughout the regions. The existence and celebration of magnificent and nationally applauded sceneries, like the Yellowstone, Niagara, or White Mountains, allowed a different approach to be taken with new parks in less sublime localities, even though some urban projects nonetheless looked to the grand natural examples as inspiration and even, in some form, as model. Furthermore, different parts of the country responded and needed to respond in very different ways to the promotion of public parks within local communities, as Jens Jensen and other midwestern designers came to

FIG. 5. Modern view in the Englischer Garten, Munich, late 1980s.

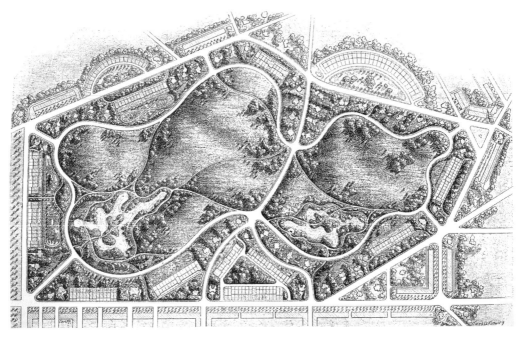

FIG. 6. Plan of Birkenhead Park, 1844. (Williamson Art Gallery and Museum, Birkenhead, Metropolitan Borough of Wirral, Cheshire)

recognize. Somebody who knew firsthand the Hudson Valley riverscape would have a rather different response to Olmsted's re-creation of it in Central Park than either a person born and bred in Manhattan or one with experience only of, say, Wisconsin. Olmsted himself objected to the reliance upon English picturesque in San Francisco, in part because it would not be a suitable language for representing that part of California.[21] The more people got to know of the grand, wild regions of North America, the more they wanted somehow to be reminded of them in sites like the Ramble of Central Park or the Ravine in Prospect Park; but equally their specific urban needs pulled them away from such often distant picturesque possibilities into the much more pragmatic mode of parks that catered to a whole variety of local civic needs. So at least by the third quarter of the nineteenth century there was no absolute idea of what any American park should look like or how it should perform: landscapes were perceived, experienced, or designed vis-à-vis other places.

Indeed, the visual documentation of American public parks established during the nineteenth century reveals the astonishing variety of their designs, uses, and associations. There is one whole narrative to be made out of the amenities and facilities deemed necessary in public parks—from boating to bandstands, from memorials to educational and civic opportunities (pavilions for nursing mothers, stations to provide fresh milk). Another concerns the variety of ways in which "nature" was interpreted locally and how those interpretations or representations of nature were calculated and indeed how they often collided with more practical obligations. The increasing establishment and invention of public parks throughout cities and suburban areas meant that designers now resumed some responsibility for what associations and experiences their visitors should enjoy. With Central Park, Olmsted could hope to stimulate memories of a larger Hudson River scenery; at Niagara, a "Cave of the Winds" could readily localize and excite appropriate reactions; at Minnehaha Park from the 1890s,

Longfellow's much-loved poem was invoked for a park designed by the Olmsted firm. Yet often the practical requirements of many such parks took precedence over any attention to how a park might engage with a person's imaginative or spiritual life. When it came to the creation of New York's pocket parks in the late nineteenth century, it was much more a question of the necessary provision of pathways, seats, comfort stations, athletic facilities, or grass and flowers to be viewed across carefully contrived iron barriers.[22] Those who escaped crowded tenements to spend time in these small open areas were (we must presume) grateful for their physical opportunities and did not harp upon *meta*physical or associative possibilities. But the scope of American public park needs and designs ensured that the once primary picturesque taste and its attendant patterns of behavior were much less in demand, or, as we now know it to be, came to be a truly contested arena of taste.

* * *

In his essay "Travelling Theory," Edward Said makes what seems an obvious point: "Like people and schools of criticism, ideas and theories travel—from person to person, from situation to situation, from one period to another. . . . Such movement into a new environment is never unimpeded. It necessarily involves processes of representation and institutionalization different from those at the point of origin."[23] Now, even if landscape itself does not "travel," for it is (after all) emphatically and by definition *grounded,* ideas and assumptions about landscape do move about. We take with us our previous experience in looking and otherwise experiencing landscape when we move into new territories. Immigrants from Europe necessarily brought with them ways of responding to the physical worlds in which they had previously existed; for some it was comforting to wrap themselves in familiar ideas and old habits of response when placed in new surroundings, for others such baggage was unnecessary and even unusable. I am struck by the fact that the reuse of European place names, familiar markers in a strange country down the East Coast of the United States, tends to peter out as immigrants moved westward and old toponyms seemed less and less apt and comfortable in those territories. Yet it must also be remembered how the native American toponyms in the Yosemite, replete with their own geographical and mythological lore, were discarded by the white men and women who needed to claim that marvelous place for themselves. What in that instance is territorial or spatial—Europe losing its hold or asserting it, as its former inhabitants advanced into the American West—is also a temporal or historical effect. Modes of regarding landscape brought over from Europe steadily morphed, melded with, or stubbornly resisted local conditions, as a result of the institutionalizing of national and state parks and of the extraordinary inventiveness of American society in devising its own repertoire of public spaces.

Notes

1. I have discussed these matters at length in *The Picturesque Garden in Europe* (London: Thames and Hudson, 2002).

2. Robert Southey, *Letters from England,* ed. Jack Simmons (London: Cresset Press, 1951), 165.

3. *The Papers of Frederick Law Olmsted,* vol. 5, *The California Frontier, 1863–1865,* ed. Victoria Post Ranney (Baltimore: Johns Hopkins University Press, 1986), 500, emphasis added.

4. William Gilpin, *A Dialogue upon the Gardens at Stow . . .* (1748), The Augustan Reprint Society Publication, no. 176, ed. John Dixon Hunt (Los Angeles: William Andrews Clark Memorial Library, University of California, 1976), 11–12.

5. Lawrence Halprin. *A Life Spent Changing Places* (Philadelphia: University of Pennsylvania Press, 2011), figs. 173–176.

6. William Aglionby, *Painting Illustrated* (London: n.p., 1685), 67.

7. *The Letters of Thomas Gainsborough,* ed. Mary Woodall (Greenwich, Conn.: New York Graphic Society, 1963), 99.

8. Richard Grusin, *Culture, Technology and the Creation of America's National Parks* (Cambridge: Cambridge University Press, 2004), 33; see also Grusin's discussions of responses to Yosemite, 39 and 42.

9. John Muir, *The Mountains of California* (1894), in John Muir, *Nature Writings* (New York: Library of America, 1997), 395.

10. Ethan Carr, *Wilderness by Design: Landscape Architecture and the National Park Service* (Lincoln: University of Nebraska Press, 1998), 12.

11. See Thomas Whately, *Observations on Modern Gardening* (1770), 150–51, for the crucial and much-cited passage on the change from what he terms "emblematic" to expressive gardening.

12. A necessary caveat here is that English painters like Constable and, above all, Turner worked to rescue landscape from its traditionally subsidiary ranking in art's hierarchies and did so by infusing historical, mythological, and symbolic meanings into them. But that is another story, though it obviously has its American parallels in the work of artists like Thomas Cole.

13. It is, however, interesting to note a reverse influence from Niagara to the writings of the German landscape critic C. C. L. Hirschfeld, who considered it the best model for waterfalls in designed landscapes.

14. John Barrell, *The Political Theory of Painting from Reynolds to Hazlitt: "The Body of the Public"* (New Haven: Yale University Press, 1986). The same is true of the exploration of American geology in paintings. See Rebecca Bedell, *The Anatomy of Nature: Geology & American Landscape Painting, 1825–1875* (Princeton, N.J.: Princeton University Press, 2001).

15. I am indebted here to Emily T. Cooperman's edition of William Birch's *The Country Seats of the United States of America* (1808; Philadelphia: Studies in Landscape Architecture, University of Pennsylvania Press, 2008), as well as to Emily T. Cooperman and Lea Carson Sherk, *William Birch: Picturing the American Scene* (Philadelphia: University of Pennsylvania Press, 2010).

16. Quotations are from the eleventh section of "An Ordinary Evening in New Haven"; but any number of Stevens's meditations on American landscapes—such as "The Idea of Order at Key West"—would reveal the same intricate dialogue that may be identified as a fundamental American preoccupation.

17. From the thirteenth *Discourse* to students of the Royal Academy (a lecture on "Representation").

18. I have written extensively elsewhere about this understanding of different types of landscape in both its Renaissance formulations and its later hold upon landscape taste and design. See chap. 3, "The Idea of a Garden and the Three Natures," in my *Greater Perfections: The Practice of Garden Theory* (Philadelphia: University of Pennsylvania Press, 2000), 32–75.

19. Roger de Piles, *Cours de Peinture par principes* (1708; Paris: Gallimard, 1989), 98–116.

20. See John Dixon Hunt, *The Venetian City Garden: Place, Typology, and Perception* (Basel: Birkhäuser, 2009), chap. 7, where I have discussed the search for viable public grounds in the Venetian city.

21. *The Papers of Frederick Law Olmsted,* vol. 7, *Parks, Politics, and Patronage, 1874–1882,* ed. Charles E. Beveridge, Carolyn F. Hoffman, and Kenneth Hawkins (Baltimore: Johns Hopkins University Press, 2007), 51.

22. See Rachel Iannacone, "Open Space for the Underclass: New York's Small Parks (1880–1915)" (Ph.D. diss., University of Pennsylvania, 2005), and Rachel Iannacone, "The Small Parks in New York City and the Civilizing Process at the Turn of the Twentieth Century," in *Gardens and Cultural Change: A Pan-American Perspective,* ed. Michel Conan and Jeffrey Quilter (Washington, D.C.: Dumbarton Oaks Research Library and Collection, 2007), 87–103.

23. Edward W. Said, *The World, the Text, and the Critic* (New York: Vintage, 1978), 226.

Romanticism and the American Landscape

Romanticism transformed human consciousness and social behavior so radically that we speak of this epochal movement as a revolution in Western European culture. Although not consciously formulated as such until the final years of the eighteenth century, it was, like all shifts in cultural values, imperceptibly continuous. Its preconditions were established in the early eighteenth century and its influence, which reached its peak in the middle of the nineteenth century, lingers even into the present.

Defining Romanticism is much more difficult than defining Classicism, which is usually considered to be its opposite. On the one hand, Classicism is typically associated with rationality, order, balance, rules, and ideal models. Romanticism, on the other hand, gives primacy to emotion and the senses. It prizes intuition and inspiration and puts a premium on the dramatic, spectacular, fantastic, and mysterious. Consciousness of the self is its hallmark. The theater of the mind is Romanticism's sphere of action, and there imagination is given free rein. Moreover, it grants unprecedented social and political importance to the individual, championing original genius, personal sentiment, and the rights of man. Democratic in spirit, Romanticism fostered the overthrow of absolute monarchy as a form of governance and the decline of aristocratic privilege as a way of life along with the concomitant rise of nationalism and patriotic sentiment.

Additionally, the Romantic era was one of tremendous economic change. It witnessed the Industrial Revolution, the rapid enlargement of cities, the rise of middle-class commerce, and along with these the social and political empowerment of the bourgeoisie. Finally, and most important for our purposes here, Romanticism defined a profoundly new attitude toward nature. Its exponents considered nature in spiritual and aesthetic terms as well as from a cosmological and scientific standpoint.

In summary, Romanticism is a compound of various and sometimes opposing beliefs held together by a new sense of the meaning of the individual, society, and nature as well as their relationship to one another. It embodies the notion of continuous change without a decisive end and views the universe as a dynamic force rather than a vast machine. Because of its fluidity and multiplicity of meanings, Romanticism is not a single movement that colors all societies with the same brush. Indeed, nations, like individuals, have temperaments, and these are brought to bear on international culture in different ways. However, in all its variants, the inspiration and consolation of nature are a paramount theme for Romantic-era philosophers, writers, and artists. Indeed, it is possible to say that the relationship of human beings to nature—and by extension, the naturalistic landscape—is the paramount concern of Romanticism.

But Romanticism as response to nature is not the same thing everywhere, nor is it an unvarying phenomenon during the course of time. Romantic thought in America was influenced by German and English philosophy and poetry, yet it is distinguished from the underlying cultural ethos of these and other European nations in large part because of the character of the American landscape.

The country's bounty, expansiveness, and wild scenic grandeur inspired romantic awe and reverence. However, even as the abundant sublimity of nature here became a source of spiritual ecstasy for some, America's natural riches stirred another kind of faith in others. The notion of a God-ordained continental conquest and the concomitant commercial exploitation of the country's mineral ores, forest timbers, lakes, and rivers represents the alternate romantic notion of human progress. This economic ideal stimulated the immigration of many people from several countries, and they inevitably brought with them the attitudes and philosophies of their homelands. Yet the uniqueness of the American opportunity, of a new beginning in a new land, held a sense of promise that was religious as well as economic. Indeed, the power of the land itself as an agent of spiritual transformation is nowhere more forcefully discerned than in America.

* * *

With a yet tenuous and endangered hold on the land, the seventeenth-century Puritans viewed the vast forest with its towering centuries-old trees as demon-haunted, a satanic menace to be subdued in accordance with the biblical injunction to take dominion over the earth. However, the eighteenth-century Calvinist theologian Jonathan Edwards (1703–1758) was sufficiently attracted to Newton's theory that the phenomena of nature were grounded in eternal law to take the daring step of reinterpreting scriptural doctrine to embrace a concept of God's revelation and grace in nature. In his autobiographical narrative, Edwards relates the circumstances of an epiphany when he was taking a solitary walk of contemplation "looking upon the sky and clouds." There came over him "so sweet a sense of the glorious *majesty* and *grace* of God, as I know not how to express." With a fervor that sounds very much like Romanticism, Edwards describes how he saw "God's excellency, His wisdom, His purity and love . . . in the sun, moon, and stars; in the clouds and blue sky; in the grass, flowers, trees; in the water and all nature."[1]

Thomas Jefferson (1743–1825), a son of the Enlightenment, set his architectural masterpiece Monticello upon an eminence with spectacular views of forested mountain ridges growing blue in the distance. Rhetorically, he queried, "Where has Nature spread so rich a mantle under the eye? Mountains, forests, rocks, rivers. With what majesty do we ride above the storms! How sublime to look down into the workhouse of nature, to see her clouds, hail, snow, thunder, all fabricated at our feet! And the glorious sun when rising as if out of distant water, just gilding the tops of the mountains and giving life to all nature."[2] However romantic in extolling the stupendous scene, Jefferson saw this grand continental vista as a bounty for future generations, with America fulfilling in reality the antique myth of a pastoral golden age by turning the immense and potentially fruitful wilderness into independently owned farms. Following the Louisiana Purchase in 1803, he extended the previous Land Ordinance of 1785, superimposing upon the natural landscape of the entire continent a mile-square surveyor's grid. This enabled the parceling of land into sale parcels of 640-acre sections and ultimately into quarter sections of 40 acres. From the air today one can see how road alignments following the national grid have etched a pattern resembling a giant piece of graph paper onto the country west of the Ohio River.

The same dichotomous view of nature in mathematical terms on the one hand and romantic terms on the other is nowhere better illustrated than in Jefferson's description of the chasm beneath the Natural Bridge in *Notes on the State of Virginia:*

The fissure, just at the bridge, is, by some admeasurements, 270 feet deep, by others only 205. It is about 45 feet wide at the bottom, and 90 feet at the top. . . . Its breadth in the middle, is about 60 feet, but more at the ends, and the thickness of the mass, at the summit of the arch, about 40 feet. . . . Though the sides of this bridge are provided in some parts with a parapet of fixed rocks, yet few men have resolution to walk to them and look into the abyss. You involuntarily fall on your hands and feet, creep to the parapet and peep over it. . . . If the view from the top be painful and intolerable, that from below is delightful in an equal extreme. It is impossible for the emotions arising from the sublime, to be felt beyond what they are here; so beautiful an arch, so elevated, so light, and springing as it were up to heaven, the rapture of the spectator is really indescribable![3]

While Jefferson's penchant for mathematical design can be seen in his placement of symmetrically aligned circular mounds within a tree-defined perfect circle radiating around an octagonal villa at Poplar Forest, the farm that served as his retreat from his incessant stream of visitors, his romantic streak is evident in the landscape of Monticello. Here the grounds were laid out as a *ferme ornée,* and in 1771 he even went so far as to fantasize a design for "a Burying place [in] some unfrequented vale in the park . . . among antient and venerable oaks." This is where he planned to erect "a small Gothic temple of antique appearance, into which would be admitted very little light, perhaps none at all, save only the feeble ray of an half extinguished lamp."[4] He also envisioned channeling a stream into a cistern, which might serve as a pool for bathing. At the mouth of the spring he would carve a grotto, to be decorated with translucent pebbles and beautiful shells and in which a sculpture of a sleeping nymph would rest on a couch of moss. However, these projects inevitably took a backseat to his more pragmatic horticultural interests. No temple ever rose at Monticello, no grotto was built to adorn a spring, and instead of the romantic burial ground, a simple square graveyard enclosed by a fence was laid out in 1773.

Born in the year of President Jefferson's Louisiana Purchase, the essayist and poet Ralph Waldo Emerson (1803–1882) became the leader of the Transcendentalist movement in America. *Nature,* his famous essay of 1836, is its manifesto. Emerson did not need to seek the sublime in nature in order to experience religious awe. It was enough to find beauty in "the charming landscape which I saw this morning, [which] is indubitably made up of some twenty or thirty farms" owned but yet not owned by any farmer because "there is a property in the horizon which no man has but he whose eye can integrate all the parts, that is, the poet."[5] The poetry Emerson had in mind was not necessarily literary, though poets and other artists could often see its forms whole and thereby celebrate the totality of nature. It was instead a system of metaphysics accessible to all who were able to comprehend the meaning of the beauty spread all around them in every season and every time of day. Beauty for Emerson was not an end in itself, a subject of aesthetic appreciation. No, he maintained, "The shows of day, the dewy morning, the rainbow, mountains, orchards in blossom, stars, moonlight, shadows in still water, and the like, if too eagerly hunted, become shows merely, and mock us with their unreality. . . . The presence of a higher, namely, of the spiritual element is essential to its perfection."[6] Beauty could be embodied in art, for "this love of beauty is Taste. . . . But beauty in nature is not ultimate. It is the herald of inward and eternal beauty, and is not alone a solid and satisfactory good. It must stand as a part, and not as yet the last or highest expression of the final cause of Nature."[7] That cause was God. With the oratorical skill honed during his brief tenure as a Unitarian minister, Emerson exhorted his readers to "see the miraculous in the common" and "kindle science with the fire of the holiest affections."[8]

It would be hard to underestimate the pervasiveness of Transcendentalism and its influence on nineteenth-century American romantic ideals. William Cullen Bryant (1794–1878) took up the theme of nature as a moral force. His poem "Thanatopsis" (1811) enjoins us to:

Go forth, under the open sky, and list.
To Nature's teachings, while from all around—.
Suddenly, we're set free . . .
Earth and her waters, and the depths of air—
Comes a still voice—.

For Bryant, the still voice was that of God, and primeval Nature had a solemn grandeur unmatched by the most magnificent architectural works of humankind. America's old-growth forests, which had not yet been cleared, represented the golden-age sanctuaries when the world was young. Here was a most worthy place of worship to which he sang this paean:

THE GROVES were God's first temples. Ere man learned
To hew the shaft, and lay the architrave,
And spread the roof above them—ere he framed
The lofty vault, to gather and roll back
The sound of anthems; in the darkling wood,
Amidst the cool and silence, he knelt down,
And offered to the Mightiest solemn thanks
And supplication. For his simple heart
Might not resist the sacred influences
Which, from the stilly twilight of the place,
And from the gray old trunks that high in heaven
Mingled their mossy boughs, and from the sound
Of the invisible breath that swayed at once
All their green tops, stole over him, and bowed
His spirit with the thought of boundless power
And inaccessible majesty. Ah, why
Should we, in the world's riper years, neglect
God's ancient sanctuaries, and adore
Only among the crowd, and under roofs
That our frail hands have raised? Let me, at least,
Here, in the shadow of this aged wood,
Offer one hymn—thrice happy if it find
Acceptance in His ear.[9]

In 1872, Bryant, then age seventy-eight, agreed to serve as the nominal editor of D. Appleton and Company's publication of *Picturesque America: A Delineation by Pen and Pencil of the Mountains, Lakes, Forests, Water-falls, Shores, Cañons, Valleys, Cities, and Other Picturesque Features.* By this time, the virgin groves he had reverently extolled a half century earlier were becoming destinations for tourists and amusement for armchair travelers as well as badges of national pride. Trumpeting the superiority of American scenery over that of Europe in his preface, Bryant chauvinistically asserted, "For those who would see Nature in her grandest forms of snow-clad mountain, deep valley, rocky pinnacle, precipice, and chasm, there is no longer any occasion to cross the ocean."[10]

The romantic sensibility so evident in *Picturesque America* was an outgrowth of the now well-established group of painters known as the Hudson River School, of which America's first great landscape painter, Thomas Cole, is considered the founder. Although, during a three-year sojourn in Europe, Cole was entranced by the romanticism of classical ruins and medieval castles "over which time and genius have suspended an imperishable halo," he heeded his close friend Bryant's pleas to retain a preference for native scenery and its associations with God. "American scenery . . . has features, and glorious ones, unknown to Europe," he declared in a paper delivered in 1835 to the American Lyceum Society in New York. "The most distinctive, and perhaps the most impressive, characteristic of American scenery is its wildness," he continued.[11] For Cole, however, wildness and civilization were not necessarily antipodes, and in the same address he foresaw that "where the wolf roams, the plough shall glisten; on the gray crag shall rise the temple and tower—mighty deeds shall be done in the new pathless wilderness."[12]

With Cole's student Frederick Edwin Church (1826–1900), American Romantic painting reached its commercial apotheosis. Inspired by the great naturalist and geographer Alexander von Humboldt's (1769–1859) five-volume *Kosmos* (1845), Church set off in the explorer's footsteps to see and paint South American flora, fauna, volcanoes, and other exotic subjects. At a time when tropical plants were novel adornments of Victorian glasshouses, Church depicted the towering palm trees he found in the lush landscapes of South America. He was a master of painting light, perhaps second only to Turner in the exploitation of its dramatic potential. Sunrise and sunset were Church's favorite times of day, and his canvases are suffused with the pearly luminescence of morning or the roseate glow of evening.

In catering to the market for representations of the exotic, Church was able to exploit an important aspect of romantic taste. In 1859 he exhibited his most famous painting, *Heart of the Andes,* in his studio on Tenth Street in New

York, charging admission for its theatrical, spotlighted presentation behind a drawn plush curtain in a room filled with South American plants. With the painting's purchase for an unprecedented $10,000 and his fame secure, Church bought a farm in Hudson, New York, and subsequently on the hill above it he acquired eighteen acres with magnificent views of the river and the Catskills. On its crest, with the help of the architect Calvert Vaux, Church built Olana, a Victorian-cum-Persian mansion with intricate interior and exterior stenciling inspired by his travels in the Middle East. As the audience for his heroically romantic works waned with the changing taste of the times, Church busied himself painting small watercolors of his home and its stupendous views, while also designing Olana's sloping grounds in a the Picturesque style. Architectural evocations of the exotic, however, lived on in the Moresque bandstands, Turkish kiosks, and similarly fanciful structures that ornamented public parks.

Other Romantic painters sought a different kind of exoticism in the landscapes of the great deserts and Rocky Mountains of the American West. In 1871 Thomas Moran (1837–1926) accompanied Ferdinand Vandiveer Hayden's (1829–1887) survey expedition, and his watercolor sketches, the basis of later oils, dramatized the strange beauty of Yellowstone's waterfalls, deep canyons, geysers, and steaming fumaroles. Moran's watercolor sketches and the photographs of William H. Jackson, also a member of the Hayden expedition, helped convince the United States Congress to pass the 1872 bill that created the country's first national park. For the owners of railroad companies, Yellowstone, the Grand Canyon, and other wonders of the West were perceived not so much as scenery to be preserved for the spiritual benefit conferred by wilderness, but, rather, as uniquely American curiosities for the future enjoyment of tourists. But for the present those who went West—trappers, miners, adventurers, soldiers, government surveyors—could scarcely be classified as Romantics.

Back East the story was a different one. There the task of imbuing the local landscape with the aesthetics of Romanticism was undertaken by Andrew Jackson Downing (1815–1852), the country's most influential mid-nineteenth-century apostle of taste. Downing's mission was advocating the creation of the rural residence as a new dwelling type enjoying the advantages of both urban proximity and immediate access to the beauties of nature. The son of a nurseryman in Newburgh, New York, he set about educating himself thoroughly about botany and landscape gardening. In 1841, while still running the family nursery business, Downing published his first book, *A Treatise on the Theory and Practice of Landscape Gardening, Adapted to North America: with a view to The Improvement of Country Residences.* Its critical and sales success as the first book of its kind in America gained him widespread recognition as a horticultural authority and tastemaker, and this confirmed him in his pursuit of a career as a writer. *Cottage Residences* (1842), *Fruits and Fruit Trees of America* (1845), and *The Architecture of Country Houses* (1850) followed. Downing's own home in Newburgh and its grounds epitomized the life of rural refinement he wished for all Americans of moderate affluence.

Downing gained a wide audience and social influence as the editor of *The Horticulturist and Journal of Rural Art and Rural Taste.* Here he was able to dispense design advice and horticultural information while also advocating solutions to important social issues of the day. Thus, alongside his other columns discussing the best methods of transplanting trees, enriching soil, fertilizing orchards, growing vegetables, producing wine, constructing ice houses and greenhouses, and designing rural villas and landscaping their grounds, he proposed the creation of a metropolitan park as a boon for the residents of rapidly growing New York City. His best articles in *The Horticulturist* were collected in a single volume published as *Rural Essays* in 1853, a year after Downing's untimely death. This book provides an important perspective on the degree of attention nineteenth-century Americans gave to landscape design as a core component of urban and regional planning, a sphere that encompassed the country's first suburbs, parks, parkways, and rural cemeteries, all of which were social responses to the rapidly industrializing new metropolis.

In one of his essays in *The Horticulturist,* Downing argued, "Does not this general interest, manifested in . . . cemeteries, prove that public gardens, established in a liberal and suitable manner, near our large cities, would be equally successful?"[13] From the beginning of the rural cemetery movement in the 1830s, those who frequented them did not necessarily go to experience the romantic sweetness of melancholy emotion. For many, cemeteries offered the opportunity for a Sunday outing in scenic surroundings. The evident enjoyment of New York's Green-Wood Cemetery as a pleasure ground as well as a place of interment caused some civic-minded New Yorkers to ask the question: Why not a people's park devoid of reminders of mortality? The creation of Central Park, America's first great public landscape design work, was thus indebted to the popularity of the Romantic-era cemetery.

As the foremost landscape designer in the country, Downing would have probably been commissioned to design Central Park had his death in 1852 not cut short his successful career. Perhaps, however, the hand of fate had decreed a more fortunate outcome, for Downing's greatest contribution to the creation of Central Park lay not in the feature-filled design he fantasized in rosy prose, but, rather, in the serendipity of his traveling to England in 1850 to search for an architect to assist him as his practice expanded throughout the Hudson River Valley. There he met and hired Calvert Vaux (1824–1895). Seven years later, after he had set up an architectural practice in New York City following Downing's death, Vaux learned of the design competition for the great metropolitan park Downing had envisioned. By then Vaux had met Frederick Law Olmsted (1822–1903). Sensing an innate talent and appreciating Olmsted's reputation as a writer and perceptive observer of scenery and social conditions, Vaux asked him to be his collaborator in the design competition, thereby launching a partnership that would imprint metropolitan landscapes all across America with a romantic beauty that remains one of their chief assets today.

Neither Olmsted nor Vaux could imagine this legacy at the time. Olmsted still thought of himself as a man of letters, having recently published accounts of his travels in England and the American South. Economic necessity had made him seek the job of superintendent of the clearing operations necessary for the building of Central Park. Unlike Vaux, Olmsted had no training as an architect, and the profession they would together found and name, landscape architecture, did not yet exist in this country. It is in Olmsted's writings, therefore, that we must seek clues to his unconscious preparation to become the author of a romantic landscape design idiom for public spaces.

Although understanding engineering technology and maintaining a working knowledge of horticultural science were essential components of Olmsted's long career as the father of American park planning, the numerous reports he wrote over the years display, in spite of their basic pragmatism, sentiments that are essentially romantic. By Olmsted's own account, his deepest religious experiences were akin to those of Wordsworth, rapt responses to nature's sublimity. From reading their books, he thought of Emerson and Ruskin as "familiar friends [who] gave me the needed respect for my own constitutional tastes and an inclination to poetical refinement in the cultivation of them that afterwards determined my profession."[14] In addition to these writers, Olmsted read the works of the Picturesque theorists Uvedale Price and William Gilpin, "books of the last century, but which I esteem so much more than any published since, as stimulating the exercise of judgment in matters of my art."[15] As his career unfolded, it was evident that Olmsted preferred their Picturesque manner of landscape design to that of the contemporary Gardenesque proponents such as John Claudius Loudon, for he was far more interested in creating naturalistic scenery than in showcasing plants.

Greensward was the name of the plan Olmsted and Vaux submitted in the 1858 Central Park design competition. In its alternation of sweeping meadows, woodlands, and lakes, their conception of Central Park was a pastoral and picturesque landscape overall. Employing a technique reminiscent of Humphry Repton, they presented to the competition jury paired images, one photographic and the other a small painting. By this means of comparing "Existing Conditions" and "Effect Proposed," Vaux and Olmsted communicated their plan for transforming bare earth and brambles into grass and swampy ground into placid waters with lush shorelines. The park's existing topography and physical features guided them. Low-lying areas were to be turned into water bodies, and the handsome outcrops of glacially polished Manhattan schist were conceived as integral elements of their landscape composition. Broad meadows with indistinct boundaries were always for Olmsted a primary desideratum in the creation of park scenery, and many thousands of carts of topsoil were ferried from Long Island and New Jersey in order to enrich the park's thin soil and grade its rough and flat terrain into gentle hills and valleys. The Sheep Meadow, with a flock of grazing sheep, recalled bucolic rural scenery, and the Ramble's circuitous paths made the ascent to Vaux's Victorian Gothic Belvedere, with its then-unobstructed distant views of the Hudson River and Long Island Sound, delightfully mysterious.

The naturalistic appearance of Central Park belies the sophistication of the technical engineering underlying it. The design competition called for the creation of four transverse roads to carry ordinary east–west city traffic across town. By sinking these below the grade of the park and creating generously planted, gently rising seven-foot-high berms alongside them, visitors passing by foot or carriage are hardly aware of any interruption in the park's surface plane. The Greensward plan gave landscape, not art, the upper hand. The stone arches that carry pedestrians under the carriage drives and the cast-iron bridges that permit them to cross over the bridle trail were carefully integrated

into the flowing circulation system, the objective of which was to provide the park visitor with uninterrupted sequences of alternating kinds of scenery. The buildings designed by Vaux were small in scale and number, and either inconspicuously sited or used to punctuate the heights of the rock outcrops, as in the case of the Belvedere and several small gazebos made of tree limbs. None of these structures were didactic tropes like those inspired by Rousseau at Ermenonville. They were here simply to provide shade and shelter, modest refreshments, rustic ornament, and vantage points for enjoying the view.

On the opposite side of America, Olmsted's greatest accomplishment during the time he spent in California as director of the Mariposa Mines lay in the landscape design reports he prepared while he was there. These included the "Preliminary Report upon the Yosemite and Big Tree Grove" (August 1865), written in his capacity as chairman of the commission "to present to the Legislature [of the State of California] a sufficient description of the property, and well considered advice as to its future management." Along with practical matters involving roads and maintenance budgets, Olmsted's report limned a romantic portrait of the scenic grandeur of Yosemite's geology, vegetation, streams, and waterfalls. For example, he described the stream flowing through the valley as "such a one as Shakespeare delighted in," where "banks of heartsease and beds of cowslips and daisies are frequent, and thickets of alder, dogwood and willow often fringe the shores. . . . Beyond the lofty walls still loftier mountains rise, some crowned by forests, others in simple rounded cones of light, gray granite. . . . After midsummer a light, transparent haze generally pervades the atmosphere, giving an indescribable softness and exquisite dreamy charm to the scenery, like that produced by the Indian summer of the East."[16]

Thanks to Calvert Vaux's encouragement, Olmsted returned to New York to resume their partnership for the purpose this time of designing Brooklyn's Prospect Park. In his capacity as "landscape architect," the term he and

Vaux invented as the best descriptor of their profession, Olmsted continued to write both practically and philosophically about the value of parks as a civilizing influence. Against the "excessive materialism" that was overtaking Western culture, he saw the Romantic-style park as a spiritually uplifting influence on the ethnically diverse populations of rapidly growing industrial cities.

Unfettered by the professional and civic responsibilities Frederick Law Olmsted shouldered and lacking Olmsted's conviction that cities and nature could be integrated by means of landscape design, John Muir (1838–1914) set out on foot from San Francisco in 1868 for Yosemite, where he found a landscape "that after all my wanderings still appears as the most beautiful I have ever beheld. . . . And after ten years of wandering and wondering in the heart of it, rejoicing in its glorious floods of light, the white beams of the morning streaming through the passes, the noonday radiance on the crystal rocks, the flush of the alpenglow, and the irised spray of countless waterfalls, it still seems above all others the Range of Light."[17]

No one perhaps has ever extolled nature's sublimity in more exalted tones than Muir. What gives his prose its special character is its combination of fervor and fact. As was the case with Thomas Jefferson, description based on close observation makes credible the romantic emotions Muir wishes to convey. This passage from *The Yosemite* (1912) will suffice as a sample:

The Bridal Veil and the Upper Yosemite Falls, on account of their height and exposure, are greatly influenced by winds. The common summer winds that come up the river cañon from the plains are seldom very strong; but the north winds do some very wild work, worrying the falls and the forests, and hanging snow-banners on the comet-peaks. One wild winter morning I was awakened by a storm-wind that was playing with the falls as if they were mere wisps of mist and making the great pines bow and sing with glorious enthusiasm. The Valley had been visited a short time before by a series of fine snow-storms, and the floor and the cliffs and all the region round about were lavishly adorned with its best winter jewelry, the air was full of fine snow-dust, and pine branches, tassels and empty cones were flying in an almost continuous flock.

Soon after sunrise, when I was seeking a place safe from flying branches, I saw the Lower Yosemite Fall thrashed and pulverized from top to bottom into one glorious mass of rainbow dust; while a thousand feet above it the main Upper Fall was suspended on the face of the cliff in the form of an inverted bow, all silvery white and fringed with short wavering strips. Then, suddenly assailed by a tremendous blast, the whole mass of the fall was blown into threads and ribbons, and driven back over the brow of the cliff whence it came, as if denied admission to the Valley.[18]

Both Central Park and America's national parks must be seen as products of Romanticism. Their creation rests squarely on the belief that nature is not merely therapeutic—the "lungs of the city"—or recreational—wilderness as tourist adventure—but, rather, that nature is a spiritual force. This, as we have seen, is an ideal embedded in this continental nation's early ethos and Transcendentalist philosophy equating scenic beauty and sublime grandeur with divinity.

Notes

This essay constitutes the substance of a lecture given in 2008, the ideas and expression of which have been incorporated into the text of Elizabeth Barlow Rogers, Elizabeth S. Eustis, and John Bidwell, *Romantic Gardens: Nature, Art, and Landscape Design* (New York: Morgan Library & Museum, in association with the Foundation for Landscape Studies and David R. Godine, 2010).

1. Jonathan Edwards, *Miserable Seeking,* p. 8, http://www.thechristian.org/resources/testimonies/edwards.pdf.

2. Letter to Maria Cosway, 1786. As quoted in Merrill D. Peterson, *Thomas Jefferson and the New Nation* (Oxford: Oxford University Press, 1970), 24.

3. Thomas Jefferson, *Notes on the State of Virginia* (1787), in *Writings* (New York: Library of America, 1984), 148.

4. See William Beiswanger, "The Temple in the Garden: Thomas Jefferson's Vision of the Monticello Landscape," *Eighteenth Century Life* 8, no. 2 (January 1983): 170–88, quotation on 172.

5. Ralph Waldo Emerson, *Nature* (1836), in *Essays and Lectures* (New York: Library of America, 1983), 9.

6. Ibid., 16.

7. Ibid., 18–19.

8. Ibid., 47.

9. William Cullen Bryant, "A Forest Hymn" (1825), lines 1–23.

10. William Cullen Bryant, ed., *Picturesque America: A Delineation by Pen and Pencil of the Mountains, Lakes, Forests, Water-falls, Shores, Cañons, Valleys, Cities, and Other Picturesque Features* (New York: D. Appleton and Company, 1872), iii.

11. Thomas Cole, "Essay on American Scenery," *Atlantic Monthly Magazine* 1 (1836): 4–5. As quoted in Roderick Nash, *Wilderness and the American Mind,* 3rd ed. (New Haven: Yale University Press, 1982), 80–81.

12. Cole, "Essay on American Scenery," 9.

13. Andrew Jackson Downing, *Rural Essays* (New York: Leavitt & Allen, 1853), 157.

14. Frederick Law Olmsted to Elizabeth Baldwin Whitney, 16 December 1890, Frederick Law Olmsted Papers, Manuscript Division, Library of Congress, Washington, D.C., Transcript courtesy of Charles E. Beveridge.

15. Ibid.

16. Olmsted, "Preliminary Report upon the Yosemite and Big Tree Grove," in *The Papers of Frederick Law Olmsted,* vol. 5, *The California Frontier, 1863–1865,* ed. Victoria Post Ranney (Baltimore: Johns Hopkins University Press, 1986), 490–91.

17. John Muir, *The Yosemite* (New York: The Century Co., 1912), 5–6.

18. Ibid., 51–52.

PART II

MOVEMENT AND LANDSCAPE

"Everyone Has Carriage Road on the Brain"

Designing for Vehicles in Pre-automotive Parks

A number of commentators have emphasized the automobile's role in shaping the national park experience. Central to most of these accounts is the implication that the automobile produced a radical reorientation of park design strategies, management practices, and visitor experiences. Critics cast the automobile as the key culprit in the purported degradation—or, as some might have it, perversion—of the park experience. According to this line of reasoning, vehicular travel and the view from the road came to dominate—and/or desecrate—a more refined, authentic, and desirable relationship with the natural environment. By inundating the parks with swarms of motorized philistines, automobiles imperiled the moral, spiritual, and social values of America's national parks, destabilizing their primeval repose and destroying their ability to serve as sanctuaries from the hustle and bustle of modern life.

While this conceit plays into long-standing anti-automobile sentiments and enables its promoters to expound on the purported paradox of the National Park Service's Faustian bargains with technology, commerce, and popular taste, it belies an imperfect understanding of the history of park design and experience, both in America and abroad. In truth, the view from the road emerged as the privileged means of enjoying scenery with the development of modern conceptions of landscape beauty in seventeenth- and eighteenth-century Europe, and the development of facilities for vehicular travel has been one of the primary goals of park designers ever since. Far from being an anomalous intrusion of the machine in the garden, the National Park Service's embrace of the automobile exemplified long-standing traditions of park design, scenic appreciation, and popular recreation.

This essay affords a more historically informed reflection on the relationship between roads, parks, and people by refocusing attention on the prominent role that vehicular travel and park road development played in the pre-automotive era. A brief synopsis of the philosophical, perceptual, and practical preeminence of roads and vehicles in European landscape design and nineteenth-century American urban parks provides the background for an account of the extent to which the design, construction, and popular embrace of roads dominated the national park experience in the pre-automotive era. The reverence for roads is evident across a broad spectrum of contemporary sources, from classic landscape design treatises, park prospectuses, and construction reports to newspaper accounts, travel literature, artworks, and a wide array of tourist ephemera ranging from guidebooks, broadsides, and postcards to photo albums, decorative plates, spoons, playing cards, and other souvenirs. The latter material not only underscores the prominence of roads and related experiences in the popular imagination but helps broaden the scholarly spectrum to encompass both the producers and the consumers of cultural landscapes.

Given their origins as royal hunting preserves, one could argue that parks have always catered to the concerns of mobile users. While their original appeal was thus practical and broadly sensorial, providing a protected realm for mounted horsemen to revel in the thrills of the chase, technological advances and the rising prominence of visual perception during the seventeenth and eighteenth centuries combined to prioritize scenic enjoyment and make the view from the road the principal concern of park designers and users. The grand allées of baroque gardens like Versailles and Vaux-le-Vicomte hinted at the future by affording exhilarating demonstrations of perspective that encouraged the eye and mind to move rapidly through space, but it was the rise of the informal or naturalistic style of landscape gardening in the mid-eighteenth century that established the precedents for modern park culture by shifting the focus from elaborate geometric set-pieces designed to be viewed from a single privileged perspective to the dynamic experience of an unfolding series of picturesque views to be enjoyed—ideally—from the seat of the sprightly new springed carriages that were rapidly gaining popularity among Europe's elite. The English philosopher Edmund Burke praised the sensation of rolling in a well-sprung carriage along the winding drives of informal landscape parks for its ability to stimulate aesthetic contemplation while relaxing the body and soul. The contemporary essayist Samuel Johnson opined that his ideal of happiness involved "being swiftly drawn in a chaise over undulating turf in the company of a beautiful and witty woman."[1]

The typical landscape park of the era was an expansive gentleman's estate, arrayed in the informal style, with a winding circuit drive providing access to a diverse array of scenic effects. The carefully orchestrated sequences were explicitly developed to appeal to the sensibilities of moving spectators. Humphry Repton, the leading practitioner of the informal style, provided extensive recommendations for designing park roads that would please the eye and the imagination when viewed from constantly shifting perspectives. Lest we assume that the audience for eighteenth-century English parks was composed entirely of artists, aesthetes, and philosophers, Repton warned that most visitors would likely be "heedless travelers" for whom "everything is lost that is not too obviously presented." He advised that "peculiar care is requisite in giving the direction of every road or walk, that we may compel the most careless to observe those parts of a design, which have a claim on their admiration."[2] Repton recommended that park roads present a diverse array of scenic experiences, wind about, ascend, and descend to produce changing perspectives and kinetic sensations, and contrast prospect and enclosure, light and shadow, picturesque woodlands and serene meadows—in short, all the tricks of twentieth-century automobile-oriented park road designers. One of his favorite strategies was to configure a road and its surroundings so that the viewer experienced the sensation of "bursting" into the open to encounter an impressive vista highlighted by some striking visual accent. In Repton's hands the focal point was often his patron's country manor, but the National Park Service employed this device to great effect to showcase scenic wonders, most spectacularly in the case of Yosemite's Wawona Tunnel overlook.[3]

Repton's ideas, along with those of his successor, the Scottish apostle of rural taste John Claudius Loudon, had an enormous impact on nineteenth-century American landscape designers. Loudon focused more on horticultural matters and practical concerns such as the dissemination of his countryman John McAdam's revolutionary methods for constructing smooth, inexpensive, and durable gravel roads, but he emphasized that carriage drives should be designed to harmonize with their surroundings while displaying existing or constructed scenery to maximum effect.[4] Loudon's American acolyte, Andrew Jackson Downing, borrowed heavily from English influences while asserting that his writings were explicitly geared to American conditions. Since there were as yet no major public parks in America, Downing's road-related advice centered on the provision of circuit drives and approaches for large estates.[5] Like Repton and Loudon, Downing considered the provision of attractive pleasure drives to be a key component of the landscape designer's art and provided advice on how to develop them to reveal the variety and extent of the owner's domain while appearing attractive and naturalistic in and of themselves. He included plans for a series of walks and drives in his 1851 proposal for the National Mall—and asserted that the project would "afford some of the most beautifully varied carriage-drives in the world"—but following his untimely death in 1852, this venture into public landscape design was only partially realized.[6]

Frederick Law Olmsted and his partner Calvert Vaux were the primary figures responsible not only for transforming nascent ideas about public park development from dream to reality but also for establishing principles and precedents for park road design that exerted widespread influence well into the twentieth century. Both in their extensive writings and in the immensely popular public spaces they designed for New York, Brooklyn, and other major cities, Olmsted and Vaux helped to articulate the form, function, and underlying social value of the American public park as well as to teach visitors how to use, enjoy, and interpret them.

Roads, of course, played a preeminent role in this process. At first glance, the primary purpose of park roads would seem to be to provide access to a park's chief attractions. In practice, roads *were* one of the park's chief attractions. Their primacy was underscored not just in the lengths park designers and guidebooks went to describe their appealing qualities, or in the fact that many late-nineteenth-century parks were often referred to as "driving parks," but also in the degree to which images of roads and their users dominated contemporary visual and verbal accounts. Early reports on Central Park in popular publications such as *Harper's New Monthly Magazine* and the *Atlantic Monthly* extolled the park's appeal to carriage users, who were depicted enjoying the newly laid out carriage drives even as the broader scenic features remained under construction. More than 80,000 carriages passed through Central Park in June 1860, when the park had just barely opened and major landscaping work was still under way. Two-thirds of the visitors

in 1863 arrived by carriage. The commissioners reported that 9,643 vehicles entered the park on a single sunny day that year, boasting that had they all been lined up in a row, the assembled equipage would extend from one end of Manhattan to the other and back again.[7] The famous John Bachman bird's-eye view of 1863 emphasized this aspect of the park's popularity, highlighting the curvilinear drives and portraying Central Park as a symphony of vehicles in motion—a Victorian "Broadway Boogie" celebrating the park's appeal to the carriage trade (fig. 1).[8] Olmsted himself touted the correlation between park development and carriage driving. "Twelve years ago there was almost no pleasure-driving in New York," he observed in 1870. With the completion of Central Park's drives, Olmsted enthused, "there are now, at least, ten thousand horses kept for pleasure-driving."[9] Local residents were so incensed when a contract dispute delayed the opening of New York's Riverside Drive in 1880 that they tore down the barricades and drove their carriages in defiance of the authorities, further underscoring the contemporary perception that a park without a drive was hardly a park at all.[10]

The mid-nineteenth-century mania for carriage driving had multiple sources. On the technological front, recent improvements in carriage design and manufacturing produced lighter, faster, and more comfortable and affordable vehicles, while the rapid adoption of McAdam's paving technique made it cheaper and easier for public authorities to provide roads to accommodate them. On the social front, the burgeoning ranks of the metropolitan bourgeoisie found the proliferation of carriage styles and accouterments an ideal means of displaying their affluence and taste (fig. 2). *Harper's* described the thronged carriage roads of Central Park as "a brilliant and inspiring spectacle, as seen upon sunny afternoons, when alive with the whirl of a thousand gay and gorgeous carriages, bearing the elite of the city on their daily outings."[11]

Even for those who could not afford to participate, the parade of fashion that filled Central Park's carriage roads in late afternoon provided

FIG. 1. Central Park, 1863, by John Bachman. (Museum of the City of New York)

an entertaining spectacle. While most chroniclers of nineteenth-century parks underscore the contemplative appeal of pastoral aesthetics and emphasize tranquil scenes such as Prospect Park's Long Meadow over the hustle and bustle of packed promenades and crowded carriage drives, the public clearly embraced these aspects. The preponderance of popular imagery celebrating the social attractions of urban parks suggests that the parsing of picturesque scenery often took a backseat to more visceral pleasures and convivial amusements.

Olmsted understood this perfectly. He repeatedly stated that the opportunities parks provided for "gregarious" recreation among a diverse and democratic citizenry were as important as the respite their sylvan scenery afforded from the harsh geometries and artificial pressures of urban life. Environmentalist and aesthetic expositors might prioritize contemplative solitude and the sharing of rarefied sentiments among a select few kindred spirits, but Olmsted valued the broader social benefits parks bestowed as places where larger groups of friends and strangers were united in healthful, attractive, informal, and emphatically American settings—whether along the carriage drives of urban parks, the dusty stagecoach roads of nineteenth-century national parks, or—by logical extension—the motorways, parking overlooks, and campgrounds of the automobile age.

Of course Olmsted and Vaux paid exacting

attention to the aesthetic experience their carriage roads were providing. Olmsted noted that people enjoyed carriage drives not just for the social and physical pleasures they provided, but because, as he put it, "the eye is gratified at the picture that constantly changes in the movement of the observer."[12] Further underscoring the emphasis he placed on the dynamic experience of scenery, Olmsted observed that his carriage roads were designed "less with the purpose of bringing the visitor to points of view at which he will enjoy set scenes or landscapes, than to provide for a constant mild enjoyment of simply pleasing rural scenery while in easy movement."[13] Rather than emphasize a small number of superlative views, or "distinct spectacles," and treat the intervening roads as utilitarian corridors, Olmsted urged that the entire road network be conceptualized as an engaging work of art in which the scenic highlights were presented as "successive incidents of a sustained landscape poem, to each of which the mind is gradually and sweetly led up, and from which it is gradually and sweetly led away, so that they become part of a consistent experience."[14] Olmsted's proposals for landscape development were often articulated as continuously unfolding scenic effects expe-

rienced from the perspective of carriage drivers tracing the primary park drives.[15] Guidebook writers took a similar approach, narrating literary excursions along popular circuits.[16]

Travel literature expounded on the sights and sensations vacationers encountered when venturing in search of picturesque scenery. From the beginnings of scenic tourism in the 1820s, Americans often seemed as intrigued with the experience of travel as with the ostensible objects of their peregrinations. They were also eager to embrace whatever means of conveyance could get them to their destinations as effortlessly as possible. The popularity of the Hudson River and Niagara Falls rose in tandem with the initiation of steamboat travel and the development of the Erie Canal, while the New England portion of the American grand tour followed the railroad's extension north from Boston and New York. Stage lines brought travelers from the docks and depots to the fashionable hotels of popular resort areas such as Saratoga, the Berkshires, and the White Mountains. A typical visit combined leisurely socializing on hotel verandas with carriage excursions through the countryside or up the summit roads that ascended peaks such as Mount Tom, Mount Mansfield, and Mount

FIG. 2. The Drive, Central Park, 1883, from *Harper's Weekly.* (Author's collection)

Washington. The Mount Washington Carriage Road was hailed as a marvel of engineering and scenic display upon its completion in 1861 and celebrated in William Cullen Bryant's *Picturesque America* and other popular media (fig. 3). The opening of the Mount Washington Cog Railway eight years later was an even more ambitious feat. Its popularity, lore, and legend underscored both the priority tourists placed on securing ready access to scenic wonders and the degree to which the means of locomotion were often considered as compelling as the natural environment itself.[17]

No such conveniences were available for visitors to the first national parks. When the federal government ceded Yosemite Valley to the State of California in 1864, the grant stipulated that "the premises shall be held for public use, resort and recreation."[18] The biggest obstacle to fulfilling this goal, most agreed, was that the existing transportation system was so inadequate that the magnificent valley could barely be considered available for public use. Intrepid travelers who braved the multiday stage trip along primitive roads often arrived so exhausted that they were hardly in the mood for resort or recreation. Olmsted decried the valley's inaccessibility in his 1865 report to the Yosemite Park commissioners. "A man travelling from Stockton to the Yosemite or the Mariposa Grove is commonly three or four days on the road," Olmsted observed, "and arrives in the majority of cases quite overcome with the fatigue and unaccustomed hardship of the journey." The result, Olmsted claimed, was that "few persons, especially few women, are able to enjoy or profit by the scenery and air for days afterward." Unfortunately, the expense of securing food and lodging in such a remote location was such that "many leave before they have recovered from their first exhaustion, and return home jaded and ill." Olmsted identified improved road access as the highest priority for park managers. He also called for the development of a carriage circuit around the valley floor to provide visitors with convenient access to scenic features. Mindful of reducing the visual impact of the road itself,

FIG. 3. The Mount Washington Road, 1872, from *Picturesque America*. (Author's collection)

he advocated a narrow, one-way track and recommended that it run along the fringe of the forest, crossing the open meadows in carefully selected locations.[19]

Olmsted's pleadings had little immediate impact. Visitors continued to make the hot, dusty, and uncomfortable stage ride to the valley rim, where they transferred to foot or horseback for the steep and somewhat dangerous descent to the valley floor. "It is impossible to repress fear," complained one early traveler. "Every nerve is tense . . . and even the bravest lean timorously toward the mountain side and away from the cliff, with foot loose in stirrup and eye alert, ready for a spring in case of peril."[20] As with Central Park, many apparently thought the visitors themselves enhanced the spectacle. Declaring that "the picturesque effect of a party of pleasure-seekers *en route*" produced "a never-failing source of pleasure," *Picturesque America* extolled the manner in which the festive sight of tourist parties enlivened the natural scenery and pointedly compared the size of the valley floor to America's other most famous public park. Lest potential visitors undertake the journey too lightly, the account went on to describe a pack train calamity that nearly killed two horses and a guide.[21]

The demand for improved roads to and through Yosemite grew stronger with the increase in western tourism that followed the completion of the transcontinental railroad in 1869. Since neither the federal nor the state government was predisposed to act, three private toll road companies undertook the task, as the outlying communities of Coulterville, Mariposa, and Big Oak Flat vied to capitalize on the Yosemite-bound trade. Observing that "everyone has carriage road on the brain," the *Mariposa Gazette* declared, "We say 'Success' to these enterprises, and we eagerly await the day we can proceed all the way to the Yo Semite in a carriage."[22] While the Coulterville and Big Oak Flat interests led the way, completing their turnpikes within a month of each other during the summer of 1874, the two roads were so close together that neither turned a profit. With its more southerly route, superior scenery, and better access to the added attraction of the Big Tree Grove, the Mariposa Road proved more successful when it opened the following year. Extolling the value of these enterprises, the Coulterville contingent's leader, John McLean, enthused that the new roadways "made access to Yosemite easy, speedy and comfortable, by wheeled vehicles, instead of tiresome, difficult, and dangerous, on horseback and over trails." Highlighting the prevailing sentiment about the significance of this achievement, McLean observed that the completion of the first toll road "was celebrated in the valley by bonfires, firing of a cannon, a procession, a public meeting, and general rejoicing."[23] Similar declarations and festivities welcomed the other turnpikes (fig. 4). The zeal for making Yosemite accessible to carriage travel was further underscored by the fact that four years before the first access roads were completed, the park guardian Galen Clark had a wagon disassembled and packed in to the

valley on mule back, so that he could transport guests around the park in proper style on a drive newly constructed for that purpose. The Yosemite promoter and entrepreneur James Hutchings followed suit the following year, packing in a small stagecoach to ferry visitors around the valley floor.[24]

"Easy, speedy and comfortable" were relative terms, of course. Road builders worked in trying conditions with primitive equipment. All three routes encompassed significant obstacles—most notably the precipitous descent to the valley floor. The Coulterville Road accomplished this feat in the simplest and most audacious manner—winding through the forest to the valley rim before dropping into the Merced River Canyon along a virtually straight two-mile 16-percent grade, much of which was laboriously hewn out of the mountainside by Chinese laborers with picks, shovels, crowbars, and black powder. The Big Oak Flat Road builders broke up the descent with an elaborate series of switchbacks supported by dry-laid rock retaining walls constructed by Italian masons. These zigzags reduced the grade appreciably but still produced an exhilarating ride that afforded striking opportunities to view the stages clattering up or down the hillside in impressive clouds of dust.[25] Such views dramatized the melding of natural and technological sublime as visitors thrilled to spectacular scenery and the frisson of danger afforded by the precipitous descents and narrow, twisting roadways, averting disaster by virtue of the teamster's superlative driving skills (fig. 5).[26] Trading on the ridiculous as well as the sublime (or perhaps a bit of both), road designers, transportation companies, and tourists conspired to create novel interactions with the park's natural wonders. Tunnels cut through giant sequoias in the Wawona and Tuolumne Groves soon became standard components of tourist itinerary (fig. 6). The prevalence of road and stagecoach imagery among the postcards, stereoscopic views, and other souvenirs that tourists collected to memorialize their visits underscored the central role that transportation played in shaping the national park experience from the outset.

FIG. 4. Opening of Mariposa Road, Yosemite Valley, 1875. (National Park Service, Yosemite National Park)

Nowhere was the correlation between the park transportation experience and the park itself stronger than in Yellowstone. Not only did the Yellowstone road system epitomize the adaption of traditional landscape design to the broader national park setting, but the public identification of the park with iconic transportation infrastructure was such that images of gateways, stagecoaches, and other road-related scenes vied with bears, geysers, and bison across a broad range of tourist artifacts and ephemera.

As was the case with Yosemite, the language of the park's 1872 authorization strongly emphasized the new reservation's recreational function, designating it "a public park or pleasuring ground for the benefit and enjoyment of the people." Roads were universally viewed as essential to this function, but Yellowstone was even larger, more remote, and less developed than Yosemite, with a harsher climate, even more challenging topography, and a more broadly scattered array of scenic features. At least the federal government expressed a modicum of interest in improving access to its first

official national park, though initial outlays and achievements were modest, at best. Employing the time-honored device of a circuit drive linking the park's primary features—an approach that Olmsted, Downing, Repton, and others had routinely applied to scenic reservations of lesser extent—Yellowstone's first superintendents, N. P. Langford and Philetus W. Norris, conceived the basic outline of the current Grand Loop Road. As with Yosemite, the slow progression from trackless wilderness to rugged pack trail to smooth, safe, and attractive road system was marked by frustrations and recriminations over trying conditions and exultation over their eventual eradication.[27]

One of the first tourists to report on Yellowstone travel conditions—and certainly the first woman—was Carrie Adell Strahorn, who traversed the park in 1880 with her husband, a journalist hired by the Northern Pacific Railroad to promote western travel. Despite this mandate, Strahorn was critical of both the basic road conditions and the skills and methods of the government's road builders. "There are no adjectives in our language that can properly define the public highway that was cut through heavy timber over rolling ground," Strahorn remonstrated, "with stumps left from two to twenty inches above the ground, and instead of grading around a hill it went straight to the top on one side and straight down on the other; whereas a few hundred dollars, properly expended, would have made it one of the finest drives in the world." Strahorn and her party were eventually forced to abandon their wagon and continue on horseback.[28]

Frustrated and embarrassed by the efforts of civilian superintendents to improve access to the park, the federal government placed the

FIG. 5. Big Oak Flat Road, Yosemite, 1903. (Julius Boysen, photographer; National Park Service, Yosemite National Park)

FIG. 6. Team and wagon with passengers, Wawona Tunnel tree, c. 1910. (Frank R. Coburn, photographer; National Park Service, Yosemite National Park)

Army Corps of Engineers in charge of the enterprise in 1883. Under the direction of Lieutenant Daniel Kingman, the corps began to upgrade the park's crude road system, retaining the concept of the Grand Loop while improving its quality and location. Langford's most notable accomplishment was the Golden Gate Viaduct, a rickety wooden structure that provided passage around a nearly insurmountable cliff and immediately became a highlight of the tour (fig. 7). Rudyard Kipling's account encapsulated the viaduct's striking contribution to the Yellowstone experience.

We heard the roar of the river, and the road went around a corner. . . . On one side piled rock and shale, that enjoined silence for fear of a general slide-down; on the other a sheer drop, and a fool of a noisy river below. Then, apparently in the middle of the road, lest any should find driving too easy, a post of rock. Nothing beyond that save the flank of a cliff. Then my stomach departed from me, as it does when you swing, for we left the dirt, which was at least some guarantee of safety, and sailed out round the curve, and up a steep incline, on a plank road built out from the cliff. The planks were nailed on the outer edge, and did not shift or creak very much—but enough, quite enough. That was the Golden Gate.[29]

The "post of rock" Kipling referred to was another celebrated feature of the Yellowstone road system. While constructing the lower approach to the trestle, Kingman's workmen manipulated a rock pillar onto the outer edge of the roadbed to form a seemingly natural gateway. This stone sentinel was immediately embraced as a cherished component of the Yellowstone experience.[30] It was relocated for similar effect during reconstructions of the viaduct in 1900, 1933, and 1977. Road builders also made creative use of natural rock arrangements in the charismatic limestone formation known as "The Hoodoos." The so-called Silver Gate became another iconic element of the Yellowstone tour. Another celebrated union of nature and culture was Obsidian Cliff, where the grade for the roadbed was created by building a bon-

fire around the base of the cliff and then dashing it with cold water to fracture the unyielding glass-like mineral. Extolling this unique combination of natural wonder and human ingenuity, the travel writer William Thayer enthused, "Glass cliffs are not usual. Sight-seers are usually satisfied with sandstone or granite ones, provided they are tall enough. But here are cliff composed of volcanic glass, with a glass road along their base. Nature made the cliffs just as they are, but *man* made the road of materials which nature furnished."[31]

Kingman completed the lower circuit of the Grand Loop, but following his departure in 1886 progress slowed dramatically and existing roads began to deteriorate from inadequate maintenance. Protesting the meager funds appropriated for road work, Captain James B. Erwin accused Washington of neglecting its commitment. "If Congress wants to make good its dedication of the park to the people of the United States as a pleasuring ground for its benefit and enjoyment," he insisted in 1898, "it should yield to the demands of the people and make additional appropriation for the construction of new roads, which will add to their pleasure and benefit by opening new and wonderful phenomena and scenery."[32] The travel writer John L. Stoddard characterized Yellowstone's shoddy roads as a national embarrassment. "Every one knows how roads in Europe climb the steepest grades in easy curves, are usually smooth as a marble table, free from obstacles, and carefully walled-in by parapets of stone," he declared. "Why should not we possess such roads, especially in our National Parks? . . . Surely, the honor of our Government demands that this unique museum of marvels should be the pride and glory of the nation, with highways equal to any in the world."[33]

Captain Hiram Chittenden is generally credited with upgrading and completing Yellowstone's road system while articulating an approach to road building that set the tone for national park development throughout the twentieth century. A West Point graduate who spent two summers supervising the park in the lean years of 1891 and 1892 before returning

FIG. 7. Golden Gate Viaduct, 1893. (F. J. Haynes, photographer; National Park Service, Yellowstone National Park)

for a longer, better-funded, and more success-ful stint from 1899 to 1906, Chittenden as-serted that the government was responsible for providing access to the park's key features but insisted that road development should be limit-ed to the minimum extent consistent with this underlying purpose. "While it is not proposed to build any roads not actually needed," he ex-plained, "nor to change in any unnecessary way the face of the country, it is proposed to make such as have to be built as perfect as any in the world."[34] By "perfect," Chittenden was referring to both the practical and the aesthetic qualities of the road system. In addition to formulating technical specifications aimed at ensuring that Yellowstone's roads would be sturdy, commodi-ous, and safe, he advised that they be located "where they would best develop the scenery," follow attractive curvilinear alignments, and employ rustic guard walls and other attractive ancillary features.[35] Enthusing that "the oppor-tunities for artistic design in harmony with the surroundings are almost endless," Chittenden expressed confidence that his successors would continue to improve and refine what he had begun.[36]

The Mount Washburn Road epitomized Chit-tenden's commitment to combining practical and aesthetic concerns. A popular side trip from the Grand Loop, the Mount Washburn Road wound gracefully around the contours of the mountain, spiraling around the summit to provide thrilling vistas from the park's most prominent peak (fig. 8). That he was able to achieve these results with hand labor and rela-tively primitive equipment was all the more remarkable.

Chittenden did employ the latest technol-ogy in the 1903 construction of a bridge over the Yellowstone River designed to provide ve-hicular access to the Artist Point lookout over the Grand Canyon of the Yellowstone. While his predecessors had called for the quicker and cheaper solution of a utilitarian metal truss, Chittenden insisted on waiting until funds could be secured for a bridge that would do jus-tice to the scenic qualities of the site. By em-ploying the newly invented Melan Arch method of reinforced-concrete construction, Chitten-den was able to produce an elegant span whose graceful profile would not have been out of place in an English garden or Olmstedian urban

FIG. 8. Mount Washburn Road, from Northern Pacific Railway, *Yellowstone National Park: America's Only Geyserland,* 1914. (Author's collection)

park (fig. 9). Further underscoring the connection between municipal landscape parks and their western national equivalents, Chittenden erected a monumental arch at the principal gateway that was expressly designed to remind visitors they were entering a vast public reservation created "for the benefit and enjoyment of the people"—words that were emblazoned above the carriageway for all to see.[37]

The entrance arch and Chittenden Bridge quickly joined the Golden and Silver Gates as icons of the Yellowstone National Park experience that tourism promoters touted and visitors, to all appearances, embraced and revered. A plethora of postcards, stereoscopic views, and other souvenirs ranging from mirrors and silver spoons to playing cards and Dresden china served as talismans of the travel landscape. As with Yosemite, the stagecoach experience itself was widely celebrated and memorialized. Commentators marveled at the extent and complexity of Yellowstone's staging operations, which employed hundreds of horses and scores of coaches to shuttle visitors around the park.[38] Even John Muir was impressed with the

system's ability to provide thousands of tourists with easy access to the park's wonders.[39] Guidebooks described the operations in detail. Typically, visitors would be met at the train by a large six-horse stagecoach or "Tally-Ho," which would carry them to their first hotel. The Grand Loop Tour was usually taken in smaller coaches drawn by four-horse teams, while lighter surreys and "mountain wagons" were available for smaller parties or excursions around the geysers or side trips to destinations like Mount Washburn. The prominence of stagecoach imagery and road-related scenes suggests that, for many visitors, this aspect of the Yellowstone experience was as memorable as the encounters with the park's celebrated natural wonders (fig. 10). The identification of Yellowstone with stagecoach travel was such that the preservation of this romantic means of travel was invoked by opponents of the government's decision to allow automobiles into the park in 1915.[40]

Opening the parks to automobiles did, of course, have enormous impacts on the roads, visitor facilities, and larger landscapes of the

FIG. 9. "Chittenden" Bridge, Yellowstone National Park, c. 1905. (F. J. Haynes, photographer; National Park Service, Yellowstone National Park)

FIG. 10. Four-horse coach at Glimpse of Upper Falls, 1900, Yellowstone National Park. (F. J. Haynes, photographer; National Park Service, Yellowstone National Park)

national parks, as well as on the national park experience itself. But these changes were more a matter of degree than a question of kind. The ideas that road development was a fundamental concern for park makers, that the experience of scenery in motion and the needs of vehicular travelers were top priorities, and that people enjoyed and valued park roads and the experience of traveling—perhaps as much as or even more than the contemplation of natural scenery and search for solitude—have been integral not just to the story of American national parks but to the broader history of landscape design. These priorities have been repeatedly expressed, both in the actions and exhortations of park designers and—perhaps more important —in the practices and preferences of park users. While the emphasis on roads and vehicles may affront contemporary cultural sensibilities, it is rooted in centuries of design theory and social practice, and is inseparable from the history of park development, scenic appreciation, and outdoor recreation.

Notes

1. Burke's reflections on the sensory pleasures of park drives are discussed in Christopher Hussey, *The Picturesque: Studies in a Point of View* (London: G. P. Putnam's Sons, 1927), 58–59; Johnson quoted in Paul Shepard, *Man and the Landscape: A Historic View of the Aesthetics of Nature* (New York: Alfred Knopf, 1967), 87.

2. Humphry Repton, "Red Book for Stoke Park: Approach from Hereford," quoted in Stephen Daniels, "On the Road with Humphry Repton," *Journal of Garden History* 16 (Autumn 1996): 179.

3. Humphry Repton, "Sketches and Hints on Landscape Gardening" (1795) and "Fragments of a Theory and Practice of Landscape Gardening" (1803), both in Humphry Repton, *The Art of Landscape Gardening,* ed. John Nolen (Boston: Houghton Mifflin, 1907), 25–27, 49–53, 122.

4. John C. Loudon, *An Encyclopedia of Gardening* (London: Long, Ree, Orme, Browne, Green, and Longman, 1834), 642–43; John C. Loudon, *A Treatise on Forming, Improving, and Managing Country Residences* (London: Longman, Hurst, Rees, and Orme, 1806), 414–416, 590–92; John C. Loudon, *Designs for Laying out Farms and Gardens in the Scotch Style*

adapted to England (London: John Harding, 1812), 24–26.

5. After gaining prominence with the publication of *A Treatise on the Theory and Practice of Landscape Gardening, Adapted to North America: with a view to The Improvement of Country Residences* (New York: Wiley and Putnam, 1841), Downing edited the influential journal *The Horticulturalist* and produced numerous related books, articles, and designs. For the definitive critical biography, see David Schuyler, *Apostle of Taste: Andrew Jackson Downing, 1815–1852* (Baltimore: Johns Hopkins University Press, 1996).

6. The quotation is from A. J. Downing, "Explanatory Notes" to 1851 Mall Plan, excerpted in John Reps, *Washington on View: The Nation's Capital since 1790* (Chapel Hill: University of North Carolina Press, 1991), 126.

7. T. Addison Richards, "The Central Park," *Harper's New Monthly Magazine* 23 (August 1861): 289–306; [Henry Bellows], "Cities and Parks: With Special Reference to the New York Central Park," *Atlantic Monthly* (April 1861): 416–29; New York City, Board of Commissioners of Central Park, *Seventh Annual Report of the Board of Commissioners of Central Park, for the Year Ending with December 31, 1863* (New York: Wm. C. Bryant and Co., 1864), 31.

8. Roy Rosenzweig and Elizabeth Blackmar discuss Central Park's carriage trade and its social implications in *The Park and the People: A History of Central Park* (Ithaca, N.Y.: Cornell University Park, 1992), 211–25.

9. Frederick Law Olmsted, "Public Parks and the Enlargement of Towns," in *The Papers of Frederick Law Olmsted, Supplementary Series,* vol. 1, *Writings on Public Parks, Parkways, and Park Systems,* ed. Charles Beveridge and Carolyn Hoffman (Baltimore: Johns Hopkins University Press, 1997), 200.

10. Martha J. Lamb, "Riverside Park: The Fashionable Drive of the Future," *The Manhattan* 4, no. 1 (July 1884): 57–58.

11. Richards, "The Central Park," 296.

12. Frederick Law Olmsted, *Forty Years of Landscape Architecture,* quoted in Irving Fisher, *Frederick Law Olmsted and the City Planning Movement in the United States* (Ann Arbor: University of Michigan Research Press, 1986), 64.

13. Frederick Law Olmsted, "Notes on the Plan of Franklin Park and Related Matters" (1886), in *The Papers of Frederick Law Olmsted, Supplementary Series,* 1:493.

14. Frederick Law Olmsted, "Mount Royal. Montreal." (1881), in *The Papers of Frederick Law Olmsted, Supplementary Series,* 1:393.

15. See, for example, Olmsted, Vaux & Company, "Report of the Landscape Architects and Superintendents to the Brooklyn Park Commissioners, January 1871," in *The Papers of Frederick Law Olmsted,* vol. 6, *The Years of Olmsted, Vaux & Company, 1865–1874,* ed. David Schuyler and Jane Turner Censer (Baltimore: Johns Hopkins University Press, 1992); and Olmsted, "Mount Royal. Montreal." (1881), 1:394–97.

16. Examples include T. Addison Richard, *Guide to Central Park* (New York: James Miller, 1866); and Sylvester Baxter, *Boston Park Guide* (Boston: The Author, 1895).

17. The rise of scenic tourism has been recounted in numerous sources, including Hans Huth, *Nature and the American: Three Centuries of Changing Attitudes,* 2nd ed., intro. Douglas Strong (Lincoln: University of Nebraska Press, 1990); and John Sears, *Sacred Places: American Tourist Attractions in the Nineteenth Century* (New York: Oxford University Press, 1989). See also William Cullen Bryant, ed., *Picturesque America: A Delineation by Pen and Pencil of the Mountains, Lakes, Forests, Water-falls, Shores, Cañons, Valleys, Cities, and Other Picturesque Features,* vol. 1 (New York: D. Appleton and Company, 1872).

18. "AN ACT AUTHORIZING A GRANT TO THE STATE OF CALIFORNIA OF THE 'YO-SEMITE VALLEY,' AND OF THE LAND EMBRACING THE 'MARIPOSA BIG TREE GROVE,' Approved June 30, 1864 (13 Stat. 325)," in Lary M. Dilsaver, *America's National Park System: The Critical Documents* (Lanham Way, Md.: Rowman and Littlefield, 1994), 11. Yosemite National Park has generated myriad historical books and reports. Excellent sources on the park's development that are particularly relevant to this study include Linda W. Greene, *Yosemite, the Park and Its Resources: A History of the Discovery, Management and Physical Development of Yosemite National Park, California,* 3 vols. (Denver, Colo.: National Park Service, Denver Service Center, 1987); Richard Quin, "Yosemite Roads and Bridges, HAER Report No. CA-117" (Washington, D.C.: National Park Service, Cultural Resources Division, Historic American Engineering Record, 1991); and Hank Johnston, *Yosemite's Yesterdays,* vol. 2 (Yosemite, Calif.: Flying Spur Press, 1991).

19. Olmsted, "Preliminary Report upon the Yosemite and Big Tree Grove" (August 1865), in *The Papers of Frederick Law Olmsted,* vol. 5, *The California Frontier, 1863–1865,* ed. Victoria Post Ranney (Baltimore: Johns Hopkins University Press, 1990), 508–9.

20. J. H. Beadle's characterization of his 1871 descent quoted in Quin, "Yosemite Roads and Bridges," 12.

21. Bryant, *Picturesque America,* 1:475–79, 490–91.

22. *Mariposa Gazette,* early 1870, quoted in Johnston, *Yosemite's Yesterdays,* 2:35.

23. John T. McLean, "A Statement Showing the wrong done to, and the pecuniary damage and losses suffered by the Coulterville and Yosemite Turnpike Company," quoted in Greene, *Yosemite the Park and its Resources,* 97.

24. Johnston, *Yosemite's Yesterdays,* 2:37.

25. Ibid., 39–47; Greene, *Yosemite, the Park and Its Resources,* 2:97–102.

26. The safety record of stagecoaches in Yosemite and other national parks was generally good, but the combination of steep, narrow, twisting roads; primitive equipment; and unpredictable means of locomotion was inherently dangerous. The Yosemite pioneer James Hutchings was killed in a carriage accident when his horses shied on the Big Oak Flat Road (Johnston, *Yosemite's Yesterdays,* 2:29). Runaways, carriage accidents, speeding, and overly aggressive driving were common problems in metropolitan parks, as witnessed by the citations listed in contemporary reports.

27. "AN ACT TO SET APART A CERTAIN TRACT OF LAND LYING NEAR THE HEADWATERS OF THE YELLOWSTONE RIVER AS A PUBLIC PARK," Approved March 1, 1872 (17 Stat. 32)," in Dilsaver, ed., *America's National Park System, The Critical Documents,* 28. Key sources on the development of Yellowstone National Park include Hiram Chittenden, *The Yellowstone National Park, Historical and Descriptive,* rev. ed. (Cincinnati, Ohio: Stewart and Kidd, 1918); Mary Shivers Culpin, *The History of the Construction of the Road System in Yellowstone National Park, 1872–1966, Historic Resource Study,* vol. 1 (Denver, Colo.: U.S. National Park Service, Rocky Mountain Region, Division of Cultural Resources, 1994); and Aubrey L. Haines, *The Yellowstone Story: A History of Our First National Park,* vol. 2, 2nd ed. (Niwot, Colo.: University Press of Colorado, 1996).

28. Carrie Adell Strahorn, *Fifteen Thousand Miles by Stage,* vol. 1, *1877–1880* (New York: Knickerbocker Press, 1911; rpt. ed. Lincoln: University of Nebraska Press, 1988), 268.

29. Rudyard Kipling, *From Sea to Sea: Letters of Travel,* vol. 2 (New York: Doubleday and McClure, 1899), 78.

30. The travel writer John Stoddard rhapsodized that "a solitary boulder, detached from its companions on the cliff, seems to be stationed at this portal like a sentinel to watch the tourists who come and go" (John L. Stoddard, *John L. Stoddard's Lectures,* vol. 10, *Southern California, Grand Canyon of the*

Colorado River, Yellowstone National Park [Chicago and Boston: Geo. L. Shuman, 1898], 235).

31. William Thayer, *Marvels of the New West* (Norwich, Conn.: The Henry Bill Publishing Company, 1892), 68.

32. Captain James B. Erwin, *Report of the Acting Superintendent of the Yellowstone National Park to the Secretary of the Department of the Interior, 1898* (Washington, D.C.: 1898), quoted in Culpin, *The History of the Construction of the Road System in Yellowstone National Park,* 1:46.

33. Stoddard, *John L. Stoddard's Lectures,* 10:222.

34. Chittenden, *The Yellowstone National Park,* 237.

35. Ibid., 237–41, quotation on 240; Culpin, *The History of the Construction of the Road System in Yellowstone National Park,* 1:47–68.

36. Chittenden, *The Yellowstone National Park,* 248–49, quotation on 249.

37. Ibid., 246–47; Haines, *The Yellowstone Story,* 221–44; Culpin, *The History of the Construction of the Road System in Yellowstone National Park,* 1:50–52.

38. Stoddard marveled: "This feature of our National Parks astonished me. I had no idea of its perfection or its magnitude. Here, for example, are vehicles enough to accommodate seven hundred tourists for a continuous journey of five days! Here, too, are five hundred horses, all of which can be harnessed at twenty-four hours notice; and since the Park is so remote, here also are the company's blacksmith shops. Within the stables, also, are the beautifully varnished coaches, varying in cost from one to two thousand dollars, and made in Concord, New Hampshire, twenty-five hundred miles away" (Stoddard, *John L. Stoddard's Lectures,* 10:230–31).

39. John Muir, *Our National Parks* (Boston: Houghton and Mifflin, 1901), 39, 51.

40. National Park Service publicist Robert Sterling Yard acknowledged the widely felt sentimental attraction of the stagecoach lines and expressed some regret about "the passing of the picturesque old horse-drawn stage-coach from its last stand in the United States," but he asserted that the speed, ease, and comfort afforded by automobile travel made for a better park experience (Robert Sterling Yard, *The Book of the National Parks* [New York: Charles Scribner's Sons, 1921], 209).

The Hegemony of the Car Culture in U.S. National Parks

Since the early twentieth century the automobile has had myriad effects on America's economy, society, and natural environment. Observers have called the automobile's sprawling influence "the car culture."[1] One product of the car culture is automobile-based tourism, which, in its origins, also gave rise to the U.S. national park system. It is true that the first national park, Yellowstone, established in 1872, existed long before the advent of the car culture. That should not confuse the point. Although the national park *idea* can be traced to an earlier time, the national park *system* and its managing agency, the National Park *Service,* both created in 1916, were born of this potent new force in American life. The car culture quickly co-opted the national park idea to suit its needs, and as the national park system matured during the twentieth century, the car culture etched itself deeply in national park policy and design.

The car in the national park setting has always had its partisans and its detractors. Its partisans have claimed that automobiles, coupled with good roads, make national parks accessible to the masses, ensuring that these special places fulfill their public purpose in providing enjoyment for the people. Furthermore, having a car in a national park allows for individual freedom and spontaneity—qualities that the automobile's champions readily associate with the American outdoor experience. Detractors, meanwhile, have focused on the problem of roads, which diminish a park's wilderness values, impair the natural scenery, and cause habitat fragmentation. They have also pointed to ways in which the car itself tends to tarnish the national park experience, isolating people from one another, separating them from nature, and creating a feeling of crowdedness in congested areas. Arguments pro and con have been mainly fashioned around two major themes in national park history: one, the problem of how to accommodate ever-increasing numbers of people, and two, the rise of ecological values in national park management.

The Birth of the National Park Service, 1910–1916

The national park system contained just fourteen national parks when it was created in 1916, and in most of those parks transportation was still in its infancy. Visitors to Yosemite National Park used a stagecoach service and toll roads that dated to the 1870s. Tourists in Yellowstone traveled by stagecoach over a road system built by the army in the last two decades of the nineteenth century. Automobiles were still seen by most people as playthings of the rich.[2]

But car ownership was spreading rapidly, especially after the introduction of the Ford Model T in 1910, which reduced the cost of a car to within reach of many non-wealthy Americans. Car owners aggressively pursued their collective interests through local automobile clubs. The auto clubs, boasting wide memberships, grew into effective lobbying organizations. Automobile clubs in the Pacific Northwest prevailed on the secretary of the interior to admit cars into Mount Rainier National Park, and when a convoy of cars rolled through the log archway at the park entrance in 1908, it marked the first automobile use of a national park in the United States. Motorists gained access to Yosemite in 1913, and to Yellowstone in 1916 (fig. 1).[3]

Between 1910 and 1916, automobile clubs became involved in a reform movement to improve the administration of national parks. They joined with local chambers of commerce, good roads associations, and national organizations led by the American Civic Association in pressing the federal government to standardize park administration and prepare the parks for the growing business of auto tourism.[4]

In 1915, the national parks reform movement found a new leader in Stephen T. Mather. A Chicago business tycoon and philanthropist, Mather entered government as assistant to the secretary of the interior and soon headed up the campaign for legislation to establish the National Park Service. Automobile enthusiasts recognized Mather as one of their own. With

his love of mountains matched by a love for the road, he was active in the American Automobile Club and the Chicago Automobile Club as well as the Sierra Club. He confidently predicted that the burgeoning car culture would do more than anything to popularize the national parks and secure the national park system in American life.[5]

Landscape architects were also central to the effort to put national park administration on a new footing. Frederick Law Olmsted Jr., probably the best-known landscape architect in the nation, drafted much of the national parks bill, including what would become the National Park Service's core mission statement, with its famously paradoxical directive to develop *and* preserve these wild places. "The fundamental purpose" of the parks, Olmsted wrote, "is to conserve the scenery and the natural and historic objects and the wild life therein and to provide for the enjoyment of the same in such

FIG. 1. A concession-operated touring car enters Mount Rainier National Park, c. 1910. As the number of park visitors per car steadily declined over the next hundred years, the number of cars in parks rose even more dramatically than the number of visitors. (Photographer unknown; National Park Service Historic Photograph Collection, Harpers Ferry Center)

manner and by such means as will leave them unimpaired for the enjoyment of future generations."[6] Landscape architects pointed the way out of this paradox by elevating scenery over ecologic values. Roads and buildings, if artfully designed, could harmonize with the natural landscape and preserve the scenery unimpaired. Landscape architects had always based their work on the principle of making movement through space an aesthetically pleasing experience, whether that movement was by foot or horse carriage. The greater speed of the automobile simply required more space and coarser design standards, such as wider radii of curves along thoroughfares. National parks provided just the kind of large public spaces that landscape architects needed to assist in making the *scenic drive* a new national pastime.[7]

National Park Development, 1916–1942

The two decades between the world wars formed the era of road building in the national parks. The National Park Service sought to make these areas accessible for the motorized public, and Congress was increasingly disposed to provide federal dollars for the purpose. In 1924, Congress provided $7.5 million for road construction in the national parks over the next three years. In 1927, it upped the ante to $51 million over the next ten years. During the New Deal, a spate of road development in the national parks occurred as part of a nationwide boom in road building that was generously funded by all levels of government. Stephen Mather, director of the National Park Service from 1916 to 1928, pronounced that his ideal was to develop one high-standard road in each park that would allow pleasurable driving to the area's most scenic vistas. But pressed by mountain clubs not to take road building too far, Mather pledged not to "gridiron" the parks with roads. Sections of each park would be preserved in a primitive condition for the enjoyment of people on foot or horseback (fig. 2).[8]

The National Park Service hailed the growing auto tourism in national parks as a fulfillment of the democratic promise contained in the national park idea. The principle at the heart of the Yellowstone National Park Act was that portions of the nation's natural heritage should be set aside in trust for all people in perpetuity. The creation of Yellowstone National Park seemed to be in fitting contrast to the landed heritage of Europeans, where wild lands were originally set aside for the pleasure of kings and a few noblemen. As one longtime publicist in the National Park Service asserted, national parks were distinctly an American idea, "a definite expression of the highest in our American code of government—equality for all."[9] But viewed in historical perspective, those claims of landscape democracy appear to have been overstated. They were based almost entirely on the national parks' accessibility by automobile, as if car ownership equated with citizenship. In fact, car ownership was far from universal. One car magazine calculated in 1921 that ownership of a $600 automobile required an income of about $1,900 for rural people and $2,800 for city dwellers—this at a time when the average household income in the United States was about $1,300.[10]

The controversy stirred up in the mid-1930s over a proposed skyline drive in Great Smoky Mountains National Park highlights the conflicting goals of supposedly democratic access and preservation of wilderness. This road was to begin at Newfound Gap, where the existing through-park road crossed over the mountain crest on the border between Tennessee and North Carolina, and it was to extend along the mountain crest westward, descending from the crest near the west edge of the park. Robert Marshall, a federal forester and leading personality in the nascent wilderness preservation movement, joined in a campaign to block the plan.[11] In an influential essay, "The Problem of the Wilderness," Marshall argued that the hiker type of nature lover derived a much more profound pleasure from hiking through wilderness than the motorist got from driving to view scenery. Motorized enjoyment by the many spoiled the intense satisfaction of the few; therefore, some wilderness areas ought to be withheld from road development and

FIG. 2. As car camping became popular in the 1920s, the Park Service developed camp-grounds to protect meadows such as this one in Yosemite National Park. (Photographer unknown; National Park Service Historic Photograph Collection, Harpers Ferry Center)

FIG. 3. Park rangers at Spence Field, Great Smoky Mountains National Park, November 1934. The controversy over the proposed skyline drive helped ignite concern about the car culture's inroads on national parks nationwide. (E. E. Exline, photographer; National Park Service, Great Smoky Mountains National Park)

protected for the recreational benefit of this relatively small constituency.[12] For Marshall, the wilderness of the Smokies was practically a matchless example of what the government ought to hold sacrosanct, since there was not much wilderness in the East left to preserve.

Arno B. Cammerer, director of the Park Service at the time, insisted that the drive along the top of the Smokies would provide immense pleasures not found anywhere else in the park. Those pleasures included being able to see the dazzling displays of flowering azaleas found only at that elevation—an experience he had enjoyed while riding horseback through the area almost a decade earlier. Without car access, the vast majority of American citizens would never see such things (fig. 3).[13]

The controversy over the skyline drive became a test case for government policy on national park road development nationwide. Secretary of the Interior Harold L. Ickes eventually sided with Bob Marshall and his co-defenders of wilderness. "This is an automobile age," Ickes said in a speech in September 1934. "But I do not have much patience with people whose idea of enjoying nature is dashing along a hard road at fifty or sixty miles an hour." Ickes ordered Cammerer to relinquish the plan for the skyline drive.[14]

National Parks under Siege, 1945–1964

Newton B. Drury, the agency's fourth director, sagely predicted that the pattern of national park visitation after World War II would be transformed by new, faster modes of transportation: commercial air service, private aircraft, and ever greater numbers of automobiles speeding over improved highways. More inclined to protect wilderness values in national parks than his predecessor Cammerer had been, Drury vowed to resist demands for the development of airports or landing strips in national parks, and he described a new park design in which the vast majority of visitors would drive in and out of the area each day, resorting to nearby communities for overnight accommodations.[15] This new emphasis on "day use" was aimed at curtailing development in-

side the national parks, a seemingly laudable goal. But it had an obvious side effect that no one cared to acknowledge: it significantly increased the number of car miles per park visit. Park visitors would spend more and more time in their cars, and park roads would have to carry more and more traffic. Driving to view scenery was further legitimized as being central to the national park experience. The "drive-in wilderness" would soon create conditions paralleling those in the cities, where people moved out to suburbs and commuted ever greater distances between home and work.[16]

After World War II, national park visitation grew apace as expected, but pressure of numbers was only half the problem that the National Park Service confronted. The other part of the problem was an infrastructure of roads and buildings that was badly deteriorated, a result of deferred maintenance during the war years. In 1955, National Park Service director Conrad L. Wirth conceived of an ambitious program of rehabilitation and new construction funded over a ten-year span, a plan that would eliminate the need to go to Congress and the Bureau of the Budget for development funds in two- and three-year driblets. The program would reach completion in 1966, coinciding with the fiftieth anniversary of the founding of the National Park Service, hence its name "Mission 66." Arguing that the program was needed to rectify nearly fifteen years of neglect resulting from budget cutbacks made during World War II and the Korean War, and that it would restore the parks to a condition capable of satisfying the growing millions of Americans who used them each year, Wirth secured political support for Mission 66 from both President Eisenhower and Congress. In affirmation that his agency was still fully in step with the car culture, Wirth launched Mission 66 at a gala banquet jointly hosted by the National Park Service and the American Automobile Association.[17]

Viewed in the context of the car culture, Mission 66 can be seen as another crucial step in the intensification of car use in national parks following World War II. A major thrust of Mission 66 plans for the many natural-area units in the national park system was to replace overnight use with day use and to move visitor facilities from the core to the periphery of each park—objectives that Drury had first articulated in 1944. The National Park Service's critics complained that Mission 66 plans for each national park placed too much emphasis on development. In fact, the premise of each plan was that the National Park Service could improve *visitor management.* The controlling metaphor in Mission 66 plans was that visitor activity in any given park was like the circulatory system in an organism. Roads, campgrounds, museums, and overlooks were the park's circulatory system, and visitors were like blood cells coursing through the system. The promise of new development was that it could spread visitor use to new areas and encourage a smooth flow of visitor movement throughout the park. New pullouts or "waysides" with permanent interpretive markers called "wayside exhibits" could hold a portion of visitors at points of interest while allowing others to pass

expeditiously by. If visitor circulation were improved, the thinking went, then a park could accommodate more people with less congestion (fig. 4).[18]

Visitor management focused heavily on making most use of the road net. Other innovations of the Mission 66 era included quick-stop visitor centers, one-way "motor nature trails," and self-guided car tours. With such improvements, one Mission 66 plan claimed, visitors would "linger longer" on the park roads, reducing pressure on the main visitor concentration areas. Yet any given point of interest would be purely optional; the self-guided car tour would still contain a modicum of whimsy. "The entire journey through the park should thus become a continuous series of new pleasures," this plan cheerily averred.[19] Such notions reinforced the National Park Service's long-standing acceptance of the scenic drive as a staple of the national park experience.

With its focus on visitor management, Mission 66 encouraged park planners and managers to view the car in the national park setting

FIG. 4. A ranger naturalist leads an "auto caravan" on a wildflower tour in Great Smoky Mountains National Park, April 1964. Auto caravans were a standard feature of interpretive programs in the Mission 66 era and were part of an effort to intensify park use while alleviating congestion. (H. W. Lix, photographer; National Park Service, Great Smoky Mountains National Park)

in a very positive light. The car expedited visitor circulation, allowing more people to flow through the park. That a greater proportion of each visit took place at speeds of 25 mph or more did not seem to matter. Even the modernist architecture of the Mission 66 era—its pavilion-like visitor centers and spiraling pedestrian ramps—suggested that the national park experience was something to be snatched on the fly. The thinking behind Mission 66 paralleled contemporary thinking in the U.S. Forest Service about forest management. Just as foresters, employing the tools of intensive forestry, promised to get more forest product out of the national forests, so too did the National Park Service, using the tools of better visitor management, expect to get more visitor use out of the national parks.

A Time of Questioning, 1964–1972

Mission 66's embrace of the car culture soon ran up against the American public's growing disenchantment with the automobile, a disenchantment fed by mostly urban-centered problems such as air pollution, urban sprawl, traffic congestion, and car safety concerns. Ultimately, Mission 66 fell out of step with the times when the American people awoke to the nation's environmental problems in the early 1960s. If clear-cuts on the national forests focused the public's ire against the Forest Service, it was Mission 66's glib acceptance of the car culture that undermined the public's confidence in the National Park Service.

Secretary of the Interior Stewart L. Udall, who helped inspire the new environmentalism with his book *The Quiet Crisis* (1963), saw need for a change of leadership in the National Park Service. He forced Wirth to retire and handpicked the former superintendent of Jefferson National Expansion Memorial, George B. Hartzog Jr., to replace him. Hartzog was a dynamic administrator with exceptional political skills. Appointed director in January 1964, he not only inherited Mission 66 at a point when the ten-year construction program had lost its luster, his appointment also came just weeks after Udall accepted the landmark Leopold Re-

port as a new basis for ecological management of the national parks. That fall, Congress enacted the Wilderness Act, which gave the agency ten years in which to recommend areas for wilderness designation in all national parks. Both the Leopold Report and the Wilderness Act called for a corrective tilt toward preservation in the agency's mission to balance preservation and use.[20]

As director from 1964 to 1972, Hartzog challenged the hegemony of the car culture in the national parks as no other leader of the agency before or since. His challenge began with a relook at road projects, which led to a series of precedent-setting decisions. In 1965, the National Park Service was studying a proposed Guadalupe Mountains National Park. The local congressman from Texas had indicated he would support the measure if the National Park Service built a road to the top of the escarpment. Hartzog sent a team to look it over with a view to building an aerial tramway instead of a road. It was the first time since the 1920s that the National Park Service seriously considered an alternative to the automobile.[21] Two years later, the agency took another step at Mesa Verde National Park. Rather than widen and improve an existing dirt road to Wetherill Mesa, Hartzog decided that the road would remain narrow, unpaved, and open to buses only—an "adventure" for the park visitor.[22] Less than a year later, Hartzog decided against building a road into the newly established Fort Bowie National Historic Site in Arizona. Since the road would have marred the hillside in plain view of the historic resource, Hartzog followed the planning team's recommendation to create only a light footpath (fig. 5).[23]

In 1967, Hartzog appointed a committee of distinguished conservationists and members of his staff to reconsider the purpose of roads in national parks. When the committee made its report, Hartzog had it printed and widely distributed. Despite its prosaic title, *Park Road Standards,* the report was an eloquent discourse on the larger issues of public access, modes of transportation, and the park experience. "The single abiding purpose of National

FIG. 5. National Park Service director George B. Hartzog Jr. and former director Horace M. Albright, 1966. Hartzog challenged the car culture in national parks as no other director before or since. (Fred Bell, photographer; National Park Service Historic Photograph Collection, Harpers Ferry Center)

Parks is to bring man and his environment into closer harmony," the authors wrote. "It is thus the *quality* of the park experience—and not the statistics of travel—which must be the primary concern." They stressed that the ideal park visit must be a leisurely experience, whether by automobile or on foot, and that the design of park roads was a key factor in setting the desired pace. They noted the fact that national parks were now suffering the same problems of congestion, noise, and pollution that plagued American cities, and that these problems had "begun to erode the quality of the park experience." Moreover, existing park roads tended to form an "ecological barrier," a problem that conservation biologists would later describe as habitat fragmentation. For these reasons, the National Park Service needed to give full consideration to alternative modes of transportation, such as aerial tramways, that did less permanent damage to the environment, and it needed to consider new roads as a "last resort in seeking solutions to park access." Faced with demands to widen or straighten park roads so as to accommodate larger vehicles, the National Park Service needed to analyze these situations one at a time and reject the notion that

all vehicles, no matter what their dimensions, were automatically admissible.[24]

Hartzog first put these principles to work in Yosemite, where the magnificent valley had become appallingly overcrowded. A shuttle bus system was introduced at the east end of the valley, the roads were converted to one-way traffic in the middle portion of the valley, cars were replaced by a sightseeing tram in the Mariposa Grove, and more than half of all campsites in the valley were eliminated. The "car reform movement," as Hartzog termed it, found more public acceptance than anticipated, but it was evident still more traffic reduction was needed. In June 1969, Secretary of the Interior Walter J. Hickel averred, "It has become increasingly obvious in many parks, especially in Yosemite National Park during the height of the summer season, that the private automobile is impairing the quality of the park experience." Acting on Hickel's advice, the National Park Service launched a comprehensive restudy of mass transit alternatives in Yosemite in 1972.[25]

While director, Hartzog also brought attention to the problem of recreational vehicles. In just four short years, from 1964 to 1968, the number of camping trailers in national parks doubled, further jamming campgrounds. RVs greatly enlarged each visitor's footprint, Hartzog explained in an article in *Popular Science.* "Increasingly, the visitor arrives in a complex, self-contained recreational vehicle, complete with color TV and air conditioning that, like its owner, demands sophisticated service facilities."[26] He told an audience in Boston, "Our national parks are not so much overcrowded with people as they are with the paraphernalia people bring with them—their cars, camper vehicles, trailers and boats."[27]

Hartzog was careful not to criticize the preferences of the individual RV user in the national parks, only to point out that RVs were becoming too numerous. But in his role as a public official, he was leading a chorus of much more vociferous critics outside of government, like the iconoclastic author Edward Abbey. "Why is the Park Service generally so anxious to accommodate that other crowd, the indolent millions born on wheels and suckled on gasoline, who expect and demand paved highways to lead them in comfort, ease and safety into every nook and corner of the national parks?" Abbey asked in *Desert Solitaire* (1968). The reason, he wrote, was that new park roads boosted the tourism economy.[28] His explanation, ironically, was similar to the argument Stephen Mather had put forward in the 1920s for the purpose of garnering congressional support for national parks. But Abbey found the National Park Service's collusion with the car culture totally unacceptable.

Even establishment groups like the National Parks Conservation Association joined in this attack on the car culture. The Public Land Law Review Commission, in its report to Congress in 1970, noted the pressure of automobiles on national parks and recommended that the National Park Service cap the number of visitors in certain areas during peak seasons. The National Parks Conservation Foundation, in *National Parks for the Future* (1972), a report commissioned by the National Park Service, agreed on the need to limit public use according to each park's "carrying capacity"; but it went further, suggesting that in a perfect world the car culture would be removed root and branch from the national park system. "Automobiles can destroy our national park heritage just as surely as they have made our cities inhumane and dangerous to limb and lung and have desecrated much of our metropolitan countryside," the Conservation Foundation stated. Short of banning cars outright, which seemed to be an impossible dream, it recommended an immediate moratorium on construction of roads and parking lots, and the appointment of a special commission to study the feasibility of developing alternative transportation systems in the parks.[29]

These criticisms of the car in the national park setting repeated arguments that had been heard earlier in the century, but with more verve. Notably, charges and countercharges of elitism resurfaced after the Conservation Foundation published *National Parks for the Future.* Secretary of the Interior Rogers C. B.

Morton remarked that he would resist changes to national park policy that tended to restrict access for young families, the elderly, and people on modest budgets. Critics shot back that the dearth of mass transportation to and within national parks already restricted the user population to people who could afford car ownership.[30]

As in the past, allegations that the car culture tarnished the visitor experience were the hardest to substantiate. Indeed, a new wave of sociological research in the parks in the 1960s purported to show that the public had more tolerance for visitor crowding and traffic congestion than critics assumed. One explanation for the surprisingly high level of satisfaction found in visitor surveys was that a gap in cultural norms had opened between the predominantly urban park users and "traditionalist" park managers. Traditionalists, for example, assumed that most campers' motivation for camping would include a desire to find quiet and solitude and the opportunity to get close to nature, whereas many campers actually went camping for the social experience and enjoyed having many comforts of home in camp.[31] Visitor attitudes about what constituted solitude or crowding, or what degree of hardship might be considered "roughing it," were constantly changing.

Many people distrusted visitor survey data because visitor surveys did not necessarily detect turnover in the user population. Many in the National Park Service began to worry that as certain areas became overcrowded, the national parks simply lost one set of visitors who did not like congestion and attracted another set of visitors who were accepting of crowds.[32]

Alternative Transportation Plans Prepared and Shelved, 1972–1980

In 1972, near the end of his tenure, Hartzog established a congressionally funded "alternative transportation systems" program. In National Park Service parlance, *alternative transportation* meant anything other than private automobile transportation. To the existing shuttle bus systems in Yosemite and Mesa

Verde, the National Park Service soon added a bus system on Mount McKinley National Park's single, eighty-six-mile-long, mostly unpaved road; a fleet of rubber-tired trailer trains in Grand Canyon National Park for ferrying people around South Rim Village and along West Rim Drive; a tram in Everglades National Park for taking people out to Shark Slough; and a handful of lesser operating systems in other units. By 1975, it had another twenty systems on the drawing board. Despite that promising start, the program soon sputtered out. Congress practically ceased funding new alternative transportation systems in the national parks in 1976.[33] Why? As will be seen, the myriad reasons had perhaps more to do with the nation's car culture than they did with the national parks. Still, the National Park Service contributed to the program's demise and must be held partly responsible for it.

The alternative transportation systems program began auspiciously because it coincided with the energy crisis. In the early 1970s, opinion leaders and policy makers began to raise concern about the nation's dependence on foreign oil and the changing world oil market. In 1973, the Arab oil embargo triggered the energy crisis of the 1970s. In 1974, President Nixon imposed a 55 mph conservation speed limit. Americans responded to rising gas prices by buying smaller cars with better gas mileage. Mass transit initiatives, whether in national parks or in cities, enjoyed a sudden vogue.

Hartzog and other proponents in the National Park Service wanted to experiment with all types of alternatives—aerial tram, monorail, and light-rail systems as well as rubber-tired buses and trams driving over existing blacktop roads. They imagined a future in which cars would be completely eliminated from some, if not all, national parks. They talked of two great advantages that alternative transportation systems would have over automobile use. First, the new systems would allow park managers to control the number of people going to certain places at certain times so that public use levels could be kept within carrying capacity. Second, the new systems, particularly elevated

systems, would have a much lighter environmental footprint. Aerial tramways, for example, would not inhibit the movement of wildlife or deface mountainsides the way road cuts did.

Some of the plans were quite bold. The 1972 master plan for Mount Rainier proposed a tramway up the mountainside to Sunrise development area, replacing the Sunrise Ridge Road, which would have been closed and obliterated. The tramway would have assured limited access and allowed more protection of the subalpine environment.[34] A transportation plan for Great Smoky Mountains National Park envisioned a light-rail line through the mountains (most of the line would have been built on old railroad beds left from the logging era) and the conversion of the Newfound Gap Road into a way for buses only. This rail-and-bus loop system was put forward with an estimated price tag of $40 million, a staggering sum by the standards of the day.[35] One of the National Park Service's top planners, William S. Rosenberg, looked even further into the future and visualized an elevated monorail system for all of Yellowstone. Visitors would debark for short walks on foot trails to points of interest, and all road surfaces would be returned to nature.[36]

Conceptualization of this brave new world rested in part on predictions that modern civilization would undergo profound transformation as oil reserves ran out. Proponents of alternative transportation argued that putting these systems in national parks would help prepare the public for sweeping changes that would inevitably occur across the entire American landscape. Planners working inside the National Park Service figured if the visiting public embraced mass transit in national parks, then the idea would spread. They christened their effort the "sustainable design initiative."[37]

Few of the National Park Service proposals for alternative transportation systems in the 1970s actually materialized. Most proposals were folded into general management plans for each park, with each separate plan or GMP being submitted in turn to an exhaustive public review process. The proposals for alternative transportation rode on a tide of public dis-enchantment with the car culture in the early and mid-1970s, but by the time each GMP was finalized some years later, the public mood had changed. Mass transit had lost its allure. As the energy crisis wore on and inflation beset the U.S. economy, Americans generally preferred to blame oil corporations for their woes rather than examine their own habits of car use and energy consumption.

Congress's actions during the seventies re-flected the shifting mood of American consum-ers. In the Clean Air Act amendments of 1970, Congress required the U.S. auto industry to cut automobile emissions by 90 percent over the next five years, and it also gave the states re-sponsibility to implement transportation and land-use plans that would improve ambient air quality. Legal challenges by the auto industry and controversial enforcement strategies by the Environmental Protection Agency (EPA) ensued, and Congress eased up pressure on the auto industry after 1975. Meanwhile, EPA at-tempts to regulate the state implementation plans ran into even stiffer opposition. Con-gress's intent was to spur, through state and local action, adoption of mass transit and zon-ing measures that would curb urban sprawl and ultimately reduce the amount of driving that Americans did in private automobiles. In the face of strong public reaction, Congress back-pedaled on these requirements in the Clean Air Act amendments of 1977.[38]

As the public mood toward the car culture swung back toward complacency, the National Park Service softened its stand on transporta-tion issues in the national parks. Sometimes it did so at the pleasure of Congress. When the National Park Service moved to eliminate motorized boat traffic on the Colorado River in Grand Canyon National Park, for example, Congress specifically forbade it from doing so. Since this proviso, a rider on the 1981 appro-priations act, overturned years of social science research and planning by the agency, it made the National Park Service gun-shy about other carrying capacity studies.[39] If national parks were not to be managed according to carrying capacities, then one of the major benefits of al-ternative transportation was gone.

After Hartzog's departure, there was no one at the top pushing for transportation reform. Although National Park Service planners re-mained enthusiastic about it, they lost power within the organization. In the Hartzog era, planning had been centered in the Eastern Office of Design and Construction (in Phila-delphia) and the Western Office of Design and Construction (in San Francisco), and the two staff groups worked relatively independently of park superintendents and regional directors. But a revision in the planning process in the mid-1970s made GMPs subject to approval by both the park superintendent and the regional director. That crucial change in procedure took power away from the planners and handed it to the superintendents and regional directors. Superintendents tended to be protective of park roads since the roads were so central to a park's budget and operations.[40] In the matter of transportation, most superintendents were traditionalists.[41]

By the end of the Carter presidency, calls for the total removal of cars from parks, the obliter-ation of park roads, and the radical implemen-tation of alternative transportation schemes —calls that had been so frequent and main-stream less than a decade earlier—had prac-tically fallen silent. When the Reagan admin-istration came to power in 1981, it found the hegemony of the car culture in national parks fully restored. As in the past, debate over the car in the national park setting mainly took its cue from what was happening in American society at large—where millions of Americans stubbornly turned a blind eye to world oil de-pletion and global warming, purchased gas-guzzling SUVs, and drove more miles per capita than ever before (fig. 6).

The Present Outlook

In the past decade, interest in alternative transportation has begun to revive. In a few units of the national park system, cars have been nearly eliminated. In Acadia National Park, a propane-powered shuttle bus service

FIG. 6. Huge RVs in Seward, Alaska, gateway community to Kenai Fjords National Park, where park managers have faced relentless pressure to upgrade road access to the Exit Glacier, one of few car-accessible attractions in Alaska's national parks, August 2008. (Author photo)

was introduced in 1999, and by its third year of operation, it carried more than two hundred thousand visitors (out of a total annual visitation of three million), clearing some eighty thousand cars from park roads.[42] In 2000 at Yosemite, the three counties surrounding the park inaugurated a regional transit service that links up with the in-park shuttle bus system. At Zion National Park, the federal government has partnered with the gateway community of Springdale in fashioning a shuttle bus system that encourages a majority of visitors to leave their cars outside the park. The beautiful Mount Carmel Road into Zion Canyon, the heart of the park, is now closed to most private vehicles, and visitors ride the free shuttle, or ride a bicycle, or walk between shuttle stops, enjoying relative tranquility as the shuttles go by at approximately eight-minute intervals. (Registered guests at the lodge may still drive their cars to the lodge and park them there, a feature that raises the old issue of elitism, but with a new twist.) These are the most impressive new additions to the National Park Service's Alternative Transportation Program, which was resurrected in 1998 after more than twenty years of dormancy.[43]

The Alternative Transportation Program dovetails with the National Park Service's grow-ing interest in climate change. In recent years, park managers have begun to ask themselves how they will respond to sweeping effects of climate change on park resources. To what extent should they intervene when sensitive species are threatened by global warming? As plant and animal species jockey into higher latitudes and higher elevations, will the National Park Service engage in "assisted migrations" to preserve isolated park populations that have nowhere left to migrate? Will it be necessary and proper, for example, to create a nursery stock and do transplanting so that Joshua trees will not vanish from Joshua Tree National Park? Faced with such issues, it is not unreasonable for park managers to point out the effects of car pollution on park resources—and how this pollution source might be contained. In Zion, for example, the conversion to mass transit rid the park of five thousand cars per day and replaced them with thirty propane-powered buses for a net reduction in greenhouse gas emissions of thirteen tons per year.[44]

Ever since Congress enacted the Clean Air Act amendments of 1977, the National Park Service has been charged with combating regional air pollution threats to national parks. Air pollution poses a variety of threats to park resources. In the Great Smoky Mountains, for example, rising ozone levels damage plant foliage, while acid rain deposition alters the chemical composition of soil and water, threatening the health of trees and aquatic life. Air pollution also impairs scenic vistas, a major source of visitor enjoyment. Fine particulate matter in the air scatters light, causing a whitish haze that obscures distant views. But while the massed automobiles driving over Newfound Gap Road in the Great Smokies contribute marginally to reduction of air quality in that park, most of the particulate matter found in the atmosphere over the Smokies comes from coal-fired power plants located hundreds of miles away.[45] The problem with protecting national parks from global warming is that the parks share the atmosphere with every other place in the world.

It is for that very reason that alternative transportation is the most effective weapon the National Park Service has for combating climate change. Just as National Park Service planners observed during the 1970s, mass transit in national parks has a social value over and above its immediate effects on park resources and visitor enjoyment. If people will come to accept use of mass transit during their visits to national parks, then they will be more likely to support it in their own communities. The National Park Service has long striven to inculcate environmental values as a central part of its educational mission. No other federal agency is better positioned to educate the public about the need to make drastic changes in how we travel and how we consume energy.

Already, in fact, the National Park Service is using its bully pulpit and the modest tools at its disposal to educate the public about climate change. Take the example of Kenai Fjords National Park in Alaska, which has been in the vanguard of a recent program called "Climate Friendly Parks." In this park, visitors ride from the gateway community of Seward to Exit Glacier in a shuttle van powered by waste vegetable oil. At Exit Glacier, they enter a newly constructed nature center that is heated and lit by an experimental solid-oxide fuel cell. On a short walk to the glacier terminus, over terrain that until recently was covered by ice, visitors listen to interpretive rangers speak informatively about climate change and its relationship to Alaska's melting glaciers. When they take a boat tour of the fjords, they may purchase a green tag that buys a "carbon offset" for their individual share of carbon emissions on the boat trip. Back at the visitor center in Seward, they learn that Kenai Fjords National Park itself has gone "carbon neutral." If visitors inquire as to what the popular shorthand term "carbon neutral" means, they learn that a tiny fraction of the park's operating budget is used to buy Renewable Energy Certificates (RECs) and carbon offsets. The RECs pay for investment in clean energy development equal to 100 percent of the park's nonrenewable energy consumption (heating oil, propane, marine gas and diesel, gas for vehicles, miles of air travel, and coal-generated electricity), while the carbon offsets pay for investment in carbon-sequestration projects equal to 100 percent of carbon emissions from the park's overall fuel combustion. In other words, while the park still relies almost entirely on fossil fuels for its operations, it is promoting development of clean energy and carbon-capturing technologies elsewhere on the planet to neutralize its effects on the world's energy supply and on the earth's atmosphere.[46]

The Climate Friendly Parks program is helpful as far as it goes, but it is based on a model that some economists describe as "weak sustainability."[47] The weakness of this sustainable development model is that it does not require anything more from people than that they contribute a small tithing for global change. It uses the power of world financial markets to maintain the status quo in one place while purporting to affect compensatory "climate friendly" change somewhere else. It exports the problem when the message ought to be that we are all in this together.

The car culture is unsustainable. According to economist Lester R. Brown, the world now has 860 million cars. In the United States, there are now three cars for every four people. Other nations with fast-growing economies, including China and India, aspire to attain similar levels of car ownership. If China alone, with its 1.46 billion people, were to replicate America's car culture, it would have 1.1 billion cars. To say nothing about their effects on the planet's atmosphere, so many cars would consume an additional 98 million barrels of petroleum a day, an amount exceeding all of the world's current daily production. In Brown's sobering words, "There go the world's oil reserves." "The overriding challenge for our generation," he says, "is to build a new economy—one that is powered largely by renewable sources of energy, that has a much more diversified transport system, and that reuses and recycles everything."[48]

The National Park Service is doing what it can to foster renewable energy sources and to recycle aggressively, but it is not doing enough to diversify transport, its Alternative Transportation Program notwithstanding. The car culture still has too firm a grip on American society. The agency needs a strong push from outside.

The nation should take a bold step toward meeting its transportation challenge by eliminating or sharply restricting car use in the national parks. What better place to reinvent our relationship to the automobile than in the national parks? Since national parks constitute one of the nation's most venerated institutions, they would provide an excellent venue for reshaping public attitudes about car use. The National Park Service already possesses a strong tradition of environmental education. It commands considerable respect from the public. No doubt many in the National Park Service would welcome a drastic reduction of car use in the national parks as a major assist toward accomplishing other management goals. National parks offer one other important advantage: they already have a unique relationship to the nation's highway system, with staffed entrance stations located on most principal roads into each park.

Congress and the National Park Service could encourage greater patronage of alternative transportation systems by replacing the current park entrance fee with a "congestion fee" for car use. Several world cities have imposed such fees on automobiles entering their core metropolitan area. The United States should get over the notion that car access to national parks is a democratic right.

Skeptics will say that the capital cost of developing alternative transportation systems in national parks is too high. The costs will be high relative to current levels of national park funding, but if these systems are serving a higher national purpose, then those costs could easily be borne. Alternative transportation only appears expensive next to car transportation if it is assumed that the car culture will continue to thrive on a steady supply of cheap oil for many years to come. That is a false basis for comparison. If we begin transforming our transportation system sooner rather than later, we will reduce the level of economic dislocation at a future time. This should be our paradigm for evaluating costs. Another argument raised against alternative transportation systems in national parks is that they require vast new parking areas for all the cars that are denied admittance. The goal of eliminating or sharply restricting cars in national parks should be aimed at persuading Americans to leave their cars at home, traveling to these places by public transportation.

At the present time, we could do well to look back at the idealism expressed by those writers in the 1960s and early to mid-1970s who dared to imagine that the historical link between national parks and the car culture might one day be severed. As the authors of the report *Park Road Standards* remind us, "The single abiding purpose of National Parks is to bring man and his environment into closer harmony."[49] In the twenty-first century, that just might mean the overthrow of the car culture.

Notes

1. James J. Flink, *The Car Culture* (Cambridge, Mass.: MIT Press, 1975). Flink coined the term "car culture" and used it interchangeably with "automobility," which, he wrote, "conveniently sums up the combined impact of the motor vehicle, the automo-

bile industry, and the highway plus the emotional connotations of this impact for Americans" (1–2).

2. Anne F. Hyde, "From Stagecoach to Packard Twin Six: Yosemite and the Changing Face of Tourism, 1880–1930," *California History* 69, no. 2 (Summer 1990): 160.

3. David Louter, *Windshield Wilderness: Cars, Roads, and Nature in Washington's National Parks* (Seattle: University of Washington Press, 2006), 24–25.

4. Department of the Interior, *Proceedings of the National Parks Conference, 1912* (Washington, D.C.: Government Printing Office, 1912).

5. Robert Shankland, *Steve Mather of the National Parks* (New York: Alfred A. Knopf, 1951), 147–48.

6. Ethan Carr, *Wilderness by Design: Landscape Architecture and the National Park Service* (Lincoln: University of Nebraska Press, 1998), 79.

7. James Sturgis Pray, "The American Society of Landscape Architects and our National Parks," *Landscape Architecture* 6, no. 3 (April 1916): 119–23; Charles W. Eliot, "The Influence of the Automobile on the Design of Park Roads," *Landscape Architecture* 13, no. 1 (October 1922): 27–37; Henry V. Hubbard and Theodora Kimball, *An Introduction to the Study of Landscape Design* (New York: MacMillan, 1927), 321–23. On landscape architects and parkways, see also Jane Holtz Kay, *Asphalt Nation: How the Automobile Took Over America, and How We Can Take It Back* (Berkeley: University of California Press, 1997), 190–91.

8. Richard West Sellars, *Preserving Nature in the National Parks: A History* (New Haven: Yale University Press, 1997), 60; Department of the Interior, *Report of the Director of the National Park Service, 1924* (Washington, D.C.: Government Printing Office, 1924), 14.

9. Isabelle F. Story, *The National Parks and Emergency Conservation* (Washington, D.C.: National Park Service, 1933), 3.

10. Flink, *The Car Culture,* 142–43.

11. Daniel S. Pierce, "The Road to Nowhere: Tourism Development versus Environmentalism in the Great Smoky Mountains," in *Southern Journeys: Tourism, History, and Culture in the Modern South,* ed. Richard D. Starnes (Tuscaloosa: University of Alabama Press, 2003), 202–3. See also Harvey Broome, "Origins of the Wilderness Society," *The Living Wilderness* 5, no. 5 (July 1940): 10–11.

12. Robert Marshall, "The Problem of the Wilderness," *Scientific Monthly* 30, no. 2 (February 1930): 141–48.

13. Arno B. Cammerer to F. Woods Beckman, 28 July 1936, Cammerer to Olcott Deming, 22 September 1936, Cammerer to Albert G. Roth, 21 September 1936, and Cammerer to Dorothy W. Haasis, 22 September 1936, File 630 Part 4, Box 1133, Central Classified Files (CCF) 1933–49, Record Group (RG) 79, National Archives (NA) II. The file contains many additional letters of a similar nature.

14. Paul S. Sutter, *Driven Wild: How the Fight against Automobiles Launched the Modern Wilderness Movement* (Seattle: University of Washington Press, 2002), 231–32; T. H. Watkins, *Righteous Pilgrim: The Life and Times of Harold L. Ickes, 1874–1952* (New York: Henry Holt, 1990), 471, 549–51. See also Pierce, "The Road to Nowhere," 202–3.

15. Newton B. Drury, "National Park Service," in *Report of the Secretary of the Interior for 1944* (Washington, D.C.: Government Printing Office, 1944), 217–19.

16. Margaret Lynn Brown, *The Wild East: A Biography of the Great Smoky Mountains* (Gainesville: University Press of Florida, 2000), chap. 6.

17. Conrad L. Wirth, *Parks, Politics, and the People* (Norman: University of Oklahoma Press, 1980), 242.

18. The park-as-circulatory-system metaphor recurs in numerous Mission 66 plans, notably the pilot study conducted for Mount Rainier National Park and the plan for Great Smoky Mountains National Park. See also Ethan Carr, *Mission 66: Modernism and the National Park Dilemma* (Amherst: University of Massachusetts Press, 2007), 71–82, 338–39.

19. National Park Service, "Mission 66 for Great Smoky Mountains National Park," File 5, Box III, Park Management Collection, Great Smoky Mountains National Park.

20. George B. Hartzog Jr., *Battling for the National Parks* (Mount Kisko, N.Y.: Moyer Bell, 1988), 33–37, 87–91.

21. John Reynolds, interview by author, 14 April 2008.

22. "Random notes on the first meeting of the National Park Service Road Committee," no date, File D30 WASO Part 1, Box 1036, Administrative Files 1949–71, RG 79, NA II.

23. Denis P. Galvin, interview by author, 2 April 2008.

24. *Park Road Standards: A Report to the Director of the National Park Service,* in U.S. Department of the Interior, National Park Service, *Administrative Policies for Natural Areas of the National Park System,* rev. ed. (Washington, D.C.: Government Printing Office, 1968), 121–24, emphasis in original.

25. George B. Hartzog Jr., "Clearing the Roads—and the Air—in Yosemite Valley," *National Parks & Conservation Magazine* 46, no. 8 (August 1972): 15–16. Hickel quoted in "Eleven Guidelines Listed,"

in U.S. Department of the Interior, National Park Service, *Newsletter* 4, no. 13 (26 June 1969): 3.

26. George B. Hartzog Jr., "Can the National Parks Meet Your Changing Needs?" *Popular Science* 200, no. 5 (May 1972): 170.

27. George B. Hartzog Jr., "The National Parks in the 1970's," speech given at Boston, Massachusetts, no date, Box K5410, Policy and Philosophy 1968–1970, National Park Service History Collection, Harpers Ferry Center, Harpers Ferry, West Virginia. Also see "Changing the National Parks to Cope with People—and Cars, Interview with George B. Hartzog, Jr., Director, National Park Service," *U.S. News & World Report* 75 (24 January 1972): 52–55.

28. Edward Abbey, *Desert Solitaire: A Season in the Wilderness* (New York: Simon and Schuster, 1968), 49.

29. "National Parks at the Crossroads: Drawing the Line Where Protection Ends and Overuse Begins," *Conservation Foundation Letter: A Report on Environmental Issues* (September 1972): 7.

30. Ibid., 4.

31. Roger N. Clark, John C. Hendee, and Frederick L. Campbell, "Values, Behavior, and Conflict in Modern Camping Culture," *Journal of Leisure Research* 3, no. 3 (Summer 1971): 143–59.

32. Reynolds interview.

33. Russell D. Butcher, "At Grand Canyon . . . You Can Leave the Driving to Them," *National Parks & Conservation Magazine* 49, no. 5 (May 1975): 4; Andrew D. Gilman, "In & Around the National Parks: Alternatives to the Auto," *National Parks & Conservation Magazine* 50, no. 7 (July 1976): 4–6; "Summary, Alternative Transportation Systems," 7 March 1975, Briefing Book, House Oversight Hearing, National Park Service History Collection, Harpers Ferry Center, Harpers Ferry, West Virginia. On Hartzog's firing, see Robert Cahn, "George B. Hartzog, Jr." (2000), at http://www.nps.gov/history/history/online_books/sontag/hartzog.htm.

34. Theodore Catton, *National Park, City Playground: Mount Rainier in the Twentieth Century* (Seattle: University of Washington Press, 2006), 156.

35. U.S. Department of the Interior, National Park Service, *Transportation Concepts, Great Smoky Mountains National Park, North Carolina–Tennessee* (Washington, D.C.: National Park Service, 1971), 34.

36. Luther J. Carter, "National Parks: Traffic Jams Turn Attention to Roads," *Science* 161, no. 3843 (23 August 1968): 772.

37. Reynolds interview.

38. Tom McCarthy, *Auto Mania: Cars, Consumers, and the Environment* (New Haven: Yale University Press, 2007), 204.

39. Patricia E. Aspland and Katherine A. Pawelko, "Carrying Capacity: Evolution of Management Concepts for the National Parks," *Trends* 20, no. 33 (1983): 23–25.

40. Gerry Patten, interview by author, 7 May 2008; Reynolds interview.

41. Of course, this is a broad generalization and there were numerous exceptions. For example, Boyd Evison, superintendent of Great Smoky Mountains National Park from 1975 to 1978, promoted bicycle use of the park, introduced "quiet walkways" to encourage drivers to get out of their vehicles, closed certain roads in the park to all car use, and had the maintenance staff cease mowing the edges of roadways to advertise the park administration's commitment to fuel conservation.

42. Jeff Rennicke, "A Climate of Change," *National Parks* 81, no. 4 (Fall 2007): 31.

43. In 2005, the Alternative Transportation Program was redesignated the Transportation Management Program. See U.S. Department of the Interior, Alternative Transportation Program, "National Park Service Accomplishments in Alternative Transportation," at http://www.nps.gov/transportation/tmp/documents; U.S. Department of the Interior, National Park Service, Transportation Management Program, "Who We Are," at http://www.nps.gov/transportation/tmp/whoweare.htm.

44. Rennicke, "A Climate of Change," 30.

45. U.S. Department of the Interior, National Park Service, Air Resources Division, *Air Quality in the National Parks,* 2nd ed. (Lakewood, Colo.: National Park Service, 2002), 10–11, 35–36.

46. "Alternate Fuel Source Tapped at Kenai Fjords," *National Parks* 78 (Fall 2004): 12–13; "Kenai Fjords National Park Uses RECs/Carbon Offsets to Go Climate Neutral," undated, and Superintendent's Annual Report, 2006, copies provided by Jeff Mow from Superintendent's Files, Kenai Fjords National Park.

47. Douglas E. Booth, *Hooked on Growth: Economic Addictions and the Environment* (Lanham, Md.: Rowman and Littlefield, 2004), 145–47.

48. Lester R. Brown, *Plan B 3.0: Mobilizing to Save Civilization* (New York: W. W. Norton, 2008), 13–14.

49. *Park Road Standards,* 121–24.

PART III

POLITICAL NATURES

Mass-Producing Nature

Municipal Parks in Second Empire Paris

Urban parks and gardens are hard to come by, and in the early nineteenth century, Paris was hardly an exception. Space was at a premium within the old walled city which until 1848 had only three public gardens—the Tuileries, the Luxembourg, and the Jardin du Roy (now known as the Jardin des Plantes). As properties of the crown, they were open to the populace on sufferance. By the mid-nineteenth century, it became increasingly clear that they were no longer in scale with the growing size of the city nor with the needs and tastes of modern society.[1] During the Second Empire (1852–70), Napoleon III and his prefect Georges-Eugène Haussmann set about to remedy this situation and gradually equipped Paris with a remarkable network of green spaces that differed radically in scale, number, and design from the princely edens of the past, and were in fact conceived as part of the new infrastructure of the French capital, along with new streets and boulevards, water supply, and sewers (fig. 1). Five new parks and some twenty-four squares came into being piecemeal, shaped by modern technology, and heavily influenced by innumerable sources in European landscape theory and design. Equally important was the revolution in horticulture which broadened the spectrum of available plants and trees and facilitated propagation, deeply transforming the very concept of landscape.

France's rich traditions in this field had kept pace with social and political change ever since the French formal garden emerged with its optical refinements and geometric splendors in the seventeenth century. Yet during the Enlightenment, Le Nôtre's magnificent creations came to be associated with absolutism, and they were challenged, though never entirely displaced, by the more informal and irregular layouts inspired by the writings of Rousseau and by the English landscape garden. Jean-Marie Morel's *Theory of Gardens* (1776), René-Louis de Girardin's *An Essay on Landscape* (1777), Claude-Henri Watelet's notions of the picturesque articulated in *Essay on Gardens* (1774), the Count of Choulot's *L'Art des jardins* (1863), and Gabriel Thouin's *Plans raisonnés de toutes les espèces de jardins* (1819), all had an impact on the Second Empire's initiatives in garden design which were strongly rooted in late-eighteenth-century theory and practice.[2]

At the same time, the municipal initiatives in this area reflected more recent forms of urban landscape that made use of new technologies brought about by modernity.[3] The July Monarchy had initiated the salutary custom of lining streets and boulevards with trees, and creating squares. French *paysagistes* were also well acquainted with the work of German colleagues like Peter Josef Lenné, and above all Hermann von Pückler-Muskau, who claimed to have had a hand in the emperor's reconfiguration of the Bois de Boulogne. English examples played a still more important role. An amateur gardener, Louis Napoleon had lived in Britain for many years and was familiar both with its aristocratic country houses and with public parks like Joseph Paxton's Birkenhead or James Pennethorne's Victoria Park.[4] London's beautiful squares, which brought greenery into the city's close-grained fabric, constituted another crucial source. Humphry Repton's work in urban areas as well as John Claudius Loudon's gardenesque provided yet other important models for the French.

But Louis Napoleon's dreams of improving the well-being of all citizens changed after his coup d'état of 1852, when the capital's new parks and gardens came to be part of his imperial agenda. As Napoleon III, he was still eager to bring about social reconciliation but only insofar as it was compatible with autocracy. The creation of conflict-free zones of leisure was part of this strategy, and had the added advantage of providing labor for the large masses of workers attracted to the city by hopes of employment in the regime's extensive public works projects. At stake was the issue of representation: the parks' undoubted environmental benefits to the population were inseparable from their importance as signifiers of the paternal and benevolent interest of the ruler in the well-being of his subjects. Urban greenery, in other words, was also intended to shore up the status quo. Yet the sheer scale of the new spaces, the diversity of uses to which they were put, their geographic distribution across the urban territory, and the many specialists involved in their implementation meant that the parks and gardens would inevitably give voice to other ideologies as well.

The very fact that Louis Napoleon wanted these parks to be urban and public necessarily entailed a close collaboration with engineers. Municipal parks had to be well connected to the city, crisscrossed by roads capable of sustaining heavy traffic, and able to provide food, shelter, and resting places for both pedestrians and horses, especially on Sundays and holidays when areas like the Bois de Boulogne received up to twenty-five thousand visitors.[5] Engineering alone, aided by modern industry and know-how, could deliver to the population vast areas of green space fully equipped with trees and flower beds, lakes and waterfalls, and drainage and roads of access. This essay will analyze the influential "new nature" manufactured by Napoleon III, Haussmann, and their experts; its

ideological implications; and the complex response of the public.

Haussmann himself was no neophyte in these matters. An able administrator with more than a passing knowledge of horticulture, he was instrumental in determining the exact number and location of the city's new parks, gardens, and squares.[6] Empiricism and tradition, he realized, were no longer capable of carrying out such ambitious tasks, and his reliance on modern engineering distinguished him from the emperor's more voluntarist approach. The spaces Haussmann had in mind called for territorial management rather than established gardening practice. Hence the need for engineers who could invent the technology required to build and maintain large-scale green spaces in urban areas. Haussmann also understood that he had to forge the municipal apparatus necessary to bring about the greening of the capital, from the legal and economic framework to the creation of a highly specialized team of experts. To this end, he founded a special bureau, the Service des Promenades et Plantations de Paris, and placed the engineer Jean-Charles Adolphe Alphand at the head of operations.

Alphand did not consult the genius of the place in all, as Alexander Pope recommended.[7] His parks were often manufactured ex nihilo, in ways that eroded the particularity of place— at times felicitously. In all the city's new promenades, as well as in his writings on the subject, Alphand proudly foregrounded the industrial infrastructure on which they were based, demystifying the illusion of unplanned nature. The self-effacement of the old-style gardener was a thing of the past: middle-class engineers were eager to advertise their technical expertise. Artifice ruled. Long-lasting industrial materials like cement lake beds and standardized cast-iron benches and railings were frankly displayed.[8] Far from being a pastoral enclave, Paris's municipal parks were hybrid creations where the urban and the suburban merged, and the city was never allowed to be forgotten. Railroads cut through four of the five municipal parks, and Alphand himself called attention

FIG. 1. Plan of Paris showing the parks, gardens, squares, and planted promenades carried out under the Second Empire, published in Alphand's *Les Promenades de Paris* (1867–73). (Marquand Library of Art and Archaeology, Princeton University)

to the ornamental role played by the plumes of smoke released by the locomotives as they raced through the Bois de Vincennes.[9] Daring bridges paraded their iron girders or cables in stark contrast to the surrounding foliage, while smokestacks spewing soot could often be seen in the background. Spectators could hardly miss the metonymic connection between landscape and industry. Such frank exposure of machinery and technology exemplified the myth of progress dear to the nineteenth century.[10]

"Nature" itself had to be mass-produced: only at this price could it be disseminated across the city, and available to large numbers of people. At the park of the Buttes Chaumont, built over old quarries of gypsum and limestone, even topsoil had to be brought to the site by rail. Water, another luxury, called for more sophisticated technology. At the Bois de Boulogne, Alphand had to drill an artesian well and also bring water by aqueduct, since it was too expensive to feed the park's lakes and waterfalls with water pumped exclusively from the Seine. The grounds were thus honeycombed with underground pipes of different length and diameter, as the all-too-evident manholes showed. Far from hiding the technological mechanisms that undergirded his initiatives, Alphand exposed them openly, to the horror of specialists like William Robinson, who studied the Second Empire's gardens in great detail. "In one case," he wrote of Alphand's matter-of-fact way of revealing his ploys, "the streamlet instead of coming from any probable source of higher rock or brushwood, starts out of a plastered hole in the grass, in a way one cannot admire."[11] Not content with exhibiting modern equipment in his gardens almost ostentatiously, Alphand went to great lengths to divulge it in print. In his sumptuous publication *Les Promenades de Paris,* subsidized by Haussmann, he explained in detail the novel techniques used to produce these different landscapes, and prodigally illustrated newfangled watering devices like hoses supported on casters so as not to damage the lawns, machines to sift gravel, and complicated pumps and pipes (fig. 2). Self-reflexive illustrations

such as these, apt to heighten rather than suspend disbelief, were hardly new. The Machine de Marly, a feat of French engineering that provided water for Louis XIV's chateau, appeared in countless prints and paintings almost immediately after it was completed in 1684, and throughout the eighteenth century books on landscape design had occasionally reproduced similar hydraulic mechanisms showing how water could be pumped to supply streams and waterfalls (fig. 3). What changed was the fact that the amount of space and importance allotted to such devices in books and articles increased significantly.

Modern and artificial means of production also affected trees and shrubs laid out in flower beds and greenswards by Jean-Pierre Barillet-Deschamps, gardener-in-chief of the city. Barillet favored spectacular, broad-leafed plants, often of tropical origin, which could now be easily propagated thanks to scientific and technological advances in botany and horticulture. He reproduced large quantities of flowers and shrubs serially in sophisticated greenhouses that quickly became tourist attractions (fig. 4). Heated by gas and steam, they were described by the architect and critic César Daly as the "largest plant factory [*usine*] in existence."[12] Horticulture narrowly conceived was not Barillet's only area of expertise. Like Paxton, he also devised much of the technology used to plant and transplant trees and flowers, such as the complicated heating systems required to raise rare species in the municipal forcing houses.[13]

Alphand refused to let his parks hide behind the fiction that the greenery was natural or even indigenous, and lavished attention on modern practices and technology. Exotic plants disappeared from view during the winter months, when they were taken indoors for protection. Trees were equally nurtured with artificial help. Bought and sold like commodities, they were ferried across the city in special vehicles designed by Barillet that permitted mature specimens to arrive fully formed in their new destinations (fig. 5). Citizens grew accustomed to seeing tall trunks or canopies passing in front

FIG. 2. Hoses on casters invented by the municipal engineers, published in Alphand's *Les Promenades de Paris* (1867–73). (Marquand Library of Art and Archaeology, Princeton University)

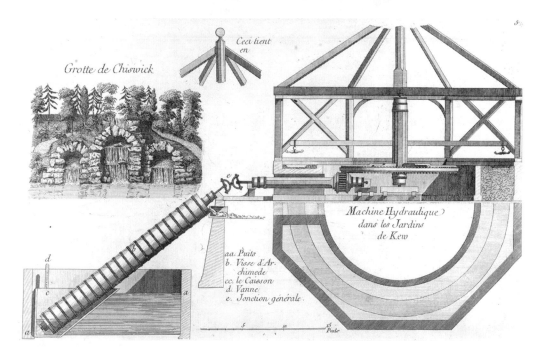

FIG. 3. Hydraulic machinery at Chiswick, published by Georges-Louis le Rouge in *Détail des nouveaux jardins à la mode* (1776–88). (Marquand Library of Art and Archaeology, Princeton University)

of third- or fourth-story windows: "Today," bemoaned a contemporary, "monuments and trees are like parcels; they are tied up, packaged, and compelled to travel."[14] As a result of new forms of cultivation instituted by modern horticulture, the city's municipal parks became veritable botanical gardens, graced with expensive and exotic species. These were not native to France but proclaimed their distant origins in France's far-flung colonies, as well as their elaborate and extravagant genesis in the municipal nurseries.[15] Costly foliage of this sort

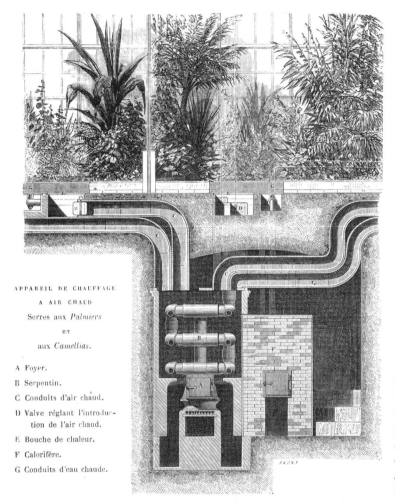

APPAREIL DE CHAUFFAGE

A AIR CHAUD

Serres aux *Palmiers*

ET

aux *Camellias.*

A Foyer.

B Serpentin.

C Conduits d'air chaud.

D Valve réglant l'introduction de l'air chaud.

E Bouche de chaleur.

F Calorifère.

G Conduits d'eau chaude.

FIG. 4. A modern green-
house in the main mu-
nicipal nursery of Paris (Le
Fleuriste de la Muette),
published in Alphand's *Les
Promenades de Paris.* (Marquand Library of Art and
Archaeology, Princeton
University)

served to detach the parks and gardens even more from the local specificity of their actual site.[16]

Ever since the late eighteenth century, no French park could be complete without rockery, the inevitable accompaniment to artificial waterfalls. Initially, huge chunks of sandstone were brought to the Bois de Boulogne from Fontainebleau at great expense, even though sandstone had nothing to do with its new surroundings geologically (fig. 6).[17] René-Louis de Girardin, Rousseau's friend, had already advocated the creation of large compositions of rocks by joining them with mortar.[18] If such practices were not unprecedented, the methods

and materials used by Alphand were. Within a few years, artificial rocks began to be fashioned out of blocks of stone welded together and covered with liquid cement to hide the sutures and make them blend more "naturally" with the environment.[19] In the case of the Buttes Chaumont, the entrepreneur Combaz fashioned rocks and stalactites by placing iron nets in the ceiling of the grottoes, and injecting liquid cement with a pump.[20] Parks and gardens became ideal testing grounds for new technologies precisely because they were far from the city and their innovative structures in concrete or cast iron could depart radically from entrenched traditions. In 1858, the engineer François Coignet erected a guardhouse at the Bois de Vincennes, built entirely out of concrete (*béton*) without the help of wooden scaffolding.[21]

Everything, it seems, was reproducible in these green spaces: rocks, trees, plants, and waterfalls. The commodification of nature took various forms. Landscape had become a form of merchandise that could be reproduced in print culture and photography, or manufactured with the use of modern technology. At the Buttes Chaumont, the beetling rock rising like a needle out of the water (fig. 7) evokes an actual site, the cliffs at Étretat, later painted by Monet and Courbet. Conversely, the city's municipal parks themselves were the object of emulation. Widely illustrated and publicized in the press, they were in turn imitated in the provinces and in other countries and continents. Quickly codified, their rhetoric of rocks and waterfalls, bridges and chalets, became set pieces, miniaturized and endlessly repeated at different scales and contexts. In the summer of 1860, for example, the popular Théâtre Saint-Martin recreated a much-abridged allusion to the Bois de Boulogne in the orchestra, complete with plants, waterfall, and rockery.

Yet even Alphand remained deeply conflicted about the role of his new nature in the parks. If he took pains, in his publications, to reveal the industrial mechanisms that undergirded his parks and gardens, he often lapsed into the old discourse of truth and authenticity, claiming, "One does not rise up with impunity against the truth that governs nature."[22] Faith in modern technology was always veined with a certain distrust. Artificial rocks, synthetic caves and stalactites, and faux wood balustrades in concrete betray a need to naturalize industrial materials that speaks volumes for the ambivalence felt by the engineers whose works these were.[23] It became increasingly hard to draw the line between "nature" and the laboriously manufactured simulacra. And if art imitated life so efficiently, life at times repaid in kind. Nature, so tightly controlled, so regimented and interfered with, occasionally came to resemble the sleek products manufactured by industry. Schooled by modern technology, Alphand's engineers and landscape architects liked their foliage neat. Not by chance did William Robinson tellingly refer to the "wrought-iron leaves" of the Wigandia, a tropical species painstakingly nurtured in the city's greenhouses.[24] Mimesis ran both ways. Paris's new green spaces complicated rather than answered the question

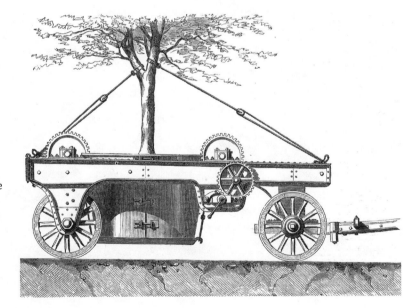

FIG. 5. Special vehicle used to transport mature trees, published in Alphand's *Les Promenades de Paris*. (Marquand Library of Art and Archaeology, Princeton University)

FIG. 6. Charles Marville, *Grande Cascade in the Bois de Boulogne.* (© Roger Viollet/The Image Works)

FIG. 7. The Park of the Buttes Chaumont. (© Roger Viollet/The Image Works)

that vexed Alphand and his contemporaries, whether friends or opponents: what did nature signify in an age of technical reproducibility?

There were no easy answers. Politically, too, the empire's green spaces were far from transparent. To begin with, they differed widely among themselves, from the predictable and pedestrian municipal style of the squares to the oneiric beauty of the Buttes Chaumont. The division of labor predicated by the parks called for collaboration between various specialists and branches—engineering, hydraulics, horticulture, and architecture—imbued with different politics and ideologies of nature. Vast, many-layered sites like the Bois de Boulogne or the Bois de Vincennes implied complex forms of collective authorship, from an autocrat like Napoleon III and his obedient experts to a socialist like François Coignet, who pioneered the use of concrete in many important avant-garde structures.[25] Municipal parks may have been decreed by fiat, but they were carried out for the benefit of the public rather than the prince. Even if they were designed in part as political propaganda for the regime and as a homeopathic form of social pacification, they always exceeded the intentions of their planners, and reflect just as much the social and economic aspirations of the rising middle classes represented by the professionals who designed them and carried them to completion. It is not by chance that these spaces reject the old humanistic codes of representation that relied on mythology and classical allusions accessible only to the elite, preferring instead to exhibit their connection to the world of the Industrial Revolution, a world at once secular and immanent, prosaic and reproducible. Serially planted trees and shrubs, artificial rocks and lakes, and bridges and viaducts displace the old garden iconography of marble gods and nymphs. The very fact that the new parks required the active participation of engineers, fired with the ideas of Saint-Simon and Fourier, helped undermine the political intentions of the emperor and his prefect.

Such varied ideological origins make the response to these parks difficult to read: the re-action of the public was not univocal, but mirrored the diversity of the population as well as the multiplicity of views represented by those who designed and carried out the new squares and gardens. On the whole, the middle and upper classes were largely in favor of the regime's green spaces. Oblivious to the ostensible display of iron and cement, they continued to see the parks in terms of the traditional discourses of nature. Intellectuals of the opposition and legitimist aristocrats, however, angered by the coup that brought an upstart to power, attacked the new initiatives, contrasting their own cultured and well-traveled views to Alphand's mass-produced scenery, often compared to the papier maché decor of the operettas in vogue at the time.[26] The parks' manufactured amenities offended the naturalist sensibilities of several writers for whom duplication and duplicity were synonymous. "Mr. Alphand," wrote Émile Zola sarcastically, "tells us calmly how his stage-hands installed each set design in its place; he even goes so far as to tell us how much each of these sets cost: so much for the oak, so much for the stream, so much for the rock."[27] George Sand anticipated his criticisms: "Do not expect to find the charms of nature anywhere in the vast spaces that Paris has given over to this fiction. Compared to the most sumptuous compositions by our Parisian *paysagistes,* the smallest rock of Fontainebleau or the wood-covered hills of Auvergne . . . have an altogether different aspect, atmosphere and powerful impact."[28] Other observers were troubled by the manifest lack of realism caused by features that defied the laws of logic and gravity. "To the north of the great lake," noted the Count of Lasteyrie contemptuously, "one is surprised to see a sheet of water situated higher than the surrounding soil."[29] To the dismay of many critics, modernity's ability to reproduce nature artificially gave new life to the old maxim associated with Le Nôtre, "forcer la nature."

These plaintive voices, often prompted by legitimate political concerns, reveal an incurable nostalgia for a lost authenticity uncontaminated by traces of urbanism or the Industrial Revolution. "The hand of man is evident everywhere," protested the writer Alphonse de Calonne in reference to the new gardens, "while liberty is nowhere to be found."[30] Clearly, Rousseau still cast a long shadow and fueled resistance to gardens that were as irregular as the philosophe might have wished, but as contrived as the formal layouts he despised. The old humanist concept of a pastoral and restorative nature resented an invasive technology which did not offer auratic consolations. Trees, streams, and topography are historical records, supports for memory, and it seemed to many contemporaries that the new parks of Paris delivered ready-made to the public—with exotic plants from other climates, newly transplanted trees, fake grottoes, and manufactured lawns—had no past, and reflected all too clearly the mobility and uprootedness of modern life. But that was precisely the point. Critics who faulted the parks as paltry surrogates for nature failed to see that the engineers and horticulturists who produced them were not imitating nature but constructing it according to the economic precepts of modernity. Far from being an exercise in mimicry, these mass-produced plantings and flower beds, cement lake beds and artificial streams, were in fact parading their own truths: they were not unique, but reproducible. The Second Empire's green spaces were a response to the changed conditions of life brought about by the modern metropolis. Their message was not altogether reassuring, perhaps, but the old nature, transcendent and restorative, was no longer within reach. The new, fungible nature was linked to spectacle, entertainment, and leisure, and these were hopelessly immanent. Nature cannot be apprehended without a code.[31] The problem here, of course, was that the old codes were no longer operative, while the new ones were still being hammered out.

Class had much to do with the broad range of reactions to the parks which were strategically disseminated throughout the city, according to the geopolitical priorities of the regime.[32] Each of the capital's green spaces addressed specific social groups in terms of design, ex-

pensive waterworks, and exotic plants, as well as the number and quality of its concessions and amenities. Alphand published the cost of each park, garden, and square in Paris, showing how clearly he differentiated them in terms of class, despite rhetoric to the contrary.[33] Although the municipal parks were extroverted, open to the city, unlike the enclosed princely gardens of aristocratic residences, equality of access was not a reality nor even a desideratum. In theory, of course, the new spaces of leisure were to be available to all. In practice, the price of transportation, long working hours of the laboring poor, and the constant vigilance of the police limited access considerably. The new urban parks were not segregated outright, but social classes used them differently over time. On weekdays, the elegant Bois de Boulogne, situated in the fashionable West End of Paris, was the playground of those who could afford horse and carriage—the rich, the emperor, and his court. On Sundays, the park was abandoned to the lower classes, or at least to those who could afford to pay for the omnibus fare or the train. For those who could not, the emperor had another park built, the Bois de Vincennes, in the eastern (and opposite) part of Paris, where most workers lived. But whether east or west, the two parks were situated at the outskirts of the city, and in general the laboring poor did not care to walk one or two miles to reach these havens of greenery. Even less did they tolerate surveillance. Haussmann himself ruefully acknowledged that the two great parks served primarily the needs of the bourgeoisie.[34] Only the Buttes Chaumont, built in one of the poorest parts of Paris, received crowds of workers, and even then only on Sundays, their day off.

One can neither reduce the emperor's initiatives to his fear of class warfare nor ignore that fear altogether. Opening up such large green spaces at the edge of the city was no doubt a visionary stroke, and Alphand and Haussmann repeatedly extolled the emperor's great generosity in creating the Bois de Vincennes for the working class.[35] Yet the contrast between the two parks could hardly have been more glaring.

In terms of expenditure and labor, the costs needed to maintain these parks were quite high. Exotic plants, artificial lakes, and lawns were labor-intensive. At the Bois de Boulogne, the social relations of production were all too visible. On weekdays, the rich rode past an army of workmen mowing huge expanses of lawn by hand, pruning hundreds of trees, and hosing down paths and alleyways.[36] It made political sense to create a class-specific playground on the opposite side of the city, and minimize the confrontation of different social groups. While the Bois de Vincennes was equipped with many of the same sorts of things as its richer counterpart, it possessed them in less expensive versions. In addition, roughly one-third of the grounds was reserved for military maneuvers so that visitors were never far from the baleful presence of the army. This enclave drove a wedge into the center of the park, separating one half from the other.

Paris's municipal parks were stamped by other class-related characteristics. Haussmann, Alphand, and their collaborators conceived them as a spectacle, an object of visual consumption. Designed to be seen rather than touched, they functioned through carefully devised Arcadian tableaux and constructed views, aimed at the spectator rather than the subject. In this, the new parks reflected the pervasive influence of the French classical tradition in landscape design which addressed the eye instead of the body.[37] In sharp contrast to the British parks, walking or sitting on the grass was not allowed. Nor was smoking. Rules and regulations, affixed to elegant cast-iron panels, and guardians of law and order enforced a code of use based on the needs and mores of the middle class. Underprivileged users were often made to feel unwelcome, particularly in the squares which, unlike the parks, were situated within the city. In consequence, the laboring poor who lived in the class-specific enclaves to the northeast of Paris, at Montmartre, Belleville, and Charonne, preferred the unkempt and unsupervised spaces of the periphery, where streets and houses ran out and the fields began, spaces they associated with freedom.[38]

Landscape can either support or call into question the way we think about our world and our place within it.[39] These parks did both. Although none of the green spaces created by the Second Empire questioned the status quo, one cannot apprehend the complexity of these modern, urban landscapes without reading them in several registers at once. No doubt the contrasts in wealth, power, and privilege made evident by these parks heightened a confrontation between social classes which would explode with greater force during the Commune. Yet not all contact between the classes was adversarial. Parks and squares also encouraged cultural emulation, an important factor in an age of rapid social mobility. The very fact that the imperial parks and gardens attracted a broad and diverse mass of people shows how these green spaces, however unequal, served as one of the many leveling forces that contributed to the gradual expansion of the middle class, and helped integrate citizens not only spatially but socially.[40]

Nor can one collapse the visitors' experiences with the ideologically driven motivations of the emperor and his men, according to the intentional fallacy. Faced with such complex, multifaceted spaces and consequent instability of meaning, not all spectators responded passively or uncritically in a purely perceptual manner. Parks always meant different things to different people: class, age, and gender, possibly religion and nationality, among other affiliations, had a bearing on how one reacted to specific spaces which had the power to exclude as well as to connect. The Second Empire's green spaces were irreducible to a single viewpoint.

Planned in painstaking detail, subject to surveillance and strict codes of conduct, the parks were expected to produce homogeneity as well as difference. The rules enforced by the parks were clearly intended to foster resigned and accommodating subjects, if not subalterns, eager to ape their betters but content to remain on a different social level. Yet workers often refused these roles and constantly transgressed regulations, picking flowers and fruits, walking on the grass, and wading in streams.[41] Consciously, perhaps, most of the population may have responded as desired—we have no way of knowing. But one cannot deny visitors a sense of agency, nor the parks some measure of emancipatory potential. The invention of leisure and its association to landscape entailed new ways of experiencing space and time. With their sylvan nooks and crannies, vast stretches of free space, and complex social structure, these parks had the wherewithal to interpellate at least some strollers, challenge their assumptions, encourage fantasy and play. In their heyday, they must have performed a central if ambiguous role in the precarious and problematic construction of modern subjectivities.

Notes

1. Lucien Augé de Lassus, *Le Bois de Boulogne* (Paris: Société générale d'éditions, 1908), 156.

2. Jean-Marie Morel, *Théorie des jardins* (Paris: Pissot, 1776); René-Louis, marquis de Girardin, *De la composition des paysages, ou Des moyens d'embellir la Nature autour des Habitations, en joignant l'agréable à l'utile* (Genève: Chez P. M. Delaguette, 1777); Claude-Henri Watelet, *Essai sur les jardins* (Paris: Prault, 1774); Paul de Lavenne, comte de Choulot, *L'Art des jardins; ou, Etudes théoriques et pratiques sur l'arrangement extérieur des habitations, suivi d'un essai sur l'architecture rurale, les cottages et la restauration des anciennes constructions* (Paris: F. Didot Frères, 1855); Gabriel Thouin, *Plans raisonnés de toutes les espèces de jardins* (Paris: Imprimerie de Lebègue, 1819).

3. Ann Komara, "Concrete and the Engineered Picturesque: The Parc des Buttes Chaumont (Paris, 1867)," *Journal of Architectural Education* 58, no. 1 (September 2004): 11. See also Ann Komara, "'Art and Industry' at the Parc des Buttes Chaumont" (master's thesis, University of Virginia, 2002).

4. Birkenhead and Victoria were published, along with Pennethorne's Battersea Park, which opened in 1858, in Adolphe Alphand, *Les Promenades de Paris* (Paris: J. Rothschild, 1867–73), 53, 56, and 52, respectively.

5. J. Lobet, *Le nouveau bois de Boulogne et ses alentours* (Paris: Hachette, 1856), 27.

6. For Georges-Eugène Haussmann's early interest in horticulture, see his *Mémoires du Baron Haussmann*, vol. 1, *Avant l'Hôtel de Ville* (Paris: Victor-Havard, 1890), 213.

7. Alphand, *Les Promenades de Paris,* xxxi. Although Alphand criticized gardens that did not take into consideration the "génie du pays," he did not follow this maxim himself, as his Parisian parks and squares reveal.

8. Alphand claims that all the cement borders in the lakes and streams were covered by a thick coat of topsoil, so grass could grow and hide the artificial bed, but the camouflage does not seem to have been successful. See Alphand, *Les Promenades de Paris,* 28. Years later, Lucien Augé de Lassus, an admirer of Napoleon III, points out how the cement beds were barely concealed. See Lucien Augé de Lassus, *Le Bois de Boulogne,* 167.

9. "Deux chemins de fer, celui de Lyon et celui d'Orléans, animent le paysage par le panache ondoyant de la fumée des locomotives." Alphand, *Les Promenades de Paris,* 165.

10. "Like the Universal Exhibitions the park becomes the site for the glorification of technology and of the machine." Maria Luisa Marceca, "Reservoir, Circulation, Residue: J. C. A. Alphand, Technological Beauty and the Green City," *Lotus International* 30 (1981): 59.

11. William Robinson, *The Parks, Promenades & Gardens of Paris, Described and Considered in Relation to the Wants of Our Own Cities and of Public and Private Gardens* (London: John Murray, 1869), 63.

12. "La plus vaste usine de plantes qui existe." César Daly, "Promenades et plantations. Parcs. Jardins publics. Squares et boulevards de Paris," *Revue Générale de l'Architecture et des Travaux Publics* 21 (1863): col. 129.

13. Barillet's use of undulating dells in all his designs was doubtless borrowed from Paxton, who was working for James de Rothschild at Boulogne-Billancourt and at the vast landscape garden surrounding the chateau of Ferrières (Seine-et-Marne).

14. "Aujourd'hui, les monuments et les arbres sont des colis; on les ficelle, on les empaquette et on les fait voyager." Victor Fournel, *Paris Nouveau et Paris Futur* (Paris: Jacques Lecoffre, 1865), 107.

15. "Plusieurs massifs ainsi composés dans un jardin, en changeront entièrement l'aspect, qui rappellera en quelque sorte celui des colonies." Jean-Pierre Barillet-Deschamps, "Des massifs à effet pour l'ornement des jardins pendant la belle saison," *Annales de la Société d'Horticulture de la Gironde* 5e année, no. 17 (April 1851): 339.

16. "Under the Second Empire, the 'natural landscape' of Alphand contributes to detach the city from

its origins." Michel Vernes, "Au jardin comme à la ville 1855–1914, le style municipal," *Parcs et promenades de Paris* (Paris: Éditions du Demi-Cercle/Pavillon de l'Arsenal, 1988), 16.

17. As Alphand himself had pointed out. See his *Les Promenades de Paris,* 31–32.

18. René-Louis de Girardin, *De la composition des paysages,* 57.

19. Michel Racine has called attention to the role played by *rocailleurs* in the invention and use of pre-stressed cement and concrete in the nineteenth century. See Michel Racine, *Jardins "au naturel." Rocailles, grotesques et art rustique* (Arles: Acte Sud, 2001), 82.

20. Ibid., 88. Little is known about these *rocailleurs,* in this case not even the complete name.

21. Ferré, "Maison de garde dans le bois de Vincennes," *L'Illustration* (31 July 1858): 68.

22. "On ne s'insurge pas impunément contre la vérité qui régit la nature." Alphand, *Les Promenades de Paris,* xviii.

23. "Within the nineteenth-century discourse on materials and production practices, the craftsmanship evident in significant elements of the park [the Buttes Chaumont] situates its presence within a cultural response to industrialization that stressed manual craftsmanship versus machine reproduction even as Alphand embraced efficiency in certain construction methods." Komara, "Concrete and the Engineered Picturesque," 10.

24. William Robinson, *Gleanings from French Gardens* (London: Frederick Warne and Co., 1868), 3.

25. For the relation between the use of cement and the utopian ideals of the French Left, see Laurent Baridon, "Béton et utopie avant 1914: Architecture et 'moule sociale,'" *RACAR, Revue d'Art Canadienne/Canadian Art Review* 31, nos. 1–2 (2007): 7–11.

26. "Chaque sujet feuillu est allé installer sa verdure, sans trouble ni erreur, précisément à la place qui lui avait été assignée! et tout cela avec la promptitude d'un changement à vue, absolument comme s'il se fût agi d'un décor d'opéra." M. L. D, ancien magistrat, *Parc des Buttes Saint-Chaumont. Guide du promeneur* (Paris: Lacroix, Verboeckhoven & Cie, 1867), 38. Théophile Gautier mentions the grottoes and the temple of Diana at the Bois de Vincennes, so reminiscent of Hubert Robert, as "an agreeable melange of architecture and landscape, of ruins, rocks and trees, disposed a bit like an opera set." See Théophile Gautier, "Le Bois de Vincennes," [1865], now in *Paris et les Parisiens* (Paris: La Boîte à Documents, 1996), 66.

27. "Et M. Alphand nous conte tranquillement comment ses machinistes ont mis chaque décor à sa place; il va jusqu'à nous dire combien la pose de chaque décor a couté: pour tel chêne, tant,—pour tel ruisseau, tant,—pour tel caillou, tant." Émile Zola, "Livres d'aujourd'hui et de demain," *Le Gaulois* (8 March 1869): n.p., but 2.

28. "Même, dans les espaces plus vastes que Paris consacre à cette fiction, n'espérez pas trouver le charme de la nature. Le plus petit recoin des roches de Fontainebleau ou des collines boisées de l'Auvergne, la plus mince cascatelle de la Gargilesse, le plus ignoré des méandres de l'Indre ont une autre tournure, une autre saveur, une autre puissance de pénétration que les plus somptueuses compositions de nos *paysagistes* de Paris!" George Sand, "La rêverie à Paris," in *Paris Guide,* vol. 2 (Paris: A. Lacroix, Verboeckhoven et Cie., 1867), 1199, emphasis in original.

29. "À l'extrémité nord du grand lac, par exemple, on s'étonne de voir la nappe d'eau plus élevée que les terrains environnants, ce qui déroute un peu les lois de la physique naturelle." Ferdinand de Lasteyrie, *Les travaux de Paris: Examen critique* (Paris: Michel Lévy Frères, 1861), 143.

30. "La main de l'homme se montre partout, la liberté nulle part." Alphonse de Calonne, "Les transformations de Paris. II—Jardins et jardinets," *Revue contemporaine* 15ème année, 2e série, 51 (Mai–Juin 1866): 746–47.

31. Bernard Kalaora, "Les salons verts: Parcours de la ville à la forêt," in *La Théorie du paysage en France (1974–1994),* ed. Alain Roger (Seyssel: Champ Vallon, 1995), 121.

32. For the correlation of politics and the siting of each park, see Heath Massey Schenker, "Parks and Politics during the Second Empire in Paris," *Landscape Journal* 14, no. 2 (Fall 1995): 201–19.

33. Alphand, *Les Promenades de Paris,* passim. He analyzes the parks, gardens, and squares one by one, itemizing the expense incurred by each.

34. "Malgré tous mes efforts pour rendre aisément accessibles à toutes les classes de la Population de Paris ces deux splendides Promenades extérieures si hautement appréciées par elle: le Bois de Boulogne et le Bois de Vincennes, je ne pus réussir à l'en faire profiter généralement, sinon les Dimanches et les Jours de Fêtes, à cause de la distance, du temps à dépenser pour la franchir, à l'aller et au retour, et des frais des transports." Georges-Eugène Haussmann, *Mémoires du Baron Haussmann,* vol. 3, *Grands Travaux de Paris* (Paris: Victor-Havard, 1893), 224.

35. "Il s'agissait ici de créer, à l'Est de Paris,

conformément aux desseins généreux de l'Empereur pour les populations laborieuses des XIe et XIIe arrondissements nouveaux et des ouvriers du Faubourg Saint-Antoine en particulier, une promenade équivalant à celle dont venaient d'être dotés, à l'Ouest, les quartiers riches, élégants, de notre Capitale." Haussmann, Ibid., 3:210. See also Alphand, *Les Promenades de Paris,* 157.

36. Ferdinand de Lasteyrie, *Les travaux de Paris,* 168.

37. Françoise Choay mentions the connection between the Second Empire's green spaces and the eye in her "Haussmann et le système des espaces verts parisiens," *Revue de l'Art,* no. 29 (1975): 96.

38. In a celebrated chapter of their novel *Germinie Lacerteux* (1865), the Goncourt brothers wrote eloquently of this association: "a breath of spaciousness and freedom came from the end of the street and from the sky" ("il venait du bout de la rue, du ciel, un souffle d'espace et de liberté"). Edmond et Jules Goncourt, *Germinie Lacerteux* (Paris: Flammarion, 1990), 114.

39. I borrow this idea from Denis Cosgrove. See Denis Cosgrove, "Prospect, Perspective and the Evolution of the Landscape Idea," *Transactions of the Institute of British Geographers* 10, no. 1 (1985): 58.

40. Michel Vernes, "Les jardins contre la ville," *Le Temps libre,* no. 9 (Printemps 1984): 51.

41. Charles Wanderer, "Promenades horticoles dans les jardins publics de Paris. Le parc des Buttes-Chaumont," *Revue Horticole* (1882): 402–5.

Playing Politics at Bear Mountain

Franklin Roosevelt, the Civilian Conservation Corps, and State Park Design during the New Deal Era

In mid-August 1934, President Franklin Roosevelt traveled fifty miles upriver from New York City into the Hudson Highlands to visit Civilian Conservation Corps (CCC) Camp SP-20 in the Pine Meadow region of Bear Mountain State Park. During his brief stay he toured the camp's grounds, most probably visiting the company barracks, the mess hall, and the camp library, which often doubled as a recreation room. He also reviewed the more than two hundred Corps enrollees stationed at the camp and publicly expressed to them his heartfelt gratitude for their hard work in the state park. Finally, before leaving, Roosevelt also inspected the company's conservation project, which at the time involved constructing a core-wall dam six hundred and fifty feet long and thirty-five feet high across the outlet of the Pine Meadow valley in order to create a swimming lake for tourists.[1] As Roosevelt explained in a letter mailed to the camp two months later, the situation at Pine Meadow in New York's Bear Mountain State Park was the political "expression of the plan of the President."[2]

While the conversion of a highland meadow into an artificial swimming lake may seem ecologically unsound today, the development of Bear Mountain State Park nevertheless suggests a variety of important historical changes set in motion by Franklin Roosevelt's New Deal. Most obvious was the dramatic transformation of the natural landscape, which Corps enrollees altered through their physical labor. The more than three million young men who joined the CCC between 1933 and 1942 undertook similarly transformative work, planting two billion trees, slowing soil erosion on forty million acres of farmland, and developing eight hundred state parks for outdoor recreation.[3] As the Corps' second director, James McEntee, explained in 1939, the CCC dramatically "altered the landscape of the United States."[4] Yet Franklin Roosevelt's visit to Camp SP-20 at Bear Mountain indicates other changes as well. The interaction of the president and working-class youths in a state park suggests that while the CCC was altering American nature, it was transforming the political landscape as well.

Throughout the early 1930s it was relatively easy for Americans to understand the vast changes in the natural landscape caused by the Civilian Conservation Corps. In Bear Mountain State Park, as in state parks throughout the country, locals and visitors alike could literally see the natural environment transforming before their eyes as Corps enrollees planted trees, halted soil erosion, and built a wide variety of outdoor recreational amenities from picnic areas and campgrounds to hiking shelters and visitor centers. Yet the political implications of these natural landscape changes were less obvious to the Great Depression–era public. What was the political meaning of a reforested stand of trees? How did a hillside that no longer eroded its soil affect local governments? When did artificial swimming lakes, built by the Corps in state parks across the country, begin to affect national politics?[5]

Although there is a rich literature on the links between natural resource conservation and the growth of the federal state, none of it examines the role played by state parks in this national state-building process. This is all the more surprising since the New Deal, an era of unprecedented state growth on the national level, gave birth to numerous conservation programs such as the Civilian Conservation Corps that undertook more work in state parks than in their national counterparts.[6] Bear Mountain State Park had more CCC camps situated within its fifty thousand acres than most national parks had within their much larger boundaries. Exploring the evolution of Corps work in Bear Mountain, from forestry projects to soil conservation efforts to park development work, will not only shed light on the role played by state parks in the rise of the modern welfare state but will also help us better understand the political implications of park design during the New Deal era.

Environmental historian William Cronon also makes a theoretical case for studying natural places such as Bear Mountain State Park. In his highly influential essay titled "The Trouble with Wilderness; or, Getting Back to the Wrong Nature," Cronon argues that Americans have been overly concerned with wild nature far removed from society in locations such as Yosemite National Park. "Wilderness gets us into trouble if we imagine that this experience of wonder and otherness is limited to the remote corners of the planet," explains Cronon.[7] Analyzing natural environments that are "closer to home," "next door," and located "in our own backyards," he argues, is more helpful for understanding American's complex relationship to the natural world. Far-off wilderness visited once in a lifetime, in other words, is less culturally significant than the nature all around us experienced each day. Bear Mountain is a case in point. Located less than an hour's drive from the most populous city in the United States, this state park in New York's Hudson Highlands, along with most state parks throughout the country, served as figurative backyards for the great majority of Depression-era Americans.

* * *

On 18 May 1933, just six weeks after Congress established the CCC at President Roosevelt's request, the first contingent of Corps enrollees began transforming the natural landscape of Bear Mountain State Park. On that day, the two hundred young men assigned to Camp SP-20 hiked up to Pine Meadow, pitched tents to be used as temporary shelters, and immediately began clearing a portion of the meadow for the construction of their camp, which would ultimately include eight wooden barracks, a mess hall and bathhouse, and a recreation room.[8] By late spring of 1933 Corps enrollees had constructed two such camps in Bear Mountain, and by the following winter the number of CCC camps in the state park had peaked at twelve before tapering off late in 1935, when the Corps removed all of the Bear Mountain camps from the state park. With approximately two hundred enrollees stationed in each company, these twelve CCC camps brought nearly twenty-five hundred young men into Bear Mountain State Park during the early to mid-1930s.[9]

The Corps enrollees hiking into Bear Mountain State Park during the spring of 1933 were but a trickle compared to the flood of young men pouring into CCC camps nationwide. During the Corps' nine-year existence, from 1933 until 1942, approximately 3.5 million young men joined the New Deal program. These men had to be 18–25 years of age, unmarried, and willing to send $25 of their $30 monthly pay back home to their families, all of which had to be listed on state relief registers. In order to avoid creating new bureaucracy, Roosevelt organized the Corps cooperatively; while the Department of Labor recruited the young men and the Department of War oversaw CCC camps, the Department of Agriculture supervised enrollee labor on projects in state and national forests and on farms, and the Department of the Interior was responsible for enrollee work in state and national parks.[10]

The Department of the Interior's National Park Service located the great majority of the CCC camps under its jurisdiction in state parks such as Bear Mountain rather than in national parks. During the Corps' first six-month enrollment period, for instance, which spanned from March through August 1933, the Park Service assigned 102 of its 172 CCC camps to state parks in twenty-six states. In 1935, the number of Corps camps in state parks skyrocketed to 475 of the Park Service's 590 allotted companies. All told, between 1933 when Congress created the CCC and 1942 when the program disbanded, the Park Service located 70 percent of all its CCC camps in state parks.[11]

The Corps camps located in Bear Mountain State Park, like most Park Service camps across the United States, initially focused their conservation efforts on forestry (fig. 1). During the first three months of 1934, Corps enrollees in Bear Mountain not only reforested areas of the park that had been heavily logged during the late nineteenth and early twentieth centuries, but the young men working out of camps at Mica Mine and Beaver Pond also felled and burned more than one thousand trees infected with Dutch elm disease.[12] These same enrollees cut dozens of miles of firebreaks through the park and built a system of fire towers, including one made of local stone atop Bear Mountain in the center of the park.[13] Corps camps nationwide did similar forestry work, planting more than two billion trees that accounted for one-half of the trees planted in U.S. history.[14]

The CCC's conservation work in Bear Mountain State Park shifted gears during the summer of 1934, when Dust Bowl winds blew soil from Great Plains farms as far east as Washington, D.C. In response, the Corps not only assigned hundreds of new camps to the Great Plains region to help farmers halt soil erosion, but the New Deal program instructed camps in other areas of the country to begin conserving soil as well. At Bear Mountain State Park, enrollees from several camps planted saplings and removed dead trees in areas of the park that had been damaged by soil erosion.[15]

During the mid-1930s, the Corps' conservation efforts in state parks expanded once again, this time to include recreational development projects. While CCC camps located in state parks had undertaken recreational work since the Corps' establishment in March 1933, labor on such projects intensified during the summer of 1935 as the Roosevelt administration became increasingly alarmed at a lack of outdoor recreational facilities for unemployed working-class Americans.[16]

In Bear Mountain, one of the most common recreational development projects undertaken by the Corps involved converting meadows, swamps, and narrow stream valleys into enormous artificial swimming lakes for visiting

FIG. 1. CCC enrollees clearing trees in Bear Mountain State Park, c. 1933. (Palisades Interstate Park Commission Archives)

tourists (figs. 2 and 3). Along with the dam constructed in Pine Meadow by camp SP-20, CCC enrollees built dams that created a 250-acre lake at Beaver Pond, two smaller swimming reservoirs in Bockey and Owl Swamps, and artificial swimming areas at Christie and Queensboro Brooks in what one park official called "a high forested region which includes the largest block of what has been practically uninhabited forest."[17] Ultimately, the CCC created ten new bodies of water in Bear Mountain that together increased the state park's water surface area by approximately one thousand acres. Nationwide the Corps built seventy-five such lakes.[18] The hard work of CCC laborers on such projects, wrote one Bear Mountain State Park commissioner in 1934, was "transforming meadows and wooded swamps and beaver ponds into clear, shining lakes."[19]

To more efficiently transport visitors to and from these new swimming lakes, CCC enrollees also labored on conservation projects that enhanced Bear Mountain's transportation network. Corps enrollees blazed dozens of miles of new hiking trails and undertook a road-building program that would have made Robert Moses proud (fig. 4). Enrollees built the George Perkins Memorial Highway to the top of Bear Mountain and a new entrance road across the western portion of the park, and also widened both Seven Lakes Drive, the main motor artery through the state park, and Popolopen Drive, which connected the park to the Bear Mountain Bridge spanning the Hudson River to the east.[20] So extensive was this road building campaign that as early as 1934 park manager Major William Welch boasted that the CCC had successfully "completed, this year, enough main motor driveways to meet the motorist demands for some years."[21] Nationally the CCC constructed more than five thousand miles of roads and trails in state parks across the country.[22]

While the CCC crisscrossed Bear Mountain with hiking trails and motor roads, enrollees also began dotting the state park with a wide variety of new spaces and structures that greatly enhanced outdoor recreational opportunities for tourists. The dozens of new picnic areas and campgrounds in Bear Mountain were but a small portion of the five thousand acres of picnic grounds and ten thousand new campgrounds developed by the CCC in state parks nationwide.[23] The Corps supplemented such work in Bear Mountain by also constructing, expanding, or improving visitor centers and trailside museums, picnic and hiking shelters, comfort stations and bathhouses, administrative offices and ranger housing, and by building a lookout tower atop Bear Mountain (fig. 5). The Corps even expanded opportunities for winter recreation when it assigned several camps to improve the Bear Mountain ski jump, which in the mid-1930s was said to have hosted more competitions than any other ski jump in America.[24]

So extensive was such development work in state parks nationwide that Park Service director Arno Cammerer stated in 1935 that "the progress in the recreational field through state park work has gone fifty years ahead of what we could have expected without the [CCC] program."[25] Overall, during the 1930s and early 1940s, the Corps created eight hundred new state parks nationwide, helped seven states establish their first state parks, and through the law establishing the CCC, which allowed the president to purchase submarginal farms and convert them into public land, expanded state park acreage nationally by more than 950,000 acres, an overall increase in state park land of 98 percent.[26]

These outdoor recreational amenities built by the Corps in Bear Mountain and other state parks during the 1930s and early 1940s reflected the National Park Service's historic design aesthetic, which since the early twentieth century entailed the use of local construction materials, the placement of indigenous plants for exterior landscaping, and the avoidance of neat, straight lines, all in an effort to blend park structures harmoniously into the surrounding natural environment.[27] In many ways Corps enrollees were the ideal labor force for this aesthetic. Because the great majority of these young men were unskilled when they joined the program, their labor while in the CCC was

FIG. 2. CCC Company 201 building a dam to create the Lake Skenonto swimming area. The CCC completed this dam in 1935. (Palisades Interstate Park Commission Archives)

FIG. 3. CCC enrollees clearing the forest and building a dam for a swimming lake in Bear Mountain State Park, c. 1933. (Palisades Interstate Park Commission Archives)

predominantly manual and therefore perfectly suited to a more naturalist architectural style. The Park Service also took steps to guide and ensure this aesthetic by assigning specialists, including architects, landscape architects, and engineers, to each CCC state park camp, and also by sending Park Service "inspectors" to tour each state park to help plan and assess Corps recreation projects.[28] While planning and design had never been as stringent in state as in national parks, during the New Deal the National Park Service used Corps labor to transfer its naturalistic design aesthetic onto the state park level.

The environmental history of the CCC in state parks thus evolved during the Great Depression. What began as forestry work during the early 1930s shifted to include soil conservation after the Dust Bowl of 1934, only to expand once again into the recreational arena in the mid-1930s. The result was a new public landscape, built from the ground up by CCC enrollees in state parks, that provided Depression-era Americans with unprecedented access to outdoor recreation right in their own "backyards." Yet the new campgrounds, hiking shel-

FIG. 4. CCC enrollees laboring on a new motor road in Bear Mountain State Park, c. 1933. (Palisades Interstate Park Commission Archives)

FIG. 5. Storm King comfort station constructed, c. 1934. (Palisades Interstate Park Commission Archives)

ters, and enormous artificial lakes constructed by the Corps in places like Bear Mountain did more than alter the natural landscapes of state parks. By drawing increasing numbers of working-class Americans into the great outdoors to camp, hike, and swim, and by infusing nearby rural economies with federal capital, this new state park landscape also began transforming the politics of both the conservation movement and the New Deal.

* * *

The early conservation work undertaken by the Corps in Bear Mountain and other state parks in 1933 and 1934 reflected the political beliefs of Progressive Era conservationists. Having become increasingly concerned at the turn of the twentieth century about industrialization's devastating impact on water, soil, and timber supplies, progressive conservationists such as Gifford Pinchot promoted federal policies to more scientifically manage such resources for future use. The Newlands Reclamation Act of 1902, the creation of the U.S. Forest Service in 1905, and the passage in 1911 of the Weeks Act, which provided for federal acquisition of private forestland, were only the most well-known attempts by conservationists to improve natural resource production nationally.[29] Franklin Roosevelt, like his close friend Pinchot, had also been a progressive conservationist, in his case when he served as state senator and governor of New York, and the Corps' earliest work planting trees and halting soil erosion in places like Bear Mountain State Park descended directly from the president's experiences with this earlier political movement.[30]

The Corps' recreational development work of the mid-1930s, however, had a very different political history, one linked not to concern for natural resources such as timber and soil in the countryside but rather to anxiety about working people in America's cities. Sparked by the late-nineteenth-century philosophy of landscape designers such as Frederick Law Olmsted, who promoted city parks as having a "harmonizing and refining" influence on the urban poor, progressive reformers involved in efforts as diverse as the city playground, city beautiful, and urban sanitation movements all promoted the notion that clean, natural environments in cities would help forge healthy, morally upright citizens. The scouting movement, which through its extensive camping program exposed urban youths to nature beyond city limits, was another such movement that believed not in good and bad people, but rather in good and bad environments.[31] Franklin Roosevelt, who during the 1910s and 1920s had extensive experience with both urban reform and the Boy Scout movement in and around greater New York City, similarly embraced the benefits of outdoor play, and later promoted it through the Corps' recreational development projects in state parks like Bear Mountain.[32]

It was this recreational development work by the CCC, with its roots in the urban parks movement, that would most forcefully transform conservation politics during the New Deal era. This process began when the Corps' publicity office in Washington, D.C., started promoting the CCC's recreation projects in state parks as conservation in its own right, albeit of a different sort. "In recent years an even broader concept of conservation has developed ... [which] has made clear the justification and necessity of preserving and conserving scenery for its social value," explained a Corps pamphlet titled *The Civilian Conservation Corps and Public Recreation*.[33] Bear Mountain's new swimming lakes were a case in point. According to the Palisades Interstate Park Commission, which oversaw the administration of Bear Mountain State Park, such projects by the CCC "will greatly improve the scenery of the region, making the water contrast among the hills and forests."[34] State parks, the CCC began suggesting in the mid-1930s as it shifted its work to recreational development, were social resources in urgent need of conservation.

In promoting recreational areas as social resources, the CCC argued that picnic shelters, campgrounds, hiking trails, and even artificial swimming lakes built by its enrollees helped restore neither forests nor fields but instead the health and vigor of the American people, particularly those residing in cities. "The strain of urban living with its quick pace in business and social activities makes escape necessary to a person's well-being," wrote the Corps' publicity department in an educational pamphlet titled *The CCC and Its Contribution to a Nation-Wide State Park Recreation Program.*[35] By undertaking "park and forest developments for recreational . . . purposes," the Corps explained in another promotional pamphlet, "the Corps is making a vitally important contribution to conservation of the human wealth of the United States." This restoration of human health, the same pamphlet concluded, "is helping to give expression to the highest meaning of conservation."[36]

While the Corps continued to promote its recreational development work in state parks as helping to conserve public health, Americans began rethinking the very meaning of conservation. "It has been on everyone's mind; it is on nearly everyone's tongue," wrote John Hatton in a magazine article titled "New Things in Conservation." Yet while the Corps' initial efforts during the early 1930s to restore the nation's timber and soil reserves had popularized the conservation of natural resources, the CCC's recreational development work in parks promoted something quite different. "Conservation is more than forests; and the highest result in the conservation effort is best expressed in human welfare," continued Hatton, who concluded his article by noting that the CCC and its park projects had popularized what he called "broader conservation."[37] "Conservation," agreed a journalist writing an article on the CCC for *Scientific American* in the mid-1930s, has become "a large word" involving concern not only for natural resources but for human resources as well.[38]

As the Corps promoted hiking trails, campgrounds, and artificial swimming lakes as key ingredients in a broader conservation involving human resources, it therefore began transforming the political ideology of the American conservation movement. No longer was conservation solely focused on natural resources such as timber, soil, and water, as it had been during the Progressive Era. Instead, Corps work

projects in state parks expanded conservationists' policy to include concern for healthful outdoor recreation, which during the Progressive Era had remained beyond the purview of conservationists. The CCC's broader conservation, however, not only wove together the ideas of conservationists like Gifford Pinchot, who focused on natural resources, and park enthusiasts such as Frederick Law Olmsted, who worried instead about human resources. By building from the ground up a new recreational landscape throughout the country, the Corps' work projects in state parks also began influencing New Deal politics.

On the most basic level, the Corps' development of places like Bear Mountain for outdoor recreation helped Franklin Roosevelt court the urban working class. Not only did poor urbanites join the CCC in astounding numbers, but city workers also began recreating in increasing numbers in state parks built up by the Corps. "As a result of CCC state park work, into these areas flocked thousands of city dwellers," explained the Corps in 1937, "for recreation amid scenes giving relief from the monotony of their everyday existence."[39] The following year, an estimated seventy million Americans, the great majority from cities, visited state parks.[40] This was certainly the case in Bear Mountain. After noting the numerous recreational amenities built by the Corps in the state park, a *New York Times* reporter celebrated the "growing legion of men and women living in the city who visit." These working-class New Yorkers, the reporter continued, crowded onto trains, buses, and boats and made the journey up the Hudson River to enjoy Bear Mountain's new "playground pavilions and picnic groves," as well as to hike on the state park's new trails, to camp in its new campgrounds, and to swim in its brand new shining lakes.[41]

President Roosevelt was well aware of the increasing popularity of state parks like Bear Mountain among urban workers, and incorporated the Corps' recreation work into his first reelection campaign strategy. In 1936, for example, the president made CCC recreational projects a staple of his stump speeches, deliberately scheduled campaign stops at or near Corps recreational project sites, and continually reminded voters of the CCC's broader conservation efforts.[42] The hiking trails, picnic areas, and campgrounds built by the Corps in the nation's parks, explained Roosevelt in a speech just three months before the 1936 election, are "part of our great program of husbandry—the joint husbandry of human resources and natural resources."[43] By the mid-1930s, in other words, state parks such as Bear Mountain had become powerful campaign advertisements for the new politics of the New Deal.

Roosevelt's campaign strategy worked. The legion of working-class urbanites hiking, camping, and swimming in Bear Mountain and other state parks across the country started flooding into the Democratic Party. During the president's 1936 reelection campaign, of the six million Americans who went to the polls for the first time, the great majority of whom were working-class immigrants from cities like New York, five million voted for Roosevelt. During the same election the incumbent also received 80 percent of the vote of the poorest Americans, and did especially well among ethnic minorities, most of whom lived in cities.[44] If the Corps' recreation work in state parks had even a partial role in Roosevelt's 1936 landslide, it seems that wooded hiking trails, visitor centers constructed from local stone, and even rustic comfort stations built by the CCC were helping to convince urban workers of the benefits of the liberal welfare state.

While Corps recreational projects in Bear Mountain were helping to make New Dealers out of poor New Yorkers, the political economy of CCC camps in places such as Bear Mountain helped the president attract rural Americans as well. Each month every Corps camp throughout the country funneled approximately $7,000 from the federal government into nearby economies through the purchase of local food, supplies, and services. Thus as the twelve camps stationed in Bear Mountain State Park in 1934 pumped $84,000 per month, or more than $1 million annually, into the Hudson Highland economy, the 475 Corps

camps assigned to state parks in 1935 infused a grand total of nearly $40 million per year into the economies of rural towns and villages that were lucky enough to have Corps camps stationed nearby.[45] "Hundreds of communities have discovered since the CCC was organized two years ago," reported *Business Week* in May 1935, "that the neighboring camp is the bright spot on their business map."[46]

The money spent locally by CCC camps stationed in Bear Mountain State Park aided every sector of the regional economy. The local building trade benefited first by supplying much of the materials used to construct the Corps' twelve Bear Mountain camps.[47] In 1933 the Haverstraw Better Laundry also won a contract to wash the sheets from nine Bear Mountain camps, and the following year Gus Lazarus's Reliable Shoe Repairing and Hat Cleaning Shop, also in nearby Haverstraw, secured a contract to "renovate and reconstruct" the "high laced leather shoes" issued to every new enrollee assigned to Bear Mountain.[48] Local gas stations fueled Corps trucks, nearby coal distributors stoked the stoves in CCC barracks, and Hudson Highlands farmers and food distributors filled the bellies of Bear Mountain's nearly twenty-five hundred enrollees with three square meals a day.[49] As the president of the Business Men's Association in nearby Suffern, New York, explained in April 1935, "local merchants directly or indirectly all feel the benefit of having the camps situated as they now are."[50] The same could be said of business owners across the country who were lucky enough to be near state parks with CCC camps.[51]

The economic changes caused by the arrival of the CCC in Bear Mountain quickly began transforming politics in the Hudson Highlands. During the early 1910s, when politicians in Albany had first proposed the creation of Bear Mountain State Park, rural business owners opposed the park not only on economic grounds but also because it signified the intrusion of the state government into local politics. Rural business interests, reported the *Rockland County Times,* were critical of the state park because it "would cause the secession of wonderfully successful commercial enterprises" involving logging and mining in the Hudson Highlands.[52] Not surprisingly, the majority of these rural business owners voted against the new state park referendum.[53] Years later, however, after the twelve CCC camps in Bear Mountain began resuscitating the region's depressed economy, local businesspeople began rethinking their aversion to outside political interference and instead clamored for increased federal aid. In 1935, when rumors circulated throughout the Highlands that the Corps had decided to remove all CCC camps from Bear Mountain, dozens of area business owners, including lumber supplier Elmer Morgan, lobbied their congressional leaders in Washington, D.C., in a futile attempt to keep CCC camps stationed in the nearby state park.[54]

When such efforts failed, rural residents of the Bear Mountain region took even more concerted political action. During the 1932 presidential election, before the arrival of the CCC, the majority of citizens from Orange County to the south of Bear Mountain and Rockland County to the north both voted Republican for president. In 1936, however, after three years of federal funds flowing from Corps camps into local bank accounts, the residents of the Hudson Highlands began recalculating their political affiliations. While Orange County again endorsed the Republican presidential candidate, Kansas governor Alf Landon, the margin of victory for the GOP dropped by 5 percent. The results were more decisive in Rockland, where locals who had given the county to Herbert Hoover in 1928 voted instead by plurality for Franklin Roosevelt.[55] A similar electoral about-face occurred in rural communities across the country that were situated near CCC camps undertaking park recreation work.[56]

* * *

In mid-August 1934, when President Roosevelt visited CCC Camp SP-20 in the Pine Meadow region of Bear Mountain, he witnessed the transformation of one state park's natural landscape. During the Great Depression, in hun-

dreds of state parks around the country, Corps enrollees undertook similar work, beginning their efforts with forestry projects in the early 1930s before also halting soil erosion in 1934 and then expanding their efforts once again to include the building of outdoor recreational amenities. In Bear Mountain, these recreational projects included the clearing of hiking trails and campgrounds, the construction of visitor centers, comfort stations, and bathhouses, and the creation of huge artificial swimming lakes that drew millions of New Yorkers to the state park both during the Depression and ever since.

Yet whereas these visitors from the nearby metropolis could literally see the grand transformation taking place in their very own "backyard," they were less conscious of the political implications of this new public landscape. The recreational projects undertaken by the CCC in Bear Mountain broadened the political ideology of the conservation movement beyond a concern for natural resources to include as well an interest in conserving human resources through healthy outdoor play. These same projects similarly influenced New Deal politics. Whereas the Corps' recreational infrastructure appealed to the urban working class, who flocked to both state parks and the Democratic Party during the Great Depression years, the federal funds flowing through CCC camps into local economies were popular with rural merchants, many of whom also became New Deal supporters. The Corps and its work projects, in other words, transformed not only the natural landscape but the political terrain as well by introducing urban workers and rural businesspeople to the modern welfare state.

Contemporary park designers and planners must remember this interwoven history of state parks and New Deal politics when contemplating the future form and function of our country's recreational infrastructure. Back during the Great Depression, the federal government hired thousands of trained architects and landscape architects to design and build, for hundreds of state parks across the country, recreational amenities that functioned to accommodate growing numbers of Americans seeking healthy outdoor activities. The rustic, naturalistic form of such structures, built by millions of young Corps enrollees by hand from local resources, instilled in the Americans visiting state parks a newfound appreciation of the federal government. Such recreational infrastructure simultaneously infused nearby economies with much-needed federal capital. As a result, beautifully landscaped campgrounds, visitor centers constructed from local stone, and picnic shelters built from native timbers all became political advertisements, of sorts, for the federal government, while hiking, camping, and swimming in state parks likewise became political acts for millions of Americans. As Americans now contemplate rebuilding much of the crumbling recreational infrastructure constructed more than seventy-five years ago by Franklin Roosevelt's Civilian Conservation Corps, park designers and planners must remember that playing outdoors in nature in the twenty-first century, as it was during the Great Depression, will be no less political.

Notes

1. For a description of FDR's visit to SP-20, see CCC camp commander E. D. O'Dea to President Franklin Roosevelt, 31 August 1934, File "SP-20, New York Pine Meadow," Entry 37 "State Park File—1933–1947," Record Group 79 "Records of the Branch of Recreation, Land Planning and State Co-operation," National Archives, Washington, D.C. For information on SP-20's work project, see E. D. O'Dea, "Emergency Conservation work Camp Report, Pine Meadow Camp SP-20," 26 March 1935, File "New York State," Entry 6 "CCC Camp Reports," Record Group 35 "Records of the Civilian Conservation Corps," NARA, Washington, D.C. Throughout this essay I use the name Bear Mountain State Park when referring to both Bear Mountain and Harriman state parks; comprising approximately 5,000 and 45,000 acres respectively, the two parks are adjacent to one another, and during the Great Depression the public and the Roosevelt administration referred to both as Bear Mountain State Park.

2. Charles H. Taylor, Assistant Director to President Franklin Roosevelt, to E. D. O'Dea, 22 September 1934, File "SP-20, New York Pine Meadow," Entry 37 "State Park File—1933–1947," Record Group 79 "Records of the Branch of Recreation,

Land Planning and State Cooperation," NARA.

3. Neil M. Maher, *Nature's New Deal: The Civilian Conservation Corps and the Roots of the American Environmental Movement* (New York: Oxford University Press, 2008), 2. The academic literature on the CCC is scant. The best administrative history of the Corps is John Salmond, *The Civilian Conservation Corps, 1933–1942: A New Deal Case Study* (Durham, N.C.: Duke University Press, 1967). For a survey of CCC work under the U.S. Forest Service, see Alison Otis, *The Forest Service and the Civilian Conservation Corps, 1933–1942* (Washington, D.C.: U.S. Forest Service, U.S. Department of Agriculture, 1986). For CCC work under the Park Service, see John Paige, *The Civilian Conservation Corps and the National Park Service: An Administrative History* (Washington, D.C.: National Park Service, U.S. Department of the Interior, 1985). For an examination of African Americans in the CCC, see Olen Cole, *The African-American Experience in the Civilian Conservation Corps* (Gainesville: University Press of Florida, 1999).

4. Robert Fechner, *Annual Report of the Director of the Civilian Conservation Corps: Fiscal Year Ended June 30, 1939* (Washington, D.C.: U.S. Government Printing Office, 1939), 7.

5. On state building and conservation, see Elmo Richardson, *The Politics of Conservation: Crusades and Controversies, 1897–1913* (Berkeley: University of California Press, 1962); Clayton Koppes, "Efficiency, Equity, Esthetics: Shifting Themes in American Conservation," in *Ends of the Earth,* ed. Donald Worster (New York: Cambridge University Press, 1988); Brian Balogh, "Scientific Forestry and the Roots of the Modern American State," *Environmental History* 7 (April 2002): 198–225. For material on the western United States, where the links between federal power and natural resource conservation were especially pronounced, see Donald Pisani, *Water and American Government: The Reclamation Bureau, National Water Policy, and the West, 1902–1935* (Berkeley: University of California Press, 2002); and Donald Worster, *Rivers of Empire: Water, Aridity, and the Growth of the American West* (New York: Pantheon Books, 1985).

6. Although there are numerous local histories on specific state parks, there is little historical literature on the state park movement in the United States. On the history of state parks in the United States, see Ney Landrum, *The State Park Movement in America: A Critical Review* (St. Louis: University of Missouri Press, 2004); Freeman Tilden, *The State Parks: Their Meaning in American Life* (New York: Knopf, 1962); Conrad Wirth, *Parks, Politics, and the People* (Norman: University of Oklahoma Press, 1980); and, especially, Linda McClelland, *Building*

the National Parks: Historic Landscape Design and Construction (Baltimore: Johns Hopkins University Press, 1998), chap. 10.

7. William Cronon, "The Trouble with Wilderness; or, Getting Back to the Wrong Nature," *Environmental History* 1, no. 1 (1996): 24. Cronon's seminal essay first appeared in William Cronon, ed., *Uncommon Ground: Rethinking the Human Place in Nature* (New York: W. W. Norton and Company, 1996).

8. On the earliest CCC enrollees in Bear Mountain State Park, see "10,000 Men at Work this Winter in Palisades Interstate Park," Palisades Interstate Park Commissioners, 4 January 1934, unarranged files, Bear Mountain Trailside Museum, Bear Mountain State Park (hereafter, BMSP); and "Civilian Conservation Corps Work Program in Palisades Interstate Park," Commissioners of the Palisades Interstate Park, undated, unarranged files, Bear Mountain Trailside Museum, BMSP.

9. On the number of camps and enrollees at Bear Mountain State Park during this period, see "Station Strength Reports," Box 1, Entry 108, Record Group 35 "Records of the Civilian Conservation Corps," NARA. Interestingly, the only CCC camp for women, called Camp Tera, was also established in Bear Mountain State Park by Eleanor Roosevelt. On Camp Tera, see "17 Jobless Women Enter New Camp," *New York Times,* 11 June 1933, N1.

10. For a more detailed account of this administrative history, see Salmond, *The Civilian Conservation Corps, 1933–1942,* 10–12. Within the Park Service, Conrad Wirth oversaw CCC state park conservation work.

11. In piecing together the statistics on camp numbers and agency affiliations, including the National Park Service, I have relied on two sources: Record Group 35 "Records of the Civilian Conservation Corps," Entry 3 "Annual, Special, and Final Reports," NARA; and Record Group 35 "Records of the Civilian Conservation Corps," Entry 108 "Station and Strength Reports," NARA. For a more detailed description of this process, see Maher, *Nature's New Deal,* 242n9.

12. "Interstate Park CCC Camps Eradicating Diseased Elms," Commissioners of the Palisades Interstate Park, undated, unarranged files, Bear Mountain Trailside Museum, BMSP.

13. "Relief Work Increases Fire Protection in Interstate Park," Commissioners of the Palisades Interstate Park, undated, unarranged files, Bear Mountain Trailside Museum, BMSP.

14. For national statistics on CCC tree planting, see Salmond, *The Civilian Conservation Corps, 1933–1942,* 121; and Phoebe Cutler, *The Public Landscape*

of the New Deal (New Haven: Yale University Press, 1986), 95.

15. On project description of the camp at Mica Mine, see "Emergency Conservation Work Camp Report, Mica Mine, SP-28," 26 March 1935, File "New York State," Entry 6 "CCC Camp Reports," Record Group 35 "Records of the Civilian Conservation Corps," NARA.

16. For additional information on this outdoor recreation crisis during the mid-1930s, see Maher, *Nature's New Deal,* 70–71.

17. On Corps lake work in Bear Mountain, see "CCC Building New Wilderness Lakes in Interstate Park," Commissioners of the Palisades Interstate Park, 1934, unarranged files, Bear Mountain Trailside Museum, BMSP.

18. On the construction by the CCC of dams for swimming lakes nationwide during the New Deal era, see Cutler, *The Public Landscape of the New Deal,* 67.

19. "CCC Building New Wilderness Lakes in Interstate Park," Commissioners of the Palisades Interstate Park, 1934, unarranged files, Bear Mountain Trailside Museum, BMSP.

20. "10,000 Men at Work this Winter in Palisades Interstate Park," Palisades Interstate Park Commissioners, 4 January 1934, unarranged files, Bear Mountain Trailside Museum, BMSP.

21. Major William Welch to President of the Palisades Interstate Park Commission J. DuPratt White, 29 January 1935, unarranged files, Bear Mountain Trailside Museum, BMSP.

22. Landrum, *The State Park Movement,* 136.

23. For national statistics of CCC picnic and campground work, see Ibid., 136.

24. On the Corps' recreational infrastructure projects in Bear Mountain State Park, see "Find Much To Do in Palisade Park: Civilian Conservation Corps Workers Are Busy in the Harriman Section," *New York Times,* 6 August 1933, RE6; "Road Opened to Top of Bear Mountain," *New York Times,* 1 November 1934, 23; E. L. Yordan, "Into the Vast Palisades Park," *New York Times,* 2 June 1935, XX1; and Commissioners of the Palisades Interstate Park (press release), "President Roosevelt Pleased with CCC Work in Interstate Park," 1934, Bear Mountain Trailside Museum, BMSP.

25. Arno Cammerer, "Remarks at the National Park Service Conference of State Park Authorities," Washington, D.C., 25 February 1935, U.S. Department of the Interior Library (SB482), Washington, D.C., 4, as quoted in Landrum, *The State Park Movement,* 135.

26. On the Corps creating eight hundred new state parks, see James McEntee, *Final Report of the Director of the Civilian Conservation Corps, April 1933 through June 30, 1942,* Entry 3 "Annual, Special, and Final

Reports," Record Group 35 "Records of the Civilian Conservation Corps," NARA, 43. On the Corps helping states to create their first state park, see James Jackson, "Living Legacy of the CCC," *American Forests* 94, nos. 9 and 10 (1988): 41. On the increase in state park acreage because of the Corps, see Fechner, *Annual Report of the Director of the Civilian Conservation Corps,* 55.

27. The National Park Service aesthetic has been written about extensively. See especially McClelland, *Building the National Parks.*

28. Ibid., 381.

29. There is a rich literature on the Progressive Era conservation movement. See especially Samuel Hays, *Conservation and the Gospel of Efficiency: The Progressive Conservation Movement, 1890–1920* (Cambridge, MA: Harvard University Press, 1959), 3; Stephen Fox, *The American Conservation Movement: John Muir and His Legacy* (Madison: University of Wisconsin Press, 1981), 107–8; James Penick Jr., "The Progressives and the Environment: Three Themes from the First Conservation Movement," in *The Progressive Era,* ed. Lewis Gould (Syracuse: Syracuse University Press, 1974); Donald Worster, *Nature's Economy: A History of Ecological Ideas* (New York: Cambridge University Press, 1977); Roderick Nash, *Wilderness and the American Mind* (New Haven: Yale University Press, 1967); Gottlieb, *Forcing the Spring;* and Samuel Hays, *Beauty, Health, and Permanence: Environmental Politics in the United States, 1955–1985* (New York: Cambridge University Press, 1987), 13.

30. On FDR's experiences as a progressive conservationist and the impact such experiences had on the creation of the CCC and its early conservation work involving trees and soil, see Maher, *Nature's New Deal,* chaps. 1 and 2.

31. Paul Boyer calls these reform efforts "environmentalist." See Paul Boyer, *Urban Masses and Moral Order in America, 1820–1920* (Cambridge, Mass.: Harvard University Press, 1978), chaps. 15–16, esp. 220–21. For more detailed accounts of various environmentalist reform efforts during the Progressive Era, see the following: on the city beautiful movement, see William Wilson, *The City Beautiful Movement* (Baltimore: Johns Hopkins University Press, 1989), and Maureen Flanagan, "The City Profitable, The City Livable: Environmental Policy, Gender, and Power in Chicago in the 1910s," *Journal of Urban History,* 22, no. 2 (January 1996): 163–190; on the urban sanitation movement, see Martin Melosi, "'Out of Site, Out of Mind': The Environment and Disposal of Municipal Refuse, 1860–1920," *Historian,* 35, no. 4 (August 1973).

32. On Franklin Roosevelt's long history with the Boy Scouts, and the influence of those experiences on the CCC, see Maher, *Nature's New Deal,* 29–41.

33. Civilian Conservation Corps, *The Civilian Conservation Corps and Public Recreation* (Washington, D.C.: U.S. Government Printing Office, 1941), 3. For additional examples of the promotion of recreational areas as natural resources in need of conservation, see Robert Fechner, *Summary Report of Director, Fiscal Year 1936* (Washington, D.C.: U.S. Government Printing Office, 1936), Entry 3 "Annual, Special and Final Reports," Record Group 35 "Records of the Civilian Conservation Corps," NARA, 29; and Robert Fechner, *Annual Report of the Director of the Civilian Conservation Corps, Fiscal Year Ended June 30, 1938,* Entry 3 "Annual, Special and Final Reports," Record Group 35 "Records of the Civilian Conservation Corps," NARA, 52; and *National Park Service, Procedure for Park, Parkway and Recreational Area Stud*y (Washington, D.C.: U.S. Government Printing Office, 1937), foreword, 3, 17.

34. "CCC Building New Wilderness Lakes in Interstate Park," Commissioners of the Palisades Interstate Park, 1934, unarranged files, Bear Mountain Trailside Museum, BMSP.

35. Civilian Conservation Corps, *The CCC and Its Contribution to a Nation-Wide State Park Recreation Program* (Washington, D.C.: U.S. Government Printing Office, 1937), 3. For other examples of promotional materials by the CCC that describe modern society as enervating, see Civilian Conservation Corps, *Recreational Developments by the CCC in National and State Forests* (Washington, D.C.: U.S. Government Printing Office, 1936), 3; and *Civilian Conservation Corps, Recreational Demonstration Projects: As Illustrated by Chopawamsic, Virginia* (Washington, D.C.: U.S. Government Printing Office, 1937), 6.

36. Civilian Conservation Corps, *The Civilian Conservation Corps and Public Recreation,* 3. On the CCC promoting its recreational work projects as helping to conserve human resources, see also Conrad Wirth, director of CCC state park work, "The Nation-Wide Program for More Recreational Areas Grows Under the CCC," *American Forests* (November 1936): 505–6; Fanning Hearon, CCC state park work administrator, "The Recreation Renaissance," *Recreation* (September 1935): 289; and Robert Fechner, "CCC Work Valued at $579,000,000," *American Forests* (February 1936): 90.

37. John Hatton, "New Things in Conservation," *The Producer: The National Live Stock Monthly* 105, no. 5 (October 1933): 3, 5. For a critique of this "broadening" of conservation, see "CCC Needs

Clearer Policy on Conservation," *American Forests* (May 1938): 224.

38. Charles Lathrop Pack, "Blister Busters," *Scientific American* (February 1934): 61.

39. Civilian Conservation Corps, *The CCC and Its Contribution to a Nation-Wide State Park Recreation Program,* 3.

40. Department of the Interior, *A Study of the Park and Recreation Problem of the United States* (Washington, D.C.: U.S. Government Printing Office, 1941), 50.

41. E. L. Yordan, "Into the Vast Palisades Park: New Throngs Are Exploring the 48,000 Wooded Acres, Where the Play Facilities Have Been Enlarged and Refurbished," *New York Times,* 2 June 1935, XXL.

42. On Roosevelt's use of the CCC in his 1936 campaign speeches, see Salmond, *The Civilian Conservation Corps, 1933–1942,* 69.

43. Speech by Roosevelt at the Dedication of Shenandoah National Park, 3 July 1936, as quoted in Edgar Nixon, *Franklin D. Roosevelt and Conservation, 1911–1945* (Hyde Park, N.Y.: Franklin D. Roosevelt Library, General Services Administration, National Archives and Records Service, 1957), 1:537–38. Roosevelt made similar speeches at North Carolina and Tennessee's Great Smoky Mountains National Park before the election of 1940; and he visited New York's Bear Mountain State Park numerous times during campaigns throughout the 1930s and early 1940s. On FDR's campaign trips to work project sites in Vermont, New Hampshire, and New York, see Jason Scott Smith, "Building New Deal Liberalism: The Political Economy of Public Works, 1933–1956" (Ph.D. diss., University of California, Berkeley, 2001), 217.

44. On Roosevelt's appeal to the urban working class during the 1936 election, see Gary Gerstle, *American Crucible: Race and Nation in the Twentieth Century* (Princeton, N.J.: Princeton University Press, 2002), 150.

45. For a breakdown of the amount of money spent each month by an individual CCC camp, see Fechner, *Summary Report of Director, Fiscal Year 1936,* Entry 3 "Annual, Special, and Final Reports," Record Group 35 "Records of the Civilian Conservation Corps," NARA, 8.

46. "CCC Also Spends," *Business Week,* 4 May 1935, 12.

47. On the local construction industry's economic ties to the Bear Mountain CCC camps, see lumber company owner Elmer Morgan to Representative Hamilton Fish, Jr., 29 March 1935, File "Bear Mountain," Box "Cities Bear Bluff—Blackwater," Entry 300 "General Correspondence 1933–1942," Record Group 35 "Records of the Civilian Conservation Corps," NARA.

48. On cleaning sheets locally, see Haverstraw Better Laundry to "Whom it May Concern," 29 November 1933, and Major William Welch to Rockland Laundry, 22 March 1934, unarranged files, Bear Mountain Trailside Museum, BMSP. On shoe repair, see "New Industry Started," *The Rockland County Times* (Haverstraw, N.Y.), 18 November 1933, 1.

49. On Bear Mountain CCC camps refueling at local gas stations, see Record Group 35 "Records of the Civilian Conservation Corps," Entry 300 "General Correspondence 1933–1942," NARA. On nearby coal being used in Bear Mountain camp barracks, see "Many Camp Improvements," *Camp Chat* 2, no. 2 (November 1934): 1, File "SP-26-New York State-State Parks," Box 103, Entry 37 "State Park File, 1933–1947," Record Group 79 "Records of the Branch of Recreation, Land Planning and State Cooperation," NARA. And for the purchase of local food by the Bear Mountain CCC camps, see Grenis Brother, Inc., Wholesale Produce, Newburgh, New York, 14 September 1934, unarranged files, Bear Mountain Trailside Museum, BMSP.

50. Louis Hammel to J. Dupratt White, 17 April 1935, unarranged files, Bear Mountain Trailside Museum, BMSP.

51. For other examples of the Corps' recreational development work in parks helping to reinvigorate local economies, see Maher, *Nature's New Deal,* 131–50.

52. For local businesses' opposition to the state park on economic grounds, see "Harriman Gift," *Rockland County Times,* 15 January 1910, 1.

53. On rural opposition to the state park referendum, see "State Park of the Highlands," *The Cornwall Local* (Cornwall, N.Y.), 15 December 1910, 8.

54. Elmer Morgan to Representative Hamilton Fish, Jr., 29 March 1935, File "Bear Mountain," Box "Cities Bear Bluff—Blackwater," Entry 300 "General Correspondence 1933–1942," Record Group 35 "Records of the Civilian Conservation Corps," NARA.

55. For voting statistics in Orange and Rockland counties during the 1932 and 1936 presidential elections, see Richard M. Scammon, ed., *America at the Polls: A Handbook of American Presidential Election Statistics, 1920–1964* (Pittsburgh: University of Pittsburgh Press, 1965), 313–15.

56. A similar political turnabout occurred in Great Smoky Mountains National Park after Corps recreational development work in that national park sparked the local Smoky Mountain economy. On the political shift in the Smokies, see Maher, *Nature's New Deal,* 148.

From Pariah to Paragon

The Redesign of Platt National Park, 1933–1940

In the late 1920s, Platt National Park was something of an anomaly among national parks. The diminutive prairie landscape had neither grand scenery nor impressive natural resources, and, located next to a bustling frontier town, featured concrete sidewalks, penned animals, and a golf course. These unusual qualities caused Horace Albright, then director of the National Park Service, to declare Platt "a travesty—a tiny mineral spring in southern Oklahoma, well below national park standards." Yet less than a decade later, in 1939, Henry Vincent Hubbard, Harvard professor and fellow of the American Society of Landscape Architects, featured Platt in *Landscape Architecture Quarterly* as an example of conservation design. In the article Platt is pictured as an equal alongside Grand Canyon, Mount Rainier, Glacier, and Zion national parks.[1]

Platt's dramatic change in status—from pariah to paragon of park design—was the result of its total redesign and reconstruction in the years 1933–40 by the Civilian Conservation Corps (CCC). Although it is just one of hundreds of local, state, and national parks built by the CCC, Platt stands out as an exceptional example of how the Park Service used the conservation program of the CCC to implement its policies of master planning and principles of naturalistic landscape design. The excellence of Platt's landscape design clearly demonstrates how effective those policies and principles, based in nineteenth-century park planning, were in improving the agency's facilities and advancing its mission. In other, western national parks, where master planning

and landscape naturalization were primarily used to obscure the evidence of human intrusion, the results of naturalistic design were often invisible in the face of world-class scenery and unparalleled natural resources. At Platt, thought at the time to be "lacking in . . . National Park Calibre," naturalistic design shone in the forefront, as it enhanced inferior scenery and, in some cases, actually created both scenery and outdoor experiences.[2] In other words, the following story of Platt National Park's CCC-era landscape design and development is less a tale of conserving a great landscape than it is of constructing one.

Early Development

Platt National Park was originally established as Sulphur Springs Reservation in 1902 to protect some thirty mineral springs with purported medicinal value. Located within the Chickasaw and Choctaw nations in Indian Territory, the springs were threatened by overdevelopment and pollution from the town of Sulphur, which had grown up around the springs. To safeguard the healing waters, the concerned tribes ceded 848 acres of land surrounding the springs to the U.S. government.[3] In 1906 the reservation was renamed in honor of Connecticut senator Orville Platt, a member of the Senate's Indian Affairs Committee.

The park's earliest development included moving the town of Sulphur from within the new park's boundaries to a new town plat nearby. Congressional appropriations also funded new roads, campgrounds, and a sewage system. Throughout the park, springs were tiled to

101

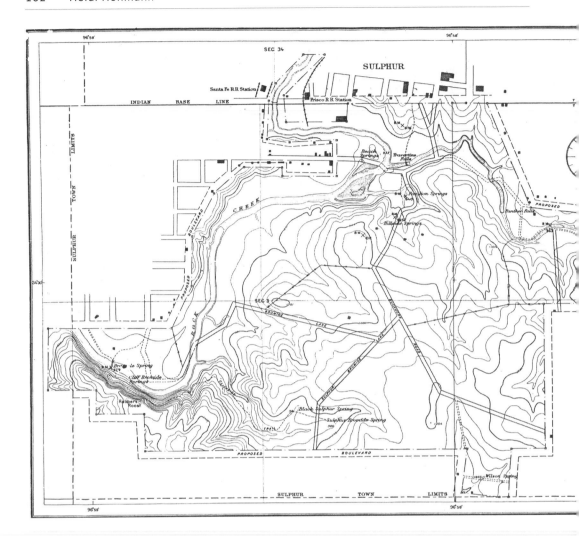

concentrate their flows, and comfort stations were erected to accommodate ever-increasing numbers of visitors. Large springhouses were built at Bromide Springs and Pavilion Springs, the latter site being particularly important as the location of seven major springs.

However, development during the park's first three decades was generally haphazard. Improvements were initiated by superintendents and park staff rather than design professionals. Even after the establishment of the National Park Service under Stephen Mather in 1916 and the creation of a Park Service planning di-

vision under Daniel Hull in 1922, Platt, located far from Park Service offices in Washington and San Francisco, was continually under-funded and under-supervised. By the late 1920s, the landscape was eclectic and a bit chaotic, barely organized by a main road running east–west along the park's Travertine and Rock Creeks and a secondary road crossing north–south through the middle of the park (fig. 1). Spurs off these routes accessed waterfalls, swimming holes, trails, and campsites. A few areas in the park—Bromide Springs, Flower Park, and Buffalo Springs—were developed as rough green-

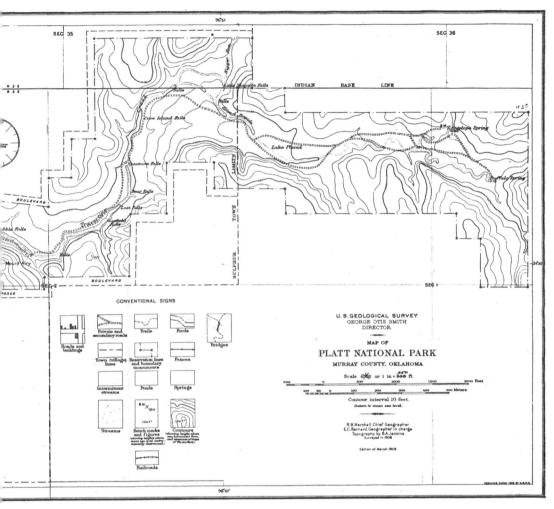

FIG. 1. "Utilities Layout," part of the "General Plan for Platt National Park," 1931, showing road and stream layout prior to master planning. (National Park Service, Chickasaw National Recreation Area Archives)

swards, dotted with trees, comfort stations, and ornamental flower beds, reflecting simplified ideas of nineteenth-century urban park design. As visitation rose, park improvements increasingly included attractions that were described as "healthful aids to the curative properties of the waters of the park," but were really entertainments. These included a collection of animals—not quite a zoo—which at times included ostriches, a caged bald eagle and penned herds of deer, elk, and bison. Between 1917 and 1923 two tennis courts and a nine-hole golf course were also added to the landscape.[4]

Such a resort-like atmosphere did not exactly meet expectations emerging from the National Park Service Act of 1916. The agency's 1918 "Statement of Policy," which defined principles for park stewardship, clearly directed that any new parks should contain "scenery of supreme and distinctive quality or some natural feature so extraordinary or unique as to be of national interest and importance." The policy also advocated maintaining "in standard, dignity, and prestige" the "national park system as now constituted." By the mid- to late 1920s, the agency's emphasis on park quality produced a movement to rid the system of "inferior" national parks. Platt was one of the parks targeted as unworthy, along with Wind Cave in South Dakota and Sully's Hill in North Dakota. Strong opposition came from the Oklahoma congressional ranks, who protected Platt from removal threats eight times between 1910 and 1940. Platt garnered support for retention not only as the singular national park in the region but also because of its consistently high visitation.[5] In 1914, Platt had more visitors than Yellowstone, and throughout the 1920s, an average of three hundred thousand visitors annually experienced the park's healing waters.[6]

With Platt resisting removal, it would fall to a developing Park Service design philosophy and an increasing staff of Park Service professionals to turn the park into a landscape worthy of the system. By the late 1920s, the Park Service had assembled a centralized field headquarters in San Francisco to advise superintendents on park development and management. This office was divided into specialty areas of civil engineering, sanitary engineering, landscape architecture, forestry, and education. In 1927, when landscape architect Thomas Vint succeeded Daniel Hull as chief of the Landscape Division, he rapidly expanded design supervision in the parks by hiring six resident landscape architects, each assigned to advise a set of national parks.[7] In addition, Vint and his staff devised a formalized park planning process, and by 1929, all parks were required to have a "general development outline"— later called a master plan. Platt National Park's first master plan was developed in 1932 by landscape architects Herbert Kreinkamp and William Carnes in consultation with Superintendent William Branch. This first official plan pragmatically focused on replacing utilities and building comfort stations. Though an unambitious design, the master plan set the stage for the park's future redevelopment: with a plan ready and waiting, Platt was well prepared to benefit from the funding and labor soon to be provided by Franklin Delano Roosevelt's New Deal.

The CCC at Platt National Park

Upon his inauguration in the midst of the Great Depression, President Franklin D. Roosevelt declared, "Our greatest primary task is to put people to work."[8] To do so, the new president and congressional leaders rapidly defined a variety of programs to stimulate the economy through massive spending on public works. Of these, two had a major impact on the National Park Service. The Public Works Administration (PWA) planned and funded civil improvements from schoolhouses and hospitals to bridges and dams nationwide. Alongside it was the Civilian Conservation Corps (CCC), authorized by the Emergency Conservation Act of 31 March 1933. This program had a dual purpose of employing impoverished youths and conserving neglected natural resources through Emergency Conservation Work (ECW), which included erosion control, fire suppression, and forestation. Implementation of the CCC was an interagency affair, with the Labor Department recruiting young men; the War Department commanding, transporting, and housing them in camps of two hundred; and the Agriculture and the Interior departments organizing their conservation activities on state and federal lands. Of 1,477 CCC camps established nationwide by early summer of 1933, the Department of the Interior supervised 245; of those, the National Park Service directed 70 in national parks and 102 in state and local parks.[9]

With astonishing speed, an ECW project was authorized for Platt National Park on 20 April 1933. By 10 May, Platt's Superintendent Branch had hired 25 "local experienced men" (LEMs)—carpenters, stonemasons, blacksmiths, electricians, and plumbers—from the Sulphur area to supervise the incoming CCC recruits. The next week 50 young men arrived by train to become CCC Company 808, the first CCC unit in Oklahoma. At its peak, Company 808 fielded 270 enrollees housed in a quadrangle of wooden army barracks at Walnut Grove along the park's Rock Creek.

The ECW program not only put urban youth to work but also hired a wide range of unemployed professionals. By mid-May a roster of technical staff was on board to guide the park's redevelopment. These men included the ECW landscape architects, first Walter Popham and later Jerome Miller, who replaced Popham when he transferred to Yellowstone in 1934. Edmund Walkowiak and George Merrill, also landscape architects, were hired as landscape foremen; they worked in the field directly supervising enrollees. Other professionals included engineers Ira Stinson and Sam Whittlesey and forester Donald Stauffer. As in all national park CCC camps, these men reported directly to the park superintendent, but their work was ultimately approved by the National Park Service offices in San Francisco. For Popham and Miller, this meant regular visits from and consultation with Charles Richey, the resident landscape architect from Vint's office (by this time known as the Branch of Plans and Design) who was assigned to Platt.[10]

It is interesting, and probably not entirely coincidental, that most of Platt's landscape architects were connected with the landscape architecture department at Iowa State College (ISC). Popham, a Harvard graduate, was a professor at ISC from 1928 until he was laid off in 1932; Miller graduated with a B.S. in 1929 and an M.S. in 1932; and Richey and Walkowiak received their B.S. degrees in 1930 and 1931, respectively. Iowa State had offered courses in landscape gardening since 1869, and after its first degree in landscape architecture was awarded in 1917 to Arthur Carhart, who became the first full-time "recreation engineer" in the U.S. Forest Service, evolved a program of "park design" focused specifically on producing foremen for public work. The ISC department chair, P. H. (Philip Homer) Elwood Jr., was also involved in the CCC program. In the summer of 1933, university budget cuts enticed Elwood to seek summer employment with the Park Service as an inspector in the Rocky Mountain District of the state park branch of ECW. Elwood, an inveterate networker, was likely influential in the hiring of his colleague Popham and his students Miller and Walkowiak for the CCC work at Platt.[11]

Between 1933 and 1940 these well-trained—if young—designers supervised the CCC recruits as they rebuilt Platt National Park from boundary to boundary. Enrollees built entirely new road and trail systems, moving tons of rock and gravel with dynamite, dump trucks, and wheelbarrows. They also built a new utility area (a quadrangle of truck shed, barn, stable, and maintenance shop); moved park residences; and rehabilitated an administrative building. Some crews did conservation work, for example, building a nine-hundred-foot-long revetment wall on the banks of Rock Creek to stop erosion. Forester Donald Stauffer's crews reforested the park, eventually planting more than five hundred thousand trees and shrubs. Other projects redeveloped the park as a natural environment for visitor use. Enrollees obliterated the golf course and tennis courts and built new picnic areas at Little Niagara Falls and Buffalo and Antelope Springs. Jerry Miller redesigned Cold Spring Campground according to the Meinecke System, with plantings for privacy and a tiered and looped layout of one-way roads. And everywhere throughout the park were brand new water features, including ornamental fountains at Bromide Springs and Flower Park; reflecting ponds at Antelope Springs; and five new dams and swimming holes in Travertine Creek. By June 1940, when the remarkable seven-year tenure of Company 808 at Platt was over, the park had been transformed from a degraded resort environment into a seemingly natural composition of forest and prairie, dotted with spring pavilions, waterfalls, and swimming holes. It had become, in the words of Palmer Boeger, a scenic and recreational "Oklahoma Oasis."[12]

The Naturalistic Landscape Design of Platt National Park

Platt's successful transformation was largely a result of Park Service policies and practices of naturalistic landscape design. Pioneered by Vint and the Landscape Division in the 1920s, key among these was master planning. Park Service master planning was a direct descendant of nineteenth-century park planning, but in application to large landscapes with unique and significant scenic resources was expanded to address complex development concerns such as sewage treatment, hotel siting, road and village planning, and impacts of automobile tourism. As initiated at Mount Rainier in 1926, the master plan was "a unified aesthetic conception . . . which limited the development of roads and other facilities, enhanced a consistent sense of place, and protected scenery from encroachments."[13] The excellence of Platt's landscape clearly owes much to its master plan, which was drastically revised by Charles Richey and Walter Popham. Richey and Popham had found the 1932 master plan to be a cursory document, lacking topographic base data and detailed drawings. Even worse, it lacked a comprehensive vision for the landscape.

Richey and Popham redressed these problems in their 1933 master plan, which was thereafter updated annually by Jerome Miller (fig. 2). In describing master planning, Thomas Vint wrote that "a park road system is the controlling element in the overall development for the park"; Richey and Popham masterfully applied this principle, completely reconfiguring the park through the simple means of a perimeter loop road.[14] By the 1930s loop roads also figured prominently in many national parks, from Acadia to Yellowstone, but had long been a standard of nineteenth-century park design. It is perhaps not surprising, then, that Richey and Popham's road design, a meandering circuit bisected by a central transverse road allowing local traffic unimpeded movement across the park, diagrammatically recapitulated the road design of Joseph Paxton's iconic nineteenth-century Birkenhead Park in Liverpool, England.

Platt's road system was obviously an organizational framework that provided easy access to all the park's features, something previously lacking. But more important, the master plan's perimeter loop fundamentally changed the park by creating an experience wherein the park landscape could be perceived as a whole. Significantly, the reorganization of the road system led to the relocation of the old buffalo and elk paddocks from the park's center

to its periphery. This bold move functionally gave the centrally located Pavilion Springs—the raison d'être for the park's establishment in 1902—the proper space for development as the major jewel in the park's crown of springs. And in so doing, the road and master plan aesthetically affirmed the idea that the park's natural waters and landscape, not imported amusements, comprised the park experience. The master plan thus brought Platt's natural features to the forefront of its design, aligning Platt with the rest of the national parks. The new master plan forcefully asserted the idea that even if Platt were not as awe-inspiring a park as Yosemite, it could still be developed in accordance with the rest of the Park Service system.

Of course, aligning Platt's development with the rest of the system required more than master planning. To support the broad visions that master planning created, Vint and the Landscape Division had also established principles of naturalistic design to protect scenery, minimize human intrusion, and ensure that built elements harmonized with their landscapes. By the late 1920s, detailed practices were codified for every type of development. To harmonize roads with the landscape, for example, designers reduced cuts and fills; deployed gracious, curving wyes at intersections; carefully excavated around trees and rock outcroppings; and modified blasting to reduce construction scarring.

Vint coined the term "landscape naturalization" to describe this combination of planting design and site work that merged human construction into its environment via screening, topographic grading, artificial rockwork, and foundation planting, all of which "enabled park designers to create or maintain the illusion that nature had experienced little disturbance from improvements." Landscape naturalization was largely based on ideas—such as pictorial composition, foundation plantings, and ecological communities—of nineteenth-century naturalistic landscape architecture as defined in Henry Vincent Hubbard and Theodora Kimball's *An Introduction to the Study of Landscape*

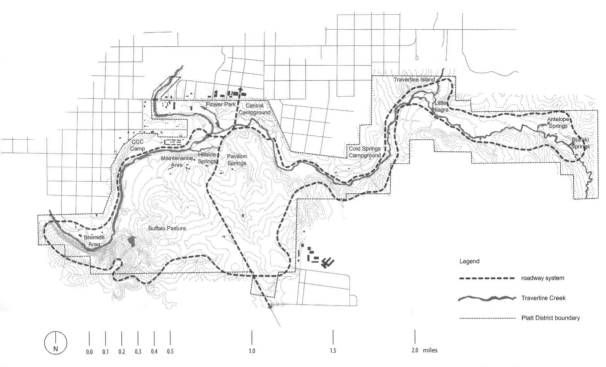

FIG. 2. Plan of Platt National Park in 1940, showing major features and overall design, including road system.

Design (1917); Frank Waugh's *The Natural Style in Landscape Gardening* (1917); and Wilhelm Miller's *Prairie Spirit in Landscape Gardening* (1915). What was new, however, was the institutionalization of these policies within a federal agency and their application at a range of scales, from plantings of ferns around a drinking fountain to thousands of acres of reforestation at Rocky Mountain national parks. And, when the CCC was established in 1933, "landscape naturalization" was easily equated with the Corps' proposed "conservation work."[15]

At Platt, the merging of CCC conservation goals with landscape naturalization was most naturally evident in the park's forestry program, where four types of plantings were designated and supervised by both Stauffer and the landscape architects. "Reforestation plantings" of thousands of oak, walnut, and red cedar planted en masse and "protective plantings" of cedars planted on steep slopes to prevent erosion met Dust Bowl conservation objectives, but were also intended to "strengthen the design"

by creating spatial enclosure, especially along the perimeter road and park trails. "Boundary plantings" were functionally similar, but hearkened back to nineteenth-century landscape tradition in screening obtrusive views of the surrounding town. Naturalistic landscape design aesthetics were, however, best expressed in so-called ornamental plantings, which helped blend structures into the surrounding forest and added seasonal interest. The circular stone spring enclosure at Buffalo Springs, for example, designed by Ed Walkowiak, was surrounded by magnolia, holly, flowering dogwood, crab apple, and redbud (fig. 3).[16]

Over time, landscape naturalization practices became the major means of implementing design at Platt. In part this occurred because most Platt projects were completed with ECW funding. In contrast, other national parks often constructed large buildings and major infrastructure with hefty appropriations from the Public Works Administration (PWA). Platt, however, received relatively little PWA money,

FIG. 3. Circular spring enclosure at Buffalo Springs, 2006. (Ken Ruhnke, photographer; National Park Service, Chickasaw National Recreation Area Archives)

and what it did get primarily funded sewer improvements and the perimeter road. Even then, the road construction was completed with ECW funds as CCC enrollees, using what Vint termed "Roadside Cleanup" techniques for healing construction scars, finished the road by grading back side slopes with "ogee" curves, constructing culverts of local stone, and planting the banks with native red cedars, dogwoods, and sumac.[17]

Platt's CCC boys used similar landscape naturalization techniques for constructing trails, which were a key aspect of the park's redesign. Richey and Popham considered the existing trail system "antiquated and totally inadequate" and laid out a new six-mile system, more than doubling its size.[18] The trails themselves were designed in situ, likely based on specifications contained in a pocket-size field guide entitled "Standards for Trail Construction" produced by the Office of the Chief Engineer in 1934. Platt's CCC crews, working under the supervision of Miller, Walkowiak, and Merrill, executed these

standards at an extremely high level; retaining and parapet walls, switchbacks, and stone gutters along Bromide Hill Trail, for example, show that the technical specifications for these features were followed exactly. Yet the trails were more than good engineering: winding along the valleys of Travertine and Rock Creeks, they were also intended to present a carefully orchestrated view and experience of Platt as a shady, watery haven in the dry Oklahoma prairie (fig. 4). Such aesthetic goals of trail design are perhaps best summarized by Frank Waugh in his 1935 *Landscape Conservation: Planning for the Restoration Conservation and Utilization of Wild Lands for Park and Forest Recreation,* written as a handbook to guide "young civilians" in implementing Emergency Conservation Work. The text states that "the scenery [along a trail] can also be made additionally attractive if it is presented by means of themes or motives arranged in 'paragraphs.' For example, if the trail leads up a narrow valley with a pleasant stream in its bed, there will be repeated pictures of a brook which will be the subject of principal interest. The stream supplies the motive to be developed. View after view, picture after picture, will be shown at the most effective points."[19] Platt's trails, which certainly presented "picture after picture" of tree-framed waterfalls, rustic log bridges, and naturalistic pools, are a perfect incarnation of Waugh's words, which summarized principles from his earlier book *The Natural Style in Landscape Gardening*. Although it is impossible to say that Richey, Miller, and Walkowiak designed Platt's trails according to Waugh's pamphlet, they certainly knew Waugh's ideas from his numerous books (all of which were in the ISC library) and his ideas on the natural style, having been taught by Elwood, who had been Waugh's colleague at the University of Massachusetts.

The influence of nineteenth-century picturesque and naturalistic park design is particularly apparent throughout Platt's landscape. Flower Park, twelve acres in extent, with its meandering pathways, "garden wall entrance treatment," and comfort station reflected in an irregularly shaped pool, was essentially a small urban park. Park administration described it, located a block from Sulphur's downtown, as intentionally "somewhat citified."[20] An equally refined landscape occurred at Bromide Springs, Platt's other town entrance, where Sulphur's Twelfth Street became a formal, Beaux-Arts-style axis, flanked by limestone entrance piers and terminated in a semicircular plaza, pool, and thirty-foot artesian water jet (fig. 5). Although the location of formalized, rather than naturalized, landscapes next to the town demonstrates the ability of Park Service designers and design policies to produce, in today's parlance, context-sensitive design, in other places such formalism was perhaps more stylistically capricious. At Hillside Springs, for instance, mineral water flowed from arched grotto fountain to patio runnel in a composition reminiscent of fifteenth-century Spanish fountains at the gardens of the Alhambra.

FIG. 4. Trail along Bromide Hill, 2006. (Ken Ruhnke, photographer; National Park Service, Chickasaw National Recreation Area Archives)

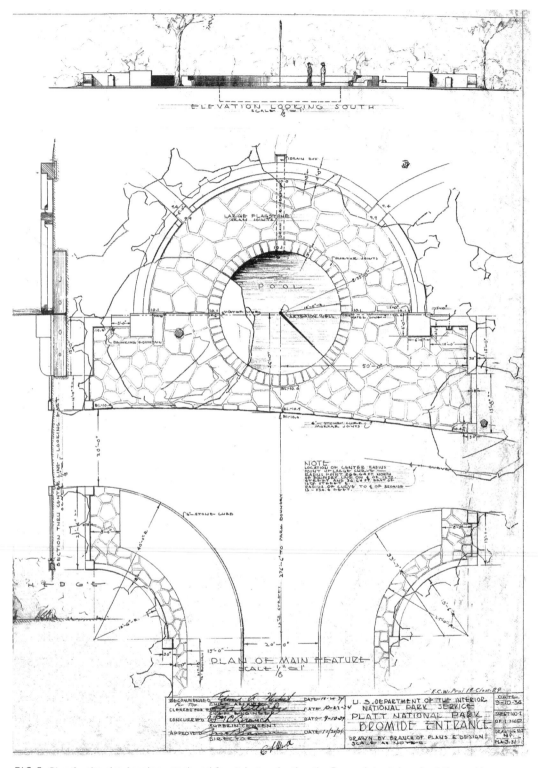

FIG. 5. Plan for the circular plaza, pool, and fountain terminating the Beaux-Arts-style axis at the park's Twelfth Street entrance, 1934. (Drawn by Jerome Miller, a portion of drawing NP-PLA-3031; National Park Service, Chickasaw National Recreation Area Archives)

Yet if references to urban, historical, and European design motifs were unusual for western national parks, they were certainly not uncommon in the eastern parks, which often utilized historical styles or motives. Charles Peterson designed Colonial Revival–style overpasses for the parkway in Colonial National Historical Park, and Norman Newton instituted a Beaux-Arts-style plaza and entrance allée at the Statue of Liberty National Historic Site. Thus the adaptation of some of these same ideas at Platt by Richey, Miller, and Walkowiak is really not surprising, especially given the emphasis on garden history and historical design styles in their curriculum at Iowa State College. In their four-year program, ISC landscape architecture students took multiple courses in landscape theory, landscape history, and architectural history, and toured great works of U.S. landscape architecture, including country estates that contained European-style formal gardens.[21]

However, such "citified" landscape features were only constructed during the CCC's first few years. After 1935, Platt's construction conformed to a decidedly "rustic" style, perhaps to emphasize the park's natural qualities over its "urban" context. By the 1930s in the Park Service the term "rustic" indicated a specific set of building techniques intended to eliminate the demarcation between nature and man-made objects, and Platt's buttressed stone comfort stations and pavilions followed these specifications faithfully. The two spring pavilions in particular demonstrated the designers' abilities to merge built form with landscape—the Bromide Springs Pavilion's flagstone terrace stepped graciously down to a wall-sheltered lawn, and the Pavilion Springs Pavilion's naturalistic, moss-covered rockwork appeared to almost flow into the ground plane. A myriad of small-scale stone architectural features such as boulder guardrails, steps and stepping-stones, trail bridges, retaining walls, picnic tables, and fire pits extended the rustic sensibility out into the rest of the landscape, furthering the consistent and cohesive naturalistic image of the park. The general excellence

of Platt's entire collection of rustic buildings and naturalized features is evident from their inclusion in Albert H. Good's *Park and Recreation Structures,* one of a number of handbooks used to inspire park architects throughout the CCC and beyond. Platt facilities featured in Good's book included the Flower Park entrance gates, the Bromide Springs Pavilion, one of the comfort stations, a wooden picnic table, and most notably, waterfalls along Travertine Creek, pools at Antelope Springs, and a set of stepping-stones.[22]

The inclusion of Platt's naturalistic water features in Good's book along with its buildings was appropriate since the park's waterways best demonstrate how landscape naturalization was a holistic approach to design. Travertine Creek, for example, was an engineering solution to hydrologic and sanitation issues, but at the same time met needs of aesthetics and recreation. At the creek's headwaters, the redesign of swampy Buffalo and Antelope Springs, as, respectively, a circular enclosure and a spring emanating from a rocky embankment, ensured the creek water's clarity and prevented contamination. Farther downstream, recreational use was addressed through the creation of the five dams and corresponding swimming holes (fig. 6). Conceived by the Office of the Chief Engineer around 1935 to provide for the regulation of creek flow and to allow for periodic cleaning, the boulder dams concealed steel-gated, concrete culverts. The dams were adapted on-site to meet local hydraulic and engineering concerns, but the landscape architects ensured that naturalistic rockwork and native plantings would blend the dams into their surroundings. When completed, the dams were almost impossible to distinguish from natural falls along the creek. To this day, park visitors are amazed to learn that many of the park's falls, dams, and banks are constructed and not "natural."

Travertine Creek's elaborate naturalization was obviously grounded in nineteenth-century traditions of rock and wild gardens made popular by British gardener William Robinson, and in early-twentieth-century urban park designs, where artificial rockwork was used along steps, as retaining walls, and, most impressively, to create rivers and swimming pools that transported urban dwellers to rural "swimming holes." Epitomized by Jens Jensen's stratified limestone pool designs for Columbus Park (1912–20) in urban Chicago, by the 1930s, naturalized swimming pools were falling out of favor in urban areas due to growing health concerns about non-chlorinated waters. However, the less crowded and less polluted nature of state and national park landscapes permitted Park Service designers to respond to Albert Good's call "for the return of the 'old swimmin' hole' of fond recollection."[23] As a result, naturalistic streams, dams, springs, and pools for swimming were relatively common in CCC-era parks, though Platt's stand among the best and most enduring.

Platt's other waterways—including a stream running through Flower Park that cascaded into Travertine Creek; Limestone Creek meandering around Travertine Island; and the outflow stream at Pavilion Springs—similarly demonstrated a high level of naturalistic design, fine masonry craftsmanship, and detailed planting. Considered as a system, however, the waterways were even more important in defining the park's new central identity—or "leading motive" as Frank Waugh termed it.[24] Stated another way, Platt was designed to be a comprehensive experience of water in all its forms, with the intent that visitors would encounter water through all of their senses. Creeks and swimming holes were created to provoke total immersion and active pursuits like fishing; trails, overlooks, and fountains to inspire the peaceful contemplation of water's sight and sound; and spring pavilions to encourage visitors to taste and smell the water. Although most national parks had a grand and obvious leading motive (whether it was volcanic geology at Yellowstone or majestic mountain scenery at Mount Rainier) which simply needed to

FIG. 6. One of the park's five constructed dams and swimming hole at Little Niagara Falls, 2004. (Katarzyna Grala, photographer)

be preserved and enhanced, at Platt, the humbler motive of plain water, buried under years of town and resort development, needed more effort to be revealed. In fact, the principles and processes of naturalistic design did not just fine-tune Platt's watery image, but essentially created it. Rock by rock, drop by drop, through small-scale interventions of trails and steps, creeks and springs, and trees and shrubs, Platt's designers and CCC boys somehow created a consistent whole where none had previously existed. And yet, despite the hard work the creative process entailed, the landscape seemed to not have been designed at all, enabling Henry Vincent Hubbard to place Platt among the best-known national parks and present it as an example "of how much effort has been bent toward preserving . . . the effect that *man has done nothing.*"[25]

One wonders if Hubbard knew that in Platt's case, more effort was bent toward creating, rather than preserving an appearance of untouched wilderness. It probably would not have mattered: in the same article Hubbard also wrote that "it is an art to conceal art."[26] And indeed, Platt National Park is a work of art, one designed expressly to conceal human genius and effort with a veneer of nature. In doing so, Platt demonstrates, perhaps better than any other park in the system, the aesthetic achievements and transformative abilities of the naturalistic landscape design of the CCC and the New Deal-era National Park Service.

Notes

1. Horace Albright and Robert Cahn, *The Birth of the National Park Service* (Salt Lake City: Howe Brothers, 1985), 223; Henry Vincent Hubbard, "Landscape Development Based on Conservation: As Practiced in the National Park Service," *Landscape Architecture Quarterly* 29, no. 3 (April 1939): 113.

2. Herbert Maier to Superintendent Wm. E. Branch, 9 July 1933, Box 7, Entry P93, RG 79, National Archives, College Park, Maryland.

3. Jacilee Wray and Alexa Roberts, *An Ethnohistory of the Relationship between the Community of Sulphur, Oklahoma, and Chickasaw National Recreation Area* (Santa Fe: National Park Service Intermountain Support Office, 2004). Chapters 1 and 2 present a detailed account of the complex negotiations leading to the reservation.

4. Superintendent of Platt National Park to Superintendent of National Parks, 12 March 1917, Chickasaw National Recreation Area (CNRA) Archives; Heidi Hohmann and Katarzyna Grala, *Cultural Landscape Report for the Platt Historic District* (Sulphur, Okla.: National Park Service, 2004), 20–25, 38–44.

5. Albright and Cahn, *The Birth of the National Park Service*, 72; Jacilee Wray and Alexa Roberts, "In Praise of Platt, Or, What is a 'Real' National Park?" *The George Wright Society Forum* 15, no. 1 (1997): 70; John Ise, *Our National Park Policy: A Critical History* (Baltimore: Johns Hopkins University Press, 1961), 136, 140–42.

6. Wray and Roberts, *An Ethnohistory of the Relationship,* 50–51, 187–89.

7. Linda Flint McClelland, *Building the National Parks: Historic Landscape Design and Construction* (Baltimore: Johns Hopkins University Press, 1998), 197–200, 329–30.

8. Franklin Delano Roosevelt, "First Inaugural Address," delivered 4 March 1933, http://www .americanrhetoric.com/speeches/fdrfirstinaugural .html.

9. John A. Salmond, *The Civilian Conservation Corps, 1933–1942: A New Deal Case Study* (Durham: Duke University Press, 1967), 121–27.

10. Hohmann and Grala, *Cultural Landscape Report,* 65.

11. *Horizons: A Resume of Departmental News, Fall Quarter 1933* (Ames: Iowa State College), 1; P. H. Elwood, Jr., "Weekly Reports, State Park Emergency Conservation Work, District Three. June–August 1933," Box 7, Entry P93, RG 79, National Archives, College Park, Maryland; Walter Metschke, "Memoir of Walter G. Metschke" (unpublished manuscript, Chicago Architects Oral History Project, The Ernest R. Graham Study Center for Architectural Drawings, Department of Architecture, The Art Institute of Chicago, 1998), 21–22, 44, 122.

12. Hohmann and Grala, *Cultural Landscape Report,* chap. 4 (on which this essay draws heavily); Palmer Boeger, *Oklahoma Oasis: From Platt National Park to Chickasaw National Recreation Area* (Muskogee: Western Heritage Books, 1987).

13. Ethan Carr, "The 'Noblest Landscape Problem': Thomas C. Vint and Landscape Preservation," in *Design with Culture: Claiming America's Landscape Heritage,* ed. Charles A. Birnbaum and Mary V. Hughes (Charlottesville: University of Virginia Press, 2005), 161.

14. Thomas Vint, "National Park Service Master Plans," reprinted from *Planning and Civic Comment* (April–June, 1946): n.p.

15. McClelland, *Building the National Parks,* 263, 3–4, 255–66, 338.

16. Charles A. Richey and Walter D. Popham, "Construction Report: Conservation Work, CCC Camp No. 808, May 16, 1933–April 1, 1934," CNRA Archives, 5, 11; Edmund B. Walkowiak, "Yearly Report: Conservation Work, First and Second Periods, May 27, 1933–April 1, 1934," CNRA Archives, n.p.

17. McClelland, *Building the National Parks,* 185–86.

18. Richey and Popham, "Construction Report," CNRA Archives, 20; Charles A. Richey and Jerome C. Miller, "Construction Report: Conservation Work, CCC Camp No. 808, October 1, 1934–March 31, 1935," CNRA Archives, 11.

19. Frank A. Waugh, *Landscape Conservation: Planning for the Restoration Conservation and Utilization of Wild Lands for Park and Forest Recreation* (Washington, D.C.: National Park Service, 1935), 10–11.

20. "Flower Park," *Platt National Park News* (undated mimeographed CCC camp newsletter),

File 000–29, Box 52, RG 79, National Archives, Fort Worth, Texas.

21. *General Catalogue, 1928–29* (Ames: Iowa State College of Agriculture and Mechanical Arts, 1928), 216–18. Catalogues subsequent to 1933 show almost identical course work. Examples of Miller's and Walkowiak's student designs utilizing axial geometries similar to the Bromide Springs Plaza can be found in Miller, "A War Memorial" (illustration), *Horizons* 5, no. 2 (1929): 25; Walkowiak, "A French Chateau" (illustration), *Horizons* 6, no. 2 (1930): 35–36.

22. Ethan Carr, *Wilderness By Design: Landscape Architecture and the National Park Service* (Lincoln: University of Nebraska Press, 1998), 283–85; Albert H. Good, *Park and Recreation Structures, Parts I, II, and III,* bound as one volume (Washington, D.C.: National Park Service, 1938), I:147, 170, II:11, 21.

23. Good, *Park and Recreation Structures,* II:120.

24. Frank A. Waugh, *The Natural Style in Landscape Gardening* (Boston: Richard G. Badger, 1917), 64.

25. Hubbard, "Landscape Development Based on Conservation," 108, emphasis in original.

26. Ibid., 105.

Urban Parks in Sweden at the Turn of the Twentieth Century

The Nature Park and the Search for National Identity

In the decades before and after 1900, a new type of urban park was introduced in Sweden: the "nature park" in which nature, or the landscape, constituted the basis for the design.[1] Appearing first as concepts in gardening journals and then created around the country, these parks were the result of a new aesthetic approach towards the layout of parks and gardens as well as a new way of thinking about nature and about national identity.

From an international perspective, all Swedish towns, with the capital as the only exception, were very small until the last decades of the nineteenth century. But the size of a town was no excuse for not making an urban park, and some towns had already planned for and laid out these parks at the beginning of the nineteenth century. They were not created in order to improve the climate, or to make the towns greener, but rather as social settings for the middle classes. In and around Stockholm, as in many other European countries, the upper classes had from the eighteenth century onward been given access to the royal parks and gardens.

The first generation of urban parks was mainly introduced in towns with a large middle-class population. From around 1860 onward, urban parks became common all around the country. Some of them were planned first and foremost for the working classes, although used by the middle classes as well. Others came into being through different associations, such as horticultural associations. Usually, the parks were planted with exotic flowers, trees, and bushes and adorned with statues, fountains, and the like. There was a strong belief that urban parks could solve many of the problems associated with the rapidly growing towns. Many park advocates argued, for example, that the urban park had a formative force, especially for children. However, it was never openly declared that a park was intended for only one group in society.

While the authorities behind the creation of midcentury parks were motivated by the idea of creating places where workers and craftsmen and their families could spend their day off enjoying themselves in a beautiful environment, gardeners were more concerned with designing the parks according to the prevailing design ideas. In creating these new social settings, the authorities were mainly influenced by British ideas, while the gardeners, having read German journals and completed their training in Germany, were mainly influenced by German ideas on design and plant material.

As industry expanded from the 1880s onward, many Swedish towns started to grow rapidly. People moved into towns from the countryside to start working at factories. With this expansion, a need for better dwellings, clean water, more urban parks, and so on, became urgent. Of course, this development could be seen all over the Western world. However, Sweden was industrialized much later than many other countries, and around 1900 about 75 percent of the Swedish population still lived in the countryside. Independent of industrialization, the urban park had become a well-established feature, and towards the end of the nineteenth century, most Swedish towns had at least one, and often several parks.

The Nature Park Makes Its Appearance

In the 1870s, when the vogue of carpet beddings was still at its height, the first signs of a change in park design could be seen. Articles entitled "Nature Parks" appeared in gardening journals. One of the first to introduce this topic was the gardener Nils Uno Blomberg, who in 1871 published an essay entitled "Om naturparker" (On nature parks). It is tempting to see a connection between Blomberg's article and William Robinson's well-known book *The Wild Garden* (1870), but it is doubtful if Robinson's book had yet been introduced in Sweden, nor was the book translated into Swedish. In addition, Blomberg's approach differed from Robinson's. Instead of planting wild flowers in a garden as Robinson recommended, Blomberg suggested that an existing wooded area or grove should be the starting point for a new park. According to Blomberg it was especially important to use already grown trees and bushes. Flower beds, on the one hand, he argued, did not fit into those settings: they belonged to the areas around houses.[2] On the other hand, the spread of wild flowers was to be encouraged, so some sort of planning was after all necessary. Blomberg, a highly qualified gardener, explicitly advocated for this new approach, in opposition to prevailing park design practice, which relied on carpet beddings and exotic trees. In the 1870s and 1880s, several essays representing ideas similar to Blomberg's were published in Swedish gardening periodicals and books, contributing to the development of this new design concept.

An interesting early example of this new type of park is Djäkneberget in Västerås, about seventy miles west of Stockholm (fig. 1). Here an amateur garden maker, Sam Lidman, a former officer who had become a schoolteacher, designed the park over a long period, from the 1860s to the 1890s. Through hard work he turned a rocky area on the outskirts of the town into a prosperous park. He chose mainly typically Swedish trees, such as oak, birch, ash, maple, common pine, and spruce, and adorned the park with hundreds of monuments. Often very simple in their construction, the monuments usually consisted of an erect granite stone with an inscription, with a more or less distinct moral message. He intended the park not only to be used for sports but to evoke a moral and aesthetic mind among the boys who attended the school, through the moral, religious, or historical inscriptions on the monuments. This park, although totally unique in its edifying content, had probably no impact on park development in the country. The town was too small, and the creator too unknown, although the first book on the park and its monuments was published in 1900.

From the 1890s onward, the concept of "nature parks" or "natural parks" dominated not only theory but the actual creation and design of new urban parks. This new approach—used in private parks and gardens, too—was advocated by county governors, city councillors, progressive gardeners and garden designers, botanists, and others. To many city authorities, in particular, the nature park seemed the best design to achieve the intended goals of urban parks.

An exact definition of what a nature park is does not exist. The definition varies from writer to writer, from town to town, and from time to time. The parks could vary in size, content, and structure, but they had some distinct features in common. Nature parks were molded from wooded hillsides or clearings and primarily restricted to plants thought to be indigenous, or at least hardy in Sweden, such as birch, rowan, and alder, and spruce and pine. The international style with carpet beddings, exotic trees, and the like, which since the 1860s had been a common feature in shaping urban parks, was now rejected in parks laid out all over the country.

Another, related type of park—also called "nature park" or sometimes "forest park"—was laid out and planted in imitation of nature. This type was less frequent, but still important in showing what park planners and city authorities thought Swedish nature should look like. Slottsparken, laid out about 1900 in Malmö, the biggest town in the south of Sweden, is probably the finest example in this category (fig. 2). Here, in an agricultural landscape, forests were (and still are) rare. This was probably one of the main reasons why the authorities desired a forest park when a new urban park was planned in the 1890s. Another reason was the authorities' strong belief that a forest park would suit the workers and craftsmen and their families better than an "artistic park." With their background in the countryside, the authorities imagined that these new settlers would feel more at home in a park looking like

FIG. 1. Djäkneberget in Västerås is an early example of the Swedish concept of the "nature park." Some of the park's characteristic monuments are shown in this c. 1900 postcard. (National Library of Sweden)

FIG. 2. Postcard from c. 1900 showing Slottsparken in Malmö with resting park visitors overlooking the lake. (National Library of Sweden)

true nature, than in an artful creation. It is difficult to determine if this assumption was correct, since there are few written sources telling us how these visitors apprehended the park.

Nationalism and Park Planning

The establishment of nature parks coincided with the formation of a national identity, not only in Sweden but in many other countries, too. The desire to give the parks a character as close to nature as possible can be viewed as a stage in this formation of a national identity: Swedish tree species represented Sweden. Farmland—with meadows, pastures, and woodland—had been a starting point for many landscape gardens in the eighteenth century; but this aesthetic approach was a new phenomenon for Swedish urban parks, as these parks, planned for the working classes, did not call on the associations to friendship, to the Roman Empire, or to foreign countries which were such prominent themes in shaping landscape gardens of the eighteenth century.

Instead, planners provided for the active use of parks, from quiet strolls to football games and skiing races, skating, and biking. Year-round games and sports for adults as well as children became more common elements in the parks. The initiative to build playgrounds and sports grounds often came from school-teachers. Since the introduction of compulsory school attendance in 1842, teachers had argued that children needed physical exercise also; otherwise they would overwork themselves and become too tired. Sports associations as well as teachers, especially in Stockholm and Gothenburg, recommended that playgrounds and sports grounds be integrated into urban parks.

These demands were often met with a negative response. In Stockholm, for example, the authorities argued that land in the city center was too valuable to be used only for children's games. However, beginning in the 1890s, city authorities around the country succumbed to the pressure to integrate playgrounds and sports grounds into urban parks.

Sports and games, skiing, and skating were seen not only as an antidote to overwork but as one way of socializing and educating children. This promotion of outdoor life in general, through sports and games, would make school-children healthier and stronger, and prepare them for excursions in nature beyond the parks. In this way, the parks served the purpose of shaping a national identity, by encouraging engagement with a landscape of mountains, rivers, and clearings seen as essentially Swedish.[3]

Swedish landscape has not always been seen in so positive a light, however. Barely two hundred years ago, the rocky landscape of the Swedish west coast, much appreciated today, was seen as something ugly, and hardly ever used for the recreational purposes that now bring visitors there. The Swedish ethnologist Orvar Löfgren has pointed out that with increasing industrialization, a landscape of production turned into a landscape of consumption. Nature was not used only for producing food, for mining, and so on, but had become a place people enjoyed visiting during their free time.[4]

From the late nineteenth century onward, a young movement for conservation asserted the importance of promoting Sweden's nature. In 1880, a first proposal for establishing national parks was made by the Finnish Swedish baron Adolf Erik Nordenskiöld (the first man to sail the length of the Northeast Passage), obviously modeled on the foundation of Yellowstone National Park some years earlier. When the Swedish Society for Nature Conservation was founded in 1909, one of the most important needs was to preserve what was seen as an unspoiled nature with species typical of Sweden. In the same year, Sweden established its first regulations for nature conservation. At the same time the first national parks were founded, nine in all. These nine national parks, situated all around the country, and thus representing different types of Swedish nature, were the first to be established in Europe. In the following decades, several more were to come. Establishing national parks was one way of teaching patriotism to Swedish men and women, to youth and children.

As love of the native land became an ingredient in nationalism, associations such as the

Swedish Touring Club and the Association for the Promotion of Outdoor Life, founded in 1885 and 1892, respectively, organized excursions on skis or on foot to the Swedish mountains and other rural places. These associations saw an active outdoor life as a possible way to foster young people and thus improve the physical and mental health of the population. Active outdoor life was also regarded as a means of national mobilization. These new ways of seeing and interacting with nature also had their impact on the park design. Like nature, the urban park could be an educational tool—not simply in the music from its bandstands or the messages on its monuments, but in the design of the park itself.

Two Nature Parks: The Slottsskogen Park in Gothenburg and the Jönköping Municipal Park

The Slottsskogen Park in Gothenburg was one of the first examples of a Swedish urban park where the starting point was nature's offering. The park was made possible thanks to a land donation from the Swedish state. A large forest area situated in a rural position just southwest of the city center was donated to the town under the condition that it would be kept as a park. It was strongly recommended that Slottsskogen should be transformed into a park as soon as possible, the authorities asserting that experience had shown that those who preferred to spend their free time in "God's open air" succeeded better both physically and morally than those who chose to stay at home. Consequently, the design of the park should emphasize that it was a healthy place that would improve people's quality of life.

City authorities in Gothenburg had a clear vision of how the park should be designed: it should be as nature intended, without "decorative elements," and walkers should themselves decide where they wanted to stroll or where to sit down for a moment's rest.[5] At that time it was an almost unheard of notion that those who chose to spend their leisure time outdoors should be allowed to walk and play on the grass. According to the plans, the park would be used for different activities throughout the year: in the winter for skating, tobogganing, and skiing, and in the summer for different games (fig. 3). In the names given sections of the park the nationalistic agenda became obvious. The hilly areas of the park were given names from Old Norse history: Bragehöjden, Valhallaberget, and Idunalunden and Balderslunden, all based on gods' names or dwelling places.

The park came into being as tourism and the open-air movement were starting to develop in Sweden. Ski races were arranged in this park, and probably in several other parks, too. Many people must have learned to ski in an urban park before embarking on more adventurous trips in the "wild" landscape. Thus, the park could be seen and used as a "preparation" for real nature.

FIG. 3. Winter motif with skiers in the Slottsskogen Park in Gothenburg shown in this c. 1900 postcard. (National Library of Sweden)

Jönköping Municipal Park in the south of Sweden, like Slottsskogen Park, was intended to look like a cleared forest glade with one or two gravel walks and a few benches offering the most beautiful views. As in Gothenburg, people were allowed to move freely on lawns, to play games, and to ski and skate. The initiator of this municipal park, the county governor, asserted that a park in a rural position like this should not contain any "luxuries"—no cut lawns, splendid flowers, or groups of deciduous shrubs, which were more suitable for parks in town centers.

Parks like these two, their layouts starting from the existing landscape, diverged radically from the current view of how an urban park should be designed. It might also be noted that they were cheaper to maintain, without expensive carpet beddings and delicate plants that required tending by a staff of gardeners. The county governor also pointed out that the workers, craftsmen, and their families at Jönköping—in the late nineteenth century an expanding town with several factories, a county residence, a prison, and other facilities—needed a park situated close to their homes to visit during their day off. The park was never

meant only for them, however, but was open to all citizens of Jönköping. The authorities even hoped that the park could bridge the class distinctions in the town. We cannot know, though, whether that goal was achieved.

The Jönköping Municipal Park also sought to promote the local cultural heritage by adding an open-air museum showing buildings typical of the farming industry. Such open-air museums displaying local culture and history became usual features in Swedish urban parks. The most well-known example is of course the open-air Skansen museum in Stockholm, which also became the model for open-air museums in Denmark and Germany. To this museum was added a collection showing all the rocks and minerals found in the county (fig. 4). The samples were provided with nameplates so that park visitors could memorize the names of the stones. Old photographs show that this collection was used in teaching children. The Jönköping Municipal Park is a first-rate example of the wish to produce a park in which a visit to health-inducing nature could be combined with exercise and education. The park, with its historical buildings, rock collection, antiquities, sports grounds, tennis courts, playgrounds, bi-

FIG. 4. Interior of Jönköping Municipal Park with some children in the so-called rock collection shown in a c. 1900 postcard. (National Library of Sweden)

cycle path, different restaurants, and the like, offered something for every visitor. The park also had a much more diversified content than most other urban parks in Sweden at that time.

Stockholm and the Debate on Nature Parks

An attentive reader might have noticed that so far I have made no references to Stockholm, the capital of Sweden. The main reason for this is that Stockholm did not have its first big urban parks until about 1900. The delay resulted mostly from a long planning process, but also from the existence of large royal parks and gardens surrounding the town, in some cases open to the public since the eighteenth century. The biggest, most important, and most beloved of these was without doubt the former royal hunting ground Djurgården. This huge area, today an important part of the Stockholm National Urban Park, is divided into two parts, North Djurgården and South Djurgården (fig. 5).[6]

The general opinion around 1900 was that there was no need for a special protection plan for Djurgården; the royal rights would suffice to preserve the park from further exploitation. This belief was suddenly proven wrong. Military regiments had for a very long period used North Djurgården for training camps; but new weapons with longer range made the area less suitable for these activities. When the regiments moved to more suitable areas, proposals were made to build on the land. According to the 1905 Djurgården Parliamentary Committee, North Djurgården was quite suitable for new dwellings, and according to one of the proposals, almost all North Djurgården could be covered with buildings.

These proposals were an eye-opener for people interested in parks and nature conservation, and preserving Djurgården as a nature park—an unspoiled landscape with a distinctive Swedish character—now became urgent. Karl Starbäck, one of the founding members of the Swedish Society for Nature Conservation in 1909, submitted a petition to parliament in 1913 for Djurgården's preservation as a nature park, stating the park's crucial importance for the citizens' recreation, since the city gardener had failed to provide the citizens with green space and urban parks. Starbäck's assertion that all sound patriotism sprang from one's love of the native landscape made the familiar connection between nature conservation and nationalism. A consequence of Starbäck's petition was the setting up of a second parliamentary committee to address the future of Djurgården. In that committee's report, made public in 1917, the experts stated the importance of Djurgården's conservation as a park: it was in the whole country's interest that Stockholm should have a well-preserved, original landscape of a typically Swedish character. The aim of this report was to save South Djurgården from further building projects, and to examine to what extent North Djurgården could be developed without any alterations when it came to the citizens' access to the area, and especially to the waterline.

At about the same time as Starbäck submitted his petition, an open disagreement on nature conservation and park design broke out in Stockholm. Professor Rutger Sernander, botanist and founding member of the Swedish Society for Nature Conservation, and Anna Lindhagen, child welfare superintendent and member of Stockholm's city council as well as founder of the Swedish allotment movement, argued that the city planners and the city gardener had failed in their park planning in not having incorporated hillocks with indigenous trees and shrubberies typical of Stockholm's landscape into the design for the new urban parks. Lindhagen suggested that what she regarded as an untouched part of the district of Södermalm should be kept as a nature park, only supplemented with some benches and a band-stand, playgrounds, and a sports ground. One of her arguments in suggesting a nature park was its cost-saving benefits. Lindhagen's proposal is a combination of nature conservation and a desire to offer the city dwellers a new type of park, inviting them to an active park visit. Anna Lindhagen was very successful in her work, although she did not manage to save the whole area.[7]

FIG. 5. North Djurgården in Stockholm, once part of a huge royal hunting ground, still looks almost as rural as in this photograph from c. 1890 by the physician Carl Curman. (National Heritage Board)

FIG. 6. Winter motif from Ålsten Park in the western suburbs of Stockholm, designed as a sort of "nature park" and as a nature conservation project, here seen in a postcard from the 1930s. (National Library of Sweden)

Professor Rutger Sernander was a key promoter of nature parks and nature conservation. Ålsten Park, in one of Stockholm's western suburbs, was another park designed, at his urging, as a "nature park," taking the existing natural landscape as a starting point (fig. 6). Some of his ideas were quite radical and controversial: that nature should be protected from human beings; that, rather than being turned into parks, unspoiled and truly Swedish nature should be allowed to develop in total freedom.

"Listen to the Wind in the Spruce by Whose Roots Your Dwelling Stands"

The aesthetic changes embodied in the design of Swedish urban parks experienced around the turn of the twentieth century have many parallels in the search for national identity within contemporary art, literature, and architecture. In the 1890s, a style called national romanticism appeared in Swedish landscape painting. Among the artists working in this style we find Prince Eugen, Karl Nordström, and Richard Bergh. Some artists, especially Bergh, saw a close connection between the Nordic countryside and its inhabitants. The pine and the birch were seen as national tree species, and specifically the pine tree—preferably at dusk—was often a focus for landscape painters at this time. Pine trees and other conifers could, as we have seen, also be the basis for a park. The landscapes painted around 1900, with their poetic and national emphasis, have many links with Swedish nationalism, associating patriotism with a love of Swedish nature.

The county of Dalecarlia was in the first decades of the twentieth century seen as a Swedish ideal, with the most typical Swedish nature, people, buildings, and the like. Dalecarlia was held in high esteem as an aesthetic ideal for a very long time, and books with titles like *Dalarna som svenskt ideal* (Dalecarlia as a Swedish ideal) were published as late as the 1930s.[8] Less industrialized than other parts of Sweden, it was seen as an idyllic part of the country. Artists, writers, historians, and others went on pilgrimages to Dalecarlia to study and be close

to its nature and culture. Others left the busy towns permanently to build houses in Dalecarlia. One of the most well-known Swedish artists who left Stockholm for Dalecarlia was Carl Larsson, who together with his wife, the artist Karin Bergöö, built and decorated perhaps the most famous Swedish home ever, Sundborn, which through Larsson's watercolors in his book *Ett hem* (A home) made the family's life and dwelling well known all over the world.[9]

For the general public, however, *Läsebok för folkskolan* (Reading for elementary schools) probably had a much stronger effect than landscape painting in associating nature with nationalism (fig. 7). A pioneer among Swedish secular books containing national poetry and sections with natural science, geography, and history, it was read throughout the country. In 1907 the book, first published in the 1860s,

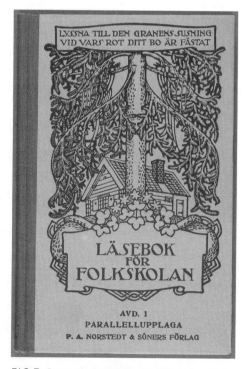

FIG. 7. Cover of *Läsebok för folkskolan* showing an idyllic image with a little cottage with blue wild anemones, a spruce, and the motto "Listen to the wind in the spruce by whose roots your dwelling stands" (1908 edition). (National Library of Sweden)

was given a new cover by the artist Olle Hjortzberg, showing a little cottage with blue wild anemones and a single spruce. The idyllic image was reinforced by the book's motto, "Listen to the wind in the spruce by whose roots your dwelling stands." The motto, traceable to Finnish proverbs, is much older than the book, but even today this expression is well known. Another link in the efforts to create a national identity through appreciation of Swedish nature is Selma Lagerlöf's well-known book *Nils Holgerssons underbara resa genom Sverige* (The wonderful adventures of Nils), written as a textbook in geography.[10]

Parallels to the Swedish nature parks can be seen in Germany, the United States, and many other countries; but in Sweden, parks are associated with a patriotic love of Swedish nature—even though the nature they call to mind, with their recurrent presentation of a forest clearing, is only one type of landscape to be found in this small, but elongated country with a great variety of climatic conditions and topography. Nevertheless, the "nature" of Sweden's nature parks embodies a nationalistic ideal that persists today, where a special fondness for nature is considered by Swedes a part of their national character.

Notes

1. This essay is mainly based on my doctoral thesis in Art History, Catharina Nolin, *Till stadsbornas nytta och förlustande. Den offentliga parken i Sverige under 1800-talet* (Stockholm: Byggförlaget, 1999), and on my research concerning the architect Lars Israel Wahlman's role as a garden designer, *En svensk lustgårdskonst. Lars Israel Wahlman som trädgårdsarkitekt* (Stockholm: Signum, 2008). Both books have summaries in English.

2. Nils Uno Blomberg, "Om naturparker," *Svenska trädgårdsföreningens tidskrift* (1871): 45–48, 77–81.

3. Catharina Nolin, "Stockholm's Urban Parks: Meeting Places and Social Contexts in the Nineteenth and Early Twentieth Centuries," in *The European City and Green Space: London, Stockholm, Helsinki and St. Petersburg, 1850–2000,* ed. Peter Clark (Aldershot, UK: Ashgate, 2006), 116–21.

4. Orvar Löfgren, "Landscapes of the Mind," *Landscape Architecture in Scandinavia. Projects from Denmark, Sweden, Norway, Finland and Iceland, Topos* (2002): 42–50.

5. *Göteborgs stadsfullmäktiges handlingar* 6 (1874): 3–4.

6. For a good introduction to the Stockholm National Urban Park, see Peter Schantz, "The Formation of National Urban Parks: a Nordic Contribution to Sustainable Development?" in Clark, ed., *The European City and Green Space,* 159–74.

7. Anna Lindhagen, "Eriksdalslunden, ett stycke ännu bevarad Stockholmsnatur," *Sveriges Natur* (1912), 36–43; Rutger Sernander, *Stockholms natur* (Uppsala, Sweden: Almqvist & Wiksell, 1926).

8. Gustaf Näsström, *Dalarna som svenskt ideal* (Stockholm: Wahlström & Widstrand, 1937).

9. Carl Larsson, *Ett hem* (Stockholm: Alb. Bonnier, 1899).

10. Selma Lagerlöf, *Nils Holgerssons underbara resa genom Sverige* was published in two volumes in 1906 and 1907 (Stockholm: Alb. Bonnier), and in English as *The Wonderful Adventures of Nils* in 1907 and 1911 (New York: Doubleday, Page & Co.).

PART IV

HISTORY AND IDENTITY

Divided Spaces, Contested Pasts

The Gallipoli Peninsula Historical National Park

The Gallipoli Peninsula Historical National Park is located at the southern tip of the Gallipoli peninsula in the northern Aegean region of Turkey. Comprising thirty-three thousand hectares of forested, grazing, and grass lands, the park sits on a spit of land that is fifty miles long and defines the European shore of the ancient Hellespont, today referred to as the Dardanelles. In Turkish the name of the strategic strait that separates the two continents of Europe and Asia is the Çanakkale Boğaz, the "throat" of Çanakkale. Across the Dardanelles from the Gallipoli Peninsula Historical National Park is the Troad, the lands where Priam's legendary city of Troy, now an archaeological park, is located (fig. 1).

The historical significance of the Gallipoli peninsula is widely recognized both in Turkey and internationally as the site of the Gallipoli campaign in World War I.[1] For at least three of the countries who participated in that campaign—Australia, New Zealand, and Turkey—this peninsula and the events that happened between 3 November, 1914 and 9 January 1916 are regarded as formative in the birth of these nations. There were soldiers from many other countries who lost their lives in the Gallipoli battles, including almost twenty-two thousand British and ten thousand French; among these Allied troops were conscripts who were Canadian, Irish, Scottish, Maltese, Welsh, Tunisian, Egyptian, Gambian, Indian, and Senegalese.[2] But for Australians and New Zealanders the ill-fated landing at dawn on 25 April 1915, below the steep cliffs of Conkbayırı at Arıburnu, and the ensuing bravery of the Australian and

New Zealand Army Corps (ANZAC) in the face of such daunting obstacles, both topographic and military, have become a particularly integral part of these two countries' larger narratives about early statehood formation.[3] As one writer has remarked, "Battlefields became physical and imaginary spaces through which the Australians declared their presence in Europe and the world, as previous generations had done on their own continent. Landscapes represented both the new experience of war and the postwar national identity for Australians in terms of the fantastic simultaneity across time and space at the heart of modern collective identity."[4]

For many Turkish citizens today, the landscape of the Gallipoli peninsula is associated first and foremost with the heroism and tenacity demonstrated by the nation's founder, Mustafa Kemal Pasha, or Atatürk, in the face of a formidable adversary: Allied Europe. Since the signing of the Treaty of Lausanne in 1923, in which the European powers returned the lands on the Gallipoli peninsula to the Turks with a proviso to keep limited jurisdiction over the foreign cemeteries there, these battlegrounds have also been associated with other aspects of Atatürk's later, postwar achievements: the struggles to create a secularist nation, to preserve the territorial integrity of the land that comprises modern-day Turkey, and to promote Kemalism, the political "ism" that encapsulates the vision that Atatürk had for the future of Turkey.[5] Every school-age child in Turkey today is familiar with the iconic images of Atatürk fighting at the Gallipoli front, and each

127

FIG. 1. Map of the Gallipoli Peninsula Historical National Park, 2011. (Reprinted with permission of Rahmi N. Çelik)

is taught about the important episodes in the war and their corresponding locations in the national park, such as the place where Atatürk made a speech in which he ordered his regiment to stand up and die for their country.[6]

The Pre–World War I History of the Gallipoli Peninsula

The Gallipoli national park has had long and rich pre– and post–World War I pasts, but these are pasts which have often been overshadowed by the fame that has been ascribed to the Gallipoli landscape because of its role as the battleground and final resting place of at least one hundred and thirty thousand soldiers who died here during that war.[7] Indeed, the Gallipoli battles of World War I, known as the Çanakkale War in Turkey, constitute a very important chapter in the history of the Gallipoli peninsula, but this is not the only historical narrative that can be told about this landscape. Comparatively little of the pre– and post–World War I pasts of the region that is now the Gallipoli Peninsula Historical National Park have been the subject of much research either in Turkey or abroad.[8]

Located in the shadow of Troy, on the opposite shore of the Dardanelles, the very limited number of archaeological excavations on the Gallipoli peninsula is striking. However, several references about the ancient past and topography of the lands that today constitute the national park can be found in the works of Herodotus, Thucydides, Strabo, Xenophon, and others.[9] All describe events that occurred on the peninsula during its classical and earlier historical eras, but most historians, philologists, and archaeologists have focused inquiries and conducted excavations on the better known sites of the opposite shore, such as Troy or Alexandria Troas.[10] Heinrich Schliemann, the renowned German archaeologist, was an exception and led a series of brief and illicit archaeological campaigns on the Gallipoli peninsula in 1882 while he was excavating at Troy.[11] Schliemann was in search of what he believed was the tomb of Protosilaus, the first of Agamemnon's soldiers to perish in the Trojan war; from ancient writers he surmised that the tomb had to be on Cape Hellas, near the entrance to the present-day village and Ottoman fortress of Seddülbahir.[12] While exploring the center of the mound, known today as Karaağaç, Schliemann was run off the peninsula because he was suspected by the Ottoman military governor of the Dardanelles of using the excavation as a pretext to inspect the nearby fortress and a line of torpedoes that the Ottomans had recently sunk in the strait.[13]

The French military conducted, by comparison, more systematic excavations on the Gallipoli peninsula during and shortly after World War I. While digging trenches in the 1915 Gallipoli campaign, the officers, some of whom had been trained as archaeologists, were assisted by their Senegalese conscripts and uncovered pottery, pithoi, and stone sarcophagi from the ancient Greek necropolis of Elaeus, which was close to their base camp at Cape Hellas.[14]

In addition to the human casualties, both the landscape and the archaeological remains on the Gallipoli peninsula suffered immense-ly as a result of the continual bombardment and trenching during the nine months of the land offensive. With the end of the war and the signing of the Moudros Armistice on 30 October 1918, the Allied forces stationed five hundred French Senegalese troops at the Ottoman fortresses of Kilitbahir and Seddülbahir early in 1919. French archaeologists were able to return during 1921, 1922, and 1923 to the location of the alleged tomb of Protosilaus where Schliemann had worked forty years earlier. At this time it was possible for them to undertake more formal, scientific excavations.[15] Rather than the tomb of the mythic Greek warrior, they discovered at the "Protosilaus mound" remains from the Early Bronze Age and Middle Byzantine periods as well as the foundations of what they believed was a small Byzantine monastery, all evidence that the Gallipoli peninsula had been of some regional importance in the postclassical era (fig. 2).[16]

FIG. 2. The French archaeological excavations outside of the village of Seddülbahir in 1923, after the Gallipoli campaign in World War I, from *Le Tumulus dit Protesilas (Fouilles de Constantinople)*.

The Ottoman Era in Gallipoli

Access to the Çanakkale Straits and the lands that bordered the strategic waterway of the Dardanelles was also coveted by the Ottomans as they expanded their holdings into Europe.[17] The capture of the peninsula played an important role in the fourteenth- and fifteenth-century expansion of the empire, giving the Turks their first foothold on the European continent. From the time of the Ottoman conquest of Thrace in the fourteenth century through the seventeenth century, the protection of the straits was of paramount importance for the Ottomans. Frequently besieged in this western frontier region by the Venetian navy, the Gallipoli peninsula became a key territory in the military and naval strategies of successive generations of sultans. Along with the construction or repair of military architecture on the peninsula, the Ottoman officials also engaged in the construction of mosques, baths, tombs, waterworks, and cemeteries to support Ottoman villages such as Eceabat, Seddülbahir, and Kilitbahir that are located within the borders of today's national park.[18]

Mehmed II, the Ottoman conqueror of Constantinople, made sure that the Dardanelles would be secure from foreign invasion by constructing a pair of fortresses at the narrowest part of the straits: Kilitbahir on the European side of the Dardanelles, which is currently within the borders of the Gallipoli park, and the Kale-i Sultaniye, or the Çimenlik fortress, on the opposite Asian shore, in the present-day city of Çanakkale. In the seventeenth century the mother of sultan Mehmed IV, Hadice Turhan Sultan, still plagued by the Venetian navy's incursions into the Dardanelles, constructed the two fortresses of Kumkale and Seddülbahir at the far western entrance to the Dardanelles. This additional pair of fortresses was intended to provide more protection to the vital channel which led to the empire's capital.[19] Throughout the eighteenth and nineteenth centuries, the Venetian threat to the lands of the Gallipoli peninsula was replaced by a Russian one, as it was hoped by the czar that the conquest of the two narrow straits—the Bosphorus and the Dardanelles—that connected the Black Sea to the Aegean would provide the Russian navy and traders with easier access to the warm water ports of the Mediterranean.

With the beginning of World War I, the Gallipoli peninsula entered a new chapter of turmoil. The Greek and Turkish civilian populations in the villages on the peninsula had fled or been evacuated just prior to the battles of 1915. The few Greeks who returned to their homes there after the battles of World War I had ended did so for a short time only, as most emigrated permanently after the Greek defeats in 1922 during the Turkish War of Independence.[20] After the signing of the Treaty of Lausanne on 24 July 1923, the migration of Turks from the Balkan regions of Eastern Europe into western Thrace, which had begun in the late nineteenth century, now accelerated as the result of the relative stability that had been brought to a region which had seen so much demographic displacement and upheaval during the Balkan Wars of 1912 and 1913, World War I, and the Turkish War of Independence.[21] Turkish refugees, the majority from Romania and Bulgaria, continued to arrive in the new lands of the Turkish Republic throughout the 1930s, and many from Romania repopulated the villages on the peninsula, while the Bulgarian Turks settled in the villages on the opposite Asian shore.[22] The oral history project conducted in this region from 1999 to 2002 revealed that most of these new migrants survived by farming among the makeshift graves of the many dead who were buried in their fields and by selling the salvaged ordnance that remained from the war. New residents built their first homes on the peninsula by harvesting the crumbling masonry structures, such as the Ottoman fortifications, and the few trees that were still standing after the war.[23] Several of the descendants of these early postwar migrants from the Balkans still live and farm in the national park, such as the Fındık family who are fiercely proud of their homeland. To commemorate the historical events that have

transpired in the national park where they re-
side, they have named their three sons Savaş,
Barış, and Zafer: War, Peace, and Victory.

Commemoration Begins: Monuments and Cemeteries for the Allies

The earliest efforts to organize formal and
permanent commemorative monuments and
cemeteries in the Gallipoli battlefields were
undertaken immediately after the armistice
in 1918 when the British Directorate of Graves
Registration and Enquiries was formed under
the direction of the Englishman Major Carbine
and the Australian Captain Hughes and Captain Biggwither from New Zealand and housed
in the barracks at the Kilitbahir fortress of
Mehmed II.[24] This first group worked for two
years on the peninsula, attempting to identify bodies and bring the remains of soldiers
to designated central burial areas. The work of
the directorate was taken over in 1920 by the
British Commonwealth War Graves Commission (CWGC), known at the time as the Imperial War Graves Commission, which planned
for thirty-one cemeteries and five Allied commemorative monuments to be constructed on
the peninsula.[25] The early British memorials on
the peninsula were created by the architect Sir
John Burnet (1857–1938), a Scot who had designed memorials and cemeteries for the Commonwealth War Graves Commission in Palestine.[26]

Many of the Ottoman subjects who remained
on the peninsula immediately after the armistice, or who had fled other war-torn areas,
including Bolshevik Russia, were employed by
the CWGC in the road building, quarrying, and
stone masonry work generated by the memorializing process of the Allies (fig. 3).[27] Thomas J.
Pemberton, an employee of the CWGC, pointed out that the commemorative architecture,
particularly at Cape Hellas, was unique in its
intentions because it was not a "stone erected as a sign of victory over a conquered race.
. . . Having suffered this splendid failure, Britain has had the courage to ignore the defeat
and commemorate in stone those who never
questioned the worth or wisdom of the idea."[28]

Acutely aware that a delicate balance had to
be struck in the religious iconography used in
any commemorative architecture erected on
the peninsula, where the majority of the fallen
had been Ottoman Muslims, Pemberton wrote
"that we have no desire to flourish the emblems
of our religion before their eyes; that in thus
commemorating our dead we do not intrude a
single note of military triumph."[29] The accomplishments of the CWGC were, Pemberton concluded hopefully, "a wonderful achievement.
Perhaps these cemeteries and these memorials
will remain as the barometer of our relations
with Islam. If they remain undisturbed we shall
know that nothing is seriously wrong in the
East" (fig. 4).[30]

Replanting the Peninsula

In addition to erecting concrete and stone
memorials and gravestones on the Gallipoli
landscape, the CWGC also made concerted efforts to cultivate several species of plants from
Australia and New Zealand under the direction of the horticulturist R. Kett.[31] Noting that
the Australian blue gum (eucalyptus) trees
had migrated to the Gallipoli peninsula in the
mid-nineteenth century, Pemberton remarked
that this invasive species of tree had pros-
pered along the European and African coast
"so much so that the new generations seem to
have forgotten that these trees are strangers,
and they claim them as their own."[32] By the
end of the war little but shrubbery remained on
the battlefields, as most usable flora had been
harvested for wartime needs. Both Kett and
Pemberton made a concerted effort to import
several antipodean species of plants to reforest
the Gallipoli peninsula, and the latter reported
enthusiastically, "Thousands of young trees
are growing in the excellent nurseries at Anzac, Kelia Bay, and Hellas, and will be planted
out in due course, but not in the cemeteries
themselves (fig. 5).[33]

Describing the monument erected by the New
Zealanders at Conkbayırı, and its surrounding
vegetation, Pemberton reveals a somewhat less
subtle delight in the more prominent mark that
he anticipated would be made upon the Gal-

FIG. 3. The stone quarries of Ulgardere were mined for the building materials needed for the commemorative architecture built on the Gallipoli peninsula, c. 1923. (Commonwealth War Graves Commission)

FIG. 4. The British War Memorial at Cape Hellas, c. 1926. (Commonwealth War Graves Commission)

lipoli landscape by the plantings of the CWGC. At the base of the monument was a "little shrub which none but a New Zealander would give particular notice. It is a *manuka* tree three feet high. . . . Next year, it is hoped, the little white flower will bloom beside those who loved it so well and who rest here."[34]

A contemporary Australian scholar, Peter Slade, has remarked on the aggressive planting agenda undertaken by the Australians on the peninsula, which included the placement of their native manuka, *Leptospermum scoparium,* at the gravesites of their dead. "Presumably they (the manuka trees) are there to keep the soldiers company. It is difficult to categorize this act. . . . Certainly the Gallipoli Peninsula looks very much like parts of the New Zealand coastline, particularly around Wellington, as if it represents an attempt to transpose a social view of a landscape to another geographical site."[35]

Pemberton's and Kett's efforts to symbolically mark the land with what would today be classified as invasive species of plants and trees, and remember the lives of Australians and New Zealanders that had been lost, were echoed in the actions of soldiers returning from the war who carried back to their native lands remembrances from the peninsula

where they had fought. Gallipoli's pine cones were among the many souvenirs that traveled across the world in the letters sent home or in the rucksacks of departing soldiers.[36]

Commemmoration Begins: The Turks

During the battles fought on the peninsula and in the immediate aftermath of the war, only a few makeshift monuments were erected by the Ottomans on the Gallipoli landscape itself to commemorate the soldiers who had died there. However, official Ottoman commemorative days were designated as early as 1916 and cemeteries were established that same year in the more protected inland towns held by the Ottomans, such as Biga, located on the Asian shore of the Sea of Marmara fifty-eight miles to the north of Çanakkale. Here, in March 1916, official Ottoman correspondence reveals that planning was underway for a cemetery to accommodate more than two hundred Ottoman soldiers who had died in the battles at Seddül-bahir and Anafartalar and the adjacent military hospital.[37] On the peninsula, at the battle site the Allies referred to as "the Nek," Pemberton describes one of the earliest makeshift examples of an Ottoman memorial as "a pyramidal block of concrete, surmounted by five live shells, and standing only some fifteen feet

FIG. 5. The post-wartime nurseries containing antipodean plants at Kelia Bay, c. 1923. (Commonwealth War Graves Commission)

in height. Its surface is rough and it is partly formed of sniper's masks."[38] This early commemorative monument, erected in 1919 at the site of one of the campaign's most ferocious battles, would become by 1934 the more permanent Turkish Monument to Sergeant Mehmet, the Mehmet Çavuş Anıtı.[39] Official committees had been formed in the late 1920s by the newly formed Turkish republican government to supervise the construction of cemeteries and commemorative monuments for those Ottoman soldiers who had lost their lives in the war, but apart from some minor Turkish monuments erected in the late 1930s and the early 1940s, the Gallipoli landscape was left relatively unadorned by the newly formed national government of Turkey. Navigating around the peninsula continued to be a challenge in these decades, and access overland to the different parts of the historic battlefields was difficult at best.[40] The Turkish military continued to have jurisdiction over the peninsula; several areas, among these the fortress of Seddülbahir at Cape Hellas, served as military bases and were completely inaccessible to the public.[41]

Plans and proposals for a larger memorial structure to honor the Turkish dead had been submitted during the 1930s, but no substantive action was taken until 1944, when the Turkish Ministry of National Defense decided that the Turks who had died on the Gallipoli peninsula should have a more substantial commemorative structure built in their honor. An architectural competition was organized to select a design for a major Turkish monument which would be called the Martyrs of the Çanakkale War.[42] Of the thirty-seven entries, the design of Doğan Erginbaş, Ismail Utkular, and Feridun Kip from Istanbul Technical University was chosen.[43] Corruption and inadequate funding plagued the project, whose first foundations were laid on 19 April 1954. Most of the monument, a square concrete baldachin that rises one hundred and thirty feet, was completed by 21 August 1960. Neither the architects nor planning board paid much heed to the fact that the great commemorative monument, and the 6,730-square-foot area planned around it, was erected on top of the ancient remains of antique Elaeus.[44]

In the 1960s several other monuments to the Turkish dead were erected at different points within the park and efforts were made to better organize the Turkish cemeteries. At this time the peninsula also became more accessible to vehicular traffic, and gradually a nationalist pilgrimage route emerged that would be followed by every Turkish schoolchild or new military recruit who came to pay respects to ancestors at this small spit of land where Turkey was born. The construction of commemorative monuments by the Turkish government in the national park has been perceived by some visitors as reflecting a kind of competition among memorializing monuments. One author has observed, "Turkish and Commonwealth memorial sites are located close to each other on the cliffs over the once disputed beaches, and giant statues of Turkish heroes stand face to face with the Commonwealth Graves Commission's neoclassical obelisks, locked in parallel monologues."[45]

The Formation of a National Park on the Gallipoli Peninsula

The groundwork was laid for the formation of national parks in Turkey in the mid-1950s with the establishment of NGOs such as the Foundation for Turkish Nature Conservation (TTKD) in 1955, and the Turkish government's signing of international agreements such as the 1951 Agreement on the Establishment of European and Mediterranean Plant Protection Organization.[46] By the 1970s the environment and its protection became an official part of Turkey's 1973–78 Five-Year Development Plan. It was during this time, in 1973, that the Gallipoli Peninsula Historical National Park was designated as a national park. An interesting chapter in the formation of Turkey's national parks is the collaboration of the United States National Park Service with the State Planning Organization in Turkey, under the direction of the head of the National Parks Department, Zekai Bayer. The project, a United States National Park Service and the United States Agency for

International Development (USAID) effort, was intended to create plans for twelve national parks in Turkey.[47] While Troy was one of the sites that was studied and proposed as a national park, Gallipoli was not included in this park planning mission, perhaps due to its sensitive status as a military area and the stipulations about the Allied burial grounds in the Lausanne Treaty. Linn Spaulding, one of the members of the U.S. team, wrote, "When we were working on Troy, one Turkish member of our team wanted to join Gallipoli and Troy in a much larger park to be named the European Aggression National Historic Park."[48] A separate planning process for the Gallipoli park was, however, initiated in the 1970s and the long-term development plan that had been used to manage the park was again updated in 1980; another twenty monuments were added to the park's commemorative repertoire.[49]

Conflicting Identities: The Gallipoli Peninsula Historical National Park since the 1990s

The Gallipoli historical park, so often associated with the policies of the Turkish government, and governed locally by the Turkish military police, has at times suffered because of its iconic status as the birthplace of the Turkish Republic and the strength of the Turkish military. On 25 July 1994, 4,049 hectares of the park's pine forests burned, and there was suspicion that the park had become the target of antigovernment arsonists. Arson continued to be a concern throughout the 1990s as strife in the southeastern region of Turkey flared up occasionally in violent acts committed on the opposite side of the country that targeted the symbolic landscape of Gallipoli. To improve the protection and management strategies of the park and deal with an increasing number of visitors, both local and foreign, another phase of updating the long-term management plan was initiated in 1996. At this time, the president of Turkey, Süleyman Demirel, became closely involved with the project and promoted the idea of hosting an international architectural competition for the Gallipoli peninsula that was

intended to create a "supra" identity for the landscape as a place of peace: a "peace park."[50]

The international architectural competition to restructure and recast the Gallipoli Peninsula Historical National Park as a peace park was organized by Professor R. Raci Bademli and his team from Middle Eastern Technical University in Ankara. The documents sent out to contestants in the competition asked those who wished to participate to think about "focusing on the landscape/seascape without altering it, creating atmospheres rather than buildings, proposing new uses and activities, helping people think and feel peace through their experiences and exploration, and sufficiently integrating local communities into the park's activities."[51] The conceptual project that won the competition was designed by the Norwegian architectural firm of Anne-Stine Reine and Lasse Hvatum Brogger, precisely because it was seen as being the least interventionist of all the entries. But because Bademli, the inspirational engine behind the Peace Park project, passed away in 2003, and the main political figure in the government who supported the project, President Süleyman Demirel, came to the end of his term, the plan was never implemented.

The extensive updated management plan for the park, called the Long-Term Development Plan (UGDP) and generated by R. Raci Bademli's team, was published in 2002 and has since then served the Turkish Ministry of Forest and Water Management and the Turkish Directorate of Nature Conservation and National Parks as a guide for the development of the park. Now more than a decade old, the plan needs to be reassessed in light of the political, social, environmental, and cultural changes that have occurred in the park. While still referred to informally as a "peace park," this title was never officially sanctioned as a supra-identity and has been downplayed by the Turkish Ministry of Forest and Water Management because it is perceived to be a romantic and inappropriate appellation with which to represent the sacrifices made by the Turkish soldiers during the war.[52]

While the winning plan of the Peace Park competition had advocated a largely noninterventionist approach to the landscape of the peninsula, the years since the competition have witnessed a much more active policy of intervention in the Gallipoli park by the current Turkish government and other stakeholders in the region. Some of this work has been a response to accommodate the growing numbers of Turkish tourists who are attending the annual commemorative ceremonies on 18 March, the day of a major Turkish naval victory over the Allies in World War I. Australian and New Zealand tourists also flock to the region each 25 April, ANZAC day; there were approximately 4,500 in 1995, 7,500 in 2009, and at least 6,000 in 2012.[53] Much controversy occurred in 2005 over the construction of new and wider roads and parking lots in the ANZAC region of the peninsula that were intended to provide better access and accommodations for the flood of tourists that visit the park on the annual commemorative dates. Erosion of the shoreline at Arıburnu continues to be a cause of concern and impetus for international cooperation.[54]

Different stakeholders, both governmental and private, have undertaken several new projects on the Gallipoli peninsula in the past decade, from the restoration of Ottoman mosques, baths, tombs, fortifications, an open prayer area and dervish convent to the creation of new museums and visitor centers. In 2005 the Turkish Ministry of Forest and Water Management opened a visitor center in Kilye, at the northern entrance to the park; an immense simulation center covering an area of 43,055 square feet replaced the original Kabatepe museum in the spring of 2012; and at least two private museums have opened in the villages of Alcıtepe and Seddülbahir. The collections in both of these private museums are comprised of war memorabilia, but the former, the Çanakkale Savaşları Canlı Tarih Galerisi (Gallery of the Living History of the Çanakkale War), has a diorama of a soldier at the front who is praying, complete with the continual recording of the prayer as part of the didactic display.[55]

Prayer has always been a part of the visit to the graves of the Turkish soldiers in Gallipoli but has become an increasingly prominent activity in the past decade; for some visitors it is the reason to go to the park. For the more devout Turkish tourist, the itinerary through the park is no longer that of a nationalist pilgrimage route of war monuments constructed by the secularist state, but now includes visits to pray at the different Islamic sites on the peninsula. For the guides who participate in this faith-based tourism, explanations about the successes and failures of the battles of World War I highlight religious devotion and angels as significant factors in the Ottoman victory. Tourist brochures distributed at the Kilye visitor center that advertise the must-see sites of the Gallipoli region and its environs show an itinerary which now conflates the traditional "secularist national" pilgrimage with a more religious one. One such tourist brochure displays at the top of the page an image of the Abide, the largest commemorative monument to the Turkish dead discussed above, but also given front-page billing is the recently restored tomb in the town of Gallipoli of a minor Muslim saint, Bayraklı Baba, or "Father Flag," from the fifteenth century, who was martyred because he ate the Ottoman flag rather than allow it to be captured by the enemy. Placed next to this tomb, now draped with the modern Turkish flag, is an open-air prayer area, or namazgah, from the fifteenth century. While the restoration of previously neglected Ottoman-era monuments is an important step in expanding and enriching the historical narrative on the peninsula, these projects have been coupled with a growing and increasingly organized faith-based tourism to the region which some feel is threatening the identity of the Gallipoli park as a symbol of the secularist beliefs that had been promoted by earlier governments in Turkey.

The annual 18 March ceremonies on the peninsula which celebrate a key naval victory of the Turks over the Allied forces in World War I have become a staging ground for a new kind of battle over the identity of the Gallipoli park. This annual ceremony is now immensely popular and is attracting large crowds of Turks from all over the nation. The slogan that is associated with this ceremony is "Çanakkale geçilmez," which means, in its original usage, that the straits—the Dardanelles—will never be breached by a foreign enemy. This is a historical reference to the Turkish opposition to the Allied forces of Europe in World War I during the latter's efforts to "Force the Narrows," the short crossing between the shores of Kilitbahir on the European side of the straits and the present-day city of Çanakkale on the opposite Asian coast. But in the 18 March ceremonies of the past decade, this slogan has taken on different meanings for the supporters of a range of Turkish political parties who see themselves either as followers of Atatürk and his secularist vision for Turkey, or as supporters of the present government which is perceived as more sympathetic to Islamic beliefs. Layered onto this already complicated rhetoric is a general protest against what is perceived as intervention by foreign powers in the national affairs of Turkey over issues that range from European Union candidacy to allegations of genocide to the Turkish role in the wars in Iraq, Syria, and other neighboring countries.

As there are no formal mechanisms in the Gallipoli park for keeping track of the numbers and origins of tourists to the peninsula, these observations are impressionistic. However, it is increasingly clear that the landscape of the Gallipoli national park is again becoming the site of various contemporary and frequently conflicting political agendas, both national and international. The potential richness that the narratives of the peninsula's "other" pasts can offer—the prehistoric, ancient, Byzantine, and Ottoman—continues to be neglected, as is the history of the region in the immediate post–World War I years, and contemporary life on the peninsula. Too often the projects built in the park, such as the 2005 Kilye visitor center and 2012 simulation center at Kabatepe, have prioritized the needs of the seasonal national and international tourists at the expense of the year-round permanent local population.

There are undoubtedly more historical lay-ers to be discovered and archaeological excavations undertaken in the Gallipoli Peninsula Historical National Park in the near future, which will further enrich our understanding of this region and its complex past. Whether peace will become one of the many layers of the park's official identities is still to be decided, but the past of the Gallipoli peninsula should not be reduced to any single narrative. Similarly any future management plan for the park should address the needs and the problems of the entire park, not only the ANZAC region, while carefully navigating the agendas of the Gallipoli park's many stakeholders. This is critical in what promises to be a challenging battle to preserve this extraordinary cultural and historical landscape.

Notes

1. For a general bibliography concerning the history of the Gallipoli campaign, see the *Imperial War Museum, Gallipoli Bibliography* at http://www.iwm .org.uk/upload/package/2/gallipoli/infoopen.htm; Fred R. Van Hartesveldt, *The Dardanelles Campaign, 1915: Historiography and Annotated Bibliography* (Westport, Conn.: Greenwood Press, 1997). In Turkey the battles fought on the Gallipoli peninsula and on the Asian side of the Dardanelles are referred to as the Çanakkale War. For a bibliography of Turkish sources, see http://www.turkeyswar.com/ bibliography/bibliography.htm.

2. David Dutton, "'Docile supernumerary': A French Perspective on Gallipoli," 86–98; Keith Jeffery, "Gallipoli and Ireland," 98–110, in *Gallipoli Making History,* ed. J. Macleod (London: Frank Cass, 2004).

3. Commonwealth Department of Veterans' Affairs, "*From Gallipoli to Dili: The Spirit of Anzac,* http://www.dva.gov.au/commemorations/ documents/education/spirit_of_anzac.pdf; Brad West, "Travel, Ritual, and Memory: Exploring International Civil Religious Pilgrimage," *Proceedings Submission, 2003 Hawaii Conference on Social Sciences* (June 2003): 1–17, http://www.hicsocial.org/ Social2003Proceedings/Brad%20West.pdf; Peter Slade, "Gallipoli Thanatourism: The Meaning of Anzac," *Annals of Tourism Research* 30, no. 4 (2003): 779–94; Bruce Scates, "In Gallipoli's Shadow: Pilgrimage, Memory, Mourning and the Great War," *Australian Historical Studies* 119 (2002): 1–21; for

the Gallipoli Association website, see http://www
.gallipoli-association.org.; and for the official Australian government website, see http://www
.anzacsite.gov.au/.

4. Peter Hoffenberg, "Landscape, Memory and
the Australian War Experience, 1915–18," *Journal
of Contemporary History* 36, no. 1 (January 2001):
111–31, quotation on 112.

5. For the stipulations in the treaty about the
war graves, see http://wwi.lib.byu.edu/index.php/
Treaty_of_Lausanne (Section II, Graves, Articles
124–136); for a history and definition of Kemalism,
see Sinan Ciddi, *Kemalism in Turkish Politics: The
Republican People's Party, Secularism and Nationalism* (New York: Routledge, 2009).

6. In Atatürk's now famous words: "I don't order
you to attack, I order you to die. In the time which
passes until we die, other troops and commanders
can take our place." Cited and translated on the official Turkish government site at http://www.atam
.gov.tr/index.php?Page=DergiIcerik&IcerikNo=942;
see also Edward Erikson, "Strength against Weakness: Ottoman Military Effectiveness at Gallipoli,
1915," *The Journal of Military History* 65, no. 4 (October 2001): 981–1011; Edward Erikson, *Ordered to
Die: A History of the Ottoman Army in the First World
War* (Westport, Conn.: Greenwood Press, 2001).

7. TC Milli Savumna Bakanlığı, *Şehitlerimiz* (Our
martyrs; Ankara: MSB Personel Daire Başkanlığı
Yayını, 1998), 5; see R. Raci Bademli and K. Burak
Sarı et al., *Gelibolu Yarımada Tarihi Milli Parkı (Barış
Parkı) Uzun Devreli Gelişme Plan Çalışmaları [UGDP]*
(The Gallipoli Peninsula Historical National Park
[Peace Park] long-term development plan; Ankara:
Middle Eastern Technical University, 2002), 48–53,
for the debates concerning the statistics for the
numbers of Turkish dead, missing, and wounded.

8. The results of the survey and excavation in
Eceabat/ Maydos, which is located at the entrance to
the Gallipoli National Park, can be found in A. Çay-
lak Türker, "The Place and Importance of Maydos in
Hellespont during the Byzantine Period," 13–20; "A
Byzantine City in the Middle Section of Hellespont:
Koila," 21–30; "Eceabat'ta Ortaçağ ve Türk Döne-
mine Ait Arkeolojik Veriler" (Archaeological finds
related to the medieval and Turkish eras in Eceabat),
31–52; Göksel Sazcı, "Tarihöncesi Dönemler'den
Antik Çağ Sonuna Kadar Eceabat/Maydos" (Eceabat/
Maydos from the prehistoric eras to the antique),
1–12, all in *Eceabat Değerleri Sempozyumu,* 18 Mart
Üniversitesi (Çanakkale: 18 Mart Üniversitesi,
2008). Prior to these surveys, Mehmet Özdoğan had
worked in the region conducting surface surveys of
the peninsula. See Mehmet Özdoğan, "Prehistoric

Sites in Gelibolu," *Anadolu Araştırmaları* 10 (1986):
51–71. For information on the joint historical
archaeological survey of the ANZAC battlefields that
was initiated in 2010 by the University of Melbourne
and 18 Mart (March) Üniversitesi in Çanakkale, see
Antonio Sagona, "The Anzac Ari Burnu Battlefield:
New Perspectives and Methodologies in History and
Archaeology," *Australian Historical Studies* 42 (2011):
313–36.

9. Herodotus, *The Histories,* trans. A. D. Godley
(Cambridge, Mass.: Harvard University Press, 1920);
Thucydides, *The Peloponnesian War,* trans Richard
Crawley (London: J. M. Dent, 1910); Strabo, *Geog-
raphy,* ed. H. C. Hamilton and W. Falconer (London:
George Bell and Sons, 1903); Xenophon, "Hellenica,"
in *Xenophon in Seven Volumes,* trans. Carleton L.
Brownson (Cambridge, Mass.: Harvard University
Press, 1985); Pausanias, *Description of Greece,* trans.
W. H. S. Jones and H. A. Ormerod (Cambridge, Mass.:
Harvard University Press, 1918).

10. W. Bates, "Archaeological News," *American
Journal of Archaeology* 20, no. 3 (1916): 357–81;
W. Bates, "Archaeological News," *American Journal of
Archaeology* 24, no. 1 (1920): 85–119.

11. Heinrich Schliemann, *Troja: Results of the Latest Researches and Discoveries on the Site of Homer's
Troy, and in the Heroic Tumuli and Other Sites Made
in the Year 1882; and a Narrative of a Journey in the
Troad in 1881* (New York: Harper and Brothers,
1884), 254–57; Heinrich Schliemann, *Troy and Its
Remains: A Narrative of Researches and Discoveries Made on the Site of Ilium and in the Trojan Plain,*
ed. Philip Smith (London: John Murray, 1875), 258,
254–62; Özdoğan, "Prehistoric Sites in Gelibolu," 54.

12. This was based on the descriptions by the
ancient writers Pausanius and Herodotus, who both
mention the tomb of Protosilaus.

13. Schliemann, *Troy and Its Remains,* 254–62.

14. This area is called Eski Hisarlık today. Elaeus
was probably an Aeolian or Attic foundation which
was established after 600 BCE. Possibly an Athenian
colony, it was issuing coins by the fourth century
BCE. See B. Isaac, *The Greek Settlements in Thrace
until the Macedonian Conquest* (Leiden: E. J. Brill,
1986), 192–93; Stanley Casson, *Macedonia, Thrace
and Illyria: Their Relations to Greece from the Earliest
Times Down to the Time of Philip Son of Amyntas*
(Oxford: Oxford University Press, 1926), 223. For the
publication of these early finds along with photographs, see the reports of J. Chamonard, F. Courby,
and E. Dhorme, "Corps Expeditionnaire d'Orient:
Fouilles archeologiques sur l'emplacement de la
nécropole d'Éléonte de Thrace" (The Expeditionary
Corps of the Orient: Archaeological excavations at

the location of the necropolis of Éléonte in Thrace), *Bulletin de Correspondance Hellenique* 39 (1915): 135–240; Angelika Waiblinger, "La Nécropole D'Éléonte," *Comptes rendu des séances de l'Académie des Inscriptions et Belles Lettres* (The Necropolis of Éléonte" Conference Proceedings of the Academy of Inscriptions and Belles Lettres)(Paris: Académie des Inscriptions et Belles Lettres, 1973), 843–57; John Boardman, *The Greeks Overseas* (London: Penguin, 1964).

15. Robert Demangel, *Le Tumulus dit Protesilas (Fouilles de Constantinople;* The Tumulus known as Protesilas [Excavations of Constantinople]; Paris: Edition de Boccard, 1926); *L' Illustration,* 5 June 1915, 579–81; Eric Zurcher, "The Ottoman Empire and the Armistice of Moudros," in *At the Eleventh Hour: Reflections, Hopes and Anxieties at the Closing of the Great War,* ed. Hugh Cecil and Peter H. Liddle (London: Leo Cooper, 1998), 266–75.

16. For information about more recent excavations, see Lucienne Thys-Şenocak, Rahmi N. Çelik, and Carolyn Aslan, "Research at the Ottoman Fortress of Seddülbahir, 2005, 2006 Seasons," in *International Archaeology, Research and Archaeometry Symposium Proceedings* (Ankara: T. C. Ministry of Culture and Tourism, 2008); Lucienne Thys-Şenocak and Carolyn Aslan "Narratives of Destruction and Construction: The Complex Cultural Heritage of the Gallipoli Peninsula," *Archaeology of Destruction,* ed. Lila Rokoczy (Cambridge: Cambridge Scholars Press, 2008), 29–47.

17. Halil Inalcik, *Encyclopedia of Islam,* 2nd ed., s.v. "Gelibolu."

18. Research on the Ottoman remains of the Gallipoli peninsula is relatively minimal and still in its infancy. For some recent work, see A. Osman Uysal, "Kilitbahir (Kilidü'l Bahr) 'de Tarihi Doku ve İki Hamam" (The historical fabric and two baths in Kilitbahir), in *Eceabat Değerleri Sempozyumu,* 53–76; A. Osman Uysal, "Gelibolu ve Çevresindeki Türk Eserleri Hakkında Tespitler" (Findings about the Turkish works in Gelibolu and its environs), in *Gelibolu Değerleri Sempozyumu* (Çanakkale: 18 Mart Üniversitesi, 2008), 101–32.

19. L. Thys-Şenocak, *Ottoman Women Builders: The Architectural Patronage of Hadice Turhan Sultan* (Aldershot: Ashgate, 2006), 106–86. See also the project website at http://www.seddülbahir-kumkale.org.

20. Justin McCarthy, *Muslims and Minorities: The Population of Ottoman Anatolia at the End of the Empire* (New York: New York University Press, 1983), 130–31. Immediately after the war, the Venizelos Greek government constructed some small houses for Greek refugees, but these homes were then abandoned and moved into by Turks. See Thomas J. Pemberton, *Gallipoli Today* (London: E. Benn, 1926), 27.

21. For the statistical analyses of this migration, see Justin McCarthy, *Population History of the Middle East and the Balkans* (Istanbul: Isis Press, 2002), 41–63.

22. Immigration statistics for the Dardanelles region show that from 1934 to 1940, 92 percent of the migrants from the Balkans were coming from Bulgaria and Romania. See ibid., 61.

23. Lucienne Thys-Şenocak and I. Cerem Cenker, "Local and National Memories of Turkish Fortresses," in *Oral History and Public Memories,* ed. Paula Hamilton and Linda Shopes (Philadelphia: Temple University Press, 2008), 65–86.

24. Pemberton, *Gallipoli Today,* 39.

25. At the end of 1918 the British Army, as a provision of the armistice, returned to the peninsula to clear the unburied bodies still on the Gallipoli battlefields.

26. The National Memorial of New Zealand at Chunuk Bair (Conkbayırı) was designed by S. Hurst Seager, a New Zealand architect.

27. Pemberton, *Gallipoli Today,* 43–44; Aydin Ibrahimov and Fetay Soykan, "Gelibolu'da Ruslar: Yaşam ve Etkisi" (The Russians in Gelibolu: Life and impact), in *Gelibolu Değerleri Sempozyumu,* 281–86.

28. Pemberton, *Gallipoli Today,* 46, 112. Most of the stones for the commemorative architecture and cemeteries were quarried from Ulgardere (Ilgardere), a site eight miles to the north of Kilya Bay; Pemberton believed that the stones that were used in the walls of Troy were also quarried from this location.

29. Ibid., 110.

30. Ibid., 111.

31. Ibid., 64.

32. Ibid., 65.

33. Ibid., 96–97.

34. Ibid.

35. Peter Slade, "Gallipoli Thanatourism: The Meaning of ANZAC," *Annals of Tourism Research* 30, no. 4 (2003): 779–94, quotation on 791.

36. "Champion Trees in Commonwealth War Cemeteries," http://www.cwgc.org/admin/files/ CHAMPIONTREES.pdf. Peter Slade has commented on the exportation of pine trees from the Gallipoli battlefields to Australia and New Zealand, and questions the claim that seeds from the Lone Pine, one of the primary battle sites of the peninsula, were taken back by soldiers to be planted throughout Australia, stating that the last tree in that area was felled on 6 August 1915 by the Turks for use as charcoal. See Slade, "Gallipoli Thanatourism," 790; Peter

Hoffenberg, "Landscape, Memory and the Australian War Experience, 1915–18," *Journal of Contemporary History* 36, no. 1 (January 2001): 125.

37. Zekeriya Türkmen, Ahmet Çalışkan, and Fatma Ilhan, *Çanakkale Savaşı Anıtları ve Şehitlikleri* (The monuments and martyrs' graves of the Çanakkale War; Ankara: Genelkurmay Basımevi, 2007). For the Biga cemetery, see BOA, (Basbakanlık Osmanlı Arşivi), DH.UMVM (Dahiliye Nezareti Umur-u Mahalliye ve Vilayat Müdüriyeti Evrak Vi137/24), 19 March 1916.

38. Pemberton, *Gallipoli Today,* 38.

39. See http://www.canakkale.gov.tr/anit_sehitlik_mezarlik/mehmet_Cavus.htm.

40. Interview on 27 June 2008 with the late Süleyman Dirvana, a physician who had served at the Seddülbahir fortress in the 1930s and who returned several times thereafter by boat to treat the residents.

41. Our surveying and documentation team, from Koç University and Istanbul Technical University, began working at the Seddülbahir fortress during the first summer that the Turkish military vacated the premises, June 1997. For more information about the project, see http://www.seddulbahir-kumkale.org.

42. "Zafer ve Meçhul Asker Anıtına ait musabaka projeleri" (Competitive projects for the Monument to the Victorious and Unknown Soldier), *Arkitekt* (March 1944): 52–65, 74–75.

43. Ertuğrul Ceylan, "Çanakkale Şehitler Anıtı" (The monument to the Çanakkale martyrs), *Cumhuriyet* 10 July 2005; interview on 10 April 2008 with Ertuğrul Ceylan, lawyer for the Committee for the Assistance for the Construction of the Monument to the Çanakkale War Martyrs.

44. Bademli and Sarı et al., *Gelibolu Yarımada Tarihi Milli Parkı (Barış Parkı) Uzun Devreli Gelişme Plan Çalışmaları (UGDP),* 90–91.

45. Rosie Ayliffe, Marc Dublin, and John Gawthrop, *Turkey: The Rough Guide* (London: Harrap Columbus, 1991), as cited in Peter Gough, "Heroes' Groves to Parks of Peace: Landscapes of Remembrance, Protest and Peace," *Vortex* 3, http://www.vortex.uwe.ac.uk/places_of_peace/peacepks.htm.

46. Kamuran Guçlu and Faris Karahan, "A Review: The History of Conservation Programs and Development of the National Parks Concept in Turkey," *Biodiversity and Conservation* 13 (2004): 1371–90.

47. E-mail correspondence on 5 March 2009 with Hugh Miller, one of the U.S. National Park Service planners who worked on this project.

48. E-mail correspondence on 28 March 2009 with Linn Spaulding, one of the U.S. National Park Service planners who worked on this project.

49. H. Aytaç "Gelibolu Yarımadası Tarihi Milli Park" (The Gelibolu Peninsula Historical National Park), http://b.domaindlx.com/omodergi/20051sy/gya_tmp.htm.

50. Bademli and Sarı et al., *Gelibolu Yarımada Tarihi Milli Parkı (Barış Parkı) Uzun Devreli Gelişme Plan Çalışmaları (UGDP),* 1–4. The goal to create a supra-identity of peace for this park is stated on the competition website: "the competition seeks from entrants an environment which will give war the place it warrants in a setting dedicated to peace. The Peace Park Competition looks to the new millennium for inspiration and aims to create a setting where alternatives to war can be imagined and encouraged." See http://vitruvius.arch.metu.edu.tr/gallipoli/gallipoli_english.html#scope.

51. Gallipoli Peace Park competition book and website, Middle East Technical University, Ankara, http://vitruvius.arch.metu.edu.tr/gallipoli/gallipoli_english.html.

52. Aytaç "Gelibolu Yarımadası Tarihi Milli Park."

53. As there is no mechanism for obtaining an accurate number of visitors to the Gallipoli Peninsula Historical National Park, these numbers are estimated. See Mustafa Doğan, "Bir Turizm Destinasyonu Olarak Gelibolu Tarihi Milli Parkı: Sorunlar ve Çözüm Önerileri" (The Gelibolu Peninsula as a tourist destination: Problems and solutions), in *Eceabat Değerleri Sempozyumu,* 271–86.

54. For the problems related to the road works in the Gallipoli park near the ANZAC cemeteries, see "Matters Relating to the Gallipoli Peninsula," The Senate, Finance and Public Administration References Committee, Commonwealth of Australia, at http://www.aph.gov.au/SEnate/committee/fapa_ctte/gallipoli/report/index.htm. For the 6 June 2011 agreements between the Turkish and Australian governments concerning the prevention of erosion at Arıburnu and improvement of the ANZAC cove area, see http://minister.dva.gov.au/media_releases/2011/jun/va039.pdf.

55. See http://www.canakkaletarihgalerisi.com/bolum10.html. See also Ayşegül Erdoğan, "A Proposal for a Maritime Museum and Underwater Archaeological Institute at the Ottoman Fortress of Seddülbahir" (master's thesis, Koç University, 2007), 92.

Enacting Discovery

Itasca State Park and the Mississippi's Mythical Source

The River itself has no beginning or end. In its beginning, it is not yet the River; in its end, it is no longer the River. What we call its headwaters is only a selection from among the innumerable sources which flow together to compose it. At what point in its course does the Mississippi become what the Mississippi *means*?
—T. S. Eliot, Introduction to *The Adventures of Huckleberry Finn,* 1950

Where does the Mississippi River begin? More than a century's worth of maps, images, and publications have pointed to Lake Itasca in northern Minnesota as the river's true source. There, a slender slip of a stream emerges from the lake's northern tip, meanders north and east through the system of lakes and streams that makes up the headwaters, and then swings south as it unfurls into the great river we know as the Mississippi. In 1891 Itasca State Park, one of the first state parks in the United States, was formed to enshrine the Mississippi's source, to preserve it in its "true natural state" for future generations. Summer after summer, thousands have journeyed into northern Minnesota to see the source. There, people gather on a sandy beach to contemplate the place known as the first clearly identifiable appearance of the Mississippi River. They watch as water spills over the stepping-stones that mark the river's beginning, and then many kick off their shoes to pick their way across the stones or wade through shallow waters where the channel is only about thirty feet wide (fig. 1). Before returning to cars or bicycles, people stop to have their pictures taken next to the marker the Civilian Conservation Corps erected in the 1930s.

This announces, in no uncertain terms, that "HERE 1475 FT ABOVE THE OCEAN THE MIGHTY MISSISSIPPI BEGINS TO FLOW ON ITS WINDING WAY 2552 MILES TO THE GULF OF MEXICO." Today the United States Geological Survey might differ on the river's length (reducing it to 2,340 miles because of various alternations in its course), but not on the validity of Lake Itasca as the place to begin measuring.[1] The park's design and signage, the stepping-stones, and the ritual of crossing combine to affirm that, yes, this is the place where the Mississippi River begins.

But is it? How do you pick a single point of origin from among the interconnected lakes, streams, wetlands, and springs that form the Mississippi River's headwaters?

Itasca State Park is one among many parks that have been formed at the headwaters of rivers and streams across the United States, ranging from Hogtown Creek in Florida to the Sacramento River in California. Yet there is no clear agreement about how to determine where any river's source is actually located. A river's source is as much a cultural construct as it is a locatable place within a complex and expansive headwaters system.[2] Parks like Itasca condense the headwaters—a particular idea of the headwaters—into a constrained and manageable space equated with the river's source, a space that can be set apart, marked, preserved, and visited. In some cases, such as Missouri Headwaters State Park in Montana, this takes the form of little more than trails, a clearing, and interpretive signage.[3] At Itasca State Park, however, the headwaters have been more elab-

141

FIG. 1. Stepping-stones and marker at the source of the Mississippi River, Itasca State
Park, c. 1955. (Minnesota Historical Society)

orately orchestrated, as visitors learn if they
walk a little farther beyond the stepping-stones
and read the signs that explain that they have
just experienced a "River Rock Illusion." In
its natural state, the river's source would be
swampy and sluggish. During the 1930s the Civilian Conservation Corps (CCC) reshaped the
site, adding a dam topped with stepping-stones
designed to "appear as natural as possible."

The CCC's imaginative reconstruction of the
Mississippi's source culminated a century of
controversy over where the river's true source
was located as one explorer after another attempted to pin it down. In 1886 Henry Gannett, one of the founders of the newly established U.S. Geological Survey, noted that "it
may easily be an open question which of a
dozen branches is the longest, when traced
through its innumerable lakes and windings,"
but acknowledged that by "*common consent . . .*
a certain branch of the Mississippi has been assumed as the river proper, and its head as Lake
Itasca, in northern central Minnesota."[4] This
"common consent" was produced amid competing claims, not only about the location of
the river's source but also about its control, its

uses, and its meanings. In this essay, I will trace
the ways these competing claims, in the space
of a century, coalesced in the CCC's fictive concept of the Mississippi's source through the
interplay of performance, representation, and
narrative. This requires moving beyond the
park's boundaries to consider the site in the
context of the complex and changing cultural
landscape of the Mississippi Headwaters.

Discovering the Source

During the nineteenth century, the quest for
the Mississippi's one true source fired the
imaginations of generations of explorers and
adventurers, scientists, and government officials who traced it to various lakes they named
(sometimes after themselves), mapped, and
claimed as their own discovery. Two of these
explorers—offering competing concepts of the
Mississippi's true source—had a lasting impact
on the way Itasca State Park eventually took
shape: Henry Rowe Schoolcraft, whose expedition narrative pervades the park's popular
significance; and Jacob V. Brower, whose hydrological study gave the park its justification
and form.

In 1832 the federal government commissioned Schoolcraft, an Indian agent for the Lake Superior region, to travel through the Northwest and the upper Mississippi to gather information, quell hostilities between the Ojibway and the Dakota, vaccinate as many as he could, and identify good locations for forts. On a mission that was primarily about advancing American control over the territory, Schoolcraft was determined to discover the Mississippi River's "veritable source." Through Indian and Euro-American trappers and traders he had heard of a lake called Omushkos or LaBiche—Elk Lake in English. With Oza Windib, an Ojibway guide who knew the region well, his party slogged through marshes and endured long portages until, finally, "What had been long sought, at last appeared suddenly. On turning out of a thicket, into a small weedy opening, the cheering sight of a transparent body of water burst upon our view. It was Itasca Lake—the source of the Mississippi." Disembarking on the lake's only island (now Schoolcraft Island), Schoolcraft planted the stars and stripes and promptly renamed the lake. The Mississippi would flow forth not from the Ojibway Omushkos or the French LaBiche, but from Itasca, an American reinvention of the Latin *veritas caput,* meaning "true head."[5] Artist Seth Eastman transformed this imageable moment, showing Schoolcraft as he pauses to contemplate the lake opening out before him, the American flag flying high (fig. 2).

Although many have claimed credit for discovering the Mississippi's source, Henry Rowe Schoolcraft has received the most lasting recognition. Others had been there before him; the Ojibway at Cass Lake provided maps that showed how to get there. But Schoolcraft performed the role of discoverer quite skillfully, translating his discovery into verifiable and mobile forms. When a member of his party, Lieutenant James Allen, mapped the lake and identified its coordinates, Schoolcraft pronounced himself satisfied that "by this discovery, the geographical point of the origin of this river is definitely fixed." Allen's map translated the lake's topography into rational terms that could be verified, replicated, and mobilized to legitimize the expedition's discovery as well as

FIG 2. Henry Rowe Schoolcraft at Lake Itasca, by artist Seth Eastman, c. 1855, from Henry Rowe Schoolcraft, *History of the Indian Tribes of the United States* (Philadelphia: J. B. Lippincott & Co., 1857). (Minnesota Historical Society)

to assert territorial control.[6] Schoolcraft also published a compelling narrative of wilderness exploration, physical challenges, and the dramatic discovery of a beautiful lake, renamed with a patriotic flourish of the stars and stripes. In later years Schoolcraft would obfuscate the origin of the name "Itasca," hinting that its source was an Indian legend:

Within a beauteous basin, fair outspread
Hesperian woodlands of the western sky,
As if in Indian myths a truth there could be read,
And these were tears indeed, by fair Itasca shed.[7]

Many others would succeed Schoolcraft, tracing the Mississippi's source beyond Itasca to ever-smaller lakes and streams. In the late 1880s, the Minnesota Historical Society commissioned Jacob Brower to put the controversy to rest, once and for all. Where Schoolcraft had ventured by canoe into territory the United States was just beginning to colonize, Brower could travel by train and then by wagon into an area mostly (though not completely) under American control.

Brower's investigation introduced a new conception of the river's source. Most of his predecessors assumed that they could follow the course of the river to one point of origin, and their narratives featured both a single, much-sought-after source and a single heroic discoverer. Brower, however, asserted his successful use of rigorous scientific methods to investigate the headwaters as a complex, hydrological system. Working with a team and an impressive array of instruments, he concluded that there was, in fact, no single source, but that the river emerged from an array of lakes, streams, and springs. At the heart of this system were two lakes to the south of Itasca, which he named Hernando de Soto and Morrison in honor of two early explorers he particularly admired. Together, these two lakes and the waters that fed them formed what Brower called the "Greater Ultimate Reservoir." He considered his conclusions to be the absolute and scientifically verifiable truth, and he presented them in a map that he considered the last word on the matter. This chart "has withstood the test

of technical scrutiny by the scientific scholars of two continents," Brower wrote.[8] As geographer Rich Heyman has argued, the production of a stable and fixed source for the Mississippi incorporated the river into a Euro-American regime of scientific knowledge that advanced the imperialistic project of constructing national territory, a process that involved the appropriation and transformation of indigenous land into uninhabited nature.[9]

Enshrining the Source

Brower's "Ultimate Reservoir" became the centerpiece of the movement to establish Itasca State Park—the first state park in Minnesota and one of the first in the nation.[10] Extolling the site both for its natural beauty and for its historical significance, the park's proponents—Brower among the most vocal—argued for preserving the park for future generations "in its natural condition of primitive beauty." Taking this further, Brower stressed the park's worldwide historical significance and its importance as a national emblem.[11] Although Brower based his argument on scientific knowledge, other factors—aesthetics, imagination, and the gradual accrual of what Gannett had referred to as "common consent"—would play equally if not more important roles in shaping the state park that would eventually enshrine the Mississippi River's source.

When Brower mapped the park, he combined his hydrographic chart with the official Public Land Survey System plat, following the rational grid that facilitated the sale and acquisition of land rather than basing the park's boundaries on topographical features. This was a decision that implicitly recognized the real estate transactions that would be crucial to making the park a reality. Although the park accommodated the Greater Ultimate Reservoir in its entirety, Brower made one curious omission. The park's northern boundary clipped off the northern tip of Lake Itasca (fig. 3). This meant that the location where the CCC would eventually place the now iconic stepping-stones was not originally included in the park at all. Brower was adamant that the Greater Ultimate Reservoir, not Lake Itasca, comprised the river's true source; he affirmed his point when he excised Lake Itasca's northern tip from the park.

In 1891, when Itasca State Park officially came into being, it was little more than an abstraction. With few resources and little backing from the state, the park's proponents had a challenge ahead of them that went well beyond acquiring the rest of the land within the park's boundaries. They needed to define a new form of cultural landscape, to shape it, give it meaning, and defend and promote its legitimacy in the face of competing claims. Itasca State Park introduced to Minnesota a new combination of recreation, aesthetics, and conservation that would have been unfamiliar to many. This concept was superimposed upon a patchwork of different forms of ownership and conflicting ways of interacting with and valuing the land. These were part of social and economic processes that extended beyond the park's boundaries, and that would continue to coincide, collide, and leave their traces well into the twentieth century.

Itasca State Park, intended to protect and enshrine the Mississippi's source(s), was a small and bounded slice of a region that was rapidly changing. The most immediate threat came from the lumber industry and the policies that supported it. In 1889, the same year Brower was charting the Mississippi's source, the Nelson Act—an "act for the relief and civilization of the Chippewa Indians in the State of Minnesota"—effectively opened tracts of Ojibway land to lumber companies.[12] The park's advocates argued that the landscape's scenic and historical value far exceeded the trees' value in lumber. But even as they worked to acquire the land and protect "primeval" forests from despoliation, clear-cutting persisted in the area around the park and then, in 1901, accelerated within its boundaries. Loggers dammed the river's outlet at the northern tip of Itasca, turning the lake into a log boom. This prompted the park's annexation of the land around the northern tip of Lake Itasca, which until then had remained outside the park's boundaries. But logs still clogged the lake in 1903, when twenty-four-year-old Mary Gibbs became park commissioner. The water rising, she defied the lumber barons and extended her hand to symbolically release the dam.[13] This performance of defiance has maintained its symbolic resonance in the park's history ever since, and was recently honored in the form of a new interpretive center named for her.

Although the battle between conservationists and lumber companies figures large in the history of Itasca State Park—and in the history of state and national parks in general—there were a number of other significant processes that intersected in the park's changing cultural landscape. The Ojibway, who were by the late nineteenth century increasingly concentrated on the White Earth, Leech Lake, Cass Lake, Red Lake, and Winnebagoshish reservations, were greatly affected by disruptions to the headwaters' ecosystem. In addition to the impact of logging and loss of land, there were the dams and reservoirs the Army Corps of Engineers had begun to construct in the early 1880s, most of them on reservation land and all of them to the east of Brower's "Ultimate Reservoir" in Itasca State Park. Hailed as feats of engineering that would make it possible to control the flow of the Mississippi farther south in the Twin Cities, these interventions changed the water levels and disturbed wild rice beds and wildlife habitat fundamental to Ojibway life. All the changes in the region made it difficult to maintain seasonal rounds to hunt, fish, and harvest wild rice irrespective of boundaries drawn on surveyors' reports. They did continue to hunt and fish in Itasca State Park, a reservation formed for other purposes. Euro-American "pot hunters" joined them, seeking fish and game for food or economic gain. Other Euro-Americans claimed land near the lake, built cabins, and soon moved on when they discovered how poor the farming was; while others streamed through the park, using its road as a public highway to head toward allotments of more fertile land.[14] And, finally, an increasing number of tourists came to enjoy canoeing, hunting, and fishing as forms of recreation and leisure. These varied uses and

experiences coincided, collided, and left their traces in the park: lumber camps and cutover land; claim shacks and cabins; Ojibway camps and tourist camps; and logging roads, public roads, and trails.

During the first two decades of Itasca State Park's history, then, several different cultural landscapes overlapped, each defined through divergent values and practices that extended beyond its boundaries. Over the next two decades, park commissioners, the Forest Service, and others would work to transform the land within the boundaries Brower charted into a "public, park, health resort, and game preserve." This required asserting control within the park's boundaries and eliminating uses that did not conform to the concept of what the park should be. In addition to acquiring the land and ousting the lumber companies, park commissioners redefined practices related to subsistence—canoeing, hunting, and fishing for food or economic gain—either as poaching or as sport, depending on who was doing it and how it was done.[15] All hunting was prohibited, and so was all fishing except with a line; this particularly affected the Ojibway, who had long employed spears and nets. After the turn of the twentieth century, Brower's successors established rules, posted them, printed them in brochures, and claimed the authority to enforce them. They also began to reshape the landscape to bring its form into alignment with its intended uses and meanings. In 1901 a wire fence went up around the park along with "gates at the entrances." In addition to asserting a modicum of control over access, these marked the park's boundaries, making them tangible and visible. Circulation also became more controlled. Although people were still "roaming all over" or streaming through, the park acquired

facing page

FIG 3. Hydrographic and Topographic chart of Itasca State Park, by Jacob V. Brower, 1892, frontispiece from Brower's *The Mississippi River and Its Source* (Minnesota Historical Collections, vol. 7; Minneapolis: Harrison & Smith, 1893). (Library of Congress)

new trails that guided visitors' paths; and the highway became a parkway designed for the leisured enjoyment of scenery. Those who preferred not to pitch a tent could stay at Douglas Lodge.[16]

By the 1920s, enough contiguous land had been acquired and enough work had been done that the park as we know it today had taken on its basic contours. Since a park of this kind was new to many Minnesotans, it needed some explanation. An early guidebook published by the Minnesota Forest Service is a particularly good example of initial interpretive strategies.[17] While highlighting the park's various features it also informed its readers about what Itasca State Park was and what it was not. It was not a Coney Island, nor was it like parks and parkways in cities, nor anything as dramatic as Yellowstone National Park. But what it did have was beauty, mystery, and uplifting scenery; abundant wildlife; and not least, the sacred source of the Mississippi River.[18] The guidebook presented the wonders of Itasca State Park as all the more valuable for their contrast with the landscape beyond the park's borders. To underscore this, the book developed a narrative that traced the visitor's journey to Itasca by train and then by automobile, passing through "broken prairie" and bleak "cut over scrub pine land," as if its stubble were a testament to what the park's lands might have become if its proponents had not won out against the "vanguard of a devastating civilization." Leaving such "discouraging scenery" behind, the visitor enters and finds renewal in the primeval world of the park, a place of peace, purity, and plenty lifted from the inexorable flow of time and change. Yet, this was also the place from which the course of history unfurled, a sacred place where the visitor could witness "that mysterious magic" of a lake that brings "forth a river that will flow for three thousand miles, molding the history of nations and the destinies of men, and irresistibly leading our imagination on to the history that is to be and back to the dim beginning of things."[19]

But where, exactly, would they find this beginning? In the 1920s, the Forest Service followed Brower's logic, arguing that although some might say that Itasca is the "cradle of the infant Mississippi," the hills around it are "collectively the only satisfactory source." But even so, the service's 1920 guidebook conceded that the small stream that emanated from the lake's northern tip "is quietly accepted as the first definite appearance of the real river."[20] By putting this in terms of a "definite *appearance*," the Forest Service acknowledged and reinforced the significance of a place that *looked* like a river's beginning. Certainly the small stream emanating from Itasca's northern tip was easier to recognize and pinpoint than Brower's more diffuse Ultimate Reservoir. Year after year as people visited, picnicked, and camped, they contributed to constructing the north end of Lake Itasca as the Mississippi River's true source. At the turn of the twentieth century, Euro-American tourists arrived by canoe and balanced on a log that spanned and marked the point where the small stream emerged from the lake. A 1926 map shows that various services accumulated near Itasca's northern tip to accommodate the growing number of visitors arriving by automobile: a store in a converted homesteader's cabin, a campground, and just

outside the park's boundaries the Park View Resort and the Headwaters Inn.[21] Eventually the old log that nestled in tall grasses at the river's outlet gave way to a more permanent log bridge and a neat boardwalk (fig. 4).

In 1932 the significance of Lake Itasca and Schoolcraft's memory gained considerable ground with the installation of pageant grounds at the north end of the lake, where thousands of visitors would watch the reenactment of Schoolcraft's discovery within sight of the river's source. Lake Itasca's popular appeal would override Brower's stringent scientific certainty. By custom, quiet acceptance, and, finally, by increasingly formalized design, the northern tip of the lake replaced Brower's Ultimate Reservoir as the Mississippi River's one true source. By the 1930s it was official: even Earl Lang, Itasca State Park's superintendent, referred to the north end of Lake Itasca as "the established source of our great river."[22]

The 1930s: Single Source, Single Narrative

On 15 June 1933, the *Farmer's Independent,* a northern Minnesota newspaper, reported that the Civilian Conservation Corps (CCC) would undertake the largest improvement in Itasca

FIG. 4. Log bridge spanning the outlet of the Mississippi River at Lake Itasca, c. 1920. (Minnesota Historical Society)

State Park in twenty years. "The famous spot where the Mississippi river leaves Lake Itasca is to be cleaned up," the paper announced.[23] The CCC's work would develop into far more than a cleanup. It became a significant re-conceptualization of the Mississippi River's source, the landscape around it, and its uses and meanings. In the 1920s the Forest Service had framed the visitor's experience as personal regeneration through the contemplation of nature. In the 1930s the focus shifted from individual contemplation to the collective performance of national regeneration.

Established to provide jobs through conservation projects, the CCC set up camp at Itasca State Park in the summer of 1933. The men and boys of the CCC worked under the combined oversight of the National Park Service, the Minnesota Department of Conservation, and the park's superintendent, Earl Lang. The Minnesota Central Design Office in St. Paul—consisting of two architects, a landscape architect, and an engineer—handled master planning and landscape and building design.[24] The Park Service, which approved their designs before they were executed, introduced new standards into the park's planning, including the development of a comprehensive vision intended to enhance the park's scenic, recreational, and symbolic value. The CCC drew a landscape where highly varied uses, values, and social practices had long coincided into a single, well-integrated scheme that revolved around the Mississippi's single source at the tip of Lake Itasca. As executed, this would be informed by a narrative of national unity and recovery performed in a series of historical pageants, by CCC workers through their labor, and by generations of visitors who came to experience the river's one true source.

Over the next nine years, the CCC did extensive work throughout the park. This required numerous reports and plans that reveal the CCC's assessment of the conditions they discovered when they arrived as well as what they did to change them, and why. One report indicated that Itasca State Park was already Minnesota's most popular park, with more than thirty

thousand acres that included "the finest stand of virgin timber" that the author had ever seen. But the cutover land surrounding much of the park presented a fire hazard along with other problems left over from all the logging. Another concern was ad hoc development throughout the park. The service buildings, dating from the "horse and buggy era," were a hodge-podge of different types and materials and all through the park there was a mix of uses that detracted from the park's natural features. Most troubling was the area around the Mississippi River's outlet at the northern tip of Lake Itasca. It was swampy, sluggish, choked with vegetation, and surrounded by all sorts of distracting development. Cars were everywhere. They were a boon to park attendance, but they were an unsightly intrusion and something would have to be done about them. The campground was also seen as a problem, for it compromised the area with the "intrusion of rather unsatisfactory tents, buildings, et cetera."[25]

To counteract these conditions, the Minnesota Central Design Office prepared plans that separated functions into different areas. They moved the campground to a new location, created picnic areas, eliminated inharmonious buildings, substituted new ones in the approved rustic style, and prescribed extensive conservation work to make the park appear "as truly natural as possible." In just three years, between July 1933 and March 1936, they put in twenty miles of trails and three and a half acres of parking and overlooks; and in 1936 alone they planted 750 native trees and shrubs.[26] They also took various measures to "renaturalize" the area they referred to as the Headwaters, the goal being to return it to what it had been before it had been sullied first by lumbering and then by the onslaught of tourists.

Historical Pageants

During the six years it took the CCC to transform the site, thousands of visitors came to the park—as many as forty thousand in one summer—to see casts of hundreds perform in a series of historical pageants held at the pageant grounds adjacent to the Mississippi's source.

The players were park employees, local people, visitors, and Civilian Conservation Corps members as well as Ojibway from nearby reservations and a white man who styled himself as Hotan-Tonka, adopted son of a Chippewa chief. These pageants created a framework for understanding the significance of the park's design. Through narratives that connected past and present, the pageants incorporated Itasca, the Mississippi, and Minnesota—and the audience members themselves—into the imagined community of the nation.[27]

The varied plots of Itasca's pageants were tailored to the locale, but the themes of national unity and progress were consistent with the historical pageants popular throughout the United States in the early twentieth century.[28] As the action unfolded, peaceful, happy Indians living in harmony with nature turned into warring tribes; fur traders swindled them; Indian braves and maidens fell in love; hearty pioneers ventured forth; and songs and narration over a loudspeaker accompanied exciting skirmishes and battles. It was here that Henry Rowe Schoolcraft really came into his own as the discoverer of the river's single true source. It was a story with all the right elements, as Schoolcraft, the individual, Euro-American hero undertakes a journey to find the source, discovers it at a particularly beautiful lake, and does all this while bringing good government to the region from the great white father in Washington, D.C.

Through all of this, the park provided both the setting for the pageants and the scenery. The park's scenic qualities—the scenery it offered for view, from a moving car, through a hike in the woods—were primary motivations for its preservation and planning. But in this context, the concept of scenery reverted to its theatrical origins, and the park's scenic qualities provided a vivid backdrop to the action. Beyond the fabricated scenery were the lake, the Indian mounds, and the forest, all borrowed views integral to the action and given new meaning through it. As Schoolcraft discovered the river's source, for example, the audience could look across the lake and see the island where he stopped to plant the flag.

In the course of the pageants, both actors and audience were immersed in a setting that accrued new layers of meaning as the action unfolded. Through plots that drew the park into the story of the nation, the pageants recounted the course of empire, the triumph of civilization, and also the scourge that threatened and decimated wilderness and with it the Indians who—in the world evoked by the pageants—had lived there in harmony with nature until the white man arrived and disrupted their way of life forever. The forces that produced modern industrial civilization were presented with ambivalence, to be sure, but they were also presented as inevitable—the conquest complete as a great civilization flowed forth, impelled by the great Father of Waters. The Ojibway, cast in the pageants as stereotyped characters, were thus put in the position of enacting their own demise (fig. 5). Their culture was relegated to a mythic past, while their present-day reality confronted a headwaters landscape that had been irrevocably disrupted by the reservoir dams; as many went hungry, the pageants offered a way to have food at least for the summer. But all of this was well out of sight in a park where a fragment of the headwaters was preserved for the descendants of the pioneers.

During the pageants, members of the audience were exhorted to feel themselves to be part of the action, that this was their story, that they were united in a common experience and identity. This message was conveyed clearly in the Diamond Jubilee pageant of 1933, which celebrated Minnesota's march to statehood: pioneers built the nation and charted the course for future generations; pioneer blood flows in the veins of our people today; and we, the participants, are a "composite of all peoples of [a] by-gone day." This was a vision of the melting pot that figuratively drew the descendants of ethnically diverse pioneers into a common bond of whiteness grounded in their shared identity as Americans.[29]

FIG. 5. Ojibway actors at Itasca State Park pageant, 1933. (Minnesota Historical Society)

Cradle of the Father of Waters

In 1938, the CCC documented both the historical pageants and its accomplishments at Itasca State Park through a film called *Cradle of the Father of Waters*.[30] The ten-minute film was one of the many short motion pictures the United States Department of the Interior Motion Picture Division produced to educate Americans about conservation while showing them the features of various parks and the nationwide program that was doing so much to conserve and improve them.[31]

Throughout the film, we are reminded that the CCC's work at Itasca is connected with a national effort of conservation, recovery, and regeneration. The film creates a historical context for the CCC's work from the beginning, linking national recovery with tradition and progress. State parks "mean a lot more than is apparent on the surface," the narrator intones. Itasca's pageants are cited for their educational value. To illustrate this, the film includes pageant footage that features industrious pioneers in fake beards before a backdrop showing a log cabin. Soon we see hardy young CCC men (some of whom also performed in the pageants) hauling logs and swinging hammers and axes, performing the old pioneer values as they erect simulacra of pioneer buildings to house park visitors—those descendents of the pioneers who return to the land on their vaca-

IT-15—Old Timer's Cabin, Itasca State Park, Minn.

FIG. 6. Old Timer's Cabin, erected by the Civilian Conservation Corps in Itasca State Park, postcard, c. 1940. (Minnesota Historical Society)

tions. The film's narrator assures us that these new cabins are built "in strict conformity with historic ones." To make them as authentic as possible, we are told, the CCC used rough logs from the immediate area. Nothing exemplified this better than the new Old Timer's Cabin constructed of gargantuan logs cut from fallen timber from "virgin forest" (fig. 6).

Log cabins were a recent memory—and for some a present reality—in northern Minnesota, and there were still a few remnants of homesteaders' cabins in the park itself (such as the Wegeman family's, converted to a store to serve tourists). But for an audience of town, suburb, and city dwellers, not to mention children who played with Lincoln Logs,[32] the park's rustic log buildings acquired new meaning, not as deteriorated signs of a harsh way of life better left behind, but as signifiers of the pioneer spirit, a rugged life lived close to nature. But not too close. The film also links the park with modernity and progress. We witness huge earthmoving machines in action and learn that the new campground has modern sanitation. Park visitors, whether they stayed in one of the new log cabins, dined at Douglas Lodge, or pitched a tent in the new campground, were invited to enjoy their own, more comfortable reenact-

ment of pioneer life and then return, restored and renewed, to the modern world.

In *Cradle of the Father of Waters,* filmed at the height of the Depression, the regenerative value of nature and physical exercise, long associated with the parks movement, is bound into the narrative of national recovery. As Neil M. Maher has shown, federal conservation policy merged a focus on natural resources with a concern for human resources, forging a "link between national building and nature."[33] Accordingly, the film features robust young men—some with shirts off to reveal well-muscled physiques—working with tireless vigor (by implication, a vigor that you too can gain in a place like Itasca). Conservation and construction at Itasca State Park, as the narrator reminds us, are part of a national effort. Through their labor, the film's narrator declares, the men and boys of the CCC are "rehabilitating a country and themselves." Maher has argued that this was also a process of Americanization for CCC enrollees. The CCC was seen as a melting pot for ethnically diverse participants who emerged having experienced and performed American values as they worked collectively to produce environments and symbols that, in themselves, furthered Americanization and national recovery.[34] This, then, brings us back to the environments they were shaping in Itasca State Park, and specifically, the area that had become the Mississippi River's one true source.

Transforming the Source

Over time the CCC had cleared away grasses and foliage, filled the marsh, and given the channel of the Mississippi greater definition. Between 1939 and 1941 the stockade, pageant grounds, and seating were removed, new parking was put in, and old parking was "renaturalized." Most memorably, CCC workers built a small dam across the "infant" river and laid a line of stepping-stones across it. The dam gives the river the more robust flow they believed a great river—even in its infancy—should have; and the stones suggested a distinct threshold where the river begins.[35] To reinforce this, the CCC planted the marker quoted at the beginning of this essay (fig. 7).

All of these elements converged to form a distinctive and memorable image of the Mississippi's source—an image that lent itself well to photographs and postcards that circulated widely. It was also an image that could be experienced and reproduced by those who came to the site itself. In 1939 the *Farmer's Independent* reported that "thousands of tourists seek out this spot every summer and the marker has been photographed more times possibly than any historical sign board in the whole northwest."[36] Offering visitors the opportunity to cross the stepping-stones and experience the narrow span of the Mississippi physically, the CCC also scripted an immersive and kinesthetic experience that combined contemplation and recreation. The stepping-stones beckon people to cross a few at a time, balancing carefully on slippery stones as they discover the Mississippi's source for themselves. It is an individual act, but the site's design also encourages shared experience as people cluster together on a small sandy beach and talk to one another—to friends, family, and strangers—comparing their experiences while children paddle in the shallow waters. Here, at the northern tip of Lake Itasca, the headwaters have been condensed and preserved within an evocative site that elicits both memory and forgetting: memory, of the expeditions of discovery that marked this place as the beginning of a great river at the heart of the nation; and forgetting, of the processes of colonization and displacement that produced the park and the nation—processes that persist more visibly throughout the expansive Mississippi headwaters system, and beyond.

FIG. 7. Mississippi Headwaters, Itasca State Park, 2010. (Author photo)

Notes

My thanks to Patrick Nunnelly for bringing the T. S. Eliot quotation to my attention and to David Pitt for sharing his deep knowledge of the park.

1. J. C. Kammerer, "Largest Rivers in the United States," United States Geological Survey, revised May 1990, http://www.pubs.usgs.gov/of/1987/ofr87-242/. The Environmental Protection Agency asserts that it is 2,320 miles long, and the Mississippi National River and Recreation Area indicates its length is 2,350 miles. See National Park Service, River Facts, at http://www.nps.gov/miss/riverfacts.htm.

2. Kammerer, "Largest Rivers in the United States." In tracing a river from mouth to source, choices need to be made where streams flow together. Which stream is a tributary and which is the river whose course you are following? Some have focused on the stream with the greatest length, while others have chosen the one with the greatest flow. This can produce dramatically different results. In the case of the Mississippi River, for instance, if the greatest length had been the main criterion the Mississippi would be considered the Missouri River's tributary rather than vice versa, and its source would likely be somewhere in Montana, not Minnesota. See Rich Heyman's fine analysis of varying perspectives in "Locating the Mississippi: Landscape, Nature, and National Territoriality at the Mississippi Headwaters," *American Quarterly* 62 (June 2010): 310, citing Ralph E. Olson, *A Geography of Water* (Dubuque, Iowa: Wm. C. Brown, 1970), 72, and a communication from Andrew Johnston, the Smithsonian Institution geographer the National Geographic Society credited in 2000 with the identification of the Amazon's source.

3. Here the Missouri River's headwaters are located at the confluence of the Jefferson, Gallatin, and Madison Rivers—a good example of how flexibly this concept has been formulated.

4. Henry Gannett, Letter to Editor, *Nature* 33 (7 January 1886): 221, emphasis added, http://www.nature.com/nature/journal/v33/n845/abs/033221c0.html.

5. Henry R. Schoolcraft, *Narrative of an Expedition through the Upper Mississippi to Itasca Lake* (New York: Harper & Brothers, 1834), 56. Schoolcraft did not mention the origin of the name in his 1834 narrative. William Boutwell, a missionary who accompanied him, confirmed that Schoolcraft discussed the Latin source of the name with him. For more on the history of the name, see the introduction and "Interview of William Boutwell with Jacob

Brower" (1890?), in *Schoolcraft's Expedition to Lake Itasca: The Discovery of the Source of the Mississippi,* ed. Philip P. Mason (East Lansing: Michigan State University Press, 1993), xxiii–xxiv, 351.

6. Henry Rowe Schoolcraft to C. Herring, Commissioner of Indian Affairs, "Official Report of the Exploratory Expedition to the Actual Source of the Mississippi River in 1832," 1 September 1832, in Henry Rowe Schoolcraft, *Summary Narrative of an Exploratory Expedition to the Sources of the Mississippi River* (Philadelphia: Lippincott, Grambo and Co., 1855), App., 573. See also Bruno Latour, "Drawing Things Together," in *Representation in Scientific Practice,* ed. Michael Lynch and Steve Woolgar (Cambridge, Mass.: MIT Press, 1990), 26–29, 42–47, passim.

7. Schoolcraft, *Summary Narrative,* 244.

8. J. V. Brower, *Itasca State Park: An Illustrated History,* Minnesota Historical Collections, vol. 11 (St. Paul: Minnesota Historical Society, 1904), 76.

9. Heyman, "Locating the Mississippi," passim.

10. Brower, *Itasca State Park.*

11. Ibid., xviii, xxi, 123, passim.

12. David Beaulieu, "A Place Among the Nations: Experiences of Indian People," in *Minnesota in a Century of Change: The State and Its People since 1900,* ed. Clifford Edward Clark (St. Paul: Minnesota Historical Society Press, 1989), 400. See also Michael David McNally, *Ojibwe Singers: Hymns, Grief, and a Native Culture in Motion* (New York: Oxford University Press, 2000), 93.

13. Brower, *Itasca State Park,* 182, 207, 229, passim.

14. Jane Lamm Carroll, "Dams and Damages: The Ojibway, the United States, and the Mississippi Headwaters Reservoirs," *Minnesota History* (Spring 1990): 3–15; Thomas Vennum Jr., *Wild Rice and the Ojibway People* (St. Paul: Minnesota Historical Society Press, 1988), 290–91; Brower, *Itasca State Park,* 72, 132, 141, 148.

15. Report from Commissioner Wm. P. Christensen to Governor Lind, 1900, reprinted in Brower, *Itasca State Park,* 169. Regarding similar processes elsewhere, see Mark David Spence, *Dispossessing the Wilderness: Indian Removal and the Making of the National Parks* (New York: Oxford University Press, 1995), and Karl Jacoby, *Crimes against Nature: Squatters, Poachers, Thieves, and the Hidden History of American Conservation* (Berkeley: University of California Press, 2001).

16. Report from Commissioner Wm. P. Christensen to Governor Lind, 1900, reprinted in Brower, *Itasca State Park,* 162, 167, 169.

17. Minnesota Forest Service, *The Source of the*

Father of Waters (St. Paul: Minnesota Forest Service, c. 1920).

18. Ibid., 6.

19. Ibid., 7, 8, 15.

20. Ibid., 8.

21. E. V. Fuller, map titled "Itasca State Park, Headwaters of the Mississippi River, The Beauty Spot of the North Woods," 1926, Collection of the Minnesota Historical Society.

22. Earl Lang, Proposed Work Plan for Unemployed, Records of the Civilian Conservation Corps, 1933–1953, Record Group 79, Box 71, NACP, quoted in Heyman, "Locating the Mississippi," 309.

23. *Farmer's Independent,* 15 June 1933, in Ben Thoma, *The Civilian Conservation Corps and Itasca State Park* (Lake Itasca: C.C.C. History Project, Itasca State Park Headquarters, 1984), 15.

24. The office included Edward W. Barber and V. C. Martin, architects; N. H. Averill, landscape architect; and Oscar Newstrom, engineer. Barbara W. Sommer, *Hard Work and a Good Deal: The Civilian Conservation Corps in Minnesota* (St. Paul: Minnesota Historical Society, 2008), 100.

25. Report submitted to Paul V. Brown, District Officer of State Park, 17 July 1934, Natural Resources Department, Parks and Recreation Division, State Parks Files, Minnesota Historical Society.

26. Ibid.; Report submitted by Floyd Tilden, Superintendent of Itasca State Park, 31 March 1936, Natural Resources Department, Parks and Recreation Division, State Park Files, Minnesota Historical Society; Thoma, *The Civilian Conservation Corps,* passim.

27. The following material is drawn from Grover M. Conzet, *The Historical Pageants Presented at Itasca State Park, 1932–33* (a report with photographs, n.d.), Natural Resources Department, Parks and Recreation Division, State Park Files, Minnesota Historical Society; *Souvenir, Schoolcraft Centennial: Commemorating the Discovery of Lake Itasca, Source of the Mississippi, 1832.* July 13, 1932 (includes "Discovery of Lake Itasca by Henry Rowe Schoolcraft, by Theodore C. Blegen"; Bemidji: Northwestern Minnesota Historical Association, 1932). On imagined

community and national identity, see Benedict Anderson, *Imagined Communities,* rev. ed. (London, New York: Verso, 1983/1991), 6–7, 33–36, passim.

28. *Cradle of the Father of Waters,* a film on Itasca State Park (United States Department of the Interior Motion Picture Division, 1938), refers to pageants performed in parks all over the United States during the 1930s. On early-twentieth-century pageants, see David Glassberg, *American Historical Pageantry: The Uses of Tradition in the Early Twentieth Century* (Chapel Hill: University of North Carolina Press, 1990).

29. Abigail Van Slyck has shown that something similar was also occurring in contemporary summer camps when children were invited to "play Indian." See Abigail Ayres Van Slyck, *A Manufactured Wilderness: Summer Camps and the Shaping of American Youth, 1890–1960* (Minneapolis: University of Minnesota Press, 2006), 212–13.

30. The film is accessible online at http://www .il.youtube.com/watch?v=cJDQlblui3A&feature= channel.

31. Neil M. Maher, *Nature's New Deal: The Civilian Conservation Corps and the Roots of the American Environmental Movement* (New York: Oxford University Press, 2008), 11, 154, 160, 162.

32. Erin Cho, "Lincoln Logs: Toying with the Frontier Myth," *History Today* 43 (April 1993): 31–34.

33. Maher, *Nature's New Deal,* 8, 15, passim.

34. Neil M. Maher, "A New Deal Body Politic: Landscape, Labor, and the Civilian Conservation Corps," *Environmental History* 7 (July 2002): 448–49.

35. For blueprints of the headwaters improvement plans, see Department of Interior, National Park Service, State Park Emergency Conservation Work, "A Plan of the Landscape Development Along the Headwaters of the Mississippi, Itasca State Park," and State of Minnesota Department of Conservation, Division of State Parks, Department of the Interior, National Park Service, Cooperating, "Mississippi Ri. Headwaters Stream & Lake Bank Protection," 6 September 1941, Minnesota Historical Society.

36. *Farmer's Independent,* 29 June 1939, in Thoma, *The Civilian Conservation Corps,* 48.

Parks Apart

African American Recreation Landscapes in Virginia

Beginning in the decades following the Civil War and continuing until the end of the era of segregation, Virginia's African American citizens created a statewide fabric of recreation sites that served as community gathering places—places that have thus far remained outside the established canon of the commonwealth's landscape history and recent scholarship focused on landscapes of slavery and on the segregation era's black community main streets.[1] This essay presents the recreation sites as a heretofore hidden layer of the Virginia landscape that offers a particularly significant opportunity to explore community conceptions of place and to uncover those shared understandings and community attachments to important everyday places not recognized by those outside the community. There is rich documentary evidence of the hidden histories of these recreation sites, an all but unexplored, unintended archive of advertisements, brochures, and family photographs, correspondence, and stories.

Many of the Virginia's African American recreation sites, including parks, picnic grounds, beaches, amusement parks, mineral springs, and fairgrounds, were places of the kind identified by historian Earl Lewis—not places of segregation, but rather places of congregation.[2] These recreational landscapes served as critically important community gathering places that offered a degree of freedom to the commonwealth's African American citizens in a time when such places were all too rare. Collectively, these sites constitute a lost landscape all but omitted from the most recent discourse that has sought to identify and recognize Virginia's landmark sites associated with the history, achievement, heritage, and culture of the commonwealth's African American citizens, a discourse that has thus far been focused almost entirely on identifying significant buildings and structures.[3]

Black churches played a pivotal role in the emergence in the late nineteenth century of Virginia's African American recreation landscape. Historians Elsa Brown and Gregg Kimball have identified black churches as "the only public spaces owned by African Americans" in the immediate post–Civil War period. During this time "churches hosted grand festivals, lawn parties, juvenile operettas, musicales, military drills, cake walks, or debates or other literary entertainments. Later . . . in the late nineteenth century . . . more facilities [including] parks, and picnic grounds became available to African Americans."[4]

From the end of the Civil War to the turn of the twentieth century, the public activities and rituals celebrated by black Virginians served as mechanisms to contest for "physical, civic, and historical space in cities throughout the state."[5] Black assertions of spatial equality in the landscape and challenges to the culture's standard narratives during this period often were played out in cities where blacks' use of the civic landscape, including sidewalks and parks, became a lightning rod for segregationist concerns. Parades, public ceremonies, and community-sponsored celebrations and events allowed black Virginians to not only claim public space for their own social purposes, relaxation, and amusement but also offered important public opportunities to challenge "dominant national narratives" and test the established "boundaries of racial etiquette that regulated public spaces."[6]

One result of African American's claiming of public space was to reinforce attempts to segregate the landscape and bar African Americans from some otherwise "public" landscapes including urban public parks. Controlling access to these landscapes became another means to exert "social control" on black Americans and further served to connect the "meaning of the landscape to racial identity."[7]

African American use of public sidewalks often became a touchstone for efforts to increase the segregation of the races. Even the simple act of smoking became a problem for the "genteel," as Dell Upton has noted:

The genteel could do little to turn back the lower class conquest of the streets. Tellingly their first response was to legislate street behavior. Since public smoking was ostensibly a habit of the rough-hewn, antismoking laws were favorite tools to drive them out of public spaces where they were not wanted. . . . [S]moking was an aggressive act that violated the genteel code of getting along and giving no offense and created a connection among people who might otherwise have avoided one another. Its connotation of equality and social presence . . . helps explain ordinances in cities such as Richmond and New Orleans that forbade African Americans to smoke in public.[8]

In this context then, by 1890 a new generation of privately developed, African American recreation sites had begun to emerge throughout the commonwealth. During the 1890s, advertisements and announcements of events at African American parks and picnic grounds regularly appeared in the state's African American–owned newspapers. Frequent advertisements appeared in the *Richmond Planet* for Bailey's Park, at the foot of Richmond's St. Peter's Street; Winddale Park, east of the city between Fair Oaks and Seven Pines; Bothwell Park in Hanover County; and Maiden's Adventure to the west of the city in Goochland. These new

parks and picnic grounds competed to host picnic and lawn parties sponsored by church groups, Sunday schools, private social clubs, businesses, and individuals.[9] The announcements and stories that describe excursions to these recreation venues offer a unique window into not only African American recreation sites but the commonwealth's black community cultural institutions, social organizations, and the rich fabric of connections between the African American business community and the network of recreation sites that developed throughout the state.

Between 1900 and 1920 advertisements for many additional parks throughout the state including Mount Pleasant near Richmond, Widewater on the Potomac, Piedmont Park in Charlottesville, Grannet Grove in Petersburg, Fulton Park in Fair Oaks, White City Park in Pine Beach, Buckroe Beach in Hampton, Bailey's Amusement Park and Little Bay Beach in Norfolk, and River View Island Park in Suffolk appeared in the commonwealth's black press. During this same period "colored" fairs emerged as annual recreational and educational events, festivals, and "homecomings" for African American communities throughout the state. The Tidewater Fair—the "official colored fair of Virginia"—was first held in Suffolk in 1909. By 1930 fairs had been held in Chesterfield County, Truxton, Norfolk, Newport News, Capron, Christiansburg, Weirwood, and Blackstone. The fair's premium books and the black press's description of the various African American recreation sites and the events held there clearly demonstrate the close connection between black leisure and recreation events and spaces and the ongoing debates in Virginia's African American communities regarding "public conduct, history and memory, and racial uplift."[10] The premium book for the 1929 Tri-County fair in Blackstone told visitors that "the purpose of the fair is to show what the colored people of Amelia, Nottaway, and Lunenburg are doing, and to stir up interest in better farming, better homes, better schools, and making better citizens."[11] The expanding network of parks, mineral springs, beaches, and fairgrounds where African American recreational activities occurred further served as essential gathering places where black families, professionals, wage workers, and members of social and religious organizations were free to reflect on grievances, share aspirations, and "[reinforce] their sense of community."[12]

Travel to many of these recreation sites, particularly the Tidewater beaches, was itself an event. Excursions, typically by train or river steamers "often sponsored by churches, social clubs, business and professional groups, and mutual benefit societies," became a central feature of the recreation experiences for many black Virginians.[13] The influence of the black churches, through their sponsorship of excursions, on the development of the recreational landscape in Virginia continued well into the twentieth century. In 1940 *The Negro in Virginia,* sponsored by the Hampton Institute, identified that "The Negro church offers pastimes for many; each denomination sponsors yearly a boat ride down the James or an excursion to Bay Shore Hotel and bathing beach. Hundreds of families pack hampers of fried chicken, hard-boiled eggs and other delicacies, take their bathing suits out of moth balls, and embark on their annual 'vacation' from the city."[14]

But the complex social circumstances of the age saw significant questions raised about the value of leisure itself, and the early excursions in particular provoked spirited debate within the African American community. During the Jim Crow era some African American leaders perceived leisure as a distraction from the hard work necessary to secure a brighter future for black Americans. Among those who questioned the positive aspects of leisure were the officials of Storer College in Harpers Ferry, West Virginia, and other reform-minded blacks who, according to historian Andrew Kahrl, "increasingly saw such excursions and vacations as a distraction from the hard labor of racial uplift, enticing blacks to pursue lifestyles unbecoming to their status in society. To them, the acts of defiance embedded in such pursuits paradoxically confirmed whites' most base stereotypes and offered further justification for their exclusion from the body politic."[15] The teachers and administrators at Storer College reacted strongly to what they perceived as the growing threat posed by the excursions. To those at Storer "the seemingly careless amusements enjoyed by the excursion parties to Harper's Ferry embodied the antithesis of the values of hard work, frugality, and conservative display. . . . So adverse to the unrespectable behavior and pretentious affectations reputedly rampant on such trips, school officials included 'pleasure excursions' on the list of banned activities."[16]

The shifting landscape of segregation throughout the early twentieth century saw more and more restrictions and limits placed on how and where the commonwealth's African American citizens could congregate. As places of congregation, the recreation parks responded directly to the "veil of segregation" that permeated not just Virginia but the entire country.[17] In Virginia, that veil became more opaque in 1926 with the passage of the Massenburg Public Assemblage Act, which made Virginia "the only state to enact a law requiring racial segregation in all places of public entertainment or assemblage."[18] The passage of the Assemblage Act followed a virulent and "emotional campaign for racial integrity that had engulfed the state of Virginia for the previous three or four years." The act was precipitated primarily by a small group of white citizens outraged that "the races were not separated when they attended events at Ogden Hall" at Hampton Institute.[19] In response, the act was "directed at both the operators of motion picture houses, theaters, and other places of public entertainment or public assemblage and the patrons of such places. Failure of an operator 'to separate the white race and the colored race' and 'to set apart and designate' certain seats to be occupied by each race was a misdemeanor punishable by a fine of $100 to $500 for each offense. Failure of patrons to occupy the seats designated for them by race was a misdemeanor punishable by a fine of $10 to $25 for each offense."[20]

In the context of the passage of the Public

Assemblage Act, an official sanctioning of existing segregation, it is not surprising that in 1926 advertisements for new African American recreation venues and for new housing developed by recreation corporations increased significantly. Norfolk Beach, Ocean Grove, and Lincoln Colored Park and Beach, all located in Tidewater, advertised heavily that year in the *Norfolk Journal and Guide,* as did Yellow Sulphur Springs in Montgomery County along with many earlier established recreation sites. In the decade and a half that followed, advertisements in the black press announced the opening of many new recreation venues including Lake Drummond in Deep Creek, Hills Point Amusement Park on the Nansemond River near Suffolk, Ellis Beach on the James River near the Jamestown Ferry in Surry County, National Memorial Beach near Williamsburg, and Belmont Lake just south of Richmond.

Understanding the emergence of the mineral springs as black recreation sites and the transformation of Yellow Sulphur Springs near Christiansburg in 1926 into a "Colored Resort" is particularly revealing. Long associated with white privilege, the Virginia mineral springs have been identified by historian Charlene Lewis as playing a key role in shaping elite southern society throughout the South—the place where in antebellum Virginia "each Summer, more elite whites congregated . . . than anywhere else in the south."[21] By the last decade of the nineteenth century, however, Virginia's African American citizens were frequenting at least some of the spring resorts, and advertisements were appearing in the *Richmond Planet* for Otterburn Lithia Springs in Amelia County, Colemanville Mineral Springs in Cumberland County, and Sweet Chalybeate Springs in Alleghany County's Sweet Springs Valley. In 1893 a "Sweet Chalybeate Letter" published in the *Richmond Planet* described Sweet Chalybeate Springs as "the paradise of Virginia Resorts. . . . [I]ts white cottages, broad lawns, green meadows, and giant shade trees stand ever ready to greet the dust worn traveler from the white city or the fleeing yellow jacket refugees, from the land of sugar cane and corn. Here all is quiet."[22]

The "Sweet Chalybeate Letter" revealed the widespread attraction of the springs within the African American community, noting visitors from Norfolk, Alexandria, Richmond, Lexington, Charlottesville, and Albemarle County in Virginia as well as guests from Chicago, Columbus, Ohio; Washington, D.C.; and Alderson and Union, West Virginia.

At first consideration it might seem odd that Virginia's black citizens would gravitate to the springs, recreation sites long associated with elite whites. However, the springs had historically depended on the labor of slaves and, in many cases, free blacks whose skills and services were essential to the daily operation of the springs. As a result, free black communities were established near some of the larger springs. Patrons and visitors to the springs often brought personal slave servants to attend them while they socialized and "took the waters." Just as white visitors to the springs met and socialized with their peers from throughout the South, slaves and free blacks at the springs "met black men and women from across the South, expanding their knowledge of others and their ties outside of their locality."[23] So too did slaves from throughout the commonwealth experience the springs and, ironically, in their limited free time, they gathered together and had "leisure experiences that were separate from, but often similar to, those of fashionable white society." In these circumstances slaves were even known to take the opportunity to act out in "imitation of their masters."[24]

The atmosphere at the springs fostered important dimensions of freedom for slaves and others, including women, who typically were "subject to the patriarchal power of elite white men."[25] Blacks at the springs had more freedom of movement, generally less supervision, and, through their various duties, some semblance of power over the daily lives of the white spring visitors.[26] Collectively then, the Virginia mineral springs were woven into the discourse of African American history, community life, and blacks' experiences of the Virginia landscape. It is not surprising that many of the state's

African American citizens would gravitate to those springs that were transformed to serve as black gathering places.

It was in this cultural and historic context that black Virginians in the late nineteenth century began to frequent a select group of mineral springs that catered specifically to African Americans. Documenting the African American presence at these springs, however, and understanding more fully the role the springs played as African American resorts and gathering places have remained elusive, requiring new and untapped sources of evidence. The standard histories that document life at the Virginia mineral springs do not include late-nineteenth- and early-twentieth-century African American recreation at the springs. These works omit the important role the springs played as African American gathering places recounted in the black press. Springs that served an exclusively African American clientele are not included among the list of commonly recognized Virginia springs. The standard histories of the white springs end when a spring finally closed its doors to its white clientele. Typical of the recent sources that fail to include the African American presence at the springs is Stan Cohen's *Historic Springs of the Virginias: A Pictorial History*. This valuable book includes one of the most complete lists of the Virginia springs, but springs that were well known in Virginia's African American communities, such as Otterburn Lithia Springs, Colemanville Mineral Springs, and Silcott Springs in Loudoun County, are not included in his accounting. Cohen's description of Sweet Chalybeate Springs in Allegheny County (also known as Red Sweet Springs) notes confidently that "the resort did not make a comeback after the Civil War. . . . Red Sweet slumbered along until it closed its doors in 1918."[27] There are no references, however, to the spring's use by an African American clientele in the 1890s. Cohen's description of Yellow Sulphur Springs near Christiansburg, Virginia, also fails to include the spring's history as an African American–owned resort. His timeline concludes that following the Civil War "for

a while the resort enjoyed considerable success, but by 1917 business had almost ceased and it closed for good in 1923."[28] It would be unfair to single out Cohen for omissions of this nature, however. None of the histories that include Yellow Sulphur Springs acknowledge its black ownership. Among those historians who omit the period of black ownership are John Gibson Worsham Jr., who wrote: "In 1923, 123 years after its founding, the Yellow Sulphur Springs resort ceased to operate. The spa then suffered several decades of neglect and was used as an indigent labor camp during the great depression."[29] Local New River Valley historian Roderick Lewis Lucas also failed to identify the black ownership of the resort even while noting that "in the 1920s a corporation was formed under the name of Yellow Sulphur Springs Incorporated."[30]

In January 1926, the same year as the passage of the Public Assemblage Act, Yellow Sulphur Springs (fig. 1) was indeed purchased by Yellow Sulphur Springs, Inc., a corporation formed by ten black businessmen from nearby Roanoke, Virginia. Advertisements for Yellow Sulphur Springs appeared in the *Norfolk Journal and Guide* throughout the summer of 1926, billing the spring as "America's Finest Colored Resort," with easy train connections on the Norfolk & Western rail line to cities throughout the state. The purchase of the spring was characterized in the *Norfolk Journal and Guide* as heralding "a new epoch in the history of the colored people," a place "where the air is pure and invigorating with an environment where race prejudice is not likely to arise."[31]

The businessmen who formed Yellow Sulphur Springs, Inc., were a remarkable cross section of black Roanoke and collectively embodied the entrepreneurial spirit, economic energy, and self-reliance that permeated black Roanoke during the era of segregation. The group included C. W. Poindexter; P. R. Cowan; lawyer J. L. Reid; Albert F. Brooks, owner of A. F. Brooks Realty; William H. Burwell, president of the Magic City Building and Loan Association and a former railroad brakeman; Henry C. Johnson, secretary/treasurer of the Magic

FIG. 1. Yellow Sulphur Springs, 2012. (Author photo)

City Building and Loan Association and manager of the Richmond Beneficial Insurance Company; C. W. Thompson, a railroad porter; Alvin L. Coleman, the chief bellman at the Hotel Roanoke; C. Tiffany Tolliver, owner of the Ideal Café, president of the Strand Theater, and former partner of pioneering black filmmaker Oscar Micheaux; and William B. F. Crowell, secretary of the Central Credit Union, grand chancellor of the Roanoke Chapter of the Knights of Pythias, and an actor in several Oscar Micheaux films.[32] Their businesses were concentrated on Henry Street (First Street), Roanoke's black main street and the economic and social heart of the Gainesboro neighborhood and greater Roanoke's black community.[33] Crowell, Brooks, and Tolliver were also co-owners of the Hampton Hotel and the Hampton Theater, both located on Henry Street.[34] The group's close connections to Henry Street illustrates the growth and development during this period of "black-owned insurance companies, banks, real estate

companies, retail outlets . . . grocery stores, pharmacies, barbershops, and other service providers [that] created downtown business districts that stabilized black communities.[35] The importance of the black commercial main street in the larger context of African American life was clearly outlined in *The Negro in Virginia:*

Every city has a "street" that serves as the social, as well as the commercial, center of Negro life. Along one or more blocks of Second Street in Richmond, Church Street in Norfolk, High Street in Portsmouth and Danville, South Avenue in Petersburg, Jefferson Avenue in Newport News, Fifth Street in Lynchburg, and Henry Street in Roanoke, the "crowd" may be found almost every evening. For a block or two everything is Negro; here is a little oasis—"our street." Race pride is triumphant; here one need bow and scrape to no one.[36]

Multiple investments and ownership roles in this complex social and business milieu appear to be typical of many black recreation entrepreneurs who retained strong connections to their community's commercial main streets. One well-known black entrepreneur who invested in Virginia's recreation landscape was John Mitchell Jr., editor of the *Richmond Planet,* who in 1919, along with four bank officers, "applied for a charter for the Unique Amusement Corporation, which had as its purpose 'to establish and conduct theaters, pleasure parks, concert halls, merry-go-rounds and things of like character to entertain and amuse the public.... [T]he company in turn purchased [Richmond's] Strand Theater."[37]

Investment in the African American recreation landscape thus might include ownership of a variety of recreation venues including parks, springs, amusement parks, movie theaters, social clubs, and restaurants, as well as new housing developments for African Americans—developments that often included proposed recreation amenities such as beaches and parks. Despite the diverse business experience of Yellow Sulphur Springs's new owners, the success of the resort appears to have been short-lived. While the reason for its demise is uncertain, Yellow Sulphur Springs was sold on the Montgomery County Courthouse steps in the spring of 1929.

Another dimension of the complexity of the African American recreation landscape during segregation is evident in the advertisements for many recreation venues. A close reading of the advertisements for Virginia's African American recreation sites can reveal the full dimensions of both the context and consequences of Virginia's landscape of segregation. Advertising claims such as "Order and Decorum Strictly Enforced" (fig. 2) by Bailey's Amusement Park in Norfolk[38] in 1917 reflect increased black middle-class concerns about "image as a sign of progress and a means of obtaining rights." Working-class public behavior during this period, including "the use of the sidewalks, streets, parks, and other spaces" and many leisure activities in these public spaces,

would lead an "increasingly privatized middle-class" to condemn the activities as "immoral and unrespectable."[39] The more insidious aspects of segregation are reflected in a 1917 newspaper advertisement in the *Journal and Guide* for River View Island Park in Suffolk, which counseled, "You need not fear" (fig. 3), and in a 1926 advertisement challenging "every Race man and woman to purchase shares in Norfolk Beach because 'It is worth it just to have somewhere to go.'"[40] But the ads reflect not only the spatial implications of the state's segregated landscape but ultimately what was really at stake for black Virginians—a powerful necessity clearly described by George Lipsitz, who observed that "struggles against the oppressions of race have by necessity also been struggles over space.... [T]hey have required blacks to literally ... *take places.*"[41] Such ads reveal that, throughout the segregation era, Virginia's African American citizens "took" places for their own use, safe places of congregation that reinforced black community identity across the commonwealth.

The "veil of segregation" also influenced the design of national parks in the commonwealth, including the Blue Ridge Parkway and Shenandoah National Park. The influence of segregation on national park design in Virginia was evident as early as 1932 when National Park Service deputy director Arno B. Cammerer proposed "provision for colored guests" at Shenandoah National Park. Soon the groundwork for an official policy of "separate, but equal" accommodations at the park was being established.[42] By 1936 the National Park Service had reluctantly recognized that, in Virginia, "to render the most satisfactory service to white and colored visitors it is generally recognized that separate rest rooms, cabin colonies and picnic ground facilities should be provided." Yet the internal conflict within the Park Service that separate but equal facilities posed was evident. In 1936 Park Service policy noted the inclusion of "separate facilities for white and colored people to the extent only as is necessary to conform with the generally accepted customs long established in Virginia."[43] As a result, by 1938

FIG. 2. Advertisement for Bailey's Amusement Park, Norfolk, Virginia, from *Journal and Guide,* 19 May 1917. (Used with permission, *The New Journal and Guide,* copyright, *The Journal and Guide,* 2013)

FIG. 3. Advertisement for River View Island Park, Suffolk, Virginia, from *Journal and Guide,* 21 July 1917. (Used with permission, *The New Journal and Guide,* copyright, *The Journal and Guide,* 2013)

plans for Shenandoah National Park included a development for "colored people" at Lewis Mountain that featured a campground, small lodge, and cabins (fig. 4).[44] Portions of these segregated facilities opened in the summer of 1939, and the first cabins and lodge were in service by summer 1940.[45]

Similar decisions regarding segregated facilities were made during the design of the Blue Ridge Parkway. In 1939 Stanley Abbott, chief landscape architect and principal designer of the parkway, noted in his *Annual Report,* "General plans crystallized during the year for provision of Negro facilities in the recreation parks."[46] By April 1939, plans had been established for separate cabin, camping, and pic-

nicking areas for Negro use in the large parks, such as Rocky Knob in Virginia and the Bluff in North Carolina, and a picnic area for joint use by both whites and Negroes at the Bluff.[47]

Facilities along the Blue Ridge Parkway were planned to include segregated comfort stations and dining rooms. But outdoor dining terraces were designed with as little separation of the races as possible, and no division in automobile service facilities, sandwich shops, lunch counters, or sales rooms were planned.

Eventually, areas for "Negro use" would be designed for Otter Creek, Pine Spur, and Rocky Knob in Virginia and at Doughton Park (the Bluff) just across the border in North Carolina. As a temporary measure, it was proposed that

African Americans be allowed to use the facilities at Smart View until the facilities at Pine Spur were completed. It is uncertain if they were ever allowed to do so.[48] Ultimately, the outbreak of World War II would reorder National Park Service priorities, and few of Virginia's segregated parkway facilities would be constructed. Only the small park, picnic area, a playing field, and the trails at Pine Spur appear to have been developed prior to the outbreak of the war.[49] After the war, the Park Service segregation policy was abandoned and the proposed facilities at Rocky Knob and Otter Creek were never constructed. Segregation issues related to the Blue Ridge Parkway would persist, however, well into the next decade, especially when questions regarding appropriate overnight accommodations were raised. In the 1950s U.S. representative Tuck from Virginia wrote National Park Service director Wirth, stating that "the people of Virginia will not stand for integration in motels, and I hope that the National Park Service will no [sic] persist in any such program or practice." "Wirth replied that the question of whether the parkway would provide overnight facilities had not yet been determined, but pointed out government contracts were required by law to carry a non-discriminatory clause."[50] The state's African American citizens did visit the Blue Ridge Parkway (fig. 5), but "the number of African Americans using parkway facilities was very low during the period segregation laws were in effect."[51]

FIG. 4. Lewis Mountain Negro Area sign, Shenandoah National Park, c. 1940s. (Shenandoah National Park)

FIG. 5. "On the Blue Ridge Parkway, c. 1950s." (Photographer unknown; Collection of Michael Blankenship; used with permission)

FIG. 6. Prince Edward State Park, c. 1955. (Prince Edward State Park Archives)

Public scrutiny focused on the proposals for segregated facilities at the commonwealth's national parks, and the black press's long-standing critiques of inequities regarding recreation opportunities available to Virginia's black citizens helped set the stage for the development of the commonwealth's first state-supported park facilities for African Americans after World War II. But by 1948, only the Goodwin Lake Recreation Area near Green Bay, which provided limited picnic bathhouse and toilet facilities for Negroes, and a small portion of Pocahontas State Park in Chesterfield County had been set aside for use by African Americans. It would take legal action to finally force Virginia to develop its first state park specifically for the state's African American citizens. In 1948, after being denied access to Staunton River State Park, Danville banker Maceo Conrad Martin filed suit to allow Negroes the "full use" of the state's existing park facilities or the use of "similar or equal" facilities. As a result of Martin's suit, Virginia, in 1950, transformed part of the Goodwin Lake Recreation Area into Prince Edward State Park, the state's first and only park "for the use of colored patrons" (fig. 6).

The opening of the newly designated Prince Edward State Park, however, did not meet with universal approval even among black Virginians. The *Journal and Guide,* which had long argued for more equitable access to all of the state's parks, described the opening of the new park as a move "designed to pacify residents of the state by giving them a 'place' to play," while "seeking to maintain the practice of 'separate but equal' facilities."[52] In a 19 August 1950 editorial, the paper noted what it believed to be "the difference between White Parks and the one for colored" when it observed that "Negroes are barred from viewing the treasured spots of natural beauty and historic significance.... [T]he scenic beauties of the seashore or the grandeur of the mountains, which may be seen in various state parks located in strategically appropriate sections of Virginia, cannot be moved to the 'colored' state park in Prince Edward County."[53]

Black Virginians' appreciation of the "treasured spots of natural beauty" and the "grandeur of the mountains" was evident more than forty years earlier, in 1906, when John Mitchell Jr., editor of the *Richmond Planet,* published "Editor Mitchell in the Mountains," a front-page story describing the journey to Pinehurst, an African American summer resort near Hot Springs, Virginia. In his travelogue, Mr. Mitchell described his experience:

Away above us were the peaks of mountain range, kissing the clouds. In some instances fleecy vapors dropped below and gave to the beholder an idea of the grandeur of nature. We had never seen anything to surpass this scene. It was only equaled by the one that greeted us upon our return drive at Lexington, Va. from a trip across the Blue Ridge. Then the valley was below, the farms cultivated, the red clay roadways, the blue foliage, the green vegetation, and the silvery waters of the streams, making a natural picture that enthused and intoxicated the beholder with its magnificence and its grandeur.[54]

In 1951, the *Journal and Guide* sharply criticized the state for continued inequity concerning park facilities for blacks and whites, noting that despite the opening of Prince Edward State Park, "Negroes were substantially in the same position as had been their lot before." The paper recognized the park "was at such a distance from most population centers that it could not be reached without great expense and long travel."[55] As a result of these inequities, privately owned recreation facilities catering to African Americans flourished in the decade after the end of World War II. Beaches, private lakes, and amusement parks catering to African Americans during this period included Ocean Breeze Beach and Amuse-

ment Park, Parker's Beach, Bay Shore Beach, and Seaview Beach in Tidewater; Mark Haven Beach near Center Cross; Wiggin's Beach near White Stone; Log Cabin Beach near Williamsburg; Sunset Lake Park in Deep Creek; City Beach in Norfolk; and Spring Lake Amusement Park in Hopewell. All advertised heavily in the state's African American newspapers. Their advertisements described sites with a range of landscape amenities including shaded groves, luxuriant foliage, picnic grounds, sandy beaches, pavilions, and private cottages along with concession stands, dining rooms, restaurants, trailer camps, and first-class hotels. Boardwalks were a common amenity at the seaside venues. Patrons of these recreation venues had access to a variety of activities including swimming, boating, fishing, crabbing, amusements, rides, merry-go-rounds, swings, archery, baseball, miniature golf, fireworks, quartet contests, and dancing. Music had a special place at many of the larger amusement parks, including Spring Lake Amusement Park, Ocean Breeze Beach and Amusement Park, and Seaview Beach. These venues became regular stops on the segregation era's black entertainment circuit, and their featured performers included a who's who of entertainment royalty, including Louis Armstrong, Dizzy Gillespie, Erskine Hawkins, Jimmie Latham, Cootie Williams, Savannah Churchill, Al Hibbler, Andy Kirk, and Cab Calloway.

Despite the importance of these recreation places, their documentation remains outside the traditional histories and archival record. The extant documentation has by and large escaped "collecting, classifying, and controlling" the traditional roles of the archivist.[56] But as historian Pierre Nora has observed, "Modern memory is, above all, archival. It relies entirely on the materiality of the trace, the immediacy of the recording, the visibility of the image."[57] Many of the physical sites of this remarkable landscape have been long abandoned and overwritten by nature's processes or later development. The traces that remain exist primarily in a dispersed, "unintended archive" of family photographs, family papers, advertise-

FIG. 7. Green Pastures Lake, Botetourt County, Virginia, 1950s. (Collage by author; photographer unknown; Peery Family Collection; used with permission)

ments and stories in the black press, the files of local black photographers, and the extant records of black churches, social clubs, and professional organizations (fig. 7). Firsthand stories that can animate these lost landscapes are embedded in the oral histories being collected in many African American communities.

Work has begun in the unintended archive to document these lost places and understand the rich landscape fabric they collectively comprised. The importance of this work extends far beyond specific understandings focused on individual communities or sites. For designers, studying and manipulating the unintended archive offers opportunities for creative design explorations focused on the larger questions of history, memory, identity, and, most important, community conceptions and constructions of place. Here explorations are not merely intended to assemble an archive from the available sources, but rather to transform the archival materials through various means including overlays, superimposition, collage, and juxtaposition to reveal the unintended archive as a "creative space" and a "discursive terrain" where interpretations are not determined but instead "invited."[58]

Studying the sites and exploring their unintended archives can transform our understanding of the commonwealth's landscape from one focused narrowly on physical sites to an expanded social and cultural "ground" of the type characterized by architect Robin Dripps—a ground that "operates with great nuance, a fragmentary ground where single, uncomplicated meanings are rare and where stories overlap and are woven together revealing patterns of physical, intellectual, poetic, and political structure."[59]

Notes

1. See Rebecca Ginsberg, Genevieve Fabre, and Robert O'Meally, eds., *History and Memory in African-American Culture* (New York: Oxford University Press, 1994), and Walter J. Hood Jr. and Mellissa Erickson, "Storing Memories in the Yard: Remaking Poplar Street, the Shifting Black Cultural Landscape," in *Sites of Memory: Perspectives on Architecture and Race,* ed. Craig Evan Barton (New York: Princeton Architectural Press, 2001).

2. Elsa B. Brown and Gregg D. Kimball, "Mapping the Terrain of Black Richmond," *Journal of Urban History* 21, no. 3 (1995): 296–346, see 342n41.

3. Calder Loth, ed., *Virginia Landmarks of Black History: Sites on the Virginia Landmarks Register and the National Register of Historic Places* (Charlottesville: University Press of Virginia, 1995).

4. Brown and Kimball, "Mapping the Terrain," 330.

5. Ibid., 308.

6. Andrew Kahrl, "The Political Work of Leisure: Class, Recreation, and African American Commemo-

ration at Harper's Ferry, West Virginia, 1881–1931," *Journal of Social History* 42, no. 1 (Fall 2008), 58.

7. Jane Dailey, *Before Jim Crow: The Politics of Race in Postemancipation Virginia* (Chapel Hill: The University of North Carolina Press, 2000), 102.

8. Dell Upton, *Another City: Urban Life and Urban Spaces in the New American Republic* (New Haven: Yale University Press, 2008), 328.

9. *Richmond Planet,* 24 June, 28 June, 15 July, and 23 August 1890.

10. Kahrl, "The Political Work of Leisure," 58.

11. Tri-County Fair Association, *Premium Book: Tri-County Colored Fair* (Blackstone, Va.: Tri-County Fair Association, 1929), 7.

12. Robin Kelly, quoted in Earl Lewis, "Connecting Memory, Self, and the Power of Place in African American Urban History," *Journal of Urban History* 21, no. 3 (1995): 161.

13. Brown and Kimball, "Mapping the Terrain," 345n79.

14. Hampton Institute, *The Negro in Virginia* (New York: Hastings House, 1940), 347.

15. Kahrl, "The Political Work of Leisure," 59.

16. Ibid., 66.

17. Ann Field Alexander, *Race Man: The Rise and Fall of the "Fighting Editor" John Mitchell Jr.* (Charlottesville: University of Virginia Press, 2002).

18. Richard B. Sherman, "Teachings at Hampton Institute: Social Equality, Racial Integrity, and the Virginia Public Assemblage Act of 1926," *The Virginia Magazine of History and Biography* 95, no. 3 (July 1987): 275.

19. Ibid., 279.

20. Ibid., 296.

21. Charlene M. Lewis, "Ladies and Gentlemen on Display: Planter Society at the Virginia Springs, 1790–1860" (Ph.D. diss., University of Virginia, 1997), ii–iii.

22. "Sweet Chalybeate Letter: A Grand Entertainment," *Richmond Planet,* 26 August 1893.

23. Charlene M. Boyer Lewis, *Ladies and Gentlemen on Display: Planter Society at the Virginia Springs, 1790–1860* (Charlottesville: University Press of Virginia, 2001), 206.

24. Ibid., 197.

25. Ibid., 9.

26. Ibid., 43, 54–55.

27. Stan Cohen, *Historic Springs of the Virginias: A Pictorial History* (Charleston, W.V.: Pictorial Histories Publishing Co., 1994), 121.

28. Ibid., 133.

29. John Gibson Worsham Jr., "A Place So Lofty and Secluded: Yellow Sulphur Springs in Montgomery County," *Virginia Cavalcade* 27, no. 1 (Summer 1977): 41.

30. Roderick Lewis Lucas, *A Valley and Its People in Montgomery County Virginia* (Blacksburg: Southern Print Co., 1975), 82.

31. "Yellow Sulphur Springs Finest Summer Resort," *Norfolk Journal and Guide,* 14 August 1926.

32. Patrick McGilligan, *Oscar Micheaux: The Great and Only* (New York: Harper Collins, 2007), 207.

33. *Hill's Roanoke City Directory,* 1926. Additional information on the owners was provided by Mr. Al Holland, in a 2007 interview with the author.

34. McGilligan, *Oscar Micheaux,* 174.

35. Mark Robert Schneider, *African Americans in the Jazz Age: A Decade of Struggle and Promise* (New York: Rowman and Littlefield, 2002), 41–42.

36. Hampton Institute, *The Negro in Virginia,* 351.

37. Alexander, *Race Man,* 186.

38. *Journal and Guide,* 19 May 1917.

39. Brown and Kimball, "Mapping the Terrain," 328–29.

40. *Journal and Guide,* 21 July 1917, and *Norfolk Journal and Guide,* 31 July 1926.

41. George Lipsitz, "The Rationalization of Space and the Spatialization of Race," *Landscape Journal* 26, no. 1 (2007): 17, emphasis in original.

42. Reed Engle, "Laboratory for Change," January 1996, newsletter, http://www.nps.gov/shen/historyculture/segregation.htm#.

43. Ibid., 1.

44. Ibid.

45. Ibid., 2.

46. Stanley Abbott, *Annual Report of the Blue Ridge Parkway, Roanoke Va. to the Director, National Park Service, June 30 1939,* 16, in "Superintendents Annual Reports, Blue Ridge Parkway 1934–1946," BLRI 440, CAT 19859, RG-1, Series 3, Box 61, I.D. 2–3, Headquarters, Blue Ridge Parkway, Asheville, North Carolina.

47. Ibid.

48. Richard Quin, Blue Ridge Parkway HAER Report No. NC-42, 1997, 211.

49. Ibid., 206.

50. Ibid., 170. The exact date of this entreaty is uncertain. The HAER report cites an "undated clipping."

51. Ibid., 169.

52. "Va. Operates 9 State Parks, But Only One for Negroes," *Journal and Guide,* 25 August 1951.

53. Ibid.

54. "Editor Mitchell in the Mountains," *Richmond Planet,* 21 July 1906.

55. "Va. Operates 9 State Parks, But Only One for Negroes," *Journal and Guide,* 25 August 1951.

56. Josephine Lanyon, "Foreword," in *Ghosting: The Role of the Archive within Contemporary Artists' Film and Video,* ed. Jane Connarty and Josephine Lanyon (Bristol, UK: Picture This Moving Image, 2006), 9.

57. Pierre Nora, "Between Memory and History," *Representations* 26 (Spring 1989): 13.

58. Neil Cummings and Marysia Lewandowska, "From Enthusiasm to Creative Commons," Interview with Anthony Spira, in *The Archive,* ed. Charles Merewether (Cambridge, Mass.: MIT Press, 2006), 150.

59. Robin Dripps, "Groundwork," in *Site Matters: Design Concepts, Histories, and Strategies,* ed. Carole J. Burns and Andrea Kahn (New York: Routledge, 2005), 71.

Conceptualizing, Representing, and Designing Nature

Cultural Constructions of the Blue Mountains, Australia

A range of cultural practices transform land into landscape, and it is through an appreciation of these practices that national park landscapes can be designed and managed most effectively. The process by which a physical space becomes a place, including those places we designate as national parks, is a multifaceted one.[1] This essay examines how the nature of national parks is inextricably linked with the evolution of cultural practices including naming, writing, image making, and spatial design. It argues that these practices must be understood as fundamental to park management due to their influence on the quality of park identity, experience, and meaning.

For the Blue Mountains, a landscape which is now recognized as a park of both national and international significance, the transition from "land" to "park" has been a gradual process of cultural transformation. The history of the Blue Mountains highlights the interconnectedness between ideas about landscape, the ways that these ideas are represented in different media through time, and how these are ultimately manifest in the physical form and symbolic content of designed landscapes. To trace the evolution of park ideals in this context is to trace multiple and intertwined narratives of colonial conquest and ambition, science and technology, art, tourism, and conservation. These histories can be traced alongside developments in the representational media used to express and influence perceptions of the landscape, from the earliest engravings to the most recent digital technologies and interactive media. Only by considering both the representation and physical modification of the Blue Mountains can the evolution of the landscape's identity be understood. This rich and diverse identity continues to evolve out of a combination of ideas, images, technologies, laws, management strategies, and design interventions.[2]

The area known as the Greater Blue Mountains consists of more than 2.47 million acres of national parks and reserves stretching in a north–south band along Australia's eastern seaboard, approximately thirty miles from the coastline and under an hour's drive from Sydney. Running in an east–west corridor across the mountains is the City of the Blue Mountains: this settled landscape occupies some five hundred and fifty square miles, and its current population of approximately seventy-two thousand people is distributed across sixty-eight miles of ridgeline in twenty-six towns and villages.[3]

The Blue Mountains reflect a rich mix of natural and cultural landscape values and practices. The area is noted for its wide and balanced representation of eucalypt habitats from wet and dry sclerophyll and mallee heathlands to swamps, wetlands, and grassland. Thirteen percent of the total of eucalypt species globally occur here. Human occupation of the area dates back more than twenty-two thousand years, when the region was populated by Gundungurra, Darug, and Wiradjuri Aboriginal tribes. The attitudes and practices of these tribes are now recognized as a fundamental element of the meaning and significance of this place; however, the history of colonization shows Aboriginal culture and rights were not always respected. Following the arrival of white settlers in 1788, indigenous ways of seeing the landscape were marginalized and inhibited, with the appropriation of their homelands, dislocation, dispersal, the loss of many languages, and the study of Aboriginals as an exotic "other."[4] Attitudes and values toward indigenous Australians, like attitudes and values toward the Australian landscape itself, continue to evolve.

Unscenic Origins: Early Inroads (1788–Mid-1800s)

During the first decades of Australia's settlement by Europeans (1788 onwards), a negative and pragmatic response to the landscape held sway, with attitudes showing little hint of the park ideals that followed. English settlers were frustrated by the foreignness of the environment they confronted. The climate, the soil, the vegetation, and the topography did not conform to their prior experience, and their attempts to navigate and cultivate the landscape were fraught with difficulty.

The Blue Mountains, visible on the horizon to the west of the settlement (Sydney), defied the lens of European logic. Early optimism and imaginative speculation about the fertile lands that might lie beyond the horizon gave way to despair as explorers repeatedly failed to find a route across the inhospitable, dry, densely vegetated, and vertiginous terrain. Eventually, more than twenty years after initial settlement was established, the settlers "discovered" a path through the mountains in 1813, by following an Aboriginal trade route. Despite this breakthrough, the mountains continued to be perceived and represented as a hostile, unforgiving place. Although a one-hundred-mile-long rough track was successfully built with convict labour to access the area, for many years the journeys this physical modification to the landscape facilitated were not enjoyed. Early travelers' journals, like the explorers' journals before them, are melancholy, describing the landscape they traversed, despite its forest cover, as "a confused and barren assemblage of mountains," monotonous and without the verdancy that characterized European vegetation.[5] These mountains were hot, dusty, and covered by the eucalypt, an unfamiliar tree that artists found difficult to represent. The steep mountain track gained a reputation for being hazardous: one writer remarked that it was "rude enough to provide drama aplenty" and accounts of the time describe bleak sights along the way, such as the bleached bones and carcasses of bullocks which had perished on previous journeys (fig. 1).[6]

To the local Aboriginal people this landscape was not barren; however, the European settlers did not recognize such knowledge and attachment to place. Colonists declared the landscape a *terra nullius,* assuming that the indigenous occupants of Australia had no legal tenure of the land on which they lived. As a result of this doctrine, Aboriginals were dispossessed of their land, their right to inhabit or use the land legally denied. (The *terra nullius* doctrine was declared legally invalid by the High Court of Australia in its Mabo judgment in 1992.)[7] To the settlers the land was an unowned and unproductive wasteland that awaited civilizing transformation. Overall, the settlers during this period conceived of the Blue Mountains landscape as a negative space, with their written descriptions and images conveying the alienation of people from place. Such attitudes were physically manifest in the track they built, a practical modification to the land which rendered it publicly trafficable but not, as yet, scenic.

Exotica, Extraction, Aesthetics, and Escapism: A Time of Transition (1820s–1870s)

During the early to late 1800s the colonists began to see and treat the Blue Mountains in a variety of ways. As the colony expanded, settlers perceived the mountains less as a barrier to be crossed and more as a landscape worthy of visiting or inhabiting in its own right. Different interest groups, including scientists, miners, artists, and the elite, learned to appreciate and appropriate the natural landscape, reflecting both progressive Enlightenment and Victorian

FIG. 1. William Govett, "Incident on road at Victoria Pass," watercolor, c. 1835, from manuscript collection, "William Govett notes and sketches taken during a surveying Expedition in N. South Wales and Blue Mountains Road by William Govett on staff of Major Mitchell, Surveyor General of New South Wales, 1830–1835." (Mitchell Library, State Library of NSW, 981/N and DSM/981/N)

romantic ideals.[8] Those seeing the landscape through Enlightenment eyes sought scientific knowledge, industrial wealth, and the progress of civilization, while those with a romantic eye sought sublime beauty, transcendence, and artistic inspiration. Such shifts in the conceptualization of place were assisted by advances in representational techniques and technologies, and were reflected in the physical modification of the land itself.

The antipodean geography and geology, once the source of such consternation, came to be viewed with interest by scientific minds. A variety of written and visual representations exist from this period, which classified and described new exotic discoveries in language ranging from the technical to the poetic. During his 1836 visit Charles Darwin studied the mountains for their unfamiliar dramatic geology and unusual vegetation, noting, "One stands on the brink of a vast precipice, and below is the grand bay or gulf (for I know not what other name to give it), thickly covered with forest. ... This kind of view was to me quite novel, and extremely magnificent."[9]

The advances in scientific understanding facilitated through geological and botanical appreciation in Western culture were paralleled by technological advances associated with mining and industry in the Blue Mountains. The extraction of mineral resources (shale and coal) had a dramatic impact on its physical landscape character. Advances in the technology of visual representation—the camera—captured the mood of progress in form and content, and while few of today's visitors to the Blue Mountains would photograph industrial infrastructure, at that time the mines were considered just as compelling subjects as the landscape setting (fig. 2).[10]

Simultaneously, a number of artists, influenced by the broader cultural movements of romanticism and particularly the sublime, saw the same landscape as an aesthetic resource. Painters such as Eugene von Guerard and photographers such as Joseph Bischoff (immigrants to the new colony who had been classically trained in Europe) illustrated the grandeur of the landscape (fig. 3). Like mining, these activities impacted on the physical terrain: records of an artists' camping trip in 1875 reveal that artists and their "axe-wielding assistants" cleared vegetation which failed to conform to their preferred pictorial conventions.[11] Others who appreciated the inherent aesthetic value of the landscape included members of Sydney's political and business elite, who established

their own private retreats in the mountains (fig. 4). These landowners modified nature to facilitate access to special scenic spots such as waterfalls. The private walking tracks which emanated from their mountain estates in the 1860s later became models for the development of public tracks within public reserves.[12]

Amid these activities lay the beginnings of the idea of the Blue Mountains as a park. From 1867 onwards, areas of unalienated crown land (public land) began to be gazetted as reserves for the purposes of public recreation. Competing interests resulted in a mix of land uses and modifications, with land being reserved for the public but also subsequently annexed

FIG. 2. Katoomba coal mine railway, c. 1890. (Blue Mountains City Library)

FIG. 3. Eugene von Guerard, *Weatherboard Creek Falls, Jamieson's Valley, New South Wales,* 1862, oil on canvas, 122.1 x 183.3 cm. (National Gallery of Victoria, Melbourne, presented through the Art Foundation of Victoria by the ANZ Banking Group Limited, Honorary Life Benefactors, 1989)

FIG. 4. F. A. Sleap, *A Visit to Sir Henry Parkes at Faulconbridge,* wood engraving, c. 1881. (La Trobe Picture Collection, State Library of Victoria)

for private use.[13] It was several decades, however, before final designation and protection of the Blue Mountains as national park were achieved, decades which were to see the landscape undergo further transformation.

Nature for the Public: Mass Tourism (1870s–1930s)

The late 1880s and early 1900s were characterized by the rise of mass recreational tourism in the Blue Mountains, assisted by an array of advertising images and physical additions that promoted and embellished it as a place for the experience of nature.[14] The difficult topography, along with the process of reserving particular scenic spots as recreational reserves, had ensured the retention of large areas of spectacular and relatively undeveloped bush, despite being so near to Sydney ("bush" is an Australian term for eucalypt forest, or generically any landscape that exists beyond urban settlement). As a result, the landscape was now one of the most important sites where Australians could engage with nature—albeit a form of nature that was mediated and modified to appeal to them as tourists.

The establishment of a public railway service through the Blue Mountains in 1867, along the same route as the original east–west road, made mass tourism possible. The railway authority was (and still is) a proactive marketer of the landscape, producing, along with local government and private tourism operators, a wealth of landscape representations including written histories and myths, guidebooks, photographs, artworks, and advertisements (fig. 5). These representations imbued the landscape with new meaning. From the early fashion for ferns, waterfalls, and canyons through to later interests in spectacular cliff top panoramas, they followed trends in taste. The notoriety of these new sights was facilitated by the shifts in technology used to produce and distribute promotional images en masse. Estimates show there have been more than one hundred different editions of guidebooks, the same number of souvenir books, and in the order of five thousand postcards produced since the 1880s, which when multiplied by the number of print runs amounts to millions of images of the Blue Mountains landscape.[15]

The effects of tourism on the physical landscape during this period were significant. A wide variety of elements were inserted within the natural setting, including paths, ladders, staircases carved into cliff faces, seats, bridges, numerous lookouts, signs, water fountains, shelter sheds, and even ornamental dams. The appearance of place names such as "Prince's Rock" and "Honeymoon Lookout" reflect some of the historic events and popular uses associated with such facilities. During tourism's heyday between World War I and World War II, the mountains were not conserved as wilderness but were considered a cultural landscape, where engaging with the natural landscape was essentially a social activity. Some historians have criticized tourism-driven modifications and additions to the landscape because of their commercial intent and "contrivance" in the face of nature.[16] Others have celebrated their cultural, historic, and aesthetic value. In a 1998 heritage report commissioned by the New South Wales National Parks and Wildlife Service (NSW NPWS), historian Jim Smith recognizes the ingenuity, creativity, craftsmanship, and environmental sensitivity of those who designed and built the eighty-seven miles of walking tracks and associated infrastructure that occur within the Blue Mountains National Park.[17] (The report also notes that the origins of some tracks, like the highway route, can be traced back to Aboriginal habitation.) In addition, tourism has historically been credited with assisting conservation efforts: historian David Mosley observed that calls for the protection of various areas of the region appeared to gain the support of local councils more readily when the areas in question were linked to established tourist sites and the towns that serviced them. The areas closest to road and rail, for example, were the first to be designated as national park, with outlying areas of the Greater Blue Mountains following some time later.[18]

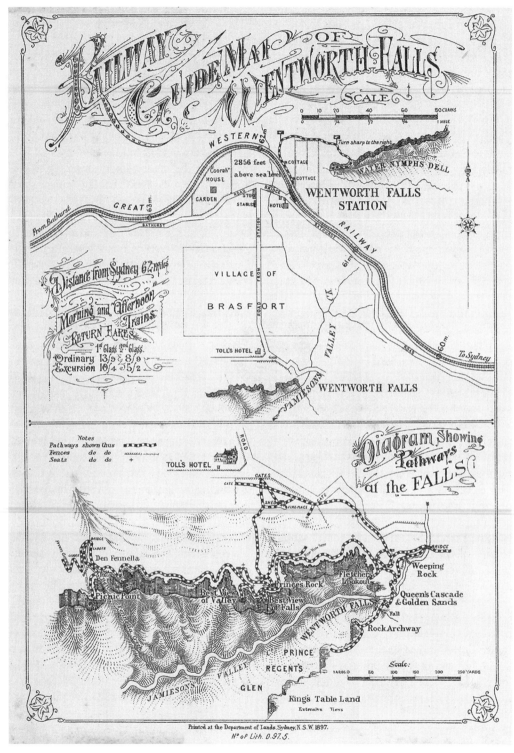

FIG. 5. Railway guide map of Wentworth Falls, 1897. (Courtesy of the State Library of NSW, A330 [Safe 1/404])

Nature Revisited: Conservation (1930s–2000)

The dominance of mass tourism as a form of engagement with the Blue Mountains landscape has, in recent decades, been superseded by conservation practices and attitudes. Following World War II, visitation to the Blue Mountains declined. It could be said that the recreational landscape became a victim of its own success: the spectacular iconic views, accessed from convenient lookouts, had become tourism clichés lacking long-term interest. As a popular beach culture developed, Sydneysiders turned eastward toward the city's coastline (most famously Bondi Beach) instead of westward to the mountains. Nevertheless, as engagement in the form of day trips and holiday makers waned, a growing number of people came to appreciate the ecological value of the mountains landscape. The Blue Mountains National Park was declared in 1959, following a conservation movement that originated with bush-walking groups in the 1930s. One of the main proponents of this movement, Miles Dunphy, successfully used the print media to advocate for the establishment of extensive areas of protected land. Dunphy's vision was largely realized in 2000, decades after his death, when the Blue Mountains National Park received World Heritage listing in December 2000 as part of the 2.47-million-acre Greater Blue Mountains World Heritage Area (GBMWHA).[19]

In the tradition of lobbying for nature conservation through the persuasive representation of landscape, filmmaker John Weiley produced the Maxvision large-screen documentary *The Edge* in 1996, at a time when the mountains were being nominated for World Heritage status.[20] *The Edge* is a nature documentary which seeks to educate viewers about the geomorphology, vegetation, Aboriginal occupation, European exploration, settlement, and conservation values within the Blue Mountains landscape. A recurring motif throughout the film is the Wollemi pine (*Wollemia nobilis*), a rare and ancient plant species discovered in a remote Blue Mountains valley in 1994. The film features individuals exploring a fragile wilderness (no walking tracks in sight) in search of the Wollemi pine, while the threat of the city of Sydney sprawling to the east looms large on the horizon. In contrast with the tourism representations of previous decades which celebrated the social qualities of nature recreation, *The Edge* presents a landscape possibly on "the edge" of environmental collapse, a wilderness needing to be treated with care.

The film illustrates a shift in the conceptual construction of nature and landscape, where new technologies are used to tell old and new narratives. As well as telling a story of conservation, this film is marketed to tourist audiences as an "edge of your seat adventure," with rock climbing shown on the custom-built six-story-high screen recalling some of the earliest Blue Mountains' themes of vertiginous danger and difficulty.[21] Throughout their experience of *The Edge,* audiences vicariously engage in a virtual simulated tour: camera movement, spectacular time-lapse imagery, and helicopter fly-through footage condense time and space and create the "illusion of actually participating" in a landscape that is larger than life.[22]

In this manner the public is encouraged to simultaneously engage in nature and leave it physically unmodified. In parallel, the park landscape itself is managed so that the provision of new infrastructure, such as paths, is limited, while the conservation, improvement, and interpretation of existing facilities (now of heritage value in their own right) are encouraged. Significantly, park staff actively participated in the making of *The Edge* movie, since the promotion of park values through outside channels (commercial filmmaking) is seen as part of an overall management strategy that extends well beyond the physical boundaries of the park landscape.[23]

Current Cultural Constructs (1990s–)

The concepts which have historically defined and shaped the Blue Mountains continue to find their expression in contemporary landscape design, representation, and management in and around the GBMWHA. More than ever, a range of practices and design interventions mediate between the national park and the next generation of mountain tourists and residents. These practices perpetuate existing narratives, transform others, and add new meanings. All use new technologies to represent and promote the landscape in conjunction with the modification of the physical sites themselves, as the following four examples elaborate.

Over time the first settler route to bisect the mountains—now the Great Western Highway—has been transformed from a "rough track" to a contemporary piece of landscape infrastructure. Most recently, in 2002, landscape architects Spackman and Mossop designed an upgrade for a 3.6-mile section of the highway which "celebrates . . . the unique drive through the mountains."[24] The handling of carriageways, cuttings, plantings, and spatial rhythms in this landscape all aims to enhance place identity as well as address the pragmatic safety issues associated with road design. The upgraded highway corridor retains remnant vegetation, uses local sandstone, makes references to local landscape gardening traditions (introduced species), and retains a sense of sweeping curves. Significantly, the road design is proudly of its time, framing the surrounding nature in a contemporary manner. As the designers explain, "Highway design can be unapologetically contemporary and yet in keeping with the natural and cultural values of the local area. . . . Respect for the character of the local area will not be achieved by the appropriation of stylistic cues or fashions from another era, but through the sensitive consideration of the location, siting and scale of the new elements."[25]

The mix of exoticism, escapism, aesthetic appreciation, and economic exploitation characteristic of the mid- to late 1800s are today reflected in the designed landscape of the Mount Tomah Botanic Garden, specifically through the inclusion of the rare Wollemi pine. The 69-acre garden is located along a main tourist route within the mountains, with expansive views of the national park that surrounds it. Designed by landscape architect Geoffrey Britten, then employed by the New South Wales Public Works Department, the botanic garden was opened in 1987 to showcase the cold climate plants that thrive at high mountain altitude. Plantings of the Wollemi pine were added following their discovery within the national park in the mid-1990s, and these are highlighted as a "feature garden" element within Mount Tomah signage, guidebooks, and their website.[26] The inclusion of these plants in this context perpetuates the scientific study of the exotic and curious landscape, as the species is presented to the public as a scientifically significant discovery that sheds light on the evolution of the Australian continent. Furthermore, the tree is an economic resource, reproduced for commercial gain; the Royal Botanic Gardens and national parks extract income from sales of the tree, which is cultivated and distributed with a commercial partner. Finally, the design of the botanic garden frames the tree as an aesthetic and symbolic object of contemplation. Just as early artists sought to inform their audience of the wonders of the landscape through the representations of nature they composed, the inclusion of this tree from the national park within a designed landscape setting is used to symbolize its ancient beauty and significance to the wider public.

The legacy of mass tourism is today most evident at Echo Point, a scenic lookout located at a cliff's edge where the township of Katoomba meets the Blue Mountains National Park. Echo Point progressed incrementally from a simple clearing one hundred years ago to a major tourist site, complete with a cantilevered concrete platform, floodlights, gates, garden, car parking, and visitor center. In 2000, the Sydney office of landscape architects Tract Consultants produced a plan for the major revitalization of the site, clearing existing outdated planting and amenities and updating them with a large sandstone plaza, new amenities area, enhanced traffic management, and new interpretive materials (designed in conjunction with the National Parks and Wildlife Service). Echo Point provides a contemporary urban window onto the adjacent scenery, making use of several devices to frame the view. Design devices include the choice of materials such as local stone, poetic and factual types of interpretive material, and a subtly choreographed experiential sequence that leads incrementally to the main viewing platform (fig. 6). Tract's design response accommodates a range of visitor patterns, from a few minutes to a few hours, making use of several functional way-finding and symbolic cues to facilitate rational circulation and access without corralling people along a directed route.

The designed landscape celebrates the contemporary spectacle and theatricality of the mass tourism lookout experience, with nature serving as a scenic backdrop for the human action in the foreground. Spectators are invited to perform the ritual of looking out on the landscape, with multiple terraces providing vantage points from where visitors can watch other visitors. The lookout "physically regulates the spectacle of the Blue Mountains landscape,"[27] and this spectatorship is itself put on display. Overlaid on this physical site is its promotion by local tourism authorities, who now represent the site via a branded website and brochures.[28]

Finally, the tension between the phenomenon of ecological conservation and the consumption of nature experiences (characterized

by *The Edge* movie) finds its physical landscape equivalent in eco-tourism resort development. The Wolgan Valley Resort and Spa, a six-star conservation-based luxury resort, opened in October 2009 following years of planning and construction by Emirates Hotels and Resorts.[29] Sydney-based landscape design firm Context developed the landscape strategy for the four-thousand-acre site that includes landscape planning, design, and management policies. The exclusive development sits in a dramatic valley surrounded by the GBMWHA, its setting emphasized in Emirates' online promotional materials. The resort consists of forty freestanding guest villa suites, serviced by a collection of main guest buildings accommodating conference facilities, restaurants, bars, a luxury spa, gift shop, and gym, all styled as interpretations of traditional rustic "Federation Period" architecture.[30] A restored heritage building from 1832 along with staff facilities in a contemporary architectural style are also included within the overall development. According to the designers the new resort structures were sited to follow the existing contours of the valley, fringed by flowing bands of predominantly endemic and native planting.

The majority of the site has been set aside by Emirates as a self-declared private conserva-

FIG. 6. Echo Point lookout, Katoomba, Tract Consultants, 2007. (Author photo)

tion area where a host of ecological measures are under way, including creek restoration, re-vegetation, and feral-proof fencing. Such a set-ting promises to provide visitors with all the highlights of the Blue Mountains in a single luxurious and convenient setting, not unlike *The Edge* movie. Indeed, like *The Edge* and the Mount Tomah Botanic Garden, the resort uses the symbolism of the Wollemi pine to promote their conservation approach, for example, by planting a commemorative specimen to mark the beginning of construction on-site and by using the Wollemi as the resort logo.

As well as giving expression to values associ-ated with nature and settler histories, all these recent projects acknowledge the Aboriginal significance of this landscape—an old narrative being retold anew. Desktop research and con-sultation with Aboriginal representative groups were undertaken by Spackman and Mossop and their client when developing the Great Western Highway plan, ensuring that no sites of archaeo-logical significance were disturbed by construc-tion works.[31] The Mount Tomah Botanic Gar-den includes a Darug Aboriginal Connections display that features storyboards at five loca-tions in the garden; these interpretive signs explain various aspects of the lives of the lo-cal Darug people, including their use of plants for bush foods. Accompanying information in a booklet and website has been endorsed by local Darug communities.[32] At Echo Point, interpre-tive signage has also been used to acknowledge the Aboriginal heritage of the area, and the Aboriginal flag flies over the Visitor Informa-tion Centre. Finally, at Wolgan Valley Resort and Spa, Context has included Aboriginal bush foods within the resort design, and the resort offers activities such as traditional storytelling, boomerang throwing, and guided Aboriginal cultural walks where archaeological sites are visited.[33]

Future Constructions

In the Blue Mountains, a range of attitudes, representational conventions, technologies, and legal frameworks have evolved alongside the physical form of the area, culminating in the current protected Greater Blue Mountains World Heritage Area and national parks net-work. Our analysis has touched on a selection of many practices and ideas associated with one particular place, sampling just some of the cultural expressions that contribute to an ongoing discourse which frames and modifies the experience and meaning of nature. This discourse both reflects and affects changes in dominant cultural attitudes. Although this analysis has been divided into five chrono-logical and thematic phases, it should be noted that in practice these phases overlap and in-terrelate. Within each phase, certain concepts and practices dominate; however, many ideas or ways of seeing persist and coexist. Further-more, current cultural practices continue to perpetuate and challenge historically domi-nant attitudes.

Conceiving parks, including national parks, as dynamic cultural landscapes whose narra-tives evolve through numerous practices has a number of practical consequences for their future design and management.

First, acknowledging the broader cultural context in which landscape narratives emerge means that national parks must look outward, beyond their physical boundaries, to under-stand and engage with that broader context. The conceptualization of the Blue Mountains as a national park has occurred through evolv-ing cultural practices such as photography, tourism advertising, and conservation lobby-ing. Surrounding or framing the national park, both physically and conceptually, are other landscapes—the road, the botanic garden, the film, and so on—each with its own evolving cultural practices. Intertextually, these all con-tinue to form a complex web of meaning and practice. This suggests that those who design and manage user areas in national parks should engage with the areas and projects adjacent to them, as the NSW NPWS did with the mak-ers of *The Edge* movie. Such initiatives ensure parks remain contextually aware and relevant, and integrated into cultural practices more generally.[34]

Second, by understanding past meanings and

uses of the landscape, designers and managers of parks can give expression to rich and important histories. Narratives from the past demonstrate the potential for change, and in so doing they open up spaces where new narratives can continue to be created. Representing multiple, and sometimes contested, narratives is important, even where so-called natural landscapes are concerned. In the Australian context, where indigenous ways of engaging with the landscape have for too long been marginalized, this is a significant challenge and opportunity.

Third, park narratives find their expression across many representational media from amateur photography to commercial film and online advertising, and as technologies evolve so too can the messages and meanings they transmit. Historically, a diverse range of meanings have been associated with nature, a diversity matched by the numerous media that have been used to give expression to them. Park managers can actively utilize a wide range of technologies to engage the wider public. Just as technologies, such as GPS, have allowed diverse and complex physical resources to be managed differently, so too should current and future technologies such as the Internet be used to manage and facilitate a diversity of park narratives.

Overall, the approaches to park design and management advocated here are fundamentally concerned with the ongoing management of landscape narratives in all their diversity. Constructing park narratives, as well as the physical form of the park itself, is a dynamic and interrelated process. Designating, describing, representing, and designing the physical landscape all have a part to play in constructing notions of what a national park can and should be.

Notes

1. Numerous cultural geography and history and landscape design texts describe the cultural construction of landscape. For example, see Cathrin Bull, *New Conversations with an Old Landscape* (Mulgrave, Vic.: Images Publishing Group, 2002);

Denis Cosgrove and Stephen Daniels, "Introduction: Iconography and Landscape," *The Iconography of Landscape,* ed. D. Cosgrove and S. Daniels (Cambridge: Cambridge University Press, 1988), 1–9; James Duncan and Nancy Duncan, "(Re)reading the Landscape," *Environment and Planning D: Society and Space* 6 (1988): 117–26; John R. Gold and George Revill, *Representing the Environment* (New York: Routledge, 2004); Matthew Potteiger and Jamie Purinton, *Landscape Narratives: Design Practices for Telling Stories* (New York: Wiley, 1998); Alexander Wilson, *The Culture of Nature: North American Landscape from Disney to the Exxon Valdez* (Cambridge, Mass.: Blackwell, 1992).

2. This approach to the cultural construction of landscapes is informed by the "circuit of culture" model. See Stuart Hall, "Introduction," in *Representation: Cultural Representations and Signifying Practices,* ed. Stuart Hall (London: Sage, in assoc. with The Open University, 1997), 1–11.

3. See http://www.visitbluemountains.com.au/about.php.

4. See Dianne Johnson, *Sacred Waters: The Story of the Blue Mountains Gully Aboriginal People* (Rushcutters Bay, NSW: Halstead Press, 2007), 21; Jim Smith, *Aboriginal Legends of the Blue Mountains* (Wentworth Falls, NSW: Jim Smith, 1991); Martin E. Thomas, *The Artificial Horizon: Imagining the Blue Mountains* (Carlton, Vic.: Melbourne University Press, 2004).

5. Historical Records of New South Wales, quoted in Kate Hartig, *Images of the Blue Mountains,* Research Monograph Series, Department of Geography (Sydney: University of Sydney, 1987), 15.

6. Ibid., 30, 33.

7. See Julia Horne, *The Pursuit of Wonder: How Australia's Landscape Was Explored, Nature Discovered and Tourism Unleashed* (Carlton, Vic.: Miegunyah Press, 2005); Jim Smith, "Blue Mountains Myths and Realities," in *The Blue Mountains: Grand Adventure for All,* ed. Peter Stanbury, 2nd ed. (Sydney: Macleay Museum, University of Sydney, 1985), 185–202; Thomas, *The Artificial Horizon.*

8. See Horne, *The Pursuit of Wonder,* 199–225.

9. Darwin, reproduced in George Mackaness, ed., *Fourteen Journeys over the Blue Mountains of New South Wales, 1813–1841* (Sydney: Horwitz-Grahame, 1965), 232.

10. Catherine Snowden, "The Take-Away Image: Photographing the Blue Mountains in the Nineteenth Century," in Stanbury, ed., *The Blue Mountains: Grand Adventure for All,* 133–56.

11. Bonyhady, quoted in Thomas, *The Artificial Horizon,* 225–26.

12. Jim Smith, *Blue Mountains National Park Walk-*

ing *Track Heritage Study* (Sydney: NSW National Parks and Wildlife Service, 1998), 11.

13. This occurred under the Crown Lands Alienation Act of 1861. See Ibid., 18–25.

14. Anne Burke, "Awesome Cliffs, Fairy Dells and Lovers Silhouetted in the Sunset: A Recreational History of the Blue Mountains, 1870–1939," in Stanbury, ed., *The Blue Mountains: Grand Adventure for All,* 99–117.

15. Smith, *Blue Mountains National Park Walking Track Heritage Study,* 93.

16. Burke, "Awesome Cliffs, Fairy Dells and Lovers Silhouetted in the Sunset."

17. Smith, *Blue Mountains National Park Walking Track Heritage Study.*

18. John Geoffrey Mosley, *Battle for the Bush: The Blue Mountains, the Australian Alps and the Origins of the Wilderness Movement* (Sydney: Envirobook and Colong Foundation for Wilderness, 1999), 118.

19. The GBMWHA is made up of seven national parks: the Blue Mountains, Wollemi, Yengo, Nattai, Kanangra-Boyd, Gardens of Stone and Thirlmere Lakes National Parks, and the Jenolan Caves Karst Conservation Reserve.

20. *The Edge,* motion picture, Heliograph Productions, Byron Bay NSW, Australia, John Weiley and R. Whittingham, Producers; John Weiley, Director, 1996.

21. *The Edge,* promotional flyer, 2004.

22. Carolynne Skinner, *The Edge—The Movie* (Wentworth Falls, NSW: OZ Arts, 1996), 27.

23. See *The Edge* movie credits; also refer to the NSW NPWS Filming and Photography Policy, at http://www.environment.nsw.gov.au/resources/parks/policyFilmingPhotography.pdf.

24. Spackman and Mossop, *The Great Western Highway Leura to Katoomba Urban Design Framework,* 2002, xii, http://www.rta.nsw.gov.au/constructionmaintenance/downloads/majorgwhleuratokatoomba_dl1.html.

25. Ibid., 56.

26. See http://www.rbgsyd.nsw.gov.au/welcome_to_bgt/mount_tomah_botanic_garden/the_garden/feature_gardens" \l"Wollemi_Pine."

27. Thomas, *The Artificial Horizon,* 222.

28. See Nicole Porter, "Landscape and Branding: The Global Market for Place," in *Globalisation and Landscape Architecture: Issues for Education and Practice,* ed. Glenn Stewart et al. (St. Petersburg: Polytechnic University Publishing House, 2007), 156–61.

29. See Urbis JHD, Emirates Luxury Resort Wolgan Valley Modified Concept Plan, November 2005.

30. See http://www.emirateshotelsresorts.com/wolgan-valley/en/resort/.

31. Spackman and Mossop, *The Great Western Highway Leura to Katoomba Urban Design Framework,* 24.

32. See the Royal Botanic Gardens Sydney website at http://www.rbgsyd.nsw.gov.au/plant_info/aboriginal_bush_foods#Darug.

33. Urbis JHD, Emirates Luxury Resort Wolgan Valley Modified Concept Plan, 62; Wolgan Valley Resort and Spa media release, October 2009.

34. For a discussion of the role of landscape design within such an approach, see James Corner, "Introduction—Recovering Landscape as a Critical Cultural Practice," in *Recovering Landscape: Essays in Contemporary Landscape Architecture,* ed. James Corner (New York: Princeton Architectural Press, 1999), 1–26.

"If Paradise Is in the Land of Israel, Its Entrance Is at the Gates of Beit Shean"

Israeli National Parks and the Fluidity of National Identity

Unlike their American precedents, which celebrate virgin nature as a source of national pride, Israeli national parks are located in the cradle of the nation's past—in the remains of King Herod's palace, in the ruins of King David's town, and in the presumed location of the biblical paradise, as wrote Reish Lakish, a third-century Jewish scholar.[1] Sixty-six national parks have been established by the State of Israel since the mid-1960s, displaying the cultural, archaeological, and historical heritage of the country, as well as some of its best outdoor environments. Nowadays, as the concept of the national state is challenged and as Israel acknowledges its more diverse, multicultural society, it is time to ask whose cultural heritage is celebrated in these parks and in what ways, if at all, they acknowledge contemporary, multicultural Israel.

National Parks and National Identity: An International Perspective

The national park idea, as conceptualized in America in the mid-nineteenth century, celebrated virgin nature as a source of national pride.[2] Half a century later, during World War I, touring America's national parks became a fashionable patriotic pastime.[3] Consequently, these sites were shaped by architects and landscape architects in order to guide the experience of park visitors and enhance their appreciation of the landscape.

The American model found its way to other countries. As early as 1895, Victorian philanthropists who were concerned about the impact of uncontrolled development and indus-

trialization set up Britain's National Trust as a guardian for the nation in the acquisition and protection of threatened coastline, countryside, and buildings. In 1931, a report issued by the National Parks Committee advocated the establishment of a series of parks in the British Isles aimed at fulfilling three objectives: "To safeguard areas of exceptional national interest against disorderly development and spoliation; to improve the means of access for pedestrians to areas of natural beauty; and to promote measures for the protection of flora and fauna."[4] Due to legislative and economic problems, the actual declaration of the British national parks was postponed until the end of World War II.

National parks were not restricted to the Western world, however, and as early as 1926, South Africa passed its National Parks Act.[5] The act was a manifestation of the Afrikaners' nationalism, which included the adoption of Afrikaans as an official language, the revival of interest in "Voortrekker"-Afrikaans and Dutch tradition, and the loosening of ties with imperial Britain. Furthermore, as Jane Carruthers has argued, the act can be seen as part of the process of systematic domination of Africans by whites.

Israel's National Parks and National Identity

The history of Israel's national parks is relatively short, but unique. Unlike the American model, Israel's national parks and landscape reserves were institutionalized under two different frameworks: the Nature Reserves Authority and the National Parks Authority (both in 1963). Their establishment was the outcome of an intensive public and parliamentary debate concerning landscape and nature preservation, cultural heritage, and tourist development.[6] Eighteen years after their establishment, in 1981, the state approved a national plan (TAMA 8) for national parks, nature reserves, and landscape reserves; and a further seventeen years later, a new amendment passed unifying the two authorities into the Israel Nature and Parks Authority (INPA, 1998), under the auspices of the Ministry of Environmental Protection. One hundred ninety nature reserves have been declared on nearly eight hundred thousand acres of land, and sixty-six national parks on more than thirty-seven thousand acres. Together, they make up about a quarter of the country's land mass.[7]

However, the idea of establishing national parks was conceived a decade before the enactment of the law, originating in an effort to promote local and international tourism within the young State of Israel. In 1956, Teddy Kollek, the director of the Prime Minister's office and in later years Jerusalem's legendary mayor, established a committee of archaeologists and former military officers in order to realize the idea. Their goal was to establish a network of parks and tourist attractions to be mainly based on restored archaeological sites, frequently including swimming facilities. This unusual combination was a perfect solution binding education and leisure, since swimming was a favored outdoor leisure activity in the hot and dry climate of Israel. The first thirteen national parks were established at prominent archaeological sites. Today, the expanded list includes historic sites, recreation areas, and scenic attractions that aim to satisfy the recreational needs of the local population, as well as to create the "tourist experience" for diaspora Jews, Christian pilgrims, and others. Furthermore, the recent inclusion of several national parks on the prestigious UNESCO List of Sites of World Heritage has secured their place in the global map of tourism.[8]

Israeli national parks were never approached as a neutral terrain for leisure activity per se. As archaeological or historical sites, or as scenic attractions, they were designed as the country's "cabinet of curiosities," a museum-like territory for enjoyment, for education, and for nourishing the soul, in accordance with the common Western park legacy of the nineteenth century. Furthermore, as "homeland museums," Israel's national parks are one of the three key institutions that Benedict Anderson defined as involved in the creation of nations in his seminal work *Imagined Communities* (1983).[9] Along with the map and the census, Anderson argues that the museum determines a nation's history and common heritage. Within this framework, archaeological sites perform the same function as museums, since they provide each nation with a deep sense of history and connection to the land.[10] The first national parks, established by the new Israeli state, reflected the ideology of the hegemonic early settler society, which was mostly of European origin. The national parks were perceived as an efficient tool in creating a new common Israeli identity by celebrating the nation's biblical history and geography, and by encouraging immigrants to take part in the actual construction of this national narrative.

Presently, between the opposing pulls of postnationalism and neo-nationalism,[11] and due to the growing influence of diverse segments of the country's population (Orthodox Jews, Palestinians, new immigrants, and distinct ethnic groups), Israeli identity is becoming fragmented and varied, less reflective of the hegemonic early settler society. The footprints of these processes are clearly marked on the local terrain, and next to traces of hegemonic Israel, which are well documented by various scholars,[12] the marks of marginalized groups have become more prominent on the landscape.[13]

Within this framework, Gan Hashlosha al-Sakhne National Park allows us to observe two different and contrasting processes in the dynamic between park design and cultural identity. On the one hand, the different elements in the park—the landscape as a concrete entity, the design process, and everyday practices and their representations—are processed to serve the construction of a hegemonic national identity. On the other hand, various groups making use of the landscape, fragment this construction and make the park a multilayered narrative. The park's management is currently negotiating between these two poles while struggling for economic viability.

Gan Hashlosha al-Sakhne National Park

"Gan Hashlosha al-Sakhne" National Park (the *garden of the three* in Hebrew, *the warm one* in Arabic) is located in the northern part of the country, at the foot of Mount Gilboa (fig. 1). It is situated in the vicinity of the biblical King's

Way, where goods, people, and, frequently, armies traveled from the Mediterranean basin to the lands of the East. At the heart of the park is a natural spring, one among several springs gushing along a deep geological fault. The water, which is slightly salty, maintains a constant temperature of 28°C (82°F) throughout the year. Its abundance enables the dense vegetation to flourish in close proximity to the stream, in contrast to the nearby bare mountains. Not surprisingly, the site is described by traditional Arab and Jewish sources as the original opening to the Garden of Eden, and by *Time* magazine as one of the world's most intriguing spots, worthy of a detour.[14]

FIG. 1. Gan Hashlosha al-Sakhne National Park, 2010. (Author photo)

As the salty water made the site unsuitable for agricultural activity, since the Roman era it was used to activate water-powered flour mills that supported the nearby prospering Roman town of Beit Shean.[15] During the Arab period, dispersed Bedouin villages dotted the landscape, and al-Sakhne was one of them. The locals built three mills next to the stream, operating year-round. Jewish settlement of the region began in 1934, when a group of settlers, the future members of Kibbutz Tel Amal (now called Nir David), began cultivating the land purchased by the Jewish National Fund. When Arab riots began one night in April 1936, the kibbutz's first wheat crop was burned and its other plants and seedlings were uprooted. Determined to return to their land, the settlers established the first "tower and stockade" settlement six months later—a fortresslike settlement that became a popular model for more than fifty other Jewish settlements in the three years that followed.

Park Design as a Zionist Project

What did Paradise look like before it was reconstructed by Jewish settlers? Zvi Bahir, a kibbutz member and the head of the National Gardeners Organization, wrote in his 1958 memories: "This lovely spot, hidden between rocky beaches, canes, reeds and thorny raspberry, which was enchanting in its savage and natural beauty, was also desolate and crowned with waste and nettles. For many years, I dreamt to redeem this lovely spot next to my home and make it a blossoming garden."[16]

Upon the establishment of the State of Israel in 1948 and the emergence of regional and national planning, the pool became a focus of more intensive development. Zvi Bahir suggested connecting all of the valley's springs, forming a long boulevard,[17] an idea ahead of its time. Several years later, Bahir and landscape architects Dan Zur and Lippa Yahalom proposed a plan which aimed to transform the dusty small pool into a "Garden of Eden" (fig. 2). Early development focused on the water as the key attraction of the park. Rolling hills covered by lawn and planted with shading trees surrounded the newly built swimming pools, creating a pastoral landscape. Among the planted trees were some old trees such as olive trees and palm trees next to new plantings of eucalyptus trees and fig trees. The latter were considered a means of financing the park by fruit marketing. Lack of a sufficient budget delayed the development, until the state decided to support the low-income, immigrant population of nearby modern Beit Shean with employment projects such as park construction. On Independence Day in 1958, as part of the celebrations for the first decade of the state, Israeli president Yitzhak Ben Zvi inaugurated the park and named it Gan Hashlosha—the Garden of the Three. The site was declared a national park in 1967.

Further initiatives brought new amenities to the site in the years that followed: a regional museum was founded in 1963, a restaurant opened in 1969, and an exact replica of Tel Amal, the first local "tower and stockade" settlement, was built within the park area in 1993. Due to limited available resources for the park's development, more ambitious projects remained on paper, and for many years Gan Hashlosha was mainly a passive recreational area.

Recently, a new master plan and detailed design schemes were prepared by landscape architects Daphna Greenstein and Gil Hargil. Their proposal addresses the management's demand to make the site more profitable, on the one hand, while maintaining its original charm, on the other.[18] They added more lighting in order to extend the hours of activity and more areas for toddlers' bathing; and they proposed playgrounds to entertain children who were bored just playing in the water. Greenstein-Hargil suggested building a spa, reviving an old idea of the early planners, in order to attract winter tourism and to upgrade the park's image as a luxurious spot (fig. 3). Other initiatives included the opening of a cave that dates back to the second century, in which Jewish rebels, fighting against the Romans, were hidden, as well as the planting of a biblical garden next to the "tower and stockade" site. (The latter would hardly be able to compete with the Australian garden in the nearby kibbutz, which also owns kangaroos and koalas [unfortunately, not mentioned in the Bible].)

In late 2008, the park inaugurated a regional initiative: the settlement's bell garden, exhibiting various bells that served the early Zionist settlements until the mid-1960s. As a main communication device, the bells woke up the pioneers, called them to attend meetings, and warned them of riots. The various bells, which vary in size and material, were collected by local residents, or were rebuilt by volunteers (fig. 4).

This short description of the park's design through almost half a century reveals the efforts of the park designers to emphasize and reinforce the Zionist identity of the park by accentuating a Zionist layer (both a physical layer and a symbolic layer of interpretation) which covers over earlier layers of the landscape, from the Israelite, Roman, and Ottoman

periods. Thanks to the ingenious design, this invented layer relates to the previous layers, takes its place among them, and thus is made to seem natural, fitting into history like a piece in a puzzle.

From the early twentieth century on, Zionist efforts to reclaim the swampy and the bare lands of Beit Shean Valley from the "desolation of generations" included not only the establishment of fields and agricultural settlements but also the improvement of the natural environment and a preference for a unique kind of development. The work of Lippa Yahalom and Dan Zur, and later Greenstein-Hargil, integrates past and future, nostalgia and utopia, biblical images and modern land uses. It is rooted in the time of the patriarchs as well as in the modern era.

Transplanting old trees, such as olive trees, palm trees, and other species mentioned in the Bible, made the place look old and "natural," not a man-made landscape. The image of an-

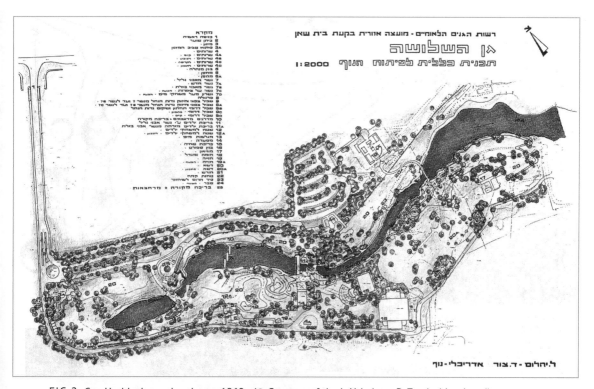

FIG. 2. Gan Hashlosha, early scheme, 1960s. (© Courtesy of the L. Yahalom–D. Zur Archive, Israel)

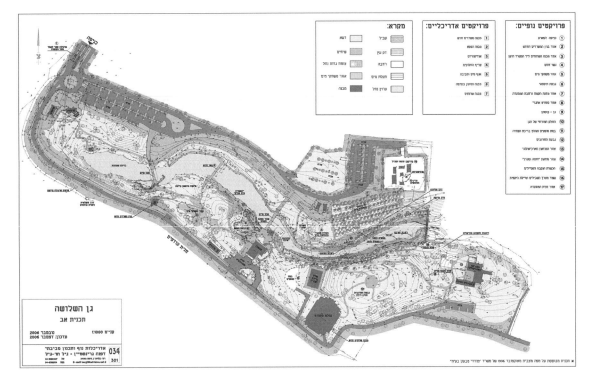

FIG. 3. Gan Hashlosha, current scheme, 2006. (Greenstein-Hargil, Landscape Architects)

tiquity, or the past, was reinforced by the exposure of the archaic layer of the Israelite village from 2000 BCE, the Roman remnants within the park, and the old mills of the Ottoman era. The archaeological exhibition in the small park's museum put the local findings such as those from the Roman Beit Shean in the regional context of the grand Mediterranean basin, including Greek, Persian, and Etruscan collections.

The Zionist layer was emphasized with the establishment of the exact replica of the "tower and stockade" Tel Amal within the park, the reproduction of the iconic pastoral landscape of the kibbutz within the park, and currently the inauguration of the settlement's bell garden. It was symbolically reinforced by the official name of the site, Gan Hashlosha—the Garden of the Three—commemorating the

FIG. 4. Gan Hashlosha, the settlement's bell garden, 2010. (Author photo)

three pioneers (modern founders of the Zionist settlements of the valley) Chaim Shturman, Aharom Etkin, and David Mosinzon, who were killed during the 1936–38 Arab riot. Zionist and archaic layers came together to present a teleological narrative, its sources in archaic Eden, or in the Israelite village, and its climax in the adjacent modern kibbutz.

Interestingly, and in contrast to other national parks around the country,[19] the Palestinian layer of the park was hardly damaged, probably due to its negligibility; after 1948, no prominent remains of the Bedouin village were left at the site, probably due to its nomadic character, and the complex of the flour mills with their Palestinian agricultural tools integrated well within the general image of the pastoral landscape. Unlike other sites all over the country, even the Arabic name of the site—al-Sakhne—was left next to the Hebrew name. This casual remainder hints at the plurality of meaning and uses of the park, which emerge despite the design efforts prioritizing Zionist historical tropes.

The Park's Mosaic of Visitors

Since its opening, Gan Hashlosha has been a successful tourist destination. Its permanently warm water made it a perfect year-round bathing place, which attracted at first the residents of the region and later people from all over the country and beyond. A recent account from a new Jewish émigré describes the site as, unsurprisingly, paradise:

In all my 38 years, I have never quite known where I would find Paradise. Until now. On an early summer trip, with our friends from Lakewood, New Jersey, we discovered Paradise; and it was not just a place, it was a state of mind. We found it right here in Israel, a little way off scenic Route 90, heading north in the Jordan Valley. . . . It was everything I imagined I would find in Paradise: tall, graceful palm trees providing shade on acres of lush, green grass, and in the center, deep, natural pools with beautiful azure waters connected to each other by dazzling waterfalls. As we walked through the site, taking in the maj-

esty all around us, we began to notice something almost as fascinating: the people. Here, lounging in Paradise was a complete mix of Israelis and Arabs; Jews, Christians and Muslims, side by side, enjoying the park together. Well, maybe not together, but side by side. In fact, with everyone in their swimming suits, splashing in the water, sometimes it was hard to tell them apart.[20]

A different perspective is presented by Esther Zandberg, a prominent Israeli critic of architecture and landscape architecture. In a 2001 newspaper article she describes Gan Hashlosha as a microcosm of the Israeli genome, a charged junction of contesting ideologies, social relations, and economic opportunities: "Gan Hashlosha represents every part of the Israeli's mosaic: Arabs and Jews, nature and cement, prophetic vision and 'Hutzpa,' mangal—the local version of barbecuing—and spa."[21] From the beginning, the social dynamics in the park reflected greater social trends. In the late 1950s, kibbutz members and Beit Shean residents got together on the lavish lawns along the water. The former were "veteran" immigrants, mostly of European origin, representing hegemonic Israel. The latter were low-income new immigrants, mostly of non-European origin, among them many park construction workers. With very limited common cultural background they struggled over the use of space, hours of activity, and style of recreation. Consequently the park, previously a direct continuation of the kibbutz yard, was fenced and separated from the kibbutz grounds, and its development directed visitors farther away from the kibbutz area. Despite the disagreements, until 1967 Gan Hashlosha continued to serve as a symbolic icon of hegemonic Israel. It was a preferred site for weekend car trips for middle-upper-class Israelis, and functioned as the ceremonious culmination of many arduous youth and military journeys in the valley. These overnight gatherings around the fire, in an Eden made by the Zionist early settlers who sacrificed their lives not far away, were very influential, strengthening self- and national identity.

After the 1967 war and the opening of the border between Israel and the Jordanian West Bank, the park became quite popular among the Arab residents of Nablus and nearby villages who found the lavish grounds and especially the water amenities very appealing. Zvi Bahir, the park founder and first manager, described their arrival as "the killing" of the park.[22] His observation was induced by the abandonment of the park by middle-upper-class visitors who used to arrive there on weekends. But his critique ignored the flourishing of the park among other segments of the population, such as the residents of Beit Shean and other locals, especially Palestinians from both sides of the border (fig 5).

Since the great immigration wave of the mid-1990s, Gan Hashlosha has become popular among Russian immigrants, who frequent the park during weekends, arriving in the early morning hours and leaving little space for other visitors. They have made the park a center for family gatherings and the site of an annual music festival.

During the 1990s, the early struggle between kibbutzim members and the residents of Beit Shean was replayed between the Palestinians and the Russian immigrants. But while the early park was designed as an undivided space for all, since the mid-1990s it has been fragmented into time and space units in order to address the contradictory demands of the park's visitors and to avoid conflicts among its users. This phenomenon was described in the local media as early as 1997: "It is worth noting that the park bustles with people of every community and origin. Veteran Russian immigrants arrive by the thousands on Saturdays, Muslims arrive on Fridays, and Christians—on Sundays. The number of swimmers is relatively small in relation to those who barbecue and entertain friends. Each according to his will."[23]

This voluntary arrangement was institutionalized by the management of the park a few years later in order to enable visits of the Jewish Ultra Orthodox community and to increase revenues from a second shift of activity. As the members of this community are strict in en-

FIG. 5. Arab matrons and teenagers from the West Bank at the edge of the pool at Gan Hashlosha, during their Friday weekend picnic in the open, late 1960s. (National Photo Collection, Government Press Office, State of Israel)

forcing separate bathing for men and women, only separate opening hours enable their bathing there.

Spatial separation is encouraged by the existing topographical conditions. The cleaner and larger upper pools are usually frequented by the Jewish visitors to the site. The lower (less clean) pools are used by the Arab visitors, and when the religious population overcrowds the site, the women are sent to bathe there separately.

Since the 1990s the focus of the park's management, in terms of development and marketing, has changed significantly from the early days, and it is reflected in the new design of Greenstein-Hargil. Adopting a more active approach, the park initiated a number of projects to appeal to the varying interests of multicultural Israel. These include a range of culturally specific programs that meet the social and economic demands and constraints of the majority of the Israeli population and foreign tourists. Throughout the 1990s, the park hosted dozens of festivals and special events such as a country music festival, jugglers' and martial arts gatherings, fashion exhibitions, and more. These activities brought thousands of visitors to the park for overnight celebrations.

Additionally, the global tourist industry has brought new communities to the site. A short magazine article in 1996 described Gan Hashlosha as a popular destination for international tourism. And after the Pope's visit to Israel in 2000, the site received the blessing of Christian pastors and became a baptism site.[24]

Summary and Discussion

As a Zionist project, the design of Gan Hashlosha al-Sakhne National Park, which integrates biblical sources and modern symbols of hegemonic Israel, was perceived as an effective tool in building and reinforcing a Zionist-Israeli identity. During the early days of statehood this narrative was relatively efficient for hegemonic Israel, a middle-class population of European origin, which until 1967 made the site part of its national lexicon, a symbolic site of pilgrimage due to its history and its various found and designed amenities.

These were less relevant for the residents of Beit Shean—a lower-class population of non-European origin—who adopted Gan Hashlosha as a site of popular celebrations devoid of national-historical meanings. Their settling process was ignored by the park's design and their local attachment to the place derived from their physical construction of the park.

The Zionist layer of the site was even less significant for the Russian immigrants. They made Gan Hashlosha a site of community gathering disconnected from the history of the place or its unique landscape (Ashkelon National Park plays a similar role for Russian immigrants from southern Israel).

Currently, and especially in comparison to the late 1960s and 1970s, Arabs feature less prominently among the park's visitors. This process began during the first Intifada (the Palestinian popular uprising from 1987–93) and has accelerated with the construction of the separation wall between Israel and the West Bank, which left only Palestinians with Israeli citizenship as potential visitors. They were gradually discouraged from visiting the park by the dominance of the Russian population as well as by park policy, which prohibited music making, on the one hand, and did not initiate any cultural programs aimed at the Arab community, on the other. Alternative bathing amenities in the Arab settlements and in other nearby springs have become more popular among this community.

Ultra Orthodox Jews and Christian pilgrims are two new elements in the park's mosaic, as they gather around the water and the biblical sources of the site.

Browsing the park's website reveals that on recent spring weekends, the park hosted Chinese and Russian circuses, an international dance group, a magic show, and more; the original amenities of the park were only mentioned under the heading "In Addition." This list of events reflects the park management's need to make the park economically viable by responding to the demands of a multiethnic, diverse market, this at the expense of fostering national identity, the park's original, declared intent. Furthermore, the park is no longer perceived as an undivided landscape where all communities meet, intermingle, and become Israeli. It remains successful as long as each community preserves its uniqueness and separation from other communities, since the parcelization of the park, and especially its peripheral area, into separate activity zones and hours of operation is currently the only way to overcome conflicts among its users.

Meanwhile, despite and perhaps against the various meanings that each of these groups projects onto the site, the park's management is reviving the pastoral image of the place as a tranquil, passive recreation area under the title "We Didn't Touch." The site is merchandised as a "natural" place, existing since primordial times (fig. 6).

FIG. 6. *We Didn't Touch,* promotion leaflet, 2008. (Gan Hashlosha Archive, Israel Nature and Parks Authority)

An advertisement for the 2008 Passover Parade along the valley's springs revives Bahir's vision of connecting all the valley's attractions and making Gan Hashlosha the gate of the project. Longing for an ideal past is expressed both visually and textually: A pastoral archaic image printed on a scroll-like background supports the text which describes Gan Hashlosha as a lovely spot from biblical time: "and it is said 'The gate of Paradise.'" Interestingly, the advertisement emphasizes the Arabic name of the site, al-Sakhne, over its Hebrew name, integrating an image of an oriental palm tree in the Hebrew letter nun, which stretches to form a river.

Recently, the local park museum hosted a three-day event in the spirit of the *"EKECHEI-RIA,"* the ancient Greek cease-fire announced during the Olympic Games. Performed mainly by Jewish schoolchildren, the local event, like similar events abroad, ended with the students declaring their commitment to peace and

friendship between nations and cultures. It seems that on the tightrope of the contemporary political situation, making peace between Sparta and Athens is the only way to handle the topic without tumbling. Hopefully, in the future, it will be possible to address directly the compartmentalization and seclusion happening within the park itself.

Notes

1. The title of this essay derives from a comment by Rabbi Shimon Ben Lakhish (Reish Lakish; c. 350 CE) found in the Talmud, Eirubin, 19a.

2. Alfred Runte, *National Parks: The American Experience* (Lincoln: University of Nebraska Press, 1987); Angela Miller, "Everywhere and Nowhere: The Making of the National Landscape," *American Literary History* 4, no. 2 (1992): 207–29.

3. Marguerite Shaffer, *See America First: Tourism and National Identity, 1880–1940* (Washington, D.C.: Smithsonian Institution Press, 2001), 107.

4. John Sheail, "The Concept of National Parks in Great Britain 1900–1950," *Transaction of the Institute of British Geographers* 66 (1975): 41–56, quotation on 42.

5. Jane Carruthers, "Creating a National Park, 1910–1926," *Journal of Southern African Studies* 15, no. 2 (1989): 188–216.

6. Daniella Arieli, "HaHavnaya HaTarbutit shel HaTeve: HaMikre shel HaHevra LeHaganat HaTeva BeIsrael" (The cultural construction of nature: The case of the Society for the Protection of Nature in Israel), *Megamot* 38 (1997): 189–206; Avner De-Shalit, "From the Political to the Objective: The Dialectics of Zionism and the Environment," *Environmental Politics* 4, no. 1 (1995): 70–87.

7. Alon Tal, "Space Matters: Historic Drivers and Turning Points in Israel's Open Space Protection Policy," *Israel Studies* 13, no. 1 (2008): 119–51, esp. 126.

8. These include the biblical archaeological hillocks of Hazor, Megiddo, and Beer Sheva (2005), the Nabatean cities of Mamshit, Shivta, Ovdat, and Haluza (2005), and Massada (2001).

9. Benedict Anderson, *Imagined Communities: Reflections on the Origin and Spread of Nationalism* (London: Verso Editions, 1983).

10. Michael Pretes, "Tourism and Nationalism," *Annals of Tourism Research* 30, no. 1 (2003): 125–42.

11. Uri Ram, "The State of the Nation: Contemporary Challenges to Zionism in Israel," *Constellations* 6, no. 3 (1999): 325–38; Adriana Kemp, Uri

Ram, David Newman, and Oren Yiftachel, *Israelis in Conflict: Hegemonies, Identities and Challenge* (Portland, Ore.: Sussex Academic Press, 2004); Baruch Kimmerling, *The Invention and Decline of Israeliness: State, Society, and the Military* (Berkeley: University of California Press, 2001); Anita Shapira, ed., *Israeli Identity in Transition* (Westport Conn.: Praeger, 2004).

12. On traces of hegemonic Israel, see Oz Almog, "Andartaot LeChalaley Milchama BeIsrael: Nituach Semiology" (War memorials in Israel: A semiological analysis), *Megamot* 34, no. 2 (1991): 179–210; Maoz Azaryahu, "From Remains to Relics: Authentic Monuments in the Israeli Landscape," *History and Memory* 5, no. 2 (1993): 82–103; Maoz Azaryahu, *State Cults: Celebrating Independence and Commemorating the Fallen in Israel, 1948–1956* (Sde Boker: Ben Gurion University of the Negev Press, 1995); Tamar Berger, "Sleep, Teddy Bear, Sleep: Independence Park, Petach Tikva: An Israeli Realm of Memory," *Israel Studies* 7, no. 2 (2002): 1–32; Yael Zerubavel, *Recovered Roots: Collective Memory and the Making of Israeli National Tradition* (Chicago: University of Chicago Press, 1995); Yael Zerubavel, "The Forest as National Icon: Literature, Politics and the Archeology of Memory," *Israel Studies* 1, no. 1 (1996): 60–99; Yael Zerubavel, "The Politics of Remembrance and the Consumption of Space: Masada in Israeli Memory," in *Memory and the Impact of Political Transformation in Public Space,* ed. Daniel J. Walkowitz and Lisa Maya Knauer (Durham, N.C.: Duke University Press, 2004), 233–52.

13. On marks of marginalized groups, see Aron Shai, "The Fate of Abandoned Arab Villages in Israel, 1965–1969," *History and Memory* 18, no. 2 (2006): 86–106; Naama Meishar, "Fragile Guardians: Nature Reserves and Forests Facing Arab Villages," in *Constructing a Sense of Place: Architecture and the Zionist Discourse,* ed. Haim Yacobi (England: Ashgate, 2004), 303–25; Yitzhak Schnell, *Ovdim Zarim BeDrom Tel Aviv-Yaffo* (Foreign workers in South Tel-Aviv-Jaffa; Jerusalem: Florsheimer Institute for Policy Research, 1999).

14. *Time* (20 May 1996); see, for example, http://www.maianot.co.il/cgiwebaxy/sal/sal.pl?lang=he&ID=930898_bbshean&act=show&dbid=Tourism_eng&dataid=96.

15. The site and its surroundings are rich in archaeological remnants dating to the middle Palaeolithic period (100,000–20,000 BCE). Within the park there are graves and a mound from the Israelite period (2000 BCE). Among the prominent remains along the stream is a Roman water theater that was hardly excavated.

16. Zvi Bahir, "Gan Hashlosha," *Gan VaNof* 18, no. 13 (1958): 236–40, quotation on 236.

17. Ariel Ranen, "Gan Hashlosha," in *Memories of Beit Shean* (Jerusalem: Beit Shean Regional Council, 1995).

18. Interview with park manager Yehuda Carmi, April 2009.

19. Shelly Egoz, "Deconstructing the Hegemony of Nationalist Narratives through Landscape Architecture," *Landscape Research* 33, no. 1 (2008): 29–50.

20. Laura Ben David, "A Peace of the Middle East," *Israelinsider* (Israel's daily newsmagazine), 2007, http://web.israelinsider.com/Views/11665.htm.

21. Esther Zandberg, "Gan Eden Maase Yedey Adam" (A manmade Eden), *Haaretz,* 4 June 2001, http://www.haaretz.com/hasen/pages/ShArt.jhtml?itemNo=025124.

22. Ibid.

23. *Babik'a* (a local magazine), December 1997 (Gan Hashlosha Archive).

24. Undated journal, Gan Hashlosha Archive.

PART V

MONUMENTS IN THE LANDSCAPE

Protecting Artifice Amid Nature

Camp Santanoni and the Adirondack Forest Preserve

On a frigid, midwinter day in 1972, the Santanoni Preserve, a 12,663-acre tract, was transferred to public ownership as a major addition to the Adirondack Forest Preserve—a great reservoir of mostly wild land, stringently protected by the state constitution.[1] Environmentalists viewed the event as a momentous one. The ceremonies occurred in the unheated 1840 Elizabethtown, New York, office of Supreme Court justice Augustus C. Hand. Hand's great, great grandson, Arthur Savage, also a lawyer, orchestrated the acquisition. For some years, Santanoni's previous owners, brothers Crandall and Myron Melvin, a prominent banker and lawyer, respectively, from Syracuse, had explored ways of divesting themselves of the preserve, which had become a serious financial burden to them. They were also concerned that the land, most of which had never experienced substantial modification by humans, remain undisturbed. At a time when the Adirondacks were experiencing unprecedented real estate development, the chance to save Santanoni Preserve was welcome not only because the acreage was so large but also because it lay tangent to the region's High Peaks, arguably the most prized portion of the Forest Preserve—a place where wildness still prevailed over a vast, unbroken territory. Besides possessing important natural attributes in its own right, the Santanoni tract would serve as a buffer for the region's crown jewels.[2]

To consummate the deal, Savage and his brother-in-law, Wayne Byrne, established a new division of the Nature Conservancy, the Adirondack Conservancy Committee, to serve as an intermediary. While the land was valued at $1.5 million, the Melvins were willing to accept two-thirds of that amount, taking the difference as a tax deduction. Most of the purchase price was covered by a grant of $875,000 from the U.S. Bureau of Outdoor Recreation, which, for the first time, allowed the equity of the land held by the applicant to be as much as 50 percent of the grant value.[3] To cover the remaining $125,000, $75,000 was donated anonymously by Harold K. Hochschild, scion of a rich mining family based in New York, longtime Adirondack summer resident, and perhaps then the foremost citizen leader in the drive to protect the natural characteristics of the Adirondacks. The conservancy, with the help of the original owner's granddaughter and her husband, raised the additional $50,000. Without this unorthodox joining of federal and private-sector sources, the Melvins would have had little choice but to sell their land to commercial interests. State officials were overjoyed with the outcome. So was the Nature Conservancy's leadership. Both contingents viewed the Santanoni transfer as an important precedent for creative collaborations in the future.

Probably no one involved gave serious consideration to protecting the stunning array of buildings that had been erected in the preserve during the late nineteenth and early twentieth centuries as a rustic retreat for a rich, patrician Albany banker, Robert Clarence Pruyn, and his family (fig. 1). Unceremoniously dubbed a camp, the immense log pile that comprised the main lodge, its flock of outbuildings, another grouping that had once served as a model farm,

FIG. 1. Camp Santanoni, Newcomb, New York, main lodge, R. H. Robertson, architect, 1892–93. Constructed aerial view, showing boathouse (*left*) and pump house (*right*), looking west toward Newcomb Lake; drawing by Paul Malo, 1999. Note that the view minimizes the land mass and omits trees standing between the lodge and lake. (Adirondack Architectural Heritage, Keeseville, N.Y.)

an imposing stone gate lodge, and a formidable infrastructure developed to sustain living on a grand scale in a rugged, remote setting was by then generally regarded as an anachronistic holdover from another era—a white elephant occupying precious land that was best returned to the elements.

Yet there was a nagging sense that Camp Santanoni might be more than cumbersome baggage. Henry L. Diamond, commissioner of the newly formed New York State Department of Environmental Conservation (DEC), under the jurisdiction of which the Forest Preserve lay, did not want to destroy the buildings, although many environmentalists believed the state constitution so mandated.[4] The DEC's predecessor agency had incurred public outcry from burning the legendary Catskill Mountain House when the state had acquired its land a decade earlier. Diamond was especially anxious to avoid a sequel since his mentor, Lau-

rance Rockefeller, embraced the preservation of historic buildings. As a result, Diamond asked his property subordinate, Norman Van-Valkenburgh, to develop a management plan for Santanoni well in advance of its acquisition. That plan stipulated that the main lodge should be retained as a DEC training and conference center; the gate lodge would be used as a facility for managing the entire tract; and some other buildings would be saved as well. In reality, no funds existed to implement such measures.[5] State officials and environmentalists alike assumed that the untended buildings would eventually be overtaken by nature. Few people even knew of the camp's existence. Its loss would be lost in the triumph of protecting the wildness of so important a part of the ancient Adirondacks.

Certainly no one in 1972 could have imagined that preserving the camp would emerge as a popular and well-publicized issue by 1980;

would be sanctioned by the governor eleven years later; and would develop into an exemplary case of interweaving the concerns of conserving natural lands and preserving historic resources by the turn of the twenty-first century. The process was a protracted one, fraught with seemingly insurmountable challenges, propelled by intense activism, aided by political savvy, and sometimes laced with acrimonious confrontation. Stoking the long-standing controversy were a host of legal issues, as well as questions of appropriate use for a place embedded in wild lands, but at the very core lay conflicting views about the value of the Adirondack Park and its future complexion. Did the region's wildness override all other concerns; was it so precious and so fragile that its protection and enhancement should guide all official policy? Or was the region also valuable as a cultural landscape, a place long manipulated by humans who had left a rich legacy that deserved to be part of the historical record understood and enjoyed by future generations? As William Cronon argued more than a decade ago, wilderness is a construct. To deny the human history of places may not only eradicate important vestiges of the past, it also establishes a false perception of nature and may foster less responsible tutelage of our own environments. Nature should not come at the expense of culture; the two are often closely related and can exist in reasonable balance.[6] Santanoni affords a particularly insightful case study of the ongoing debate between natural and cultural affinities; it also demonstrates how that debate can and should be tempered— how both spheres can exist in harmonious relationship with each other.

The Making of Santanoni Preserve

The fact that so much privately held land remained in so wild a state into the third quarter of the twentieth century was no accident. Santanoni Preserve indeed ranked among the most ambitious conservation projects in the Adirondacks at the time of its inception in 1890. Over the following eight years land parcels were assembled by Robert Pruyn, who, with his wife,

Anna Williams Pruyn, shared a deep love of nature.[7] While most of the land they purchased in the town (i.e., township) of Newcomb remained pristine, the potential for change was by no means small. The demand for all kinds of timber was then swelling in proportion to the nation's insatiable appetite for pulp and lumber; some of the Pruyns' tract had been heavily logged by a previous owner. As the extraction of natural resources from the region was nearing its peak, creating Santanoni Preserve was a decisive countermeasure.

Although ideas for preserving the wildness of the Adirondacks had been advanced since the mid-nineteenth century, state legislators entertained virtually no concrete measures to ensure that agenda. Lawmakers in Albany *had* withdrawn the region's remaining state-owned land from sale in 1883. Two years later, they designated that land as the Adirondack Forest Preserve, which comprised around 640,000 acres in hundreds of parcels scattered throughout an area roughly the size of Vermont. Yet no stipulations were made as to how these fragments were to be protected or how they might be expanded and consolidated. The Forest Preserve was considered more of a land bank to protect supplies of timber and fresh water than the makings of a true park. State officials, moreover, were notoriously beholden to business interests. A growing contingent of citizens feared the Adirondacks were headed for ecological disaster. Extensive tree cutting for pulp was causing large-scale erosion, and the detritus left in its wake was generating unusually numerous and intense forest fires. Nervousness mounted that the prolonged effects of these phenomena could adversely affect land—and business—well beyond the region. Within the contexts of backroom political deals and escalating destruction, the Forest Preserve seemed little more than a ruse.[8]

Due to intensifying public pressure, more concerted measures were taken to protect the region concurrent with Pruyn's development of his estate. In Albany, the legislature resolved in 1890 to enlarge the Forest Preserve through additional purchases. A bill was passed two years later to create the Adirondack Park, comprised of some 2.8 million acres, and to expand the Forest Preserve, which then comprised less than a fifth of that territory. By 1905, Forest Preserve land had more than doubled in acreage, but remained geographically scattered, without a systematic plan for consolidation.[9] Unlike national and most state parks, then, the Forest Preserve was not a coherent entity, but a diffuse array of holdings large and small and in many cases not readily accessible from public rights of way.

The Forest Preserve also differed from other holdings that came into federal or state stewardship by virtue of the near absence of recreational infrastructure. Hotels, restaurants, ski facilities, picnic grounds, scenic drives, and many other features that increasingly characterized rural parkland were banned; only dirt access roads, trails, and occasional camping shelters were permitted.[10] This unusual protection of wildness stemmed from the state's new constitution of 1894, which included a provision (Article VII, Section 7; reconstituted as Article XIV, Section 1 in 1938) stipulating that the Forest Preserve "be forever kept wild forest lands. They shall not be leased, sold or exchanged, or be taken by any corporation, public or private, nor shall the timber thereon be sold, removed or destroyed." Any buildings or other man-made artifacts on acquired land would be burned, demolished, moved, or left to decay.[11] This mandate was the first substantive step to counter the then-still-increasing exploitation of timber and mineral resources. Some proponents of Article XIV may have envisioned the day when the Forest Preserve would encompass most of the Adirondacks, but it is doubtful if anyone intended the region to become an entirely wild land. Its protection was in large part for human enjoyment through hiking, hunting, fishing, and other leisure pursuits. Yet the fact that the Adirondacks had long been a place of human habitation was accorded little consideration in the law. Though sparsely settled by East Coast standards and still boasting vast acreage untouched by any people, the region was far from being a true wilderness.

Like others, the Pruyns embraced protecting land for enjoyment. While they were not the first to create Adirondack preserves for this purpose, they fashioned their holdings in a distinct way. The Brandreths and the Whitneys amassed enormous tracts in the central part of the region beginning in 1851 and 1887, respectively, but their parks, as they were called, were developed primarily as a male sporting ground. Santanoni Preserve, conversely, was a place for the family and for guests of all ages and both genders.[12] Three years before Pruyn began his purchases, the Adirondack Mountain Reserve (AMR) was formed to acquire from timber interests more than twenty thousand acres around the Ausable lakes, encompassing some of the most spectacular landscape in the High Peaks. But that organization was comprised of stockholders, who with their families resided at a nearby hotel or in cottages around that establishment. The AMR was used for hiking and fishing (but not hunting), with nights sometimes spent in modest lakeside campsites. And, unlike virtually all other such private reservations in the Adirondacks, the AMR allowed the general public access to the mountain trails within its confines.[13]

In contrast, Santanoni was a very private residence occupied by a relatively small number of people. It was developed on an epic scale, unprecedented in the Adirondacks. The main camp, comprised of an enormous lodge and subsidiary buildings—including a boathouse, studio, caretaker's residence, barn and stable, icehouse, and, later, garage and chauffeur's house—was reached by a five-mile drive from Newcomb's hamlet center. The site's isolation was apparently the wish of Anna Pruyn, who had a special fondness for residing amid the wilds. About a third of the way on this route lay a farm compound, with a barn, shop, creamery, smokehouse, icehouse, hen houses and coops, piggery, sheep barn, duck house, slaughterhouse, and eventually three residences (fig. 2). The farm was developed out of necessity, as importing fresh food to the camp was difficult by horse and wagon and remained challenging after the introduction of motorized transport.

Robert Pruyn, who was more partial to pastoral than wild settings, took special interest in farm operations. At the entrance to the estate lay an imposing gate lodge, as well as carriage house, barn, chicken coop, boathouse, and residence (fig. 3). Elaborate camps had been built in the Adirondacks since the late 1870s, but never before on so large or isolated a tract. Even with much larger camps undertaken around the turn of the twentieth century, the size and extent of infrastructure attained at Santanoni was seldom matched and even more rarely exceeded.[14]

If Camp Santanoni can be seen as an epic fin-de-siècle gesture, defying its isolation and allowing perhaps as many as twenty members of the family and their guests to live in comfort amid the wilds, it can also been seen as a conservative enterprise where the impact upon its setting was minimal and largely benign. Grounds were not cultivated and seldom even cleared save for the raising of food to sustain the household, staff, and livestock. Space around the main complex was sufficiently open to inhibit prolonged moisture penetration, but the

FIG. 2. Camp Santanoni, farm complex, looking south, showing, *right to left,* dairy barn (1896, 1902–4, Edward Burnett, architect; burned 2004), piggery (probably by Burnett), creamery (1904, att. Delano & Aldrich, architects), icehouse (*to rear*), "new" farmhouse (1896), and refrigeration plant (*to rear*). Photo early twentieth century. (Adirondack Architectural Heritage, Keeseville, N.Y.)

FIG. 3. Camp Santanoni, gate lodge, 1905, Delano & Aldrich, architects. View looking west, with Rich Lake in background (*right*). Photo early twentieth century. (Adirondack Museum/Susan Pruyn King)

FIG. 4. Camp Santanoni, main lodge, view of central pavilion (living and dining areas). Photo early twentieth century. (Adirondack Museum/Susan Pruyn King)

FIG. 5. Camp Santanoni, main lodge, view of rear, showing, *left to right,* kitchen wing, central pavilion, guest cabin, and bachelor's cabin. Photo 1895. (Adirondack Museum/ Susan Pruyn King)

FIG. 6. Camp Santanoni, boating party, probably comprised of Pruyn children and their friends. Photo early twentieth century. (Adirondack Museum/Susan Pruyn King)

effect was still of buildings in the woods, with trees screening the nearby lake from all but fragmented views (figs. 4, 5). Daily life, when the Pruyns were in residence, was largely spent outdoors—boating, swimming, hiking, fishing, playing ball games, having picnics, and visiting the farm (figs. 6, 7, 8). Hunting was generally limited to a fall party. Geographically, these pursuits were for the most part confined to an area within a mile radius of the main lodge or along the drive. After Robert Pruyn's death in 1934, some selective harvesting of timber was done to offset the formidable costs of maintenance, but most of the land experienced little, if any, human presence.

FIG. 7. Camp Santanoni, camping party at Moose Pond lean-to, probably comprised of Pruyn children and their friends. Photo early twentieth century. (Adirondack Museum/Susan Pruyn King)

FIG. 8. Camp Santanoni, members of Pruyn family and/or guests at shore of Newcomb Lake, near main lodge. Photo early twentieth century. (Adirondack Museum/Susan Pruyn King)

The Rise of Historic Preservation

The campaign to preserve Camp Santanoni would never have coalesced without a series of unrelated events that began to bring the historical significance of Adirondack camps into the public limelight. For most of the twentieth century, these rustic retreats were primarily known just to those who occupied, visited, or serviced them. That situation began to change in 1975 when Syracuse University proposed to sell Sagamore, a 1,500-acre tract that it owned near Raquette Lake. Erected in 1897–98 by William West Durant and sold in 1901 to Alfred G. Vanderbilt, the camp that lay in the heart of the preserve matched Santanoni in its grand scale, and the main lodge surpassed it in its theatricality.[15] Armed with funds for land acquisition appropriated in a 1972 bond issue, the DEC was the only party to make an offer. To stave off the inevitable loss of this complex were it to become part of the Forest Preserve, the newly formed Preservation League of New York State worked with the DEC to find an outside purchaser for the 7.5-acre area in which most of the buildings lay. Barbara Glaser and Howard Kirschenbaum offered a viable proposal to use the complex as an education and conference center, the same basic function it had served for the university and one most environmentalists considered acceptable for a remote place that lay three miles from a public road.[16]

Sagamore was not the only Adirondack preservation issue. Marjorie Merriweather Post's lavish Camp Topridge on Upper St. Regis Lake was bequeathed to the state in 1973. Wishing to avoid further controversy, state officials placed the property under the Office of General Services instead of the DEC. Topridge became a conference center, but proved too costly to operate and went on the market in 1984, putting its future in jeopardy.[17] During the mid-1970s, too, heirs to William Seward Webb's Ne-Ha-Sa-Ne Park negotiated with the DEC to sell most of the 14,664-acre tract, stipulating that its buildings, dating from the mid-1890s and by the same architect as Camp Santanoni, be destroyed after the transfer.[18]

But the most concerted struggle emerged in 1983 over Sagamore's service complex. Kirschenbaum had wanted to include it in the original purchase, but the DEC's VanValkenburgh had balked, believing that it would be too intrusive on the Forest Preserve. Now the threat of destruction prompted preservationists to go on the offensive. That summer the Preservation League, working closely with Kirschenbaum, established a coalition that courted the region's Republican politicians, always interested in countering the power of state agencies, and also acquired a two-hundred-acre tract of privately held land to exchange for the ten acres occupied by the service buildings. The transfer required an amendment to the state constitution, but the state's gain in land coupled with rescuing what was now seen as a key component of the camp proved a winning combination. The episode also proved to be an important training experience for Santanoni, the fate of which became ever more an issue amid the mounting drive to protect Adirondack camps.[19]

That such concern could be expressed over Sagamore's service complex reflected a maturing historic preservation movement. The growth and increasing professionalization of that movement following passage of the National Historic Preservation Act of 1966 occurred more or less concurrently with the recrafting of historical inquiry to encompass a much broader segment of the past, with attention focused on representative, as well as exceptional, heritage.[20] In the Adirondacks, the Preservation League sponsored a 1975 conference on the challenges of protecting the region's camps and in 1978 completed a historical survey of thirty-five of them.[21] Knowledge of the remarkable characteristics of many camps and the challenges of preserving them was advanced, in writings by Craig Gilborn, director of the Adirondack Museum, and Paul Malo, the Preservation League's first president, among others. Harvey Kaiser's *Great Camps of the Adirondacks* (1982), a lavishly illustrated popular history, was particularly instrumental in bringing the subject to a large, national audience.[22]

A shift in state attitudes was also discernible.

In 1978, the lieutenant governor convened a conference, "Cultural Heritage in the Wilds," which was held at Camp Topridge. In the opening address, Peter Berle, DEC commissioner and a prominent environmentalist, stressed the need to have a comprehensive inventory of historic places in the Adirondacks and doubted there would be many instances where the goals of historic preservation would conflict with those of the Forest Preserve. He also recognized Santanoni as "one of the finest examples of wilderness estate architecture" and vowed to maintain the buildings until their future was resolved. At the conclusion of the conference, a resolution was passed that preserving historic buildings was in the public interest and thus should become a priority of the DEC.[23] But as the discussions at Topridge made clear, the legal difficulties involved and the degree to which views differed on the subject were substantial. No monies were forthcoming for a region-wide survey, nor had any real progress been made on other fronts when a second conference on the subject was convened at Union College in 1982.[24]

The Concerns of Environmentalists

Many of those dedicated to protecting the Forest Preserve regarded the move to preserve historic properties on state land from quite a different perspective, one that saw the Adirondacks as a region under siege. The increasingly perceived need to protect wild areas throughout the United States during the post–World War II era, most publicly manifested in the passage of the Wilderness Act of 1964, was confronted in the Adirondacks by fast-mounting threats of development.[25] Although conservationists had opposed it, an amendment to the state constitution in 1959 allowed Interstate 87—the Adirondack Northway—to go through the park's eastern side. When it opened eight years later, the highway enabled vacationers from both the New York and Boston metropolitan areas to reach the Adirondacks within four hours and those from Montreal within half that time. The resulting pressures for developing seasonal residences, especially along lakefronts, was unprecedented. The village of Lake Placid was fast being transformed from a genteel enclave into a mass resort. Overdevelopment was already considered rampant along the southwestern shore of Lake George. The environmentalists' concern for what they deemed inappropriate uses of privately held land was matched by pressures on the Forest Preserve and, by extension, the sanctity of Article XIV. The rapid growth in popularity of mountain climbing, canoeing, camping, and other outdoor recreational activities, for example, was subjecting Forest Preserve land in the High Peaks to far more intense use than it had previously experienced.[26]

The park's fragility was underscored when Laurance Rockefeller proposed in 1967 that a major segment be transferred to the federal government as a national park. Environmentalists were incensed that their efforts of many decades might be undercut by a move that could increase public access.[27] As a countermeasure, Governor Nelson Rockefeller established a temporary commission, eventually chaired by Hochschild, to delineate measures needed for long-range park protection. The commission's report, released in 1970, stressed the urgency of taking decisive measures to save the park from ruin. Its recommendations led to the establishment of the Adirondack Park Agency (APA) in 1971, one of the nation's first regional planning authorities, which was given jurisdiction over the use of publicly and privately held lands alike. The following year the APA issued the State Land Master Plan for the Forest Preserve, designating most of the Forest Preserve as wilderness (997,970 acres), wild forest (1,150,000 acres), or primitive area (about 75,000 acres). But the drive to keep the Adirondacks wild and especially the APA's efforts to control development through zoning were met with passionate, occasionally violent, opposition from many year-round residents, who had long felt excluded from decision-making processes affecting their region and had felt especially threatened by the national park proposal, which would have forced substantial numbers of them from their homes.[28]

The ferocity of the response to the APA as well as the many environmental challenges facing the park spurred the formation of the Adirondack Council in 1975. Established by an alliance of regional and national groups, with Hochschild a leading proponent, the organization was set up to lobby and litigate. It would keep watch over environmental conditions in the park and defend the APA's planning program, but also keep watch over the actions of that agency, the DEC, and other government entities to ensure they acted in the public interest.[29] The Adirondack Council's leadership regarded efforts to preserve camps that lay on state lands as an unwelcome development in several ways. Such actions were among the latest in a long history of attempts to erode the forever-wild provisions of Article XIV, attempts that had been almost entirely rebuffed over the years. The mantle of preservation as being for the public good, however, may have seemed to pose a special threat to the constitution. Equally alarming was the fear that preserved camps could become a "deep woods nuisance"—major tourist destinations, introducing a level of human intervention far greater than these sanctuaries had ever experienced before.[30] Some other environmentalists shared that view. Hochschild apparently dreaded the possibility that Santanoni would become another large campground for the Adirondack Mountain Club. New York attorney Peter Paine Jr., who had served with him on the temporary commission and had served on the APA's board since its inception, described the road to Santanoni as "a dagger [thrust] into the heart of the wilderness."[31]

Dilemma and Transition

Throughout the 1980s, the future of Santanoni remained a dilemma, for which no progress was made toward resolution. The buildings themselves were steadily deteriorating from lack of maintenance. As decay accelerated, the DEC found itself ever less equipped to reverse the process.[32] The agency did not have the resources to rehabilitate and use the camp, and, even if it did, the controversy such steps might induce became readily apparent when some consideration was given to converting the gate lodge for use as one of two Adirondack visitor information centers, which were authorized in 1985. The Adirondack Council's George Davis emphasized to a member of the governor's staff that such a step would raise "the spectre of the environmental community's worst fears."[33] State officials were by no means uniform in their viewpoints. On the one hand, the state's Office of Parks, Recreation, and Historic Preservation (OPRHP) spearheaded Camp Santanoni's listing on the National Register of Historic Places in 1987. On the other hand, the Forest Preserve Advisory Committee voted the previous year to recommend that the complex be demolished in its entirety.[34]

The Sagamore experience had turned Kirschenbaum into a committed preservationist, who now set his eyes on finding a viable solution for Santanoni's long-term use. Beginning in 1984, he sought to demonstrate that the camp could be repaired and maintained by outside parties at little or no cost to the state. Lobbying DEC and other officials, he proposed that it be used as a lodge or youth hostel. However, these forays only aggravated environmentalists about overly intrusive use of Forest Preserve land.[35] In a public appeal, Kirschenbaum remarked that "Santanoni . . . has become a thorny issue for state agencies and environmental organizations, none of which wants to go on record as advocating the camp's destruction, yet none of which desires a major constitutional controversy over any attempt to save it or utilize it." In January 1989, a writer for the National Geographic Society framed the situation more dramatically: "Santanoni is dying, caught in a web of conflicting laws and good intentions," to which J. Winthrop Aldrich, who had become Santanoni's advocate within the DEC, added that it was "Exhibit A for where two very significant and very popular policies are in direct conflict."[36]

Santanoni would have succumbed to the elements, had not Kirschenbaum decided to form an organization to save it, Adirondack Architectural Heritage (AARCH), and become its first chairman, serving six years.[37] While AARCH's mandate was broad, the Santanoni issue was urgent. During the next five months a special committee was formed and its recommendations submitted and then adopted.[38] Kirschenbaum lobbied members of the state assembly and the governor's staff and created alliances with a spectrum of regional and local organizations, including a partnership with the Town of Newcomb. Knowing how polarized the situation had become, Kirschenbaum's strategy was to gain the upper hand through creating a sizable coalition with a sound plan of action. Only then would parties in opposition be engaged.[39]

AARCH's leadership benefited from the professional expertise of seasonal and year-round residents.[40] Equally important was a contingent comprised of elected officials and civic leaders from the region, who considered AARCH's mission—to understand, celebrate, and protect the region's human-made heritage—a welcome antidote to the demands of environmentalists. AARCH's key leader in this regard was George Canon, who had become Newcomb's town supervisor the previous year and was directing his energies to aid his community's survival.[41] Newcomb had never been a recreational destination. With the closing of a large mining operation nearby and the retreat of the forest products industry, the town lost most of its employment base. Eighty percent of town lands were owned by the state or under conservation easement. Canon shrewdly understood that increasing tourism compatible with Newcomb's expansive natural setting was essential to sustaining the community. Preserving Santanoni was central to that agenda. Many of his constituents were partial to the idea. In a town of fewer than six hundred residents, some households had direct ties with, and many had sentimental attachment to, the camp, which they considered an important part of the town's heritage.

And AARCH's lobbying efforts paid off.[42] During the summer of 1991, support from legislators, OPRHP, the Preservation League, and other groups appears to have led the DEC to commit to saving most of the main camp complex. Soon after the DEC's announcement, Kirschenbaum offered town monies and some volunteer labor for stabilization of the now rapidly deteriorating buildings. AARCH contributed volunteers as well. OPRHP offered technical assistance and the Preservation League commissioned a historian-architect team to make a preliminary assessment of the building components that demanded immediate attention. The momentum was sufficient that on 10 October 1991, Governor Mario Cuomo proclaimed that Santanoni would be preserved.[43]

Consummation

The path from Cuomo's pledge to resolving the legal issues, determining appropriate use of the site, and the extent of physical work to be done, as well as securing the funds necessary to realize the project, consumed nearly a decade. A major concern of the DEC and environmental groups alike had been the legal means of preserving the camp without eroding the strength of Article XIV.[44] Amending the constitution to create a land bank comprised of a maximum total acreage within the Forest Preserve to protect historic properties was entertained by many preservationists, including Kirschenbaum, but was criticized by others as potentially taking ever more land from its "natural" state.[45] Some parties believed that utilizing a 1983 law crafted to create "historic" areas on state land within the Adirondack Park, which a contingent of environmentalists believed to be unconstitutional, was a much easier and acceptable method.[46]

Once Santanoni was placed on the National Register and it became apparent that the buildings would not just be left to decay, Paine, who had coauthored the State Land Master Plan, successfully pressed for the APA's leadership to resolve the camp's legal status by according it the plan's "historic" category. By February 1992, DEC officials had decided in favor of this last option and to draft a unit management plan accordingly. AARCH and its allies accepted that position. But it continued to be debated, especially by the Adirondack Council, concerned lest the plan undermine Article XIV.[47]

A citizens advisory committee was created by the DEC in March 1995 so that all interested parties might express their concerns and aid the agency in crafting the unit management plan.[48] Kirschenbaum and Canon, especially, hoped that the camp could serve as a museum, presenting the story of a grand rustic retreat.[49] Michael DiNunzio of the Adirondack Council feared that any museum function would be too intensive a use. The interpretation should be of the "evolution of the land from a private resort to forest preserve," he maintained, adding: "The real story was that the camp became a white elephant, the farm failed and that the best use of the land turned out to be forest."[50] Similarly, the idea that the farm buildings house livestock and sustain some modest agricultural function was opposed because of the impact on wildlife and the intrusion of supply vehicles. There were, however, no serious disagreements over using the gate lodge as an interpretative center since the building lay at the edge of the Forest Preserve.[51]

How much of the camp complex should be preserved was also vigorously debated. AARCH took the offensive to retain all extant buildings so that the camp's extent and multiple functions would be clearly evident. Adirondack Council representatives regarded the extensive work necessary to save the collapsing boathouse and to repair the fast-decaying porch of the main lodge as overly interventional.[52] Environmentalists wished minimal change to the overgrown conditions that had occurred since the camp had come into state hands, while preservationists called for bringing back some of the openness that had characterized the farm historically. Ultimately, practical matters dictated some practices. If buildings were to be repaired and kept in reasonable condition, some of the forest that had grown up around many of the farm buildings, especially, had to be cleared.

In the fall of 1999, the DEC issued a unit management plan that enabled remaining portions of the camp to be preserved in their entirety. If it excluded all commercial functions and any motorized vehicles, the plan nonetheless went against many environmentalists' wishes for a greater sense of wildness at the buildings' expense.[53] The strong support base that AARCH had been able to build over the years, however, proved crucial to the acceptance of the plan by state officials, including the governor, in August 2000. The drive to validate its significance was fully realized when the camp was declared a national historic landmark three months earlier.[54] Since 1992, AARCH had been leading tours of the camp and had sponsored summer interns on the site to assist visitors in its interpretation beginning in the previous year.[55]

Equally important was the concrete work that had been undertaken since 1993. Historic structure reports, funded by the Preservation League and AARCH, provided the basis for setting priorities. In 1997, AARCH entered an agreement with the DEC to establish the Friends of Camp Santanoni for fund-raising. Money came from AARCH, mostly through the Friends group, and from the Town of Newcomb, private organizations, the DEC, and the state's Environmental Protection Fund.[56] In 2006, Governor Pataki pledged $1 million to the effort, monies that continue to fund work six years later.[57] The state was now a full participant in the process. The mountain had come to Mohammed.

In the late 2000s, as many as fifteen thousand visitors explore the site annually—walking, skiing, biking, riding horses, or hiring one of two wagon teams to traverse the five-mile drive to the main lodge. The "compromise" solution that the DEC developed with the unit management plan may in fact be the optimal one. The buildings, most of them now in sound condition, stand on their own, with low-key interpretative assistance. The minimalism, especially at a time when some interpretative facilities seem to overwhelm the resource, drives home the remoteness, the isolation, the solitude, and the wonder of the site. Standing on the main lodge's porch, peering through the trees to Newcomb Lake, one can sense the vastness of the wild lands that abound in the Adirondacks. One can also get a dramatic sense of how the Pruyns at once defied that wildness and built (and lived) in harmony with it. In all seasons and in all kinds of weather the experience is moving. There would be no Camp Santanoni left were it not for Kirschenbaum and AARCH, and Canon and his constituents. But the persistent concerns of environmentalists and the reverence all parties have shared for the Forest Preserve helped frame a remarkably powerful testament to artifice and nature in balance.

Maintaining that balance may prove as challenging as any other component of the preservation campaign to date. The complexity of the task has only become fully understood in recent years. The loss of the barn to fire in 2004 underscored the fragility of conditions. AARCH is committed to its reconstruction, but the means to accomplish that objective are far from certain.[58] While volunteers and contracted workforces have accomplished much, the need for a year-round site manager and staff is pronounced. And will the site continue to draw substantial numbers of visitors without offering more for them to experience? Might a living history farm that Canon has always hoped would take shape be a viable option? Not in the minds of many environmentalists, who still fear any such endeavor would intrude on the wild lands all around.[59] Pursuing any such projects has seemed the more problematic in recent years because the DEC remains a reluctant steward of historic properties—a role that seems far afield of its primary mission.[60]

The natural heritage of the Adirondacks is as precious as it is remarkable in its many aspects, not the least of which is the regeneration process that has occurred in the wake of massive deforestation in the nineteenth and early twentieth centuries. But the cultural legacy is also a long-standing one, with a rich heritage stemming from two hundred years of permanent settlement. The more these spheres can be harmoniously related, the more we can understand and appreciate each. By the mid-1990s, environmentalists and state policy makers alike were becoming more sensitive to involving year-round residents, to local economic concerns, and to forging alliances with property owners to pursue environmentally sensitive land management practices. Paper companies, for example, are no longer seen as alien interests but as partners in sustaining an ecologically sound park.[61] There has also been a significant rise in awareness of the rich and varied nature of the park's built environment, a shift to which AARCH has contributed in many ways. Our need to protect wild lands cannot come at the expense of human history—in the Adirondacks or elsewhere. The Santanoni accord deserves our attention for how one can achieve reconciliation under the most difficult circumstances.

Notes

I am grateful to Steven Engelhart, Susan Arena, Bonnie DeGolyer, and Ellen Ryan at AARCH; Elaine Burke at the Adirondack Council; and Connie Pickett at the Adirondack Chapter of the Nature Conservancy for sharing their extensive files with me. Additional material was gathered at the public libraries in Glens Falls, Plattsburgh, Saranac Lake, and Schenectady and at the Adirondack Museum in Blue Mountain Lake, where I am indebted to Jerold Pepper for information and to Angela Syne for illustrations. J. Winthrop Aldrich, former preservation officer for the DEC and deputy commissioner for historic preservation, OPRHP; Tim Barnett, former director of the Adirondack Chapter, Nature Conservancy; George Canon, supervisor of the Town of Newcomb; Howard Kirschenbaum, former codirector of the Sagamore Institute and founder and past chairman of AARCH; Peter S. Paine Jr., former member of the Temporary Study Commission on the Adirondacks and of the APA; Arthur Savage, cofounder of the Adirondack Chapter, Nature Conservancy; John Sheehan, communications director of the Adirondack Council; and Norman VanValkenburgh, former director of the Division of Lands and Forests, DEC, all graciously allowed me to interview them. AARCH and the Adirondack Museum supplied me with most of the photographs, the cost of which, along with other expenses incurred with this project, were covered by a grant from George Washington University's University Facilitating Fund. J. Winthrop Aldrich, Steven Engelhart, Howard Kirschenbaum, and Philip Terrie were kind enough to read a draft of the manuscript and offer numerous helpful comments.

I confess to knowing most of the people I interviewed, some of whom are friends and one of whom is a relative through marriage. I have served on the board of AARCH and am a member of the Adirondack Council and the Nature Conservancy. Despite these personal ties, I have sought to provide a balanced account that illuminates the differing concerns of those individuals and groups involved.

ABBREVIATIONS

Organizations: AARCH = Adirondack Architectural Heritage, AC = Adirondack Council, APA = Adirondack Park Agency, CAC = Santanoni Historic Area Citizens Advisory Committee, DEC = New York State Department of Environmental Conservation, OPRHP = New York State Office of Parks, Recreation, and Historic Preservation, PLNYS = Preservation League of New York State

People: BM = Bernard Melewski, AC; CG = Craig Gilborn, director, Adirondack Museum; CS = Clark Strickland, director, PLNYS; CV = Charles Vandrei, historic preservation officer, DEC; DG = David Gibson, AC; FC = Fred Cawley, director, PLNYS; GC = George Canon, supervisor, Town of Newcomb; HC = Herman ("Woody") Cole, chairman, APA; HK = Howard Kirschenbaum, codirector, Sagamore Institute, and chairman, AARCH; HW = Henry G. Williams, commissioner, DEC; JS = Julia Stokes, deputy commissioner for historic preservation, OPRHP; JWA = J. Winthrop Aldrich, special assistant to the commissioner, DEC; NVV = Norman VanValkenburgh, director, Division of Lands and Forests, DEC; PM = Paul Malo, director, PLNYS, and board member, AARCH; RB = Robert Bendick, deputy commissioner, DEC; RC = Richard Cipperly, assistant regional forester, DEC; SE = Steven Engelhart, director, AARCH; TJ = Thomas Jorling, commissioner, DEC [Note: positions were those at time of correspondence]

Publications: AAN = Adirondack Architectural Heritage, *Newsletter; ACN = Adirondack Council Newsletter; ADE = Adirondack Daily Enterprise* [Saranac Lake]; *AE = Adirondack Explorer; AJES = Adirondack Journal of Environmental Studies; AL = Adirondack Life; LPN = Lake Placid News;* PLN = Preservation League of New York State, *Newsletter; NYT = New York Times; PR = Press-Republican* [Plattsburgh]; *PS = Post-Star* [Glens Falls]; *TU = Times-Union* [Albany]; AAA = Santanoni files compiled by AARCH, DEC, and HK, AARCH Archives, Keeseville; ACA = Santanoni files, AC Archives, Elizabethtown

For purposes of brevity, newspaper and non-scholarly journal article titles have been abbreviated and writers' names, when noted in the former sources, are omitted. All communities are in New York State unless otherwise noted.

1. Throughout the text I use "Santanoni Preserve" to refer to the tract in its entirety. "Camp Santanoni" and "Santanoni" refer to the residential and related infrastructural development that lies within that tract. Little Santanoni Mountain and the taller Santanoni Peak, however, lie outside Santanoni Preserve.

2. "A-95 Review DEC Acquisition of Santanoni Preserve," Lake Champlain–Lake George Regional Planning Board, 2 Dec. 1971, AAA; "State Forest Preserve," *NYT,* 5 Dec. 1971, 52; "Adirondack Conservancy Committee Formed," *Adirondac* 36 (Jan.–Feb. 1972): 18–19; "State Takes Santanoni," *PR,* 19 Feb. 1972, 1; "13,000-Acre Wilderness Tract," *NYT,* 19 Feb. 1972, 35; "State Acquires," *PS,* 19 Feb. 1972, 1; "Conservancy Acquires Santanoni Tract," *Conservationist* 26 (Feb.–Mar. 1972): 24–25; "Santanoni Preserve," *Adirondac* 36 (Mar.–Apr. 1972): 35–36; interview with Arthur Savage, St. Huberts, 4 Aug. 2008.

3. Interviews with Norman VanValkenburgh, Saugerties, 4 Sep. 2008; J. Winthrop Aldrich and Tim Barnett, Keene Valley, 18 Aug. 2008. Aldrich thinks the Melvins may have purchased Santanoni on speculation, but one of the brothers became very attached to the place and eventually wanted to ensure the land's preservation.

4. The DEC was formed in 1970, combining the former Conservation Department, Water Resources Commission, Air Pollution Control Board, and other entities as a reform measure to integrate state oversight of environmental issues. See "Conservationists Ask," *NYT,* 21 Feb. 1970, 48; "State Plan Given," *NYT,* 15 Mar. 1970, 44; "Governor Creates Department," and "New Environmental Conservation Law," *Conservationist* 24 (June–July 1970): 2–5, 6–7, resp.; "New Department, New Commissioner," *Adirondac* 34 (July–Aug. 1970): 73–74; and "Environmental Watchdogs," *NYT,* 1 Oct. 1972, R1, R14.

5. VanValkenburgh interview; "Management and Use Plan, Santanoni Preserve," Division of Lands and Forests, DEC, 22 Oct. 1971, AAA. VanValkenburgh wielded considerable power in determining what lands might be acquired for the Forest Preserve. For background, see Eleanor F. Brown, "He Worked for Wilderness," *Adirondac* 50 (Oct.–Nov. 1986): 14–16.

6. William Cronon, "The Trouble with Wilderness; or, Getting Back to the Wrong Nature," in *Uncommon Ground: Rethinking the Human Place in*

Nature, ed. William Cronon (New York: W. W. Norton, 1996), 69–90, 479–82; William Cronon, "The Riddle of the Apostle Islands: How Do You Manage a Wilderness Filled with Human Stories?" *Orion* 22 (May–June 2003): 36–42. See also Loretta Neumann and Kathleen M. Reinburg, "Cultural Resources and Wilderness: The White Hats versus the White Hats," *Journal of Forestry* 87 (Oct. 1989): 10–16.

7. By far the most detailed account of the camp is Robert Engel, Howard Kirschenbaum, and Paul Malo, *Santanoni: From Japanese Temple to Adirondack Great Camp,* 2000; updated ed. (Keeseville, N.Y.: Adirondack Architectural Heritage, 2009). See also Harvey H. Kaiser, *Great Camps of the Adirondacks* (Boston: David R. Godine, 1982), 169–74; and Craig Gilborn, *Adirondack Camps: Homes Away from Home, 1850–1950* (Blue Mountain Lake, N.Y.: Adirondack Museum, and Syracuse: Syracuse University Press, 2000), 227–32. The final chapter of *Santanoni* offers a detailed account of its preservation from Kirschenbaum's firsthand perspective. I have tried to develop this essay as a complementary piece.

8. For background, see Frank Graham Jr., *The Adirondack Park: A Political History* (Syracuse: Syracuse University Press, 1978), chaps. 10–13; Philip G. Terrie, *Contested Terrain: A New History of Nature and People in the Adirondacks,* 1997; exp. ed. (Blue Mountain Lake, N.Y.: Adirondack Museum, and Syracuse: Syracuse University Press, 2008), chap. 5; Barbara McMartin, *The Great Forest of the Adirondacks* (Utica: North Country Books, 1994), chap. 5; and Barbara McMartin, "The Constitution and the Adirondack Forest," in "Celebrating the Constitutional Protection of the Forest Preserve, 1884–1994," Silver Bay Symposium, Lake George, 30 Sep. 1994, 55–63.

9. Graham, *The Adirondack Park,* chap. 14; Terrie, *Contested Terrain,* 97–102; Norman J. VanValkenburgh, *The Adirondack Forest Preserve* (Blue Mountain Lake, N.Y.: Adirondack Museum, 1979); and Norman J. VanValkenburgh, *Land Acquisition in New York State: An Historical Perspective* (Arkville, N.Y.: Catskill Center, 1985) provide detailed accounts of the land acquisition process. See also Jerry Jenkins, with Andy Neal, *The Adirondack Atlas: A Geographic Portrait of the Adirondack Park* (Syracuse: Syracuse University Press, and Blue Mountain Lake, N.Y.: Adirondack Museum, 2004), 26–27.

10. The Adirondack region has been advanced as important training ground for the wilderness movement. See Ed Zahnizer, "The Adirondacks Roots of America's Wilderness Preservation Movement," *AJES* 5 (Spring–Summer 1998): 14–18.

11. VanValkenburgh, *The Adirondack Forest Preserve,* App. 5. See also Alfred S. Forsyth, *The Forest and the Law* (New York: Sierra Club, Association for the Protection of the Adirondacks, and Adirondack Mountain Club, 1970); Graham, *The Adirondack Park,* chap. 15; Philip G. Terrie, *Forever Wild: Environmental Aesthetics and the Adirondack Forest Preserve* (Philadelphia: Temple University Press, 1985), chap. 8; Terrie, *Contested Terrain,* 102–3; McMartin, *The Great Forest,* chap. 6; and Joseph D. Tekulsky, "Forever Wild–'The Law's Delay,'" *Adirondac* 58 (Nov.–Dec. 1994): 14–19.

12. Gilborn, *Adirondack Camps,* 89–97, 120–25; Barbara McMartin, *The Privately Owned Adirondacks: Sporting and Family Clubs, Private Parks and Preserves, Timberlands and Easements* (Canada Lake, N.Y.: Lake View Press, 2004), 13–14, 79–82, 97–103, 115–16; Edward Comstock Jr., "The Role of Private Preserves in the Adirondacks," *AJES* 2 (Fall–Winter 1995): 32–39.

13. Edith Pilcher, *Up the Lake Road: The First Hundred Years of the Adirondack Mountain Reserve* (Keene Valley, N.Y.: Adirondack Mountain Reserve, 1987); McMartin, *The Privately Owned Adirondacks,* 74–75.

14. Harold K. Hochschild, *Life and Leisure in the Adirondack Backwoods* (Blue Mountain Lake, N.Y.: Adirondack Museum, 1962); Craig Gilborn, *Durant: The Fortunes and Woodland Camps of a Family in the Adirondacks* (Sylvan Beach, N.Y.: North Country Books, and Blue Mountain Lake, N.Y.: Adirondack Museum, 1981). See also Kaiser, *Great Camps,* chaps. 5, 6; and Gilborn, *Adirondack Camps,* 125–32, 220–25.

15. Historical accounts of Sagamore include those cited in ibid.; and Howard Kirschenbaum, *The Story of Sagamore* (Raquette Lake, N.Y.: Sagamore Institute, 1990).

16. "State Buys," *NYT,* 7 Oct. 1975, 37, 45; "Vanderbilt Camp," *NYT,* 9 Nov. 1975, 38; "Preservation League Conference," *PLN* 1 (Dec. 1975): 1–2; interview with Howard Kirschenbaum, Raquette Lake, 6 Aug. 2008.

17. CG to Mary Anne Krupsak, 20 Apr. 1978, AAA; "Millionaire's Retreat," *NYT,* 5 June 1978, NJ13; "Luxury Camp," *NYT,* 19 Aug. 1984, 49; "Forest Preserve Threatened," *ACN* 8 (Oct. 1984): 2; "State, Citing Cost," *NYT,* 24 Mar. 1985, 46; Howard Kirschenbaum, "Camp Topridge for Sale?" *AL* 16 (Mar.–Apr. 1985): 17–19; "State Sells," *NYT,* 1 Aug. 1985, B2; "'Great Camp' in Adirondacks," *NYT,* 14 Nov. 1985, C10. Concerning the buildings, see Kaiser, *Great Camps,* 207–14.

18. CG to Peter Berle, 1 Feb. 1978; PM to Peter

Borrelli, 9 Feb. 1978, AAA; "State Is Adding," *NYT,* 17 Dec. 1978, 51. Concerning the buildings, see Kaiser, *Great Camps,* 182–87; and Gilborn, *Adirondack Camps,* 225–27. According to Kirschenbaum, preservationists did not rally to save the complex because Sagamore and Santanoni seemed much higher priorities that were enormously challenging unto themselves and because the family stipulated that it not be preserved. Kirschenbaum interview.

19. Frederick L. Rath, Jr. to Peter Borrelli, 23 Feb. 1978, AAA; "Coalition Garners Support," *PLN* 9 (July–Aug. 1983): 1; "Voters to Decide," *NYT,* 5 Sep. 1983, 40; "Adirondack Camps," *NYT,* 13 Sep. 1983, A22; "The Sagamore Amendment," *Adirondac* 47 (Oct.–Nov. 1983): 15; "Camp Sagamore," *NYT,* 8 Aug. 1985, C3; Kirschenbaum and VanValkenburgh interviews. According to Kirschenbaum, the Preservation League deserved the credit for insisting the complex be saved in situ and in its entirety.

20. As is evident in numerous preservation-related publications of the period, a particularly instructive example of which is National Trust for Historic Preservation et al., *America's Forgotten Architecture* (New York: Pantheon, 1974). For a retrospective analysis, see Richard Longstreth, "Architectural History and the Practice of Historic Preservation in the United States," *Journal of the Society of Architectural Historians* 58 (Sep. 1999): 326–33.

21. "Preservation League Begins," *PLN* 3 (Nov. 1977): 1; "League Documents," *PLN* 5 (Mar. 1979): 1; "Adirondack Update," *PLN* 6 (Jan. 1990): 5; FC to TJ, 17 Oct. 1989, AAA; "Research Report on the Great Camps of the Adirondacks," PLNYS, June 1978.

22. Craig Gilborn, "Oh For a Lodge in Some Vast Wilderness," *Nineteenth Century* 2 (Summer 1976): 23–29; Paul Malo, "The Great Camps of the Adirondacks," in *Saving Large Estates,* ed. William C. Shopsin and Grania Bolton Marcus (Setauket, N.Y.: Society for the Preservation of Long Island Antiquities, 1977), 173–78; Kaiser, *Great Camps.* See also Philip Langdon, "Compromise with Nature," *Historic Preservation* 31 (Sep.–Oct. 1979): 13–21; and Barbara McMartin, "Historic Preservation and the Forest Preserve," *Adirondac* 46 (May 1982): 8–9.

23. "Cultural Heritage in the Wilds, Conference Report," New York Office of Parks and Recreation and Office of Environmental Conservation, 1978, 8–11, quotation on 10, 75. Concerning Berle, see Rick Karlin, "Adirondack Park Loses a Champion," *AE* 10 (Jan.–Feb. 2008): 16–17.

24. Thomas L. Cobb, ed., "Historic Preservation in the Adirondack Park, Conference Proceedings," Adirondack Research Center, Union College, Schenectady, New York, 1982.

25. Roderick Nash, *Wilderness and the American Mind,* 1967; 3rd ed. (New Haven: Yale University Press, 1982), chap. 13; Max Oelschlaeger, *The Idea of Wilderness: From Prehistory to the Age of Ecology* (New Haven: Yale University Press, 1991), chap. 9; Carolyn Merchant, ed., *Major Problems in American Environmental History* (Lexington, Mass.: D. C. Heath, 1993), chap. 14; J. Baird Callicott and Michael P. Nelson, eds., *The Great Wilderness Debate* (Athens: University of Georgia Press, 1998), pt. 3; Paul S. Sutter, *Driven Wild: How the Fight against Automobiles Launched the Modern Wilderness Movement* (Seattle: University of Washington Press, 2002), epilogue.

26. Graham, *The Adirondack Park,* 211–13; Terrie, *Contested Terrain,* 160–65; "Ecologists See," *NYT,* 8 Nov. 1959, 59; "Blueprint for Leisure," *NYT,* 21 June 1970, 376; "'Taming' of Adirondack Feared," *NYT,* 21 Dec. 1970, 37; "Wood, Field and Stream," *NYT,* 22 Jan. 1971, 48.

27. Conrad L. Wirth et al., "A Report on a Proposed Adirondack Mountains National Park," New York, 27 July 1967; Graham, *The Adirondack Park,* chap. 24. Wirth had been director of the National Park Service and architect of Mission 66, a major infrastructural development program for the system under his tutelage.

28. "The Future of the Adirondack Park," Temporary Study Commission on the Future of the Adirondacks, 1970; "New Policy Urged," *NYT,* 3 Jan. 1971, 1, 60; "Governor Urges," *NYT,* 9 May 1977, 57; "Assembly Backs Control," *NYT,* 8 June 1971, 21; "Adirondack Plan," *NYT,* 9 May 1972, 30; Courtney Jones, "Master Plan for the Adirondacks," *Conservationist* 27 (Oct.–Nov. 1972): 9–11, 46; Graham, *The Adirondack Park,* chaps. 25, 26; Richard A. Liroff and G. Gordon Davis, *Protecting Open Space: Land Use Control in the Adirondack Park* (Cambridge, Mass.: Ballinger Publishing, 1981), chaps. 2, 6; Terrie, *Contested Terrain,* 166–83; Eleanor Brown, "42%/58% and Counting," and Neil F. Woodworth, "A Park in Danger," *Adirondac* 56 (May–June 1992): 16–22, 30–32, resp.; Catherine Henshaw Knorr, *Living with the Adirondack Forest: Local Perspectives on Land Use Conflicts* (Ithaca: Cornell University Press, 1998), 69–72; Barbara McMartin, *Perspectives on the Adirondacks: A Thirty-Year Struggle by People Protecting Their Treasure* (Syracuse: Syracuse University Press), 2002, chaps. 1–4. See also "Public Control Growing," *NYT,* 3 Sep. 1973, 1, 4. Concerning local resistance, see "Adirondack State Park," *NYT,* 24 Aug. 1971, 39, 75; "Opposition to the Adirondacks Plan," *NYT,* 22 Jan. 1973, 35; Anthony N. D'Elia, *The Adirondack Rebellion: A Political, Economic and Social Exposé of the Adirondack State Park* (Loon Lake, N.Y.: By the

author, 1979); "For 100 Years," *NYT,* 19 May 1992, B1, B2; Will Nixon, "Fear & Loathing in the Adirondacks," *E: The Environmental Magazine* 3 (Sep.–Oct. 1992): 28–35; and Walter M. Aikman, "To Us It's Home: Confrontation and Community Change in the Adirondack Property Rights Movement" (Ph.D. diss., Cornell University, 1998).

29. For background, see McMartin, *Perspectives,* 54–56; John Sheehan, "History of the Adirondack Council 1975 to 2000," *AJES* 11 (Winter 2004): 10–20; and "Forever Wild?" *ACN* 4 (Feb. 1980): entire issue. The coalition that created the council included the National Audubon Society, Natural Resources Defense Council, Wilderness Society, and Association for the Protection of the Adirondacks. The last of these organizations was formed at the turn of the twentieth century (Pruyn was an early member), but in recent years had taken a less activist role.

30. Interview with John Sheehan, Albany, 2 Oct. 2008. At first the Adirondack Council was noncommittal on the issues; see "The Dilemma of Historic Preservation," *ACN* 7 (Jan. 1983): 2–3. Later correspondence reveals the organization's concerns, ACA, AAA.

31. Savage interview; Arthur Savage to John Cahill and Richard Lefebvre, 15 June 2000; Peter Paine, Jr. to RC, 10 Sep. [1995], AAA.

32. Alan Darling, "Santanoni," *AL* 12 (Sep.–Oct. 1981): 10–13, 40; "Santanoni in Disrepair," *PS,* 18 Aug. 1984, 14; Howard Kirschenbaum, "To Save Santanoni," *AL* 17 (Jan.–Feb. 1986): 53–54.

33. George Davis to Francis Murray, 21 Nov. 1985, AAA. See also "Remote Newcomb," *ADE,* 26 Aug. 1985, 1, 12; "Cuomo Selects," *TU,* 15 Nov. 1985, B1, B6; "Adirondack Council Protests," *PR,* 23 Nov. 1985, 15; JWA memo to Janice Corr, 15 Nov. 1985; HC to HW, 5 Dec. 1985; and HW to HC, 16 Jan. 1986, AAA.

34. NVV memo to HW, 12 Mar. 1985; JWA memo to NVV, 2 May 1985; David Newhouse to HW, n.d. (before 21 Feb. 1986); JWA memo to HW, 14 Mar. 1986; NVV to David Newhouse, 24 Mar. 1986; JS to JWA, 30 Sep. 1986; JS memo to Orin Lehman, 30 Oct. 1986; James Gold memo to HK, 2 June 1988; JWA to Robert Binnewies, 23 Oct. 1989; JWA memo to Langdon Marsh, 25 May 1990, AAA. See also J. Winthrop Aldrich, "Sagamore—Santanoni—Topridge," in Cobb, ed., "Historic Preservation," 6–14. George Canon, supervisor of the Town of Newcomb since 1990 and a key figure in the saving of Camp Santanoni, regards Aldrich as the major DEC staff member partial to retaining the buildings and the key inside figure during the 1980s. Interview with George Canon, Newcomb, 12 Aug. 2008.

35. HK memo to HW et al., 21 June 1984; Robert Glennon memo to HC, 1 Aug. 1984; HK to HC, 18 Aug. 1985; HK to Sagamore Institute board, 29 Aug. 1985; George Davis to HW, 19 Sep. 1985; Jack Drury to HW, 23 Oct. 1985; HW to George Davis, 24 Oct. 1985, AAA.

36. Kirschenbaum, "To Save Santanoni," 53: Donald Smith, "Legal Conflict Imperils," National Geographic Society press release, 1 Jan. 1989, AAA.

37. Preservation remained a sideline for Kirschenbaum, who started a consulting practice on human development and later taught at SUNY Brockport and the University of Rochester.

38. HK to FC, 13 Dec. 1989; "Forming an Adirondack Preservation Organization, Summary of May 4, 1990 Meeting"; "Organizational Meeting of Adirondack Architectural Heritage," 26 June 1990; "Recommendations of the Santanoni Committee of Adirondack Architectural Heritage," 20 Aug. 1990; "Board Resolution on Camp Santanoni," 11 Sep. 1990; AARCH board min., 11 Sep. and 11 Dec. 1990, AAA. See also "Adirondack Group Urges," *PR,* 24 Jan. 1991, 13; "Architectural Group Formed," *ADE,* 1 Feb. 1991, 7; "Group Tries to Secure," *TU,* 10 Feb. 1991, G-4; and "Preserving Park's Cultural Legacy," *PS,* 10 Feb. 1991, C8.

39. See HK to Stafford, Casale, and Hinchey, and Bendick, all 15 Nov. 1990; "Notes from December 17 [1990] Meeting with DEC"; HK to Martens, 22 Dec. 1990; HK to FC, 15 Jan. 1991; HK memos to AARCH board, 18 Jan. and 8 Feb. 1991; HK to RB, 14 Feb. and 8 Apr. 1991; HK to Mario Cuomo, 1 Mar. 1991; HK memo to AARCH board, 23 July 1991; HK to RB, 17 Sep. 1991, AAA. Organizations and jurisdictions courted included the Preservation League, Adirondack Museum, Town of Newcomb, and Essex County. See HK to FC, 21 Aug., 17 Sep., and 24 Oct. 1990, and 15 Jan. 1991; HK to GC, 17 Sep. 1990; and HK to CG, 17 Sep. 1990, AAA.

40. Among the first board members were Paul Malo, a Syracuse architect and first president of the PLNYS; historical architect Carl Stearns; University of Pennsylvania historian Anthony N. B. Garvan, whose parents had long owned Kamp Kill Kare, one of the region's most lavish seasonal residences; Steven Engelhart, stonemason and preservation activist in Keeseville; Craig Gilborn, director of the Adirondack Museum; Mary Hotaling, historian and preservationist in Saranac Lake; and William Johnston, planner for Essex County.

41. "George Canon," PLNYS, Annual Report, 1996, n.p.; "Newcomb at Crossroads," *AE* 9 (Nov.–Dec. 2007): 8–9, 44–45; Canon interview.

42. Mary Hotaling to HK, 13 Dec. 1990; [PM] to

HK, 23 Dec. 1990; HK to PM, 3 Jan. [1991]; HK to JWA, 16 Aug. 1991, AAA; Kirschenbaum interview. See also AARCH board min., 11 June, 23 July, and 10 Sep. 1991; HK to AARCH board, 20 Aug. 1991; Anthony Garvan to HK, 15 Aug. 1991; PM to HK, 24 Aug. 1991; AARCH executive committee min., 14 Jan. 1992; HK to Tania Werbizky, 24 Apr. 1992; HK to GC, 26 June 1992, AAA.

43. JS to JWA, 27 Aug. 1991; GC to JWA, 3 Sep. 1991; Wesley Haynes to CS, 28 Sep. 1991; "Camp Santanoni: Emergency Stabilization Priorities," n.d. [before 17 Sep. 1991]; CS to JWA, 8 Oct. 1991; HK memo to AARCH board, 10 Oct. 1991; David Gillespie to RB, 22 Oct. 1991, AAA; "Santanoni Still Shows," and "Let's Preserve," *PR,* 7 July 1991, C-1, C-10, resp.; "Way Sought," *PR,* 18 Sep. 1991, 11; "State Resolves," *Schenectady Gazette,* 20 Oct. 1991, B1, B7; "Effort Mounted," *PR,* 22 Nov. 1993, 17.

44. "Adirondack Camp Restoration," *Schenectady Gazette,* date uncertain, 1991–92, AAA. Among the most forceful advocates for maintaining the efficacy of Article XIV in the face of historic preservation efforts was Robert Glennon, counsel for, and later director of, the APA. See Robert C. Glennon, "State Acquisition in the Adirondack: The Inconsistent Purpose Doctrine and Related Legal Issues," in Cobb, ed., "Historic Preservation," 41–51; and Thomas L. Cobb, "Inconsistent Acquisition and Article XIV," *Adirondac* 47 (Apr. 1983): 14–23.

45. This and other options were outlined in detail in Norman VanValkenburgh, "The Santanoni Preserve: Some Options for the Future," typescript, 13 Nov. 1991, which may have been prepared for the AC, ACA.

46. The APA and the Adirondack Mountain Club supported this option (Charles Scrafford to State Land Master Plan Subcommittee, 4 Sep. 1991; Neil Woodworth to TJ and Robert Glennon, 12 Nov. 1991), while the Association for the Protection of the Adirondacks was opposed (DG to RB, 23 Oct. 1991). Concerning the DEC's decision to take this option, see Marc Gerstman memo to Langdon Marsh, 12 Feb. 1992; RB memo to R. Bathrick, 21 Feb. 1992; Daniel Luciano to BM, 10 Mar. 1992; and Marc Gerstman memo to RB, 7 May 1992, AAA.

47. Interview with Peter Paine Jr., New York, 7 Mar. 2009.

48. First convened on 2 May 1995, the CAC included representatives of AARCH, AC, Adirondack Nature Conservancy, Adirondack Mountain Club, Adirondack Museum, APA, Association for the Protections of the Adirondacks, DEC, Essex Community Heritage Organization, Essex County Planning Office, OPRHP, and PLNYS. See "Citizens Groups

Help," *ADE,* 1 May 1995, 3; and "Historic Resources & Nature," *New York State Preservationist* 1 (Spring 1997): 7.

49. CAC min., 2 May, 13 June, and 24 July 1995, 24 Jan., 27 Feb., and 10 Oct. 1996, AAA. See also "Santanoni," *Chronicle* [Glens Falls], 16–23 Sep. 1992, 31.

50. As paraphrased in CAC min., 27 Feb. 1996, AAA.

51. CAC min., 2 May, 13 June, 24 July, and 14 Sep. 1995, 27 Feb., 28 Mar., and 10 Oct. 1996; AARCH board min., 9 Jan., 9 Apr., and 29 June 1996, AAA; Sheehan interview.

52. CAC min., 24 Jan., 27 Feb., and 10 Oct. 1996, AAA. The debate had gone on for some years; see "Trying to Save," *PS,* 5 Jan. 1992, C-1, C-6.

53. "Adirondack 'Great Camp,'" *Schenectady Gazette,* 13 Oct. 1999, D6; "A Lodge for Everyman," *AE* 2 (Jan. 2000): 21. See also "Draft Plan for Santanoni," *Hamilton County News,* 2 Nov. 1999, 1, 4; "Great Camp Debate," *AE* 1 (Dec. 1999): 12, 13; "After Thirty Years," *Hamilton County News,* 7 Mar. 2000, 7; "Great Camp Santanoni," *LPN,* 5 May 2000, 6; "Camp Santanoni Plan," *ADE,* 13 May 2000, B1; "Santanoni Debate," *ADE,* 15 May 2000, 1, 8; "Newcomb Packed," *ADE,* 16 May 2000, 1, 7; and Michael DiNunzio to John Banta, 24 May 2000, ACA. AARCH's leadership was not entirely happy with the plan either; see SE to Robert Lefebvre, 11 July 2000; AARCH board min., 18 Oct. 1999, and 10 Jan. and 17 July 2000, AAA.

54. "Camp Santanoni Historic Area Unit Management Plan," Division of Lands and Forests, New York State Department of Environmental Conservation, August 2000; "Great Camp," *PS,* 10 July 2000, B1, B6; "APA Committee," *ADE,* 14 July 2000, 1, 16; "APA Vote," *PR,* 14 July 2000, A3; "APA: Yes, to Santanoni," *ADE,* 15 July 2000, 1, 5; "Camp Santanoni," *Hamilton County News,* 19 Sep. 2000, 14, 15; "National Recognition," *New York State Preservationist* 4 (Fall–Winter 2000): 9; "A Milestone Year," *AAN* 10 (Winter 2000): 1, 3; "Making History," *AL* 21 (Dec. 2000): 12, 13; AARCH board retreat summary, 5–6 Dec. 2001; AARCH board min., 23 Feb. 2004, AAA.

55. AARCH board min., 11 June and 23 July 1991, and 14 Apr. 1992, AAA. "Internship 1995," *AAN* 4 (Fall 1995): 5. Kirschenbaum saw a significant change in the DEC's approach to the project beginning with the election of George Pataki as governor in 1995. Kirschenbaum interview; see also AARCH board min., 8 July 1995, AAA.

56. GC to JWA, 3 Sep. 1991; Herbert Lamb memo to JWA, 11 Dec. 1991; HK to RB, 4 Sep. 1992; Wesley Haynes to CS, 28 Sep. 1992; HK to RB, 12 Mar. and 25 July 1993; Thomas Monroe memo to Robert

Wilson and Dale Huyck, 10 Sep. 1993; JWA to JS, 24 Sep. 1993; JS to JWA, 4 Oct. 1993; AARCH board min., 12 Oct. 1993, and 11 Jan. and 9 July 1994; HK to RC, 11 July 1994; CV to JWA, 26 July 1994; AARCH board min., 11 Oct. 1994; 10 Jan., 11 Apr., and 20 Oct. 1995; 14 Jan., 8 Apr., 12 July, and 18 Oct. 1997; 13 Oct. 1998; 18 Oct. 1999, AAA; "Slow and Steady," *AAN* 1 (Fall 1992): 4; "Santanoni Restoration," *AAN* 2 (Fall 1993): 4; "Serious Restoration," *AAN* 3 (Fall 1994): 4; "Exciting Progress," *AAN* 4 (Spring 1995): 2; "AARCH Awarded," *LPN,* 17 Nov. 1995, 2; "HSR Complete," *AAN* 5 (Nov. 1996): 1, 3; "Santanoni," AARCH, Annual Report, 1997, 2–3; "Santanoni," AARCH, Annual Report, 1998, 2–3; "What's New," *AAN* 7 (Fall 1998): 2. The most detailed accounts of work done are in the *Friends of Camp Santanoni Newsletter,* published annually beginning with the winter 1999–2000 issue.

57. "Great Again," *PS,* 11 Aug. 2002, A1, A4; "Camp Santanoni," *Observer-Dispatch* [Utica], 31 Aug. 2002, 10; "Camp Santanoni," *AAN* 12 (Winter 2003–4): 12; "Santanoni," *TU,* 25 Jan. 2004, J6; AARCH board min., 3 Feb. 2004 and 26 July 2006, AAA; "Tragedy and Progress," *AAN* 13 (Winter 2004–5): 1, 3. Figures are based on material supplied by Steven Engelhart and culled from AARCH documents.

58. AARCH board min., 9 Aug. and 27 Sep. 2004, AAA; "Tragedy and Progress," *AAN* 13 (Winter 2004–5): 1, 3.

59. The matter deserves further study. Since the 1940s, the North Country School has maintained farming operations, with an array of livestock, adjacent to the Sentinel Range wilderness area in the High Peaks without causing environmental problems.

60. AARCH board min., 31 Jan. and 31 Oct. 2005, and 26 July and 20 Oct. 2006, AAA.

61. John F. Sheehan, ed., *Managing Growth and Development in Unique, Natural Settings* (Elizabethtown: N.Y.: Adirondack Council, n.d. [c. 1991]); Linda M. Champagne, ed., *Wilderness and People: The Future of the Adirondack Park* (Schenectady: Association for the Protection of the Adirondacks, n.d. [c. 1994]); Thomas Pasquallo et al., "Wilderness and the Working Landscape," *AJES* 1 (Winter 1994): 19–23; Philip G. Terrie, "The Adirondack Park: A Look Back, A Look Ahead," *AJES* 2 (Fall–Winter 1995): 9–17; *2020 Vision: Fulfilling the Promise of the Adirondack Park,* vol. 4, *Private Land Stewardship* ([Elizabethtown, N.Y.]: Adirondack Council, 2007).

A Grand Experiment

The Jackson Lake Lodge

Upon completion in 1955, the Jackson Lake Lodge in Grand Teton National Park, Wyoming, was met with a barrage of criticism. Jackson Lake Lodge is "the ugliest building in the park and monument system," wrote Devereux Butcher, a National Parks Association board member, going on to compare the new lodge to Alcatraz.[1] Another critic called it "a concrete monstrosity built for that sub-species of Homo sapiens called the tourist," highlighting the tensions between people in nature as well as the controversy over architecture.[2] Jack Goodman perhaps best captured the feelings surrounding the lodge in a 1955 *New York Times* article in which he wrote, "Those who bitterly deride the appearance of the fifty-room main lodge building and its 250 adjacent guest cottages level their aesthetic barbs at the mammoth central structure chiefly because it does not look 'rustic.'"[3]

As many of its detractors noted, Jackson Lake Lodge was a modern building in a wilderness setting. Departing from its grand rustic predecessors, the new hotel drew on elements of the rising International Style. Capable of housing up to 750 guests, the development was originally comprised of a central lodge, several one-story guest cottages, a large landscaped parking area, a stable, a service station, and a small telephone utility building. Marked by clean lines and a simplified facade, the lodge was made up of a series of interlocking rectangular blocks with shallow shed roofs. Bands of ribbon windows complemented by a large, flat porte-cochere highlighted the long horizontal emphasis of the building, typical of the Inter-

national Style. Constructed of steel and poured concrete, the building was modern in look and construction, which was exactly what critics condemned. As a Jackson Hole local confided in an oral history interview, the building "could have been built a little more rustic like" (fig. 1).[4]

Unfortunately, the modern exterior has led historians to dismiss the building without probing further into the complexities of its design. While a few rustic details are pointed to as the only connections between early-twentieth-century lodges and the Jackson Lake Lodge, to argue that all tradition was forsaken at the later structure is misleading. Instead, at the Jackson Lake Lodge, the architect, Gilbert Stanley Underwood (1890–1960), attempted to create a balance between the past and the present. Completed one year prior to the launch of Mission 66, the building reflects the tradition of the great national park lodges of the early twentieth century, while also demonstrating the new, modern aesthetic that came to dominate American architecture after World War II—a shift in national park architecture that raises questions about the treatment of design in the American wilderness.

Primarily known for his design of immense rustic lodges, Underwood's early career was defined by his work for the National Park Service in Yosemite National Park, and his work for the Union Pacific Railroad in Bryce, Zion, and Grand Canyon National Parks. Recommended by his friend Daniel Hull, Underwood began work developing a complex for the Yosemite Valley in 1923, the same year he graduated with an M.A. from Harvard and established his own firm in Los Angeles.[5] Both National Park Service director Stephen Mather and the Commission of Fine Arts in Washington, D.C., rejected his sketches, however, asserting that they were too decorative and removed from the site. The Commission of Fine Arts even noted, "With all the rock in the valley there was not enough rock used in the building."[6]

Despite this initial failure, Underwood adapted his work to suit the rustic idiom dominating national park design. At the Zion Lodge in Zion National Park (1924), the Bryce Canyon Lodge in Bryce Canyon National Park (1925), and later at the Ahwahnee Hotel in Yosemite (1927) and the Grand Canyon Lodge on the North Rim of the Grand Canyon (1929), Underwood developed a distinct rustic aesthetic, setting a standard for national park architecture across the West. By combining native materials, exaggerated steeply sloping roofs, dormer windows, and other rustic elements of earlier lodges such as the Old Faithful Inn (1901) and the El Tovar

Hotel (1903), he produced a simple yet dramatic style that remained true to the Park Service's rustic ideals. His designs were picturesque, complementing their unique and spectacular landscapes, while offering luxurious accommodations for national park guests. As a Union Pacific spokesman boasted in a brochure, the Grand Canyon Lodge "harmonizes perfectly with its surroundings and seems itself a work of nature."[7] While Underwood is often criticized for abandoning his rustic knowledge at the Jackson Lake Lodge, it is important to note that more than twenty-five years separated the completion of the Grand Canyon Lodge in 1929 and the completion of the Jackson Lake Lodge in 1955.

With the onset of the Great Depression, Underwood's stream of work for the National Park Service and Union Pacific Railroad came to an end, and he was forced to look elsewhere for commissions. In 1932 he joined the Federal Architects Project as a consulting architect, and

FIG. 1. Jackson Lake Lodge complex, c. 1966. (Collection of the Jackson Hole Historical Society and Museum)

two years later finally gave up his practice in L.A. and moved his family to Washington, D.C.[8] He remained in D.C. until 1950, serving as federal supervisory architect from 1947 to 1949.[9] During his years of government service Underwood served as federal architect in the West, and produced preliminary designs for the Timberline Lodge at Mount Hood, Oregon, as well as more than twenty post offices, two federal buildings, and the U.S. State Department Building (1941).[10] In most cases his designs reflected the contemporary institution of Art Deco architecture, although his post offices varied from location to location, employing the Mission Revival in his design for the Burbank Post Office in California in 1937, and again for the Los Angeles Terminal Annex Post Office in 1939.

Underwood was greatly affected by his years in Washington. Exposed on a large scale to the increasingly popular modern strains of architecture and the designs of architects such as Louis A. Simon, who was supervising architect when Underwood first arrived in D.C., and George Howe, with whom Underwood served on a panel called General Principles to Be Considered in the Design of Government Architecture, Underwood's work tended more and more towards the modern. Influenced particularly by Paul P. Cret, another consulting architect in the Federal Architects Project, Underwood experimented through the 1930s with starved classicism and modern materials and volumes.[11] His State Department Building (originally occupied by the War Department) was designed with fellow federal employee William Dewey Foster and followed Cret's lead, modernizing classical elements with simple wall surfaces and buff limestone.[12]

While Underwood was experimenting with stark classical buildings, he was also embracing the developing International Style. As was evident in structures like his 1938 post office for Nome, Alaska, by the late 1930s and early 1940s Underwood was replacing the heavy vertical elements with lighter, horizontal features in his work. This lighter and simpler approach is unmistakable in his 1942 dormitory designs. Assigned to the development of tem-

porary emergency housing in D.C., his work was praised in the *Washington Post* as "well planned" and reflective of the "artist's taste."[13] Designed for the Public Buildings Administration, his dorms were clear experiments in International Style design. Modern in character, they combined vertical ribbons of windows, flat roofs, and central lobbies in a manner remarkably similar to his later design at Jackson Lake Lodge. The dorms molded "utility and economy into a suitable and functional composition," according to the *Architectural Record* in 1942, again a characteristic he would later employ at Jackson Lake Lodge.[14]

The nearly twenty years Underwood spent in Washington, D.C., were significant in shaping the architect's work. In D.C., Underwood was in close contact with modern architects and developing modern architecture, shifting his style closer to the popular modes of design being cultivated on the East Coast.

Underwood's architecture was also impacted by the huge cultural shifts that had taken place between 1930 and 1950. Americans had survived the Great Depression and World War II, and personal automobiles were on the rise, changing the landscape of America in dramatic ways. These changes were particularly felt in the national parks, where postwar visitation rose sharply, highlighting poor conditions. In Grand Teton National Park specifically, visitation rose from 189,286 visitors in 1950 to 785,343 only two years later, while the number of housing units remained at only 150.[15]

In his proposal for facilities in Grand Teton National Park, submitted in 1950, Underwood addressed these changes and the challenges of national park concessions, dividing his recommendations for a Jackson Lake Lodge into two alternatives. Stage No. 1, as he identified it, included supplementing all the existing buildings at Jackson Lake Lodge with all the movable buildings from Moran, a small town within the park boundaries, to create a new lodge center. Stage No. 2, which was ultimately chosen, consisted of building an entirely new lodge and a large number of new cabins, replacing the existing Jackson Lake Lodge completely.[16] This plan, Underwood explained, addressed the question of efficiency, allowing the hotel to operate at low-level periods without opening the guest lodges and supporting facilities. It also addressed the needs of the new traveling public, providing ample parking and allowing tourists to park within feet of their cabin doors. As explained in a letter to the contractors, Morrison-Knudsen Company, Inc., of Boise, Idaho, the project involved "the construction of a 600-room hotel, somewhat on the nature of the Ahwahnee in Yosemite, at an estimated cost of three or four million dollars."[17] A year later Underwood contradicted this assertion, confiding in a letter that he was "trying to stop our clients from doing another deal like the Ahwahnee with a hundred rooms and public space for a thousand people."[18] This clash of old and new drove the design of Jackson Lake Lodge, resulting in the construction of a grand lodge complex that successfully integrated rustic detail into the context of American modernism.

Underwood's surface treatment is a case in point. Substituting the natural materials he had used at Bryce, Zion, and the North Rim of the Grand Canyon with stained and molded concrete, Underwood produced an effect he labeled "shadowood" (fig. 2). Obtained by sand-blasting plywood to raise the wood grain, then placing it in the concrete forms and allowing the concrete to set up against the plywood, the effect left a distinct wood grain impression on the concrete. The technique was similar to that employed at the Ahwahnee Hotel, yet the visual impact was modern and distinct. While the effect offered the appearance of wood grain, the product was never meant to completely conceal the actual material. The stain was matte and the plywood was applied in squares, leaving a repetitive blocky pattern. While the form of the Jackson Lake Lodge was highly organized and simplified, the shadowood molding gave the exterior texture, a key component in rustic design, while still being a clear expression of concrete.

FIG. 2. "Shadowood" construction at Jackson Lake Lodge, c. 1954. (Collection of the Jackson Hole Historical Society and Museum, Gift of Herb and Quita Pownall)

Similarly interpreted from Underwood's previous lodges was the large porte-cochere. Winding up from U.S. highway 89/287 (now the John D. Rockefeller Jr. Memorial Highway), the driveway loops under the long porte-cochere supported by concrete-encased steel beams and posts remarkably similar in volume and effect to those of the original Zion Lodge. As at Zion, the posts support a large flat deck off the second floor that looks out over the parking lot. Unlike at Zion, however, the porte-cochere was capable of accommodating up to eight vehicles, demonstrating Underwood's intense interest in providing for the new automobile tourist. Between 1940 and 1960 the number of registered vehicles in the United States more than doubled from 32,453,200 to 73,868,600, and the miles of paved road increased from 1,367,000 to 2,557,000, making cross-country travel accessible to American families as never before.[19] The design of Jackson Lake Lodge addressed these modern concerns, including a convenient service station and extensive parking in the overall plan.

While the modern features seemed to clash with traditional expectations for appropriate architecture in national parks, the overall layout was the same as at Bryce, Zion, and the North Rim of the Grand Canyon, where Underwood paired a central lodge with satellite cabins. Likewise, the interior of the lodge offered a similar progression through space and retained much of the traditional detailing of earlier national park lodges.

Entering from the porte-cochere, a guest crossed into the primarily utilitarian, cramped first floor. The principal activities of the hotel were focused on the second floor, where the lounge, restaurants and conference center were located. Climbing the narrow terrazzo staircase from the lobby, a visitor ascended to the main lounge and was confronted immediately by the light, double-height space and breathtaking views through three enormous picture windows. Measuring 60 x 36 feet, the picture windows dominate the western facade: Not only are they accentuated by their scale, but the height of the building rises around them

and the facade is popped out by two additional windows on either side, offering a 180-degree view of the valley and the Teton Range (fig. 3). This transition from the dark, cramped business lobby to the light, double-story lounge created a dramatic experience for the visitor, almost identical to the effect Underwood produced at his earlier lodges, where windows were arranged around spectacular scenery and excitement was obtained by contrasting light and dark spaces.

This effect was enhanced by the decorative scheme for the lodge, created by the New York firm of James McCutcheon's & Co., a department store founded in 1855 specializing in linen. Chandler Cudlipp, vice president and director of the firm, headed the project, although his associate William Ulrichs was responsible for the actual design.[20] Ulrichs was on-site to select color schemes ("seashore gray" for the coffee shop, "redwood" for the lounge and convention hall), and to ensure all treatments were executed to the firm's expectations.

On 1 July 1954, a meeting was held in the empty shell of the Jackson Lake Lodge to decide on a program for the interior.[21] The directors considered a number of themes for the interior, including guest activities, the historical periods of the valley, and wildlife and flowers—none significantly modern in conception. They finally decided on a trapper theme, focusing their attention on the period between 1810 and 1840, with specific instructions to make the furnishings harmonize with the character of the building and the environment.[22]

In each room this theme was approached in a slightly different manner. In the main lounge, the showcase of the entire lodge with the impressive picture windows, little trapper decoration was included, with the exception of a number of animal paintings by Carl Rungus. Due to the scale of the room (60 x 100 feet), all the furniture was custom designed in the most elegant and modern fashion. Large curving couches fit together around coffee tables, and two centerpieces of dried wood and branches on animal skin rugs divided the room into small clusters of seating areas. The enormous

FIG. 3. Main lounge at Jackson Lake Lodge, c. 1966. (Collection of the Jackson Hole Historical Society and Museum)

picture windows dominated the decoration of the room, looking out to the spectacular view of Mount Moran and the Tetons, while small alcoves on either side of the lounge offered "shelter . . . from the tremendous power and beauty of the Grand Teton Range."[23]

Despite the lack of explicit trapper references in the décor, the lounge is perhaps the most rustic room in architectural detail. Large stone walls rise to meet massive shadowood beams that span the ceiling and more than anywhere else in the hotel resemble the molded-concrete beams of the Ahwahnee Hotel. Two enormous fireplaces stand in the back corners of the lounge, again reflecting the tradition of grand hotel lounges, with large moose-head andirons made out of old railroad ties, an unintentionally ironic reflection of the state of the great railroads that would previously have played patron in the construction of such a lodge.

In addition to the main lounge, the three original restaurants on the second floor highlight the balance between traditional and modern. The Pioneer Grill, the informal eatery, was styled after an oversized 1950s diner, with green upholstered, stationary, stainless steel stools and stainless steel cake holders and menu stands, the epitome of 1950s modern.[24] Sharing a kitchen with the Pioneer Grill was the Mural Room, the formal dining room, which was decorated with murals of the fur traders and trappers of the early West. Painted by Syracuse University professor Carl Roters, the murals, completed in 1959, consisted of ten panels and portrayed early Native American and mountain man scenes.[25]

Contrasting both of these eateries, the third restaurant, the Stockade Bar, pandered to every rustic stereotype for a western resort (fig. 4). The room was modeled after a western stockade and was decorated with skins, axes, and trapper materials illustrating the life of the trapper. The walls were lined with lodgepole pine, and the ceiling was painted blue to give the appearance of an open sky. The structural steel columns in the space were surrounded with conifers, and discussions between Cudlipp and Underwood even raised the idea of hiring "a scenic man up from Hollywood to do the [decoration]."[26] The room was indeed a stage set, with rugged and simple furniture and curtains constructed of leather hides sewn together. The bar departed from the simplicity of design carried through the rest of the hotel, but drew strongly on traditional expressions.

Examination of the interior reveals the many similarities between Underwood's work in the 1920s and his design for Jackson Lake Lodge. Both in the circulation and the decoration, the architect and his associates shaped a hotel reminiscent of the great rustic lodges. By merging components from his early experience in the national parks with a modern aesthetic developed during his time in Washington, Underwood designed a building that was at once innovative and familiar. His careful balance between the two created a unique experience that was carried into the landscape design with equal attention.

While Underwood's experiment in combining old and new was typically met with vehemently negative reactions, a few critics still praised the lodge. The *New York Times* wrote that "the handsome new Jackson Lake Lodge" was "modified modern in architecture, having been designed to take full advantage of the site above gem-like Jackson Lake without obtruding on the landscape."[27] "Only the front of the Lodge is visible from the highway and the 250 guest cottages nestle behind the Lodge to make as little intrusion as possible on the native landscape," the *Jackson Hole Guide* stated.[28] The recurring concern with structure and site in these articles underscores the changes occurring in 1950s America regarding perceptions about the appropriate relationship between culture and nature. Constructing nonintrusive buildings that harmonized with their surroundings was still the primary concern in national park development; however, the definitions of those terms were changing.

The majority of those criticizing the lodge, as *New York Times* reporter Jack Goodman identified, despised the building because it did not "harmonize" with the landscape. "Lodges like the one at Old Faithful in near-by Yellowstone Park are built of local timber and have peaked roofs, therefore 'blending with the scenery.'"[29]

FIG. 4. Former Stockade Bar at Jackson Lake Lodge, 1956. (Courtesy of the Rockefeller Archive Center)

These rustic lodges, however, did not "blend," as Goodman marked in quotations; rather, they were picturesque enormities meant to complement the scenery by being a crucial part of the view. Built for the few well-heeled sightseers, lodges like the Ahwahnee and the Grand Canyon Lodge indulged the romantic American criteria for structures in nature. Pairing beautiful architecture with breathtaking scenery, the lodges at Bryce, Zion, Yosemite, and the North Rim of the Grand Canyon established a harmonious balance between man and nature that solidified national park design goals: They harmonized with the surroundings, relating to the site by utilizing natural materials and rough surfaces, and referencing local heritage.

Despite visual differences, the Jackson Lake Lodge was constructed within the same set of goals as the earlier lodges. Set on a raised plateau at the south end of Jackson Lake, the lodge looked over the marshy willow flats of the valley and across at the Grand Teton mountain range. As at the earlier lodges, the view, and the orientation towards the view, was paramount. The dramatic experience created by circulation, placement of public rooms and large windows towards the views, and careful consideration of how the building fit within its site were elements Underwood considered in all of his national park lodges in order to direct the visitors' focus beyond the building. As he explained in his initial report for Jackson Lake Lodge: "The location of the Lodge Center on the peninsular site will provide a highly dramatic and commanding view. It will, on the other hand, permit the Lodge Center to grow into the site and offer no offence against the skyline viewed from Jackson Lake or against the scenery from closer approach. A low-lying, flat, spread out structure will almost completely merge into the natural scenery. It should be helped to this end by planting."[30]

While at Jackson Lake Lodge natural materials were replaced with concrete and steel, Underwood's concern with connecting the building to the site was still critical. "Harmony," in discussions, had been replaced with the desire to "merge" the man-made structures into the scenery, through the use of a "low-lying, flat, spread out structure" and natural coloring rather than through native materials. Instead of constructing a building that "grow[s] *out* of the site," as the Union Pacific claimed of the Grand Canyon Lodge in a promotional brochure, Underwood designed one that "grow[s] *into* the site."[31] The goals of the design at the 1920s hotels and the Jackson Lake Lodge are very much alike. Both sought to merge the man-made and the natural, creating a union of the ancient landscape and the modern hotel. The way of obtaining this connection, however, had changed dramatically by the mid-1950s.

At the Jackson Lake Lodge, Underwood's approach to the environment was also different, indicative of a new awareness and understanding of the natural world. Reporters quoting the architect's intentions called both the Ahwahnee Hotel and the Grand Canyon Lodge "environmental" hotels. "Architect Underwood characterizes the style of building as environmental. Though constructed of concrete and steel the hotel will have a rustic appearance in harmony with its setting," the *Los Angeles Times* wrote of the Ahwahnee Hotel in 1926.[32] In using the term "environmental" they referred to how the building related to the surroundings through the use of natural materials, natural coloring, and textured surfaces, not green building techniques or conservation efforts. While Jackson Lake Lodge was no more sustainable as a building, construction planning highlighted the growing awareness for environmental preservation, taking into account the impact of such a large project on the landscape. A monumental assessment was provided on the site, and surveys were completed that resulted in the preservation of 40–50 percent of the existing trees, particularly around the cabins. This was no small project, and the lodge had to be squeezed into the site in order to avoid substantial damage to the immediate landscape.[33]

Planting was critical in creating this relationship between structure and site. "I'm sure we can put in enough planting to ultimately . . . conceal the Ground Floor story," Underwood noted in a 1953 site plan.[34] A year after the building opened, Raymond Lillie, vice president and general manager of the Grand Teton Lodge and Transportation Co., reported that "the shrub planting program is in full progress around Jackson Lake Lodge. . . . In a year or two, this will make a great difference in our appearance."[35] With the extensive criticism of the architecture, however, "a year or two" proved too long a period to wait, and by 1957 Kenneth Chorley, president of the Grand Teton Lodge and Transportation Co., was writing to National Park Service director Conrad Wirth asking for more landscaping support: "Frankly, all of us feel very definitely that there is something lacking. Also as you know, there has been a certain amount of very severe criticism of the architecture of the building and the landscaping. . . . [W]e had a number of conferences about this whole situation and we finally came to the conclusion that the whole project could be very materially improved if there was much more extensive landscaping."[36] The call for additional planting was a direct response to the architectural criticism the lodge faced. The building was too urban, some reviewers commented, too much like the business hotels of everyday life and not enough of an escape. In an attempt to remedy this shared concern, in 1957 the Grand Teton Lodge and Transportation Co. hired Ted Spencer of Spencer & Lee, Architects in San Francisco to examine the situation and put together a report that "would completely change the character of the entire area for the better."[37]

The proposal Ted Spencer submitted included plans for new plantings around the cabins and main lodge, such as shrubs, natural ground cover, lawn, and trees. He suggested bringing in trees between 10 and 20 feet tall, and maintained the Park Service ideal to use only local species in the landscaping. Spencer also recommended an experiment in planting the large central parking lot. Mortimore and Wirth, the National Park Service landscape architects responsible for the initial landscaping, had placed a number of pines and aspens in the dividers between the parking areas. Spencer built

on this foundation, constructing a buck-and-rail fence and planting sagebrush and a variety of other low-grade vegetation in the strips between the parking areas.[38] The result, as the vegetation filled in, comprehensively camouflaged the 277-space public parking area, successfully softening the urban appearance of the facility.

Although Underwood's lodge was harshly criticized for not blending with the topography, the brown coloring of the concrete and the use of native plants in the landscaping reveal the care and calculations that went into making sure the building disappeared into the landscape. While the strong horizontals of the building seem to clash with the jagged peaks of the Tetons, by its placement on a raised plateau in the flat Jackson Hole Valley, the structure ultimately reflects the landscape to which it is anchored. Viewed from the west the Jackson Lake Lodge does not compete with the rough mountains but crouches unobtrusively into the scenery (fig. 5). Additionally, while plantings around the cabins and the parking lot in front of the lodge eventually concealed the east side of the buildings in order to focus arriving visitors' view on the mountains in the distance, plantings in the back on the western side of the buildings would have conflicted with the view of the Tetons through the picture windows. From inside and out the view of the mountains dominates the visitor's experience. The entire building, much like more rustic Park Service lodges, is arranged around the scenery. Thus while Underwood's landscape scheme failed, his entire Jackson Lake Lodge design was aimed at uniting architecture and landscape, revealing his care, concern, and familiarity with the problem of constructing tourist facilities in a national park setting.

As landscape historian Ethan Carr expressed in an article on Mission 66, "The goals of National Park planning and design have remained remarkably constant since the earliest days of the National Park Service: park buildings and other structures should be kept to a minimum and be designed so that they 'harmonize' with their landscape settings. . . . [W]hat has changed,

FIG. 5. Jackson Lake Lodge, 2008. (Courtesy of Anders Engle)

over time, is what we mean by 'harmonize.'"[39] This is particularly evident at the Jackson Lake Lodge where the underlying objectives were the same as those of the 1920s lodges. The new lodge was meant to harmonize with its surroundings, provide for a specific demographic of visitors, and blend with the scenery.

At Jackson Lake Lodge, Underwood adapted the traditional rustic national park idiom to address prevailing trends in American architecture and tourism, particularly the increasing popularity of the International Style and the needs of the private automobile as the primary means of transportation. He also produced a lodge that reflected his career, incorporating aspects and lessons from his early lodges with elements characteristic of his mature work in D.C. The distinct shell, the interior decoration, and the significant concern for the site and environment reflected Underwood's attention to detail and the consideration that produced the completed project.

The construction of Jackson Lake Lodge tested American expectations. By reinterpreting traditional rustic elements in a modern framework, Gilbert Stanley Underwood opened the door for modernism in the national parks, making way for Mission 66, a decade-long initiative launched in 1956 in response to deteriorating conditions in the national parks.[40] Known as "The Grand Experiment," the developments in Grand Teton National Park set a standard for construction and planning in national parks, redefining the long-standing question of the relationship between design and wilderness. As the contractor for the project perhaps best explained, the new Jackson Lake Lodge was "as modern as tomorrow, yet rustic enough to harmonize with the natural beauty of the park."[41] Thus as both the last great rustic lodge and the first modern park hotel, the Jackson Lake Lodge represents a shift in national park architecture within traditional theoretical ideals, reflecting the changes occurring in post–World War II America.

Notes

1. Devereux Butcher, "Sunshine and Blizzard," *National Parks Magazine* 31, no. 128 (January 1957): 24–33.

2. Ernest Swift, "Parks—Or Resorts?" *National Parks Magazine* 31, no. 131 (October 1957): 147–48.

3. Jack Goodman, "Controversy Over Lodge In West," *New York Times,* 7 August 1955, X27.

4. Interview with Mr. Homer Richards. Conducted by Ed Edwin, 18 July 1966, Oral History Collection of Columbia University, 34.

5. Joyce Zaitlin, *Gilbert Stanley Underwood, His Rustic, Art Deco, and Federal Architecture* (Malibu, Calif.: J. Simon/Pangloss Press, 1989), 14.

6. Ibid., 25.

7. Union Pacific Railroad Company, *Zion National Park, Grand Canyon National Park, Bryce Canyon, Cedar Breaks, Kaibab National Forest* (Omaha, Neb.: Union Pacific System, 1928).

8. Zaitlin, *Gilbert Stanley Underwood,* 134.

9. Rodd L. Wheaton, "National Park Service: The First 75 Years," *The National Park Service* (1 December 2000), National Park Service, http://www.nps.gov/history/history/online_books/sontag/underwood.htm.

10. Ibid., 1.

11. Robert A. M. Stern, *George Howe: Toward a Modern American Architecture* (New Haven, Conn.: Yale University Press, 1975), 203.

12. Antoinette J. Lee, *Architect to the Nation* (New York: Oxford University Press, 2000), 283.

13. Zaitlin, *Gilbert Stanley Underwood,* 114; Jane Watson, "Critic Finds U.S. Housing Attractive," *Washington Post,* 23 May 1943, 48.

14. "PBA Residence Halls for Women, Washington, D.C., Designed to Meet the Acute Housing Problem," *Architectural Record* 92 (July 1942): 40–43.

15. National Park Service Public Use Statistics Office, "NPS Stats: National Park Service Public Use Statistics Online," *National Park Service* (30 September 2004), National Park Service, Department of the Interior, http://www.nature.nps.gov/stats/viewReport.cfm; Memorandum, undated, No Folder, Box 1, Family Related—Organizations series, Record Group 27, Grand Teton Lodge Company (GTLC), Special Collections, Rockefeller Archives Center, Sleepy Hollow, New York (RAC).

16. Gilbert Stanley Underwood, "A Scheme for the Development of the Public Concessions in Grand Teton National Park, Wyoming," 1 December 1950, Folder 831, Box 90, Cultural Interest series, Record Group 2, Office of Messieurs Rockefeller (OMR), Rockefeller Family Archives (RFA), RAC.

17. To "Harry"? from H. W. Morrison, President of Morrison-Knudsen Company, Inc., 29 November 1952, Folder 1303, Box 8, Family Related—Organizations series, Record Group 27, GTLC, Special Collections, RAC.

18. Gilbert Stanley Underwood to Frank Sullivan, 7 February 1953, Folder 1302-C, Box 8, Family Related—Organizations series, Record Group 27, GTLC, Special Collections, RAC.

19. United States Census Bureau, "Statistical Abstract: Historical Statistics," *U.S. Census Bureau* (6 November 2007), U.S. Census Bureau, http://www.census.gov/compendia/statab/hist_stats.html.

20. Chandler Cudlipp to Gilbert Stanley Underwood, 24 August 1954, Folder Furnishings, Box 8, Family Related—Organizations series, Record Group 27, GTLC, Special Collections, RAC.

21. "Notes of Meeting of July 1, 1954 on Main Lodge Decorations," Folder: Furnishings, Jackson Lake Lodge Construction, Box 8, Family Related—Organizations series, Record Group 27, GTLC, Special Collections, RAC.

22. Presentation Board Outlining Interior Decoration, JHPI, Oversized Material, Presentation Boards (on Jackson Lake Lodge) for Design Competition, 1956, RAC.

23. Harold Fabian, "Jackson Lake Lodge Development," report, 1954, Folder 347, Box 30, Family Related Individuals series, Record Group 7.2, Harold P. Fabian Papers, Teton Companies, Special Collections, RAC.

24. Gregory D. Kendrick, *National Historic Landmark Nomination: Jackson Lake Lodge,* 2002.

25. David M. Burwen and Susan Jo Burwen, *Carl Roters and the Rendezvous Murals* (Mountain View, Calif.: Venture Development Group, 2004), 18.

26. Chandler Cudlipp to Gilbert Stanley Underwood, 22 July 1954, Folder Furnishings, Box 8, Family Related—Organizations series, Record Group 27, GTLC, Special Collections, RAC.

27. Jack Goodman, "Jackson Lake Lodge to Open June 15 with Accommodations for 750," *New York Times,* 8 May 1955, XX39.

28. "Everyone Invited to Open House at New Jackson Lake Lodge," *Jackson Hole Guide,* 2 June 1955, 1.

29. Goodman, "Controversy Over Lodge In West," X27.

30. Underwood, "A Scheme for the Development of the Public Concessions," 3.

31. Union Pacific Railroad Company, *Zion National Park, Grand Canyon National Park;* Underwood, "A Scheme for the Development of the Public Concessions," 1, emphasis added.

32. "Park Hotel Under Way," *Los Angeles Times,* 25 July 1926, E1.

33. Interview with Mr. Theodore J. Wirth, FASLA, former president of ASLA. Conducted by Elizabeth Flint and assisted by Mrs. Joan Berthiaume, 6 October 2008.

34. Gilbert Stanley Underwood to Harold Fabian, 28 January 1953, Folder 1302 C, Box 8, Family Re-

lated—Organizations series, Record Group 27, GTLC, Special Collections, RAC.

35. Raymond Lillie to Kenneth Chorley, 16 June 1956, Courtesy of Mary McKinney, GTLC historian.

36. Kenneth Chorley to Conrad Wirth, 13 March 1957, Folder Landscaping work, JLL, Box 8, Family Related—Organizations series, Record Group 27 GTLC, Special Collections, RAC.

37. Ibid.

38. Spencer & Lee, Architects, "Landscape Development Plans, Jackson Lake Lodge," 3 July 1958, National Park Service Technical Information Center, Denver, Colorado.

39. Ethan Carr, "Mission 66 and 'Rustication,'" *CRM* (bulletin) 22, no. 9 (1999): 16.

40. Ethan Carr, *Mission 66: Modernism and the National Park Dilemma* (Amherst: University of Massachusetts Press in association with Library of American Landscape History, 2007), 4.

41. "The EM-Kayan, the Magazine of 'M-K,'" December 1953, p. 16, Folder 346, Box 30, Family Related Individuals series, Record Group 7.2, Harold P. Fabian Papers, Teton Companies, Special Collections, RAC.

The Visitor Center as Monument

Recontextualizing Richard Neutra's 1962 Cyclorama Center within the Commemorative Landscape of the Gettysburg Battlefield

The 1962 Cyclorama Building at Gettysburg National Military Park, designed by modernist architects Richard Neutra and Robert Alexander, was once heralded as a landmark structure representative of the federal government's post–World War II architectural identity. In a glowing review, the *New York Times* declared the structure the "first port of call for all visitors" to Gettysburg and predicted the innovative new visitor center was "likely to become one of the showplaces of the National Park System" (fig. 1). In the intervening years, however, the building lost this privileged status in the eyes of its patron agency and the public.[1] Officials with the National Park Service now insist that removal of this mid-twentieth-century building is critical to their plans to restore the 1863 battlefield where Americans fought and died during the Civil War. The decision to excise this building from the "sacred ground" of the battlefield, however, fails to acknowledge the original intent for the building within the context of the memorial landscape, as well as the significance of the building as one of Neutra's most important public commissions and as a signature commission of the Park Service's historic Mission 66 program. The architects and the Park Service intended the strikingly contemporary Cyclorama Building to function both as a flagship visitor center representing the large-scale achievements of the Mission 66 program and as a commemorative gathering place, a modern-day memorial set upon one of our nation's most hallowed sites (fig. 2).[2]

Gettysburg, located near the southern border of central Pennsylvania, is a small town surrounded by a rich cultural landscape. This area played a critical role during the Civil War, as more than fifty-one thousand men fell in battle or died during the three days of conflict between the Union and Confederate forces in July 1863. Mourners, collectors, photographers, and sightseers converged upon the site in the immediate aftermath of the engagement, arriving before the government cleared the field of bodies. That November, the formal process of commemoration began when President Abraham Lincoln ascended the podium for delivery of his address at the dedication of the nearby Soldiers National Cemetery. During his landmark speech, Lincoln asserted that "we cannot dedicate—we cannot consecrate—we cannot hallow—this ground. The brave men, living and dead, who struggled here, have consecrated it, far above our poor power to add or detract." Despite these words, each succeeding generation of Americans and stewards have felt compelled to add a series of physical memorials to the site, in part to interpret the event from their own perspective but also as an effort to protect the boundaries of the battlefield and preserve the "blood-soaked ground" upon which the soldiers walked, fought, and died.[3]

The Pennsylvania legislature worked quickly to secure the long-term future of the site by conferring to the Gettysburg Battlefield Memorial Association the right "to hold and preserve" the battlefield and oversee "such memorial structures as a generous and patriotic people may add to erect, to commemorate the heroic deeds, the struggles, and the triumphs of their brave defenders." The association, founded in April 1864, transferred its title to the federal government in 1895, after Congress approved the creation of Gettysburg National Military Park. In this, and in the case of many Civil War battlefields at the turn of the twentieth century, the War Department was charged with managing and interpreting the site, supervising the addition of hundreds of markers, statues, and plaques by veterans groups and state organizations, and creating a system of tour roads throughout the park to enhance interpretation.[4]

By the time the War Department transferred the battlefield to the Park Service in 1933, the landscape had become one of America's most prominent "memory places," a site for national commemoration, historical interpretation, and heritage tourism. Despite the worldwide prominence of the battlefield, and an ever-increasing number of visitors, the Park Service did not immediately undertake the construction of new facilities. Instead, the agency relied upon an off-site information center in nearby downtown Gettysburg. Entrepreneurial commercial establishments quickly filled the void created by the absence of an official governmental presence. Privately owned "museums," conspicuously located on major highways, provided tourists with appealing, and sometimes dubious, interpretations of park history. For many years the white-columned "National Museum," located across from the Soldiers National Cemetery, at-

FIG. 1. The Cyclorama Center, looking west, 2004. The National Park Service selected a central site on the battlefield to increase rates of interaction between visitors and park staff, consolidate park operations, and provide a gallery for the Battle of Gettysburg cyclorama painting at approximately the same vantage point expressed on the canvas. (Jack Boucher, photographer; Library of Congress, Prints and Photographs Division, Historic American Buildings Survey, HABS PA-6709-7)

MONUMENTS, MARKERS, AND TABLETS

1   4TH OHIO INFANTRY LEFT FLANK MARKER
2   4TH OHIO INFANTRY MONUMENT
3   4TH OHIO INFANTRY RIGHT FLANK MARKER
4   "HANCOCK AVENUE" WAR DEPARTMENT ID TABLET
5   107TH PENNSYLVANIA INFANTRY POSITION MARKER
6   111TH NEW YORK INFANTRY RIGHT FLANK MARKER
7   12TH NEW JERSEY INFANTRY RIGHT FLANK MARKER
8   111TH NEW YORK INFANTRY MONUMENT
9   11TH MISSISSIPPI INFANTRY MONUMENT
10 111TH NEW YORK INFANTRY LEFT FLANK MARKER
11 12TH NEW JERSEY INFANTRY MONUMENT
12 12TH NEW JERSEY INFANTRY LEFT FLANK MARKER
13 "PETTIGREW'S CHARGE" INFORMATION SIGN
14 2ND DELAWARE INFANTRY POSITION MARKER
15 125TH NEW YORK INFANTRY MONUMENT
16 125TH NEW YORK INFANTRY RIGHT FLANK MARKER
17 "HAY'S U.S. DIVISION" TABLET
18 "WILLARD'S BRIGADE" TABLET
19 "BRYAN HOUSE" WAR DEPARTMENT ID TABLET
20 "BRYAN HOUSE" INFORMATION SIGN
21 "HIGH WATER MARK TRAIL" INFORMATION SIGN
22 108TH NEW YORK INFANTRY LEFT FLANK MARKER
23 9TH MASS. ARTILLERY TABLET (BIGELOW'S BATTERY)
24 "SONS OF UNION VETERANS" TABLET
25 GRAND ARMY OF THE REPUBLIC MEMORIAL
26 BATTERY I 1ST US ARTILLERY TABLET (WOODRUFF'S BATTERY)
27 108TH NEW YORK INFANTRY MONUMENT
28 108TH NEW YORK INFANTRY RIGHT FLANK MARKER
29 BATTERY F 5TH ARTILLERY TABLET (MARTIN'S BATTERY)
30 BATTERY G 2ND US ARTILLERY TABLET (BUTLER'S BATTERY)
31 126TH NEW YORK INFANTRY LEFT FLANK MARKER
32 TOPOGRAPHIC BASELINE MONUMENT
33 126TH NEW YORK INFANTRY MONUMENT
34 HAYS MONUMENT
35 "ZIEGLER'S GROVE" WAR DEPARTMENT ID TABLET
36 GETTYSBURG NATIONAL MILITARY PARK MONUMENT
37 126TH NEW YORK INFANTRY RIGHT FLANK MARKER
38 90TH PENNSYLVANIA INFANTRY LEFT FLANK MARKER
39 90TH PENNSYLVANIA INFANTRY MONUMENT
40 1ST MASS. SHARPSHOOTERS POSITION MARKER
41 90TH PENNSYLVANIA INFANTRY RIGHT FLANK MARKER
42 88TH PENNSYLVANIA INFANTRY POSITION MARKER
43 12TH MASS. INFANTRY (WEBSTER REGIMENT) POSITION MARKER
44 3RD NEW YORK ARTILLERY RIGHT FLANK MARKER
45 3RD NEW YORK ARTILLERY MONUMENT
46 3RD NEW YORK ARTILLERY LEFT FLANK MARKER
47 MARYLAND STATE MONUMENT
48 DELAWARE STATE MONUMENT
49 7TH WEST VIRGINIA INFANTRY POSITION MARKER
60 6TH NEW YORK INDEPENDENT BATTERY MONUMENT

PLANT LIST

KEY	BOTANICAL NAME	COMMON NAME
AP	ACER PLATANOIDES	NORWAY MAPLE
AR	ACER RUBRUM	RED MAPLE
ASo	ACER SACCHARUM	SUGAR MAPLE
ASp	AMELANCHIER SPECIES	SERVICEBERRY
BS	BUXUS SEMPERVIRENS	BOXWOOD
CB	CATALPA BIGNONIOIDES	CATALPA
CF	CORNUS FLORIDA	FLOWERING DOGWOOD
CH	CORYLUS HAMAMELIS	WITCH HAZEL
FA	FRAXINUS AMERICANA	WHITE ASH
FG	FAGUS GRANDIFOLIA	AMERICAN BEECH
GB	GINKO BILOBA	GINKO
IO	ILEX OPACA	AMERICAN HOLLY
LT	LIRIODENDRON TULIPIFERA	TULIP POPLAR
MS	MALUS SPECIES	APPLE
NS	NYSSA SYLVATICA	BLACK GUM
OV	OSTRYA VIRGINIANA	IRONWOOD
PO	PLATANUS OCCIDENTALIS	SYCAMORE
PS	PRUNUS SEROTINA	BLACK CHERRY
QPa	QUERCUS PALUSTRIS	PIN OAK
QPh	QUERCUS PHELLOS	WILLOW OAK
QR	QUERCUS RUBRA	RED OAK
SA	SASSAFRAS ALBIDUM	SASSAFRAS
TC	TAXUS CANADENSIS	AMERICAN YEW
TS	THUJA SPECIES	ARBORVITAE
VA	VIBURNUM ACERIFOLIUM	ARROWWOOD VIBURNUM
VP	VIBURNUM PRUNIFOLIUM	BLACKHAW VIBURNUM

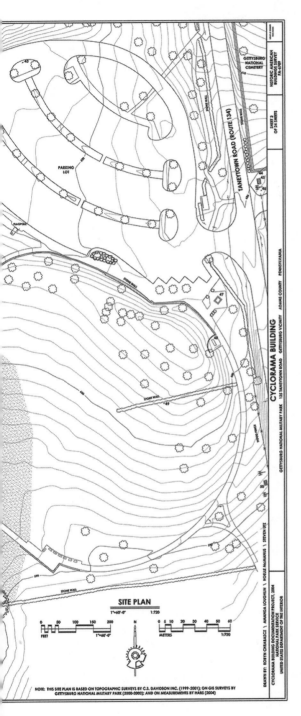

FIG. 2. Current site map of the Cyclorama Center area. The Cyclorama Center sits at the southern edge of Ziegler's Grove; above the office wing is an extended open-air platform providing expansive views of the battlefield. The privately owned "Gettysburg National Museum" (also referred to as the "Rosensteel Building," later the Visitor Center for the park) was just north of the Cyclorama Center parking area. That building was demolished in 2008. (Library of Congress, Prints and Photographs Division, Historic American Buildings Survey, HABS PA-6709)

tracted travelers who mistakenly thought the building was a Park Service facility. One visitor wrote: "Following our road map which included a sectional map of the city of Gettysburg, we arrived at 'The National Museum' expecting to find the usual high standards we've come to expect of fine National Park Service organization and preservation of treasured historical and natural wonders throughout the country. Imagine our reaction to find the 'Museum' to be privately owned and commercialized to the 'nth' degree, in a manner totally unfitting to bear the 'National' title."[5] Clearly the public expected the Park Service to provide facilities for their "use and enjoyment" of park resources, or, at the least, to maintain a high standard for visitor services in the area without relying upon the kitsch of battlefield tourism.

In 1942, the National Park Service added to its collection at Gettysburg with the acquisition of a gigantic painted canvas known as a "cyclorama." The artwork, completed by French artist Paul Philippoteaux in 1883, depicted his interpretation of the military action on the third day of the Battle of Gettysburg, 3 July 1863. The "circular panorama" painting, with diorama-like constructions placed at the base of the canvas to create a three-dimensional effect, attracted large crowds from across the country and around the world. With popular subjects of the era including urban conflagrations, epic battles, and the Crucifixion of Christ, this particular cyclorama painting was first displayed in a custom-designed building in Boston, an imposing brick structure capped with battlements designed by the firm of Cummings and Sears in 1884. By 1889, however, waning interest in the painting prompted its removal from the building, to be replaced by a cyclorama depicting "Custer's Last Stand."

After numerous ownership transfers, each time accompanied by a manipulation and cutting of the canvas to fit a variety of display spaces, the painting was bought by a private party and installed in a squat silo-like structure in Gettysburg. The Park Service purchased the painting and the building in 1942. With no other options available, the enormous canvas, measuring approximately 360 feet in length and 26 feet in height (cut down from an original height of 40 feet), remained in the unheated, poorly lit building with a leaky roof. "There is urgent need for museum development at Gettysburg," stated the park historian in 1956, "especially for a building to properly house, preserve, and interpret the great cyclorama painting . . . and through the media of exhibits to better explain and interpret the events which happened here."[6]

The historian's plight was echoed at parks nationwide, as a perfect storm of too many visitors, an aging infrastructure, and no funding gains strained the Park Service to the breaking point. The post–World War II visiting public, mobilized by a thriving economy and a surge in nationalist propaganda that equated tourism with patriotism, eagerly sought out the parks as a welcome respite from the foreign crises of the era. But the parks were unprepared for the onslaught. In a widely circulated exposé, entitled "The Shocking Truth About Our National Parks," *Reader's Digest* editor Charles Stevenson sent out a dire admonition to vacationing Americans. "One out of three persons in the United States will visit some part of our national-park system during 1955. To these visitors I must pass along a warning: Your trip is likely to be fraught with discomfort, disappointment, even danger." Stevenson found "appalling" conditions throughout the parks during his yearlong national survey, citing dilapidated buildings, crumbling roads, rampant littering, and a proliferation of petty crimes.[7]

The fusillade of bad press and public pressure on the government to stem deterioration and vandalism in the parks increased throughout the 1950s; yet Congress continued to turn a deaf ear to the problem. Critics likened the National Park Service to "a favorite figure of American legendry, the widow who scrapes and patches and ekes out, who by desperate expedients succeeds in bringing up her children to be a credit to our culture."[8]

Conrad L. Wirth resolved to alter the grim outlook for the postwar parks when he assumed the directorship of the National Park Service in 1951. "Low scale, piecemeal progress" caused by consistently skimpy appropriations forced the Park Service "year by year" to fall "farther behind in its capacity to serve the Nation," according to Wirth. Desperate for a solution to the park system's pervasive "financial malnutrition" and decades of benign neglect, Wirth set forth a bold initiative to modernize park facilities and, on a grand scale, restore the luster to America's dilapidated national treasures. Congress, and the president, approved, signing off on a ten-year, billion-dollar building program. "Mission 66," scheduled for completion in 1966 to coincide with the fiftieth anniversary of the Park Service, effectively captured America's ambitious spirit at midcentury and promised a new era for its national parks.[9]

The abandonment of traditional approaches to developing and interpreting the parks became a project trademark within Mission 66. Wirth encouraged his staff to "feel free to question anything [they] thought could be done in a better way." "Nothing was to be sacred," Wirth later recalled, "except the ultimate purpose to be served. Men, method, and time-honored practices were to be accorded no vested deference. Old traditions seem to have determined standards far beyond their time."[10]

The "rustic" tradition in park architecture appeared to be one casualty in Wirth's nationwide effort to modernize. Yet, the transition from rustic to modern, a switch that seemed to happen overnight, fomented and grew for decades before the beginning of the Mission 66 program. The next generation of architects and designers—led by veterans of the pre–World War II parks era, such as Wirth—longed to creatively forge ahead with a new style of architecture. But change was slow, inconsistent, and subjective. Wirth himself had previously passed over a major opportunity to recast the architectural character of park structures with the addition of what could have been a remarkable building. In 1954, he and other park administrators rejected a restaurant design submitted by Frank Lloyd Wright at Yosemite National Park. Wirth referred to the design as a "mushroom-dome type of thing" discarded for its "modernized" statement that did not "fit into the scenery." Frank Lloyd Wright, upon hearing the news, responded, "It's politics." Yet, less than one year later, Wirth hailed the opening of the modernist Jackson Lake Lodge in Grand Teton National Park as "the first major post-war construction in any Federal parkland."[11]

Gilbert Stanley Underwood's glass-and-concrete lodge generated controversy and heated exchanges. In a "wordy fracas," reported in the *New York Times,* followers of Underwood applauded the "blending of practical, modern architecture with western motifs" as appropriate to a park wilderness area, while critics called the structure a "slab-sided concrete abomination." At the opening ceremonies, Conrad Wirth referred to the Mission 66 program for infrastructure improvements, at that point not yet announced to the general public, and proposed the new lodge as a model for similar projects in the parks.[12]

Mission 66 began as a bold initiative to bring the national park system into the modern age, but the program lacked a flagship component, a compelling architectural feature that would promote the new identity of the agency and incorporate all of Mission 66's ambitious goals for public service and park preservation. Conrad Wirth and his planning committees found their eureka moment in the creation of the visitor center. The contemporary buildings, designed to occupy prime tourist territory at more than one hundred parks nationwide, showcased the Park Service's renewed commitment to interpreting and protecting the nation's most valuable sites and quickly became the structure most looked for, relied upon, and remembered by park guests.

The visitor center building program focused primarily on the construction of entirely new structures; all designs shunned the traditional "rustic" look and tapped into the modernist ethos of post–World War II America. National Park Service architects Cecil Doty, Walter Roth, Benjamin Biderman, and Donald F. Benson led the in-house design effort. At most parks, these architects worked with small local firms to streamline the design and construction process. For a limited number of high-profile projects, however, the Park Service commissioned prominent private firms to create showpiece buildings. Gettysburg, a crown jewel of the park system, was selected as one of five sites nationwide that would receive special architectural treatment.

Initially, the Park Service considered the Cyclorama Building and the Visitor Center as two different building projects, with the gallery for the painting to be placed near the Soldiers National Cemetery and the Visitor Center at a separate location "where incoming visitors can be intercepted." At a 1957 planning meeting, the Park Service issued a clear directive stating that "the Cyclorama relates to a specific event and should be located near the site of the event." Eventually, the building functions were consolidated into one structure to be built near Ziegler's Grove at the northern boundary of the park. In this case, the centrally located site, occupied by a seventy-foot-tall 1895 observation tower (later demolished), lay conveniently close to the National Cemetery and the problematic "National Museum," providing the best "one-stop" access to the battlefield desired by the typical visitor. Additionally, the new building established a solid Park Service presence at this critical point of tourist activity.[13]

After calling for, and rejecting, building plans from its staff architects, the National Park Service handpicked the firm of Neutra and Alexander of Los Angeles to design the visitor center. Richard Neutra, an Austrian-born immigrant who became one of the most significant architects of the twentieth century worldwide, excitedly accepted the commission. Neutra is best known for his Southern California houses, most notably the Lovell "Health" House in Los Angeles (1927–29) and the Kaufmann "Desert" House in Palm Springs (1946–47), high-end projects that influenced residential design throughout the country. A self-proclaimed "bio-realist," Neutra worked tirelessly for more than sixty years to create built environments that enhanced basic human relationships and promoted people's connection to their surroundings. At Gettysburg, the Park Service presented Neutra with a rare late-career opportunity to explore his theories on a monumental scale. The architect seized upon this rare chance to contribute to a monumental American landscape and immersed himself in the creation of a building that enhanced, and exceeded, the expectations of the client.

At the time, Neutra and Alexander had two projects for the National Park Service on the table—Gettysburg and a visitor center with staff housing for Petrified Forest National Park in Arizona. Neutra and his architect son, Dion, assisted by architect Thaddeus Longstreth, quickly took the lead in Pennsylvania. The project began as a Museum and Auditorium, "first programmed as a center" for visitors "who make a pilgrimage to the famous battlefield of supreme sacrifice," according to Neutra. His vision for the site took another course, however, after a conversation with a newspaper editor in Arizona named John Riddick. Riddick, a transplanted Virginian, was with Neutra when he received the news of this honored architectural commission. After completing the call to Washington, D.C., Neutra enthusiastically related his future aspirations for Gettysburg to the skeptical newsman. Expecting congratulations, Neutra was shocked to hear instead that Southerners still viewed Gettysburg as a site of defeat rather than reconciliation.[14]

Following that experience, Neutra envisioned a mission far above that accorded to the typical park visitor center. He believed that he was "a servant of the human community," called

in by the Park Service "to find for the project a much enriched significance." He referred to the site in a tone of reverence appropriate to a memorial battlefield. Lincoln's Gettysburg Address was "immortal," the cemetery a "sacred spot," and the whole encompassing the "solemn memory of a nation." Neutra went so far as to credit the Civil War outcome as contributing to the United States' supremacy in world politics of the time, creating an America "so fateful to this planet three generations later." In his notes, the architect referred to the building variously as a "Shrine of a Free World," the "Lincoln Memorial Museum and Visitors' Center," and a "Shrine of Our Nation Reunited."[15]

Despite his dedication to the memorial concept, Neutra proclaimed impatience with the profusion of neoclassical statuary and figurative monuments present on the battlefield. "I don't like the nationalistic, untied-shoe Lincoln or the classic Roman-togaed Lincoln," he wrote. "This memorial should not stand for the man, or the war, or any side. It is for the Address. This place has become universal because of a one minute, 40-second speech." As for his own contribution to the landscape, he mused that "perhaps an architect and a building could help to signify the world's historical multinational necessities on a shrunken globe." Neutra dedicated his full energies to this honored project; he kept copious notes of his aspirations and referred to the Cyclorama Building as the structure "closest to my heart."[16]

The National Park Service had a similarly modern objective in mind for the Cyclorama Building. The agency had already approved the move away from the reinterpretation of classical architecture for memorials in 1947 with their acceptance of Eero Saarinen's Jefferson National Expansion Memorial Gateway Arch, designed as a "symbol of national recovery." Interestingly, Neutra, along with a number of other notable modernists, served on the committee that approved Saarinen's design, which was not completed until funding was appropriated under Mission 66. At Gettysburg, the new visitor center, located close to a number of historic memorials, including the massive neoclassical-inspired Pennsylvania Memorial, needed to address the commemorative nature of the site while speaking clearly to its own era and function. According to historian Sarah Allaback, the agency expected Neutra's design to "meet the criteria of both a sacred monument and a utilitarian public facility."[17]

This unusual conception of the visitor center as a memorial worked in harmony with the existing commemorative landscape. Scholar Edward Tabor Linenthal describes Gettysburg as a "rich cultural archive of various modes of remembrance." Actual images of the dead are far too graphic for effective postwar symbolism—the honor of dying for the cause is obscured by the reality of the dismembered and bloated bodies on the landscape, as captured in Alexander Gardner's and Matthew Brady's haunting photographs taken immediately after the battle. The populace instead drew upon a long legacy of commemoration, erecting a cornucopia of monuments on the battlefield, dedicated by every generation from the Civil War onward and frequently timed to coincide with the original event's anniversary calendar. For instance, the cornerstone for the Soldiers' National Monument, a gray granite shaft that features four allegorical statutes in white marble representing War, History, Peace, and Plenty, was laid on the first anniversary of the battle and dedicated on 1 July 1869. In January 1912, the Gettysburg Park Commission erected the Lincoln Address Memorial near the Soldiers National Cemetery. The battle was further commemorated in "three outstanding anniversary celebrations" on the twenty-fifth-year and fiftieth-year marks. A strong number of men even made it to the seventy-fifth anniversary of the event in 1938 to witness the dedication of the Eternal Light Peace Memorial, when 1,845 veterans (of approximately 8,000 then living) arrived at the battlefield. The average age of these last survivors: ninety-four years old.[18]

One hundred and fifty years after Lincoln's birth, designs for the Cyclorama Building were approved on 12 February 1959. The building program posed considerable challenges to the architects. On a practical level, the visitor center had to include offices, restrooms, an auditorium, a museum, and a clear-span gallery for the "circular panorama" painting. Neutra addressed basic design principles, such as streamlining public flow through the structure, as well as creating a "successful esthetic solution" for housing the enormous painting. Yet, he went further and "added the very interesting possibilities of a prophetic 'Rostrum'" for speeches and proposed housing these "manifold activities" in a "monumental form befitting the historic site." Construction estimates of $1 million were given. An estimated 1.25 million people were expected to visit Gettysburg in 1966, with the building able to accommodate up to 29,000 people "in a single peak day."[19]

In plan, the building resembles the shape of a keyhole (fig. 3). At the north end a series of concentric circles is created by the curved shape of the auditorium and the outer wall of a stark white, cast-in-place concrete rotunda which houses the painting gallery and exhibit area. Extending to the south is a low-lying rectangular office wing of concrete and glass topped by a generous observation deck intended to provide tourists with an immediate, three-dimensional vision of the landscape rendered in the cyclorama painting. Descriptive plaques along the deck helped visitors link the tangled story of the battle with the panoramic view laid out before them. The wing featured two signature Neutra devices: a screen of movable metal sun louvers installed to create a comfortable interior environment for park staff and a concrete "spider leg" extending from a wall of native Pennsylvania stone that cleverly disguises the scale and presence of the building when viewed from the battlefield.

Neutra carefully manipulated reflective light and battlefield vistas, both outside and inside the building, to blur the boundaries of the physicality of today and call to mind an ethereal emotion of the past. He designed the visitor center to harmonize with the century-old cultural landscape, promising that the building would "play itself into the background, behind a pool reflecting the everlasting sky over all of

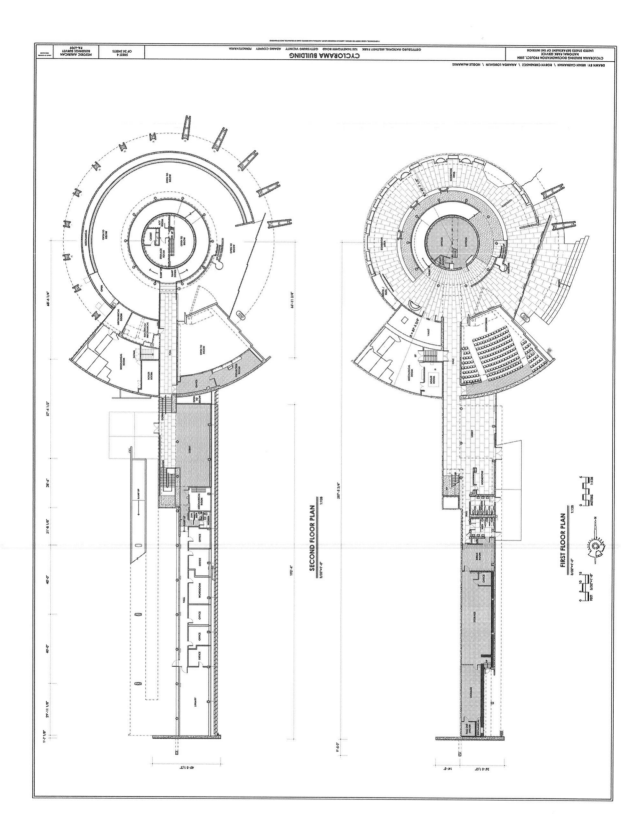

HISTORIC AMERICAN
BUILDINGS SURVEY
PA-6709

SHEET 4
OF 24 SHEETS

CYCLORAMA BUILDING

GETTYSBURG NATIONAL MILITARY PARK   135 TANEYTOWN ROAD   GETTYSBURG VICINITY   ADAMS COUNTY   PENNSYLVANIA

UNITED STATES DEPARTMENT OF THE INTERIOR
NATIONAL PARK SERVICE
CYCLORAMA BUILDING DOCUMENTATION PROJECT, 2004

DRAWN BY: BRIAN CASANANAN \ ROBYN CHERASCIZ \ AMANDA LOSCHIUN \ NOELLE McMANUS

SECOND FLOOR PLAN

FIRST FLOOR PLAN

facing page

FIG. 3. Plan of the first (*right*) and second (*left*) floors of the Cyclorama Center. The cyclorama painting is housed in the circular gallery to the right, with the semicircular auditorium wing, visitor services, and park operations extending to the left in this drawing. (Library of Congress, Prints and Photographs Division, Historic American Buildings Survey, HABS PA-6709)

us—and it will not shout out any novelty or datedness." Water ran in a shallow pool along the length of the observation platform, spilling over into a separate pool near the junction of the rotunda and the main entry, mirroring the adjacent drum (housing the cyclorama canvas) and fracturing the visible line between building and landscape. Mica chips mixed into the white paint of the drum refracted the sunlight and created a star-like effect across the striated concrete surfaces.[20]

Inside, the floors were covered with dark, reflective terrazzo which visually dematerialized the building's foundation. The ceiling was lit by concealed sources, while a continuous light strip at floor level illuminated the central ramp. The whole effect of the building foretold the arrival at one of the main attractions—the cyclorama painting (fig. 4). To reach the viewing platform inside the circular canvas, Neutra created a slow, anticipatory climb up the spiraling ramp. "The breathing lungs, the palpitating heart . . . while we turn and rise . . . are fused with a vast multitude of memories," he wrote. Visitors would catch bright flashing glimpses of the battlefield through a screen of slender rods before arriving at double doors that led to the painting gallery. After viewing the presentation, consisting of an automated narrative, the visitors exited over an open-grid sky ramp to the second-floor lobby and the outside entrance to the observation deck (fig. 5).[21]

The memorial homage to Lincoln and the contemporary cause for worldwide reconciliation culminated in the "Rostrum of the Prophetic Voice." This elevated platform, standing at the juncture of two curved walls, one

bearing the words "Shall Not Perish From the Earth," became "the climax of the composition" for Neutra (fig. 6). According to his notes, the architect believed that this speaker's platform represented a "visible symbol for contemplation, that is probably the highest good of memory which can be taken away from a battlefield of the past." Enormous glass walls in front of the rostrum rolled out of the way on small wheels and the adjacent auditorium wall pivoted open so that people seated indoors and gathered in the outdoor assembly area would mutually face the podium.[22]

Richard Neutra drew inspiration from symbolic spaces of the past, creating a twentieth-century memorial intended to encourage quiet contemplation and facilitate new conversations about the meaning of Lincoln's timeless words. The visionary architect imagined that a procession of world leaders, such as India's Jawaharlal Nehru, Brazil's Juscelino Kubitschek, or China's Chou En-Lai, would use the rostrum to present stirring speeches promoting global unanimity. "We should invite every year one of the great statesmen of the Nations," he wrote in his notes. "It may be even a 'Cold War' enemy nation to speak before thirty thousand people about: 'What Shall Not Perish from the Earth.'"[23] Where Lincoln spoke poignantly of the shattered Union between the Northern and Southern states, the National Park Service dedicated Neutra's latter-day "Lincoln Memorial" to the cause of international harmony in a world threatened with atomic annihilation.

Neutra's million-dollar memorial opened to great acclaim in 1962. The dedication ceremony, planned—as tradition called for—on the anniversary of the Gettysburg Address, featured a speech by National Park Service director Conrad Wirth himself. Wolf Von Eckardt of the *Washington Post* praised the "quietly monumental but entirely unsentimental" Neutra design. He cited the Gettysburg building as one of a set of "exceptionally distinguished and fearlessly modern" buildings in the national parks, each deserving of an architectural excellence award. The American Institute of Architects agreed, honoring Mission 66 and the Park

FIG. 4. The 1883 cyclorama painting and viewing platform inside the Cyclorama Center rotunda, 2004. To reach the painting, visitors ascended a circular, darkened ramp. Neutra created the quiet, confined space to prepare people for the solemnity of the scene unveiled in the gallery: a full-color panorama depicting the third day of the Battle of Gettysburg. (Jack Boucher, photographer; Library of Congress, Prints and Photographs Division, Historic American Buildings Survey, HABS PA-6709-69)

Service for the innovative development of modern facilities "in harmony with the architectural theme" of each park.[24] By the 1970s, however, park officials had grown disenchanted with the building. Although the visitor center/memorial building, set upon a premier commemorative site, initially resonated with America's international ambitions at midcentury, changing sociopolitical environments quickly rendered its message ineffective. The architects' vision of the Cyclorama Center as a "Shrine of Our Nation Reunited" failed to materialize. The Park Service hosted only one major event at the building—its dedication—before quietly abandoning the commemorative concept (fig. 7).

The rousing success of Mission 66 modernism weakened nationwide as the original contexts of the mid-twentieth-century buildings

facing page

FIG. 5. Cross-section of the Cyclorama Center. Bethlehem Steel of Pennsylvania provided the materials for the clear-span cyclorama gallery. An eighteen-foot-high center column serves as the hub of the hung roof, with steel purlins that radiate outward from the upper end and bridge strands that extend from the lower end. The entry ramp for the painting gallery wraps around a hollow concrete cylinder at the bottom. (Library of Congress, Prints and Photographs Division, Historic American Buildings Survey, HABS PA-6709)

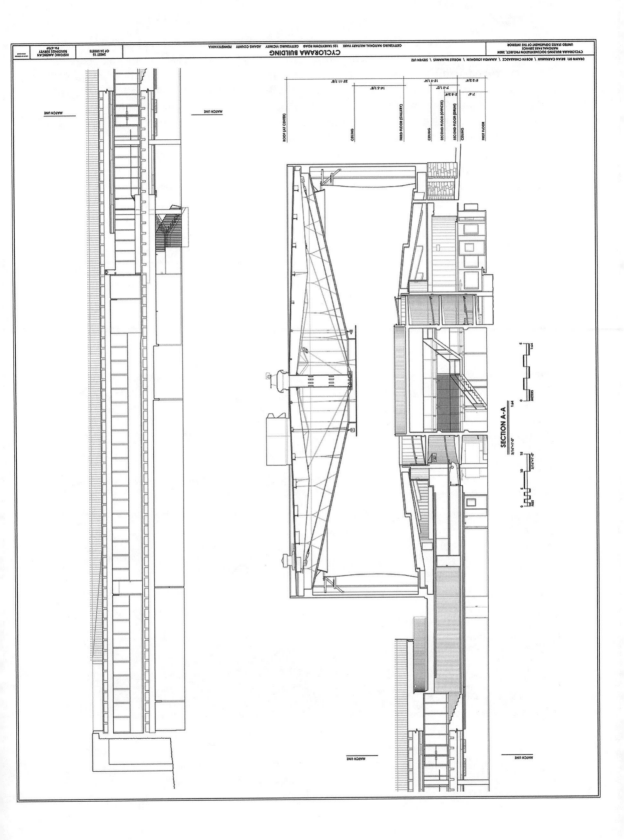

CYCLORAMA BUILDING

GETTYSBURG NATIONAL MILITARY PARK   125 TANEYTOWN ROAD   GETTYSBURG VICINITY   ADAMS COUNTY   PENNSYLVANIA

SHEET 16
OF 24 SHEETS

HISTORIC AMERICAN
BUILDINGS SURVEY
PA-6709

CYCLORAMA BUILDING DOCUMENTATION PROJECT, 2004
NATIONAL PARK SERVICE
UNITED STATES DEPARTMENT OF THE INTERIOR

DRAWN BY: BRIAN CARNAHAN \ ROBYN CHIARADOZ \ AMANDA LOUGHLIN \ NOELLE McMANUS \ STEVEN UTZ

ROOF (AT CENTER)

CEILING

THIRD FLOOR (GALLERY)

CEILING

SECOND FLOOR (OFFICES)

SECOND FLOOR (DRUM)

CEILING

FIRST FLOOR

SECTION A-A

—material symbols of a unified and reenergized park system—slowly faded from memory. Changing economies drew money away from the parks, resulting in spotty structural maintenance of the new buildings. Post-program critics of the Mission 66 legacy derided modernist buildings as counter to the "parkitecture" ideal that the Civilian Conservation Corps had established in the 1930s; the modernist park buildings, often built adjacent to earlier "rustic" structures, appeared anomalous in the continuing architectural lineage of the national parks. Dislike turned to contempt as the visitor centers and other midcentury improvements inevitably showed their age.

In 1973, the National Park Service removed the main visitor center functions from the Cyclorama Building to the newly acquired "National Museum" nearby. In the mid-1990s the Park Service (and its supervisory agency, the U.S. Department of the Interior) agreed with an in-house analysis that the building lacked merit and approved its demolition. Yet the Park Service remained divided on the issue of the Cyclorama's significance, if not its preservation. In September 1998, the Keeper of the National Register overruled park and state authorities and declared the Cyclorama Building a structure of "exceptional historic and architectural significance," adding that the building was a "rare example of Neutra's institutional design on the east coast and one of his very few Federal commissions." Recognizing the significant contribution of Mission 66 design in the park, the keeper also declared four other visitor centers eligible for the National Register: Anshen and Allen's Quarry Visitor Center at Dinosaur National Monument in Utah (1956–

FIG. 6. Interior view of the Cyclorama Center, looking north, 2004. Neutra considered the "Rostrum of the Prophetic Voice" (elevated podium at center, wrapped by waist-height metal bars) as the centerpiece of the building program. Glass walls to the right opened up to the battlefield; the topographical map at the lower half of the image is a modern addition. (Jack Boucher, photographer; Library of Congress, Prints and Photographs Division, Historic American Buildings Survey, HABS PA-6709-53)

FIG. 7. Exterior view of the Cyclorama Center, looking northwest, 2004. The glass walls of the exhibit area at the center and the metal walls of the auditorium at the left opened to the battlefield. The "Rostrum of the Prophetic Voice" faced this open area; attendees in the auditorium and on the battlefield could gather here annually to listen to inspirational words based on sentiments Abraham Lincoln expressed in the Gettysburg Address. The small rectangular opening in the rotunda (above the glass walls) once held an audio speaker for such events. (Jack Boucher, photographer; Library of Congress, Prints and Photographs Division, Historic American Buildings Survey, HABS PA-6709-16)

57); Mitchell/Giurgola's Wright Brothers National Memorial in North Carolina (1957–59), once scheduled for demolition, now preserved; Taliesin Associated Architects' Beaver Meadows Headquarters at Rocky Mountain National Park in Colorado (1964–67); and Neutra and Alexander's Painted Desert Community (including the Visitor Center) at Petrified Forest National Park in Arizona (1959–61).[25]

After the determination of eligibility, the Advisory Council on Historic Preservation reviewed the park plans to demolish the building, with total removal of the structure considered an "adverse effect" under preservation statutes. But where preservationists had hoped to see a victory, there was none. As early as 1977, the council had recommended "reloca-

tion" of Neutra's building. In its 1999 report, the Advisory Council described the Gettysburg case as a "difficult choice" between "three competing historical resources." According to the council, the National Military Park, the cyclorama painting, and the Cyclorama Building could not move into the future together. This *Problem of Common Ground,* as the council entitled the report, resulted from an analysis that relied upon "weighing the historical values represented by each resource." Additionally, the Advisory Council declined to reverse their support for their original 1977 assessment that recommended removal of the building, absent "any compelling reason to do so." Therefore, the report concluded, the "continued existence of the building is consequently pre-empted by another controlling historic preservation objective." Final decision: "The Building must yield."[26]

In an attempt to secure the future of Neutra's Cyclorama Building, the Society of Architectural Historians completed a nomination in December 1999 for National Historic Landmark status in conjunction with the Park Service's nomination of the Dinosaur, Wright Brothers, and Rocky Mountain visitor centers of Mission 66 as landmarks. At this point, however, Park Service administrators formally adopted a general management plan for Gettysburg that described the Cyclorama Building as an intrusion and called for its removal. The NHL petition for the building, coincidentally, was eventually denied despite public support and a favorable recommendation from the Park System Advisory Board National Landmarks Committee.[27]

Despite these interpretive inconsistencies, the building remains a critical component in our understanding of the National Park Service's institutional and architectural histories. Under Mission 66, the Park Service successfully adopted modernism as both a catalyst toward and a symbol of cultural accomplishment. The promise of modern buildings in the parks—not just new but Modern—won the approval of the president, Congress, and the American public. The widespread promotion of a singular aesthetic approach unified an enormous collection of disparate sites without diluting the unique character of each area. The high-profile Mission 66 project, with its massive public relations campaign and resulting increase in tourism, strengthened the legislative boundaries of the parks against incursion and reinvigorated their overall mission to protect and interpret significant American venues.

The persistent reluctance to accept the Cyclorama Building at Gettysburg as one in a series of commemorative monuments might arise, in part, from a long-standing gap between differing perceptions of the battlefield in American history. Author Tony Horwitz delved into the enduring legacy of the Civil War in his sometimes biting commentary *Confederates in the Attic*. Many of the individuals he encoun-tered took solace in remembering this era of America's past as a "talisman against modernity" within a context of "pastoral, preindustrial landscape[s]."[28] Neutra did not harbor this nostalgic view of the Civil War. He approached the battlefield as he saw it in the late 1950s—as a century-old site of memory, covered with monuments, statues, plaques, and markers dedicated to wartime heroism and prophetic words that could continue to inspire people worldwide. This message, manifested in the design and program for the Cyclorama Building, was a timely one for the generations living through the Cold War. The U.S. Civil War Centennial Commission, created in 1957, emphasized that the upcoming celebrations at Gettysburg and elsewhere would be devoted to "national unity and ideals and keeping peace through international understanding."[29] Neutra followed this command by designing a modernist building that could help us learn from history while living in the present.

Richard Neutra's wife, Dione, in a letter to a friend in Germany, defended the humanist extension of the visitor center into a memorial. She wrote that "an architect can and always ought to interpret a program to gain in significance and fascination." At Gettysburg, Neutra had changed "a battle scene of 'a war in the colonies'... into a world panorama of today and the future, a panorama of the historic struggle for mankind's greater union." She hoped that the visitor center and memorial would "resound for centuries and echo hopes and aspirations for a peaceful unity in a free world."[30]

No matter how we proceed at Gettysburg, one fact remains: the battlefield can never recover its "original 1863 condition" because the very event we commemorate, and the process of that commemoration, forever changed the purpose of the site. Gettysburg National Military Park is now home to the largest collection of outdoor statuary in the world, with more than thirteen hundred monuments and four hundred cannon.[31] This "common ground" showcases memorials dedicated by many generations, from the Civil War, through the Cold War, and into the present day.[32] Architect Richard Neutra and the National Park Service contributed to this rich tapestry by conveying "the solemn memory of a nation" at the centennial of the pivotal event.[33] The Cyclorama Building has hosted visitors for one-third of the commemorative landscape's 150-year history. Removing the structure from the landscape will not bring back the old battlefield, nor will it make the war more comprehensible to visitors. Many architects and scholars, including such noteworthy petitioners as Robert A. M. Stern, Frank Gehry, Sir Norman Foster, and the World Monuments Fund, still hope that the Park Service will change its course and claim their responsibility to care for this architectural monument.

Notes

1. Ward Allan Howe, "A Date to Recall: Gettysburg Centennial Will Be Marked by Special Ceremonies July 1–4," *New York Times,* 9 June 1963, 451.

2. Ibid.

3. Abraham Lincoln, Gettysburg Address, 19 November 1863 (Gettysburg, Pennsylvania), Transcript of the "Nicolay Draft" of the Gettysburg Address, Series 3, General Correspondence 1837–1897, the Abraham Lincoln Papers at the Library of Congress, Manuscript Division, Washington, D.C.

4. Frederick Tilberg, *Gettysburg National Military Park, Pennsylvania,* National Park Service Historical Handbook Series, No. 9 (Washington, D.C.: National Park Service, 1954; rev. ed., 1962), 47.

5. Rhoda Mason, Cedar Rapids, Iowa, to National Park Service, Washington, D.C., 27 July 1959, letter, photocopied; and Revised Prospectuses, Mission 66, 1960–61, both in Record Group (RG) 79, National Archives Building, Washington, D.C.

6. Park historian Frederick Tilberg, revision of museum prospectus, 1956, quoted in Richard Segars and Kathy Harrison, *Determination of Eligibility: Gettysburg Visitor Center and Cyclorama Building* (Gettysburg, Pa.: U.S. Department of the Interior, National Park Service, 1998), 40.

7. Charles Stevenson, "The Shocking Truth About Our National Parks," *Reader's Digest* (January 1955): 45, 47. This article was also published in *Landscape Architecture* 45 (January 1955): 57–60, under the same title.

8. Bernard DeVoto, "Let's Close the National Parks," *Harper's Magazine* 207 (October 1953): 51.

9. Howard Stagner, "Mission 66 Revisited: A report submitted by Conrad L. Wirth, Former Director, National Park Service, on the occasion of the 20th anniversary of the launching of Mission 66 and the 60th anniversary of the establishment of the National Park Service, 1976," TMs, 3 of 16 pages, Department of the Interior, Washington, D.C.

10. Conrad L. Wirth, *Parks, Politics, and the People* (Norman: University of Oklahoma Press, 1980), 242.

11. Staff writer, "Yosemite Rejects Design by Frank Lloyd Wright," *New York Times,* 1 December 1954, 25L.

12. Jack Goodman, "Controversy Over Lodge in the West," *New York Times,* 7 August 1955, X27.

13. U.S. Department of the Interior, National Park Service, "Memorandum to Director from Regional Director, Subject: Gettysburg Conference," Philadelphia, Pennsylvania, 16 May 1957, RG 79, E2, B8, Copy held at the National Archives.

14. Richard J. Neutra, The Gettysburg Museum and Auditorium, typewritten note, undated, Neutra Collection 1179, Box 810, Young Research Library, University of California, Los Angeles.

15. Ibid.

16. Richard J. Neutra, *Life and Shape* (New York: Appleton-Century-Crofts, 1962), 311; Neutra Collection 1179, Box 810, Young Research Library, University of California, Los Angeles.

17. Sarah Allaback, *Mission 66 Visitor Centers: The History of a Building Type* (Washington, D.C.: U.S. Department of the Interior, National Park Service, Park Historic Structures and Cultural Landscapes Program, 2000), 1, 101.

18. Edward Tabor Linenthal, *Sacred Ground: Americans and Their Battlefields* (Chicago: University of Illinois Press, 1993), 89; Tilberg, *Gettysburg National Military Park,* 47.

19. Richard J. Neutra, Gettysburg Visitors' Center, typewritten note, undated; and Richard J. Neutra, "Gettysburg Visitor's Center and Cyclorama Building—Scheme 'O,' Site Study #7, October 31, 1958," both in Neutra Collection 1179, Box 810, Young Research Library, University of California, Los Angeles.

20. Neutra, *Life and Shape,* 311.

21. Richard J. Neutra, Los Angeles, to Lee Miller, Gardena, California, 17 January 1962, Neutra Collection 1179, Box 810, Young Research Library, University of California, Los Angeles.

22. Richard J. Neutra, Gettysburg Visitors' Center, typewritten note, undated, Neutra Collection 1179, Box 810, Young Research Library, University of California, Los Angeles.

23. Ibid.

24. Howe, "A Date to Recall," 451; Wolf Von Eckardt, "The Park Service Dares to Build Well,"

Washington Post, Times Herald, 29 March 1964, G6; Robert Hawk, Chairman, Committee on Awards and Exhibits, Washington-Metropolitan Chapter of the American Institute of Architects, Inc., Washington, D.C., to Norman C. Fletcher, FAIA, Chairman, Committee on Institute Honors, "Citation of an Organization for Achievement in Architecture and Planning," n.d., American Institute of Architects Library, Washington, D.C.

25. U.S. Department of the Interior, National Park Service, Washington, D.C., National Register of Historic Places, Determination of Eligibility Notification for the Cyclorama Building, September 1998, Washington, D.C.

26. Advisory Council on Historic Preservation, *A Problem of Common Ground,* 14 May 1999, Washington, D.C.

27. U.S. Department of the Interior, National Park Service, *General Management Plan/Draft Environmental Impact Statement, Gettysburg National Military Park, PA* (Washington, D.C.: Government Printing Office, 1998), 221; Letter from James V. Hansen, Chairman, Subcommittee on National Parks and Public Lands, to John Berry, Assistant Secretary, Policy, Management and Budget, U.S. Department of the Interior, supporting review of the Cyclorama Building as a National Historic Landmark by the National Park System Advisory Board, 16 May 2000.

28. Tony Horwitz, *Confederates in the Attic* (New York: Pantheon Books, 1998), 386, 383.

29. Linenthal, *Sacred Ground,* 98.

30. Dione Neutra, Los Angeles, to Richard Heyken, Duisburg, Germany, 28 February 1959, Neutra Collection 1179, Young Research Library, University of California, Los Angeles.

31. Bentley Boyd, "Gettysburg is popular, but not protected," *Daily Press,* 17 August 2007, http://www.dailypress.com/news/local/dp01152sy0aug17,0,4140051.story.

32. Linenthal, *Sacred Ground,* 89.

33. Richard J. Neutra, The Gettysburg Museum and Auditorium, typewritten note, undated, Neutra Collection 1179, Box 810, Young Research Library, University of California, Los Angeles.

CONTRIBUTORS

Tal Alon-Mozes is a landscape architect and an Associate Professor in the Landscape Architecture program, the faculty of Architecture and Town Planning, Technion, Israel Institute of Technology. Her areas of interest include history and theory of gardens and landscape architecture, landscape and culture, and especially the cultural dimensions of landscape production in Palestine and Israel. Among the topics of her work are the history of gardens of pre-state Israel and its current landscapes, planning and design of Israel's national parks, memorial parks, the narrative approach in the design studio, and the culture of urban agriculture in contemporary Israel.

Catherin Bull, MLArch (Melbourne), DrDes (Harvard), AM FAILA MAICD, is Emeritus Professor of Landscape Architecture at the University of Melbourne and Adjunct Professor at Queensland University of Technology. She has led national and international consultancies in landscape architecture and urban design, has been a commissioner in the Land and Environment Court of NSW, and has been an academic for more than twenty years, teaching, researching, and supervising doctoral students, most recently as the Elisabeth Murdoch Professor of Landscape Architecture. She has published two books and more than fifty papers in Australia and internationally. As an advocate for better-quality planning and design, she chairs and serves on planning and design review panels and boards across Australia, advising government and industry on open space and urban design matters. She was made a member of the

Order of Australia in 2009 in recognition of her contribution to landscape architecture and urban design.

Ethan Carr is an Associate Professor at the University of Massachusetts, Amherst, where he teaches courses in heritage landscape research, management, and interpretation. He is the author of *Wilderness by Design* (winner of the American Society of Landscape Architects Honor Award), and *Mission 66: Modernism and the National Park Dilemma* (winner of the J. B. Jackson Book Award, Foundation for Landscape Studies, and the Elisabeth Blair MacDougall Award, Society of Architectural Historians). Carr is the volume editor of Volume 8 of *The Papers of Frederick Law Olmsted: The Early Boston Years, 1882–1890.* He has degrees in art history and landscape architecture, and before becoming an academic he worked for the New York City Parks Department and the National Park Service.

Theodore Catton is an Associate Research Professor in the History Department at the University of Montana. He is the author of numerous books, articles, and reports on the national parks, including *Inhabited Wilderness: Indians, Eskimos, and National Parks in Alaska,* and *National Park, City Playground: Mount Rainier in the Twentieth Century.* In 2010 he received a Fulbright Senior Scholar award to make a comparative study of U.S. and New Zealand national parks, featuring case studies of Glacier National Park in Montana and Arthur's Pass National Park in South Island. Catton resides in

Missoula, Montana, with his wife and sometime writing partner, Diane Krahe. His other interests include backpacking in the Northern Rockies and walking vacations in the British Isles.

Esther da Costa Meyer is Professor in the Department of Art and Archaeology at Princeton University. A specialist in the history of modern architecture, she has published on modern and contemporary architecture, with a special focus on architecture and memory, issues of gender, and the interface between architecture and the other arts. More recently, she has worked with the challenges that globalization has posed to architectural history. She is the author of *The Architecture of Antonio Sant'Elia: Retreat into the Future* and *Frank Gehry: On Line,* and the coeditor, together with Fred Wasserman, of *Schoenberg, Kandinsky, and the Blue Rider.*

Timothy Davis is a historian for the U.S. National Park Service. His writings on the American landscape have appeared in numerous publications including *America's National Park Roads and Parkways: Drawings from the Historic American Engineering Record, Inventing for the Environment, The World Beyond the Windshield, Landscape Journal, Perspectives in Vernacular Architecture,* and *Studies in the History of Gardens & Designed Landscapes.* He has also taught courses on landscape history, theory, and preservation at the University of Texas, the University of Maryland, and the Bard Graduate Center for Studies in Decorative Arts, Design and Culture.

Elizabeth Flint Engle is an Architectural Historian for the Western Center for Historic Preservation in Grand Teton National Park. She earned a graduate certificate in historic preservation from Savannah College of Art and Design in 2012, and holds an M.A. in Architectural History from the University of Virginia and a B.A. from Williams College. Her current research focuses on early Mission 66 developments throughout the national park system. She was a recipient of a Rockefeller Archives Grant-in-Aid in 2011 for her research on Colter Bay Village, a Mission 66 development in Grand Teton National Park.

Shaun Eyring is Chief of the Division of Resource Planning and Compliance of the Northeast Region for the National Park Service, and the coeditor of *Re-creating the American Past: Essays on the Colonial Revival* (with Richard Guy Wilson and Kenny Marotta).

Christine Madrid French, a historian and advocate for the preservation of American modern buildings, was born and raised in Los Angeles. She graduated from the University of Utah in Architectural Studies in 1992 and worked for the National Park Service as a historian in Washington, D.C. Ms. French earned an M.A. in Architectural History from the University of Virginia in 1998. She is also a writer and photographer, with her work appearing in *U.S. News & World Report, Virginia Living, Modernism Magazine,* and *Landscape Architecture.* In 2000, she cofounded the Recent Past Preservation Network and served as the president for nine years. She is an expert member of the Scientific Committee on Twentieth-Century Heritage for the International Council on Monuments and Sites (ICOMOS) and is completing a book on mid-twentieth-century Mission 66 visitor centers in our national parks.

Heidi Hohmann is a registered landscape architect and an Associate Professor of Landscape Architecture at Iowa State University. She has worked as a preservation planner and landscape architect for the National Park Service and for planning and design firms on the East Coast and in the Midwest.

John Dixon Hunt is the Emeritus Professor of the History and Theory of Landscape in the School of Design at the University of Pennsylvania. He is the editor of both the journal *Studies in the History of Gardens and Designed Landscapes* and of the series Penn Studies in Landscape Architecture, in which thirty titles have so far appeared. He is the author of more than a dozen books, most recently *Nature Over Again: The Garden Art of Ian Hamilton Finlay* and *A World of Gardens,* and the author of many articles in books and journals on both landscape history and the relationship of word and image; until 2010 he was for twenty years the senior editor of *Word & Image: A Journal of Verbal/Visual Enquiry.* With Michael Leslie (Rhodes College) he has jointly edited *The Cultural History of Gardens,* in six volumes.

Brian Katen is an Associate Professor and Chair of the Landscape Architecture Program, School of Architecture + Design at Virginia Tech. His research centers on the archival and liminal dimensions of landscape and the persistence and materiality of memory in everyday, vernacular, and ephemeral landscapes. His current work is focused on understanding and documenting the trace record of Virginia's African American landscapes during the eras of Jim Crow and segregation.

Richard Longstreth is Professor of American Studies and Director of the Graduate Program in Historic Preservation at George Washington University. He is a past president of the Society of Architectural Historians and vice president of the Vernacular Architecture Forum. Currently he chairs the Maryland Governor's Consulting Committee on the National Register of Historic Places and serves as the secretary of the Frank Lloyd Wright Building Conservancy and on the board of the Fort Ticonderoga Association. From 1998 until 2010, he served on the board of Adirondack Architectural Heritage. Longstreth's wife's extended family began going to the Adirondacks in the mid-nineteenth century. He has been a summer resident there for more than thirty-five years.

Longstreth's recent books include *The American Department Store Transformed, 1920–1960* and three edited volumes: *Sustainability & Historic Preservation: Toward a Holistic View, Housing Washington: Two Centuries of Residential Development and Planning in the National Capital Area,* and *Nature and Culture and Change: Cultural Landscapes and Historic Preservation.* His *City Center to Regional Mall: Architecture, the Automobile, and Retailing in Los Angeles, 1920–1950* and a complementary

study, *The Drive-In, the Supermarket, and the Transformation of Commercial Space in Los Angeles, 1914–1941,* won four national awards in the fields of architectural history, urban history, and historic preservation. Currently he is working on a volume, *Looking Beyond the Icons: A Legacy of Architecture and Landscape from the Recent Past,* to be published by the University of Virginia Press.

Neil M. Maher is an Associate Professor in the Federated History Department at the New Jersey Institute of Technology and Rutgers University at Newark. His book *Nature's New Deal: The Civilian Conservation Corps and the Roots of the American Environmental Movement* received the Charles A. Weyerhaeuser Book Award for the best monograph in conservation history. He has also edited a collection of essays by historians, scientists, and policy analysts titled *New Jersey's Environments: Past, Present, and Future,* and coedited a special issue of the *Radical History Review* titled "Transnational Environments: Rethinking the Political Economy of Nature in a Global Age." He is currently working on a book-length project on the environmental and political history of the space race during the 1960s and 1970s.

Catharina Nolin is Associate Professor and Senior Lecturer in the Department of Art History, Stockholm University, Sweden, where she lectures mainly on architecture, landscape architecture, and cultural heritage. In her research she has specialized in the study of gardens and designed landscapes. Her doctoral dissertation explored the urban park in Sweden in the nineteenth century (*Till stadsbornas nytta och förlustande. Den offentliga parken i Sverige under 1800-talet,* with an English summary). Her research has been published in English in *Garden History* and in *The European City and Green Space: London, Stockholm, Helsinki and St. Petersburg, 1850–2000.* She is the coauthor of a book on the sculptor Carl Milles's home and garden (*Millesgården. Arkitektur och trädgård*) and the author of the book *En svensk lustgårdskonst. Lars Israel Wahlman som trädgårdsarkitekt* (with an English summary). She is currently investigating women landscape architects in Sweden c. 1900–1950.

Nicole Porter, Ph.D., M.Arch, BPD, Grad. Cert. L.Arch (Melbourne) RLA, AILA is a Lecturer in Architecture at the University of Nottingham. She has taught built environment design at the University of Canberra and the University of Melbourne, and has worked in the public sector and private practice. Her research interests include landscape design, landscape representation, and place branding. She completed her doctoral thesis, "The Promotion and Production of Contemporary Landscape," at the University of Melbourne in 2009. This thesis interrogated the cultural construction of landscape as practiced by creative industries including landscape architecture, place branding, and new media communications. Nicole is also interested in creative practice and expression in allied areas such as urban design, urban installations, and public art.

Elizabeth Barlow Rogers is the President of the Foundation for Landscape Studies. A native of San Antonio, Texas, Rogers earned a B.A. degree from Wellesley College and an M.A. in City Planning from Yale University. In 1979, she was appointed Central Park administrator, and in 1981 she was instrumental in founding the Central Park Conservancy. As president, she led the conservancy until 1996, at which time she founded the Cityscape Institute. In 2002, she created a curriculum of Garden History and Landscape Studies at the Bard Graduate Center. Her published works include *The Forests and Wetlands of New York City, Frederick Law Olmsted's New York, Rebuilding Central Park: A Management and Restoration Plan, Landscape Design: A Cultural and Architectural History,* and *Romantic Gardens: Nature, Art, and Landscape Design.* Rogers is a life trustee of the Central Park Conservancy and a member of the boards of the Battery Conservancy and the Library of American Landscape History. She is a fellow of the American Academy of Arts and Sciences, an honorary member of the American Society of Landscape Architects, and the winner of the ASLA's 2005 LaGasse Medal.

Katherine Solomonson is an Associate Professor in the School of Architecture at the University of Minnesota, where she is also affiliated with programs in American Studies, Art History, and Comparative Studies in Discourse and Society. A historian of American buildings, landscapes, and material culture, she is the author of *The Chicago Tribune Tower Competition: Skyscraper Design and Cultural Change in the 1920s,* recipient of the Alice Davis Hitchcock Award from the Society of Architectural Historians. She coedits a book series called Architecture, Landscape, and American Culture published by the University of Minnesota Press.

Lucienne Thys-Şenocak is an Associate Professor in the Archaeology and the History of Art department at Koç University, Istanbul, where she has taught courses on cultural heritage site management, museum studies, visual culture, and Ottoman architectural history since 1993. She is the author of several publications related to these fields, including *Ottoman Women Builders: The Architectural Patronage of Hadice Turhan Sultan,* a study of the architectural patronage undertaken in Istanbul and the Gallipoli region of Turkey by the mother of an Ottoman sultan who lived in the latter half of the seventeenth century. Her second book, *Divided Spaces, Contested Pasts: The Heritage of the Gallipoli Peninsula,* will be published in 2014. From 1997 to 2010 she directed surveying, conservation, and oral history projects in the Gallipoli Peninsula Historical National Park at the Ottoman fortress of Seddülbahir. She is a member of ICOMOS Turkey.

Richard Guy Wilson holds the Commonwealth Professor's Chair in Architectural History at the University of Virginia. A frequent lecturer and a television commentator, he has also published widely on different aspects of American and modern architecture. His books include *The Making of Virginia Architecture, Thomas Jefferson's Academical Village, Campus Guide: University of Virginia, Richmond's Monument Avenue, Buildings of Virginia: Tidewater and Piedmont,* and *Re-creating the American Past: Essays on the Colonial Revival* (with Shaun Eyring and Kenny Marotta).

INDEX